Children and Youth in Crisis

Children and Youth in Crisis

Protecting and Promoting Human Development in Times of Economic Shocks

Mattias Lundberg and Alice Wuermli
Editors

THE WORLD BANK
Washington, D.C.

ISBN (paper): 978-0-8213-9547-9
ISBN (electronic): 978-0-8213-9548-6
DOI: 10.1596/978-0-8213-9547-9

Cover photos: *Clockwise, starting from top left:* © Arne Hoel/The World Bank; © Scott Wallace/The World Bank; © Arne Hoel/The World Bank; © Arne Hoel/The World Bank; © Scott Wallace/The World Bank.

Library of Congress Cataloging-in-Publication Data
Children and youth in crisis : protecting and promoting human development in times of economic shocks.
    p. cm. — (Directions in development)
  Includes bibliographical references.
  ISBN 978-0-8213-9547-9 (alk. paper) — ISBN 978-0-8213-9548-6
  1. Child welfare—Economic aspects. 2. Children—Social conditions. 3. Youth—Social conditions. 4. Financial crises—Social aspects. 5. Business cycles—Social aspects. I. World Bank.
  HV713.C3964 2012
  362.7—dc23
                                                          2012011905

Contents

Foreword   *xi*
About the Contributors   *xvii*
Acknowledgments   *xxi*

PART I   **Introduction and Framing**   **1**

Chapter 1   Introduction   3
                  Mattias Lundberg and Alice Wuermli

                  Objective of This Volume   4
                  Structure   7
                  Summary   8
                  Conclusions   21
                  Notes   22
                  References   22

Chapter 2   A Conceptual Framework   29
                  Alice Wuermli, Rainer K. Silbereisen,
                  Mattias Lundberg, Michèle Lamont,
                  Jere R. Behrman, and Larry Aber

Overview   29
Shocks, Crises, Business Cycles, Recessions,
    Depressions, and Busts   32
The Economics of Human Capital   37
Human Development and a Bioecological Model   47
Shocks, Transmission Mechanisms, and the
    Dynamics of Human Development   66
Policy Implications of an Integrated Approach   79
Notes   85
References   87

PART II   **The Empirical Evidence of the Impact of**
                 Economic Crises on Children and Youth   103

Chapter 3   **Aggregate Economic Shocks in Utero and**
                 during Early Childhood   105
                 Early Childhood Development: An Introduction
                     Carly Tubbs and Dana Charles McCoy   106
                 Shocks, Health, and Nutrition during Early
                     Childhood
                     Sarah Baird, Kathleen Beegle, and Jed Friedman   116
                 Economic Crises and Early Childhood
                     Cognitive and Socioemotional Development
                     Carly Tubbs   127
                 Conclusions   132
                 Notes   135
                 References   135

Chapter 4   **Aggregate Economic Shocks during**
                 Middle Childhood   149
                 Susan Parker and Carly Tubbs

                 Middle Childhood Development: An
                     Introduction   149
                 Economic Crisis and Schooling during
                     Middle Childhood   153
                 The Long-Term Impacts of Economic Crisis
                     on Cognitive and Socioemotional
                     Developmental Outcomes   167

Conclusions		177
Notes		179
References		179

Chapter 5	**Aggregate Economic Shocks during Adolescence:**	
	Transitions, Mental Health, and Behaviors	**189**
	Adolescent Development: An Introduction	
	Alice Wuermli	190
	Economic Crisis and School-to-Work Transition	
	Suzanne Duryea	195
	Economic Crisis and Adolescent Mental Health	
	Sarah Baird, Kathleen Beegle, and	
	Jed Friedman	206
	Economic Crisis and Risky Adolescent Behavior	
	Mattias Lundberg	210
	Conclusions	214
	Notes	216
	References	217

| **PART III** | **Policy** | **227** |

Chapter 6	**Policies to Protect and Promote Young People's**	
	Development during Crisis	**229**
	Alice Wuermli, Kevin Hempel, Larry Aber,	
	and Mattias Lundberg	
	Introduction to Policies during Economic Crisis	229
	Moving beyond Traditional Safety	
	Net Programs	232
	Early Childhood	242
	Middle Childhood	251
	Adolescence	257
	Conclusions	264
	Notes	267
	References	268

Appendix A	The Theory of Human Capital Investment	
	Decisions	279
	Notes	283
	References	284

Appendix B   Measurement and Identification of Aggregate
Shocks: Problems of Comparability
between Studies   285
Note   287
References   287

Glossary   289

Boxes

2.1   Short List of Resilience Factors, with Implicated
Human Adaptive Systems   63
3.1   Prenatal Health and Development   107
3.2   Biological and Environmental Transactions in
Children's Development   110
4.1   Parenting in a Cultural Context and the Family
Stress Model   157
4.2   Economic Crisis and Child Labor   171
6.1   *Jefes y Jefas de Hogar Desempleados*: Argentina's
Response to the 2001–02 Financial Crisis   244
6.2   Social Resilience and Human Development   248

Figures

2.1   A Bioecological Model of Human Development   49
2.2   The Developmental Course of Human Brain
Development by Months, Years, and Decades   58
2.3   Distinction between Resilience and Risk Reduction
and Protection   61
6.1   A Developmental Approach to Policy during
Economic Crisis   235
A.1   Private Marginal Benefits and Private Marginal
Costs of Human Capital Investments, with Higher
and Lower Marginal Benefits   280
A.2   Private Marginal Benefits and Private Marginal
Costs of Human Capital Investments, with Higher
and Lower Marginal Costs   280

Tables

2.1   Global Incidence of Shocks, Selected Years, 1946–2010   35
2.2   Stage-Salient Human Developmental Tasks, by Age   57

5.1   Long-Term Effect on Employment of Entering the
        Labor Market during Poor Economic Conditions in
        Six Countries: Argentina (1980–2010), Brazil
        (1978–2002), Chile (1957–2005), Germany
        (1975–2001), Norway (1993–2000), and the
        United Kingdom (1981–97)   205
5.1a   Less-Educated and Highly Educated Males and Females
        in High-Income Countries   205
5.1b   All Males and Females and Less-Educated and Highly
        Educated Males and Females in Middle-Income Countries   205
5.2   Estimated Duration of Adverse Effects on Employment
        of Entering the Labor Market during Poor Economic
        Conditions for Argentina and the United Kingdom   205
6.1   Transmission Mechanisms (Mediators) by Life Stage
        and System Level   238
6.2   Negative Outcomes by Life Stage: Time of Exposure
        and Time of Outcome Measured   240

Foreword

Katherine J. Conger and Rand D. Conger

"Science is focused on what we do not know. Social policy and the delivery of health and human services are focused on what we should do" (Shonkoff, 2000). "Our challenge then is to examine what is being done in light of what we think we know, and how the two inform each other" (Authors).

Economists, sociologists, psychologists, and others in the social sciences have long been concerned with the plight of individuals and families in the wake of economic and other types of crises. An overarching goal of social scientists has been to find more effective strategies for reducing the adverse effects of such crises in both the short and the long term. Ideally, scientists and practitioners will learn how to avoid many of these crises, such as major economic downturns or the negative consequences they may produce. In this process, the hope is to provide communities, families, and individuals with better tools for handling or avoiding significant economic and other crises in the future.

As demonstrated in the present volume, achieving these goals requires the efforts of both researchers and practitioners, as well as policy makers who must work together to improve our ability to deal effectively with the kinds of crises that can have a disruptive influence on families and children. Although the underlying goals are quite similar, researchers, program providers, and policy makers often work at cross-purposes because they do not have a common working model or even a common language with which to communicate ideas and implement programs. A major contribution of the present volume is that it takes an important step toward building a shared understanding of how crises influence individuals, families, and communities. It proposes a working model based on perspectives from economics and human development that provides a shared foundation for developing programs of research, application, and intervention designed to address the negative consequences of economic and other major crises around the world.

With these goals in mind, in 2010 researchers and policy makers responsible for this report came together in an attempt to improve the understanding of the impact of economic crises on humans, especially vulnerable people in developing countries. Financial crises seem to be ubiquitous and to happen every 20 years or so, as discussed in chapter 1. However, a strictly economic response does not fully address the many significant challenges faced by individuals and families when economic crises occur. Consistent with this idea, Lundberg and Wuermli pose the central thesis that animates this book: "Human development is at the core of economic development.... Shortfalls or setbacks at any stage of the life course may have severe consequences for individual development as well as for the growth and development of successful communities." This observation and the support provided for it by the chapters in this volume provide an important antidote to the idea that only a single discipline can adequately address the too frequent economic downturns that seriously affect people in their daily lives.

Especially important, the dedicated professionals in economics, human development, sociology, psychology, education, and other fields responsible for this report have created a blueprint that underscores the need for this multidisciplinary perspective on economic crises. Across disciplines and professional interests (that is, research, policy, and practice), the authors have focused on how to take what we know—and we do know a few things—and use that knowledge to improve the health and well-being of individuals, families, and communities around the world, even in the face of seemingly insurmountable challenges. We were fortunate to be part of this interdisciplinary process as it played out in a conference held in Marbach, Germany, in May 2011. And although the lessons gleaned from our often intense discussions around the table at that conference were primarily focused on developing nations, many of these lessons can be applied to families experiencing financial hardship regardless of where they live. Thus, this volume will have broad application in fostering more robust public-private partnerships that can be used to improve the lives of children and youth in both developing and industrial societies.

We are pleased to see in this final report the interweaving of ideas from the several disciplines represented at the Marbach conference. For example, our research on the consequences of economic hardship across generations (see K. Conger et al. 2012) and within different ethnic groups (R. Conger et al. 2012) helped inform this report by noting many of the ways in which economic change can affect individuals and families. The authors of this volume have done a superb job of integrating this work with the observations from other disciplines to generate a better understanding of how economic crises affect human development. Joining with scientists and policy makers from the World Bank and the Jacobs Foundation forced all the participants at the conference—some of whom are authors of this volume—to step outside their disciplinary silos (that is, their research comfort zones) and look at the impact of socioeconomic changes on individuals and families from a broader perspective. In other words, everyone who worked on this project had the experience of crossing academic boundaries, considering new disciplinary approaches, and rethinking organizing principles of research, policy, and programs to fully appreciate the wide-reaching impact of designing and implementing interventions around the world in response to economic crises.

The end result of this process was the generation of this volume, which reflects new insights that would not have been possible if it had been pursued from the vantage point of a single discipline. For example, economists as well as psychologists at the conference were presented with the challenge of taking both timing and stage-salient development into account as they considered the effects of economic crises on infants, children, and adolescents (see part II of the volume). The empirical examples presented in chapters 3–5 also reflect this multidisciplinary integration by providing a broad understanding of the wide-ranging effects of economic crises on nutrition, cognition, socioemotional development, and educational outcomes from infancy through adolescence. Thus, the entire volume suggests many new and innovative approaches to developing more effective programs for handling economic and other crises in a fashion that can improve the lives of children and their families. These insights would not have been generated without the broad interdisciplinary theme that drove both the Marbach conference and the present volume.

As we look at the history of boom-and-bust cycles involving recessions, depressions, and regional downturns, it is tempting to focus on only one small problem and ignore the larger context. We often engage in the "if only" game—if only we had more money, more resources, or more support, we could design a great program to address the fundamental, underlying structural deficits in the problem of the moment. Sometimes we get lost in the *if only* syndrome of thinking we can do nothing because the scope of the problem is so broad or intense. This book suggests—in fact, demands—that we as scientists, practitioners, and policy shapers keep the small steps in place that provide immediate relief while at the same time consider options for dealing with larger, more fundamental issues. Building resilience and protecting development through a crisis with one big idea is not likely feasible: indeed, one size does not fit all. However, many small programs—like supportive community-based parenting programs or antenatal programs that address the stresses experienced during times of economic turmoil—can be tailored to fit the needs, culture, and customs of specific regions. And small steps can begin to add up to larger gains that can ripple through and spill over into all areas of family and community life.

Just as research using our Family Stress Model demonstrated how economic hardship and family distress can spill over into all aspects of family relationships and affect child and adult well-being (R. Conger et al. 2010), evidence from the broad range of studies considered in this volume suggests that adaptive responses and proactive strategies can spill over and promote positive interactions and improved health and well-being for children and adults living in difficult circumstances around the world. This report provides an invaluable resource for promoting that approach in dealing with the crises that affect children's lives.

References

Conger, Katherine J., Monica Martin, Ben T. Reeb, Wendy M. Little, Jessie L. Craine, Barbara Shebloski, and Rand D. Conger. 2012. "Economic Hardship and Its Consequences across Generations." In *NICHD/Oxford Handbook of Child Development and Poverty*, ed. Valerie Maholmes and Rosalind Kingpp, 37–53. New York: Oxford University Press.

Conger, Rand D., Katherine J. Conger, and Monica Martin. 2010. "Socioeconomic Status, Family Processes, and Individual Development." *Journal of Marriage and Family* 72: 686–705.

Conger, Rand D., Hairong Song, Gary D. Stockdale, Emilio Ferrer, Keith F. Widaman, and Ana M. Cauce. 2012. "Resilience and Vulnerability of Mexican

Origin Youth and Their Families: A Test of a Culturally-Informed Model of Family Economic Stress." In *Adolescence and Beyond: Family Processes and Development*, ed. Patricia K. Kerig, M. S. Schultz, and Stuart T. Hauser, 268–86. New York: Oxford University Press.

Shonkoff, John P. 2000. "Science, Policy, and Practice: Three Cultures in Search of a Shared Mission." *Child Development* 71: 181–87.

About the Contributors

Larry Aber is Distinguished Professor of Applied Psychology and Public Policy at the Steinhardt School of Culture, Education, and Human Development, New York University, and board chair of its Institute for Human Development and Social Change. His research focuses on the influence of poverty and violence, at the family and community levels, on the social, emotional, behavioral, cognitive, and academic development of children and youth.

Sarah Baird is assistant professor of Global Health and Economics at the George Washington University. Her work focuses on analyzing health and education issues in developing countries through careful program design and evaluation. More specifically, her research focuses on the health of infants and youth, as well as on issues related to HIV/AIDS. She has conducted field work in Kenya, Malawi, and Tanzania.

Kathleen Beegle is a senior economist in the Development Research Group of the World Bank. Her current work focuses on poverty, socio-economic status, and gender in Sub-Saharan Africa. She is deputy director for the *World Bank World Development Report 2013* on jobs. She has expertise in the design and implementation of household survey operations and the use of household surveys for poverty and policy analysis.

Jere R. Behrman is the William R. Kenan Professor of Economics and a research associate at University of Pennsylvania Population Studies Center. He serves as the economics and social science member of the National Advisory Council of the National Institute of Child Health and Development of the National Institutes of Health. His research focuses on determinants of later-life outcomes, the role of endowments and early-life experiences over the life cycle, and how households invest in their children to reinforce or to compensate for endowment differentials among siblings.

Dana Charles McCoy is a doctoral student in psychology and social intervention in the Steinhardt School of Culture, Education, and Human Development at New York University. Her research focuses on understanding how low-income children's families, neighborhoods, and school environments affect the development of their cognitive, behavioral, and emotional self-regulatory skills.

Suzanne Duryea is a principal research economist in the Social Sector at the Inter-American Development Bank. Her current work focuses on youth development in Latin America and the Caribbean. She has studied the effects of economic fluctuations on children's school attendance and labor supply in Brazil, and has investigated the mechanisms through which parents' schooling affects investments in children and fertility.

Eric Edmonds is an associate professor of economics and chair of international studies at Dartmouth College, director of the Child Labor Network at the Institute for the Study of Labor, a faculty research fellow at the National Bureau of Economic Research, and an associate editor for *Economic Development and Cultural Change*. His current work includes developing strategies to deter child and forced labor in Uzbekistan's cotton sector and understanding child and forced labor in the carpet sector in the Indian subcontinent.

Jed Friedman is a senior economist in the Development Research Group of the World Bank. He is working on the effectiveness of malaria control programs in India, Nigeria, and Zambia; national health financing reforms in the Kyrgyz Republic, Zambia, and Zimbabwe; and conditional cash transfers in the Philippines.

Kevin Hempel works in the Social Protection and Labor Unit of the Human Development Network at the World Bank. Prior to joining the World Bank, he worked for the Inter-American Development Bank in Mexico, the GIZ in Bolivia, and the UN Economic Commission for Latin America in Chile. His recent work has focused on youth employment and entrepreneurship, youth violence, and monitoring and evaluation of youth-focused interventions.

Michèle Lamont is Robert I. Goldman Professor of European Studies and professor of sociology and African and African American Studies at Harvard University. She is a fellow of the Canadian Institute for Advanced Research and is codirector of its research program on Successful Societies. Her work focuses on group boundaries, racism, and antiracism, how culture matters for poverty, shared criteria of evaluation for qualitative social sciences, disciplinary cultures, and interdisciplinary collaboration.

Mattias Lundberg is senior economist in the Social Protection and Labor Unit of the Human Development Network at the World Bank. He is leading research on the school-to-work transition, youth voice and violence, and youth employment. His published research has focused on the impact on households of crises such as HIV/AIDS and flood exposure; he has published numerous other articles on the relationship between income distribution and growth and on public service delivery, slum upgrading, and many other topics.

Ryann Manning is a doctoral student in organizational behavior and sociology at Harvard University. She has research and management experience in international development and global health, and has lived in El Salvador, Mexico, Sierra Leone, South Africa, and Uruguay. Her research interests include organizational effectiveness, change, and innovation in the international development sector and in public institutions.

Susan W. Parker is professor of economics at the Center for Research and Teaching in Economics in Mexico City (*Centro de Investigación y Docencia Económicas*) and adjunct professor at the RAND Corporation. Her research focuses principally on education, labor markets, and social program evaluation in developing countries, with a particular emphasis on conditional cash transfer programs.

Rainer K. Silbereisen is professor and head of the Department of Developmental Psychology at the University of Jena (Germany), adjunct professor of human development and family studies at the Pennsylvania State University (United States), and director of the Center for Applied Developmental Science. His research work focuses on human development across the life span and, in particular, on the role of social change in positive and maladaptive human development, utilizing a cross-cultural and biopsychosocial format.

Carly Tubbs is a doctoral student in the psychology and social intervention program in the Steinhardt School of Culture, Education, and Human Development at New York University. Her research focuses on examining the pathways through which large-scale alterations in technological, economic, and ideological systems in societies affect adolescent development.

Alice Wuermli currently works in the Social Protection and Labor Unit of the Human Development Network of the World Bank. Her work has focused on how economic crises affect young people's developmental processes, with a particular emphasis on interventions to build resilience in the face of adversity. She has conducted extensive reviews of the literature on youth interventions to support young people's transition from school to work.

Acknowledgments

The authors would like to thank workshop and seminar participants in Washington, DC, and Marbach, Germany, including Urs Arnold, Kathy Conger, Rand Conger, Wendy Cunningham, Eric Edmonds, Gelgia Fetz, Kamola Khusnutdinova, Iliana Kohler, David Lam, Murray Liebrandt, Daniel Loschinger, Constanze Lullies, Elise De Neubourg, David Newhouse, Ashkan Niknia, Simon Sommer, and Luca Tiberti; peer reviewers Mohammed Ihsan Ajwad, Harold Alderman, and Maureen Lewis; and others who provided support, comments, and guidance during the process, including Juliana Arbelaez, Arup Banerji, Ann Masten, Hideki Mori, Anne Petersen, Vijayendra Rao, and Lonnie Sherrod. This project would not have been possible without the generous support of the Jacobs Foundation, and the World Bank's Rapid Social Response Fund and Trust Fund for Environmentally and Socially Sustainable Development.

PART I

Introduction and Framing

CHAPTER 1

Introduction

Mattias Lundberg and Alice Wuermli

Financial crises, at both the global and the national level, are ubiquitous. Reinhart and Rogoff (2009) provide the invaluable lesson that over the past 800 years a major crisis has happened roughly once every 20 years. This pattern raises concern about the human impacts of crises, especially among more vulnerable people in developing countries. During the most recent global financial crisis, international organizations, bilateral development agencies, and civil society organizations all expressed concern about the ongoing "human crisis" (see, for instance, World Bank 2009). The global community has become alarmed that the crisis could reverse recent progress in poverty reduction and the achievement of the Millennium Development Goals.[1]

Human development is at the core of economic development. Human capital accumulation at all stages—from the antenatal environment through early childhood and adolescence—helps facilitate the transition to a healthy and productive adulthood and break the intergenerational transmission of poverty. Shortfalls or setbacks at any stage of the life course may have severe consequences for individual development as well as for the growth and development of successful communities.

Objective of This Volume

Motivated by the need to understand how crises affect human development in diverse segments of the population, this book explores how individuals and households cope with the changes and stresses induced by economic crises. It examines how these impacts and coping mechanisms differ across cultural and institutional contexts and looks at how best to protect the most vulnerable from lasting harm and the degradation of human capital.

Several recent articles and reports review the existing literature on the impact of shocks on human capital development (see Ferreira and Schady 2009; Fasih et al. 2009; Harper et al. 2009). For instance, Harper et al. (2009, 1) find that "children and young people suffer disproportionately [and that] increases in child mortality and morbidity, child labour, child exploitation, violence against children and women and other forms of abuse, alongside declines in school attendance and the quality of education, nurture, care and emotional well-being, can all be traced to times of economic crisis." Ferreira and Schady (2009) have a more nuanced view and find both pro- and countercyclical correlations, depending on the aggregate level of income. Friedman and Sturdy (2011) show that economic crises may affect physical and cognitive development during early childhood through nutritional as well as environmental pathways. Finally, World Bank (2011a) and Cho and Newhouse (2011) present evidence that the global recession of 2007–09 can affect both educational attainment and success in the labor market.

Those studies and others show that children and youth are among the most vulnerable to crises because of their lack of agency and, more importantly, because of the sensitive developmental milestones they must achieve during those years. The studies examine the impact of crises on separate and distinct outcomes—whether in the decision to stay in school, or to make healthy choices, or in the ability to enter and remain in productive employment. But human development is by nature cross-sectoral, involving complex interactions among different domains of development that only imprecisely map into these three sectoral outcomes. In addition, the study and design of interventions to facilitate human development is naturally interdisciplinary; it lies at the intersections of neurology, sociology, genetics, psychology, biology and economics. In other words, health, education, and labor market success are manifest outcomes of complex processes spanning neurobiological and physiological development, genetic expressions in response to environmental influences, and socioemotional-behavioral-cognitive functioning within a particular social and institutional context.

The work presented in this volume deepens our understanding of how shocks affect children and youth in two ways. First, we aggregate the evidence on various developmental outcomes across developmental stages from conception to adulthood (broadly defined by the transition to work). Second, we show that the impact of crises will differ according to the social and environmental contexts in which the child or young person grows and that shocks can in turn affect those contexts. We hope to understand the short- and long-term impacts of crises, and whether we can identify particular protective factors that support children's recovery from the worst ravages of the crisis. The focus on transmission mechanisms, the pathways of influence, leads to a set of broad policy recommendations for enhancing both protection and recovery.

This volume incorporates the knowledge and evidence on shocks and human development from a variety of disciplinary perspectives, from economics to sociology, anthropology, and social and developmental psychology. The treatment of different topics across the disciplines is uneven, reflecting the diverse foci of disciplinary endeavor and empirical research. For example, studies in developmental sciences have explored socioemotional development during early childhood, mostly from countries in the Organisation for Economic Co-operation and Development (OECD). Studies from developing countries have focused more on children's school attendance or dropout rate, but little is known about their socioemotional and behavioral development or even their underlying cognitive development. The interdisciplinary approach permits a broader scope than would have been possible if confined to one discipline. Nevertheless, significant gaps remain in the evidence and in our understanding of human development and shocks in a wide range of contexts.

Most of the evidence on shocks and human development in developing countries has come from the early childhood years (roughly conception to 5 years), where the focus has been on health and nutrition. Among older children, the attention shifts to education and cognitive development (roughly 6–16 years). For older youth, over 16, the vast majority of research has focused on the transition to work. This division reflects the relative importance generally placed on particular domains during different stages of development. Physiology takes precedence over social and emotional development among very young children; cognitive and academic achievements are the main developmental concerns during middle childhood, when children seem less vulnerable to factors leading to deficiencies in physiological development. Whether these divisions truly reflect the relative importance of different domains at different stages remains to be seen. What is more important is that changes in one domain of human development determine, and are determined by, changes in other domains.

The complex and multifaceted nature of human development necessitates the use of a broader range of tools than is normally brought to bear on questions of economic policy. However, interdisciplinary endeavors can become stuck in semantic and methodological quicksand. Questions of causality, the constitution of sufficient proof, the choice of outcomes and variables, and methods of measurement, just to name a few, often prevent complete agreement among researchers from different disciplines. On the one hand, we present research from economics that may satisfy high (albeit narrow) standards of causality and attribution. On the other hand, we also present studies from other disciplines that yield invaluable insights into the processes and interactions of complex developmental systems, some of which might not live up to the same standards of methodological scrutiny.

As noted earlier, this volume is limited in the origins and therefore the applicability of much of the empirical evidence. Although considerable evidence on the links among human capital, poverty, and economic growth comes from developing countries, human developmental research is generally limited to OECD countries. The importance of context and of sociocultural and political influences on perceptions, aspirations, behaviors, and decision making makes it difficult to apply the lessons learned from research on child development in one context to another. For example, similar family structures and values in child-rearing practices among OECD countries allow for a certain degree of cross-country comparability. However, where the structures and cultures of child rearing differ—for example, where polygamy is the norm or where age-specific expectations of developmental tasks differ—policies and interventions to enrich or protect child development warrant significant adaptation. These subtle complexities require a multidisciplinary approach to the research and to the design of policies.

This project began by reaching out to the broader research community to bring together unpublished research from these different fields of study to enlarge both the analytical toolkit and the evidence base. An open call was issued for papers to be presented at a conference in May 2011; of 87 submissions, 9 were invited for presentation at the conference. Most of that material has been incorporated in the present volume. The conference, held under the auspices of the Jacobs Foundation, brought together researchers and policy specialists from these diverse disciplines to discuss methods, evidence, questions, problems, and policies to protect and enhance human capital development in a crisis.

That said, this volume does not attempt to sort out disciplinary disputes or disagreements on methods and measurement. The goal, and method, of this exercise is to draw upon the strengths and evidence of diverse disciplines and advance our understanding of economic crisis and the development of young people. We came to understand the difficulties and complexities that interdisciplinary collaboration entails, from semantics to methodology. But we also came to appreciate the benefits of reaching beyond disciplinary boundaries.

Structure

Different organizations, as well as different disciplines, approach child and youth development differently. Most, including the World Bank, divide the topic into sectoral pillars, examining and designing interventions to deal independently with education, health, and so on. However, as we note, this approach does not deal adequately with the enormously complex and interconnected processes of human development. For example, while the literature on young children most often focuses on health, the literature looking at education focuses on older children and is often examined in conjunction with child labor. Similarly, the literature on education is not easily separated into age-specific or schooling-level categories. As will become clearer throughout the chapters, however, the age and grade levels will have different implications both for development and for policy. In addition, examining health exclusively in early childhood may cause us to miss the health aspects of other stages, from neurological maturation to the development of autonomy and self-control later on during middle childhood and adolescence. Certainly, concerns about mental health shift from parent to child during later childhood and adolescence. Therefore, if all health aspects were isolated in one chapter on health, the relationship between mental health and a successful transition to work and adulthood would have been more difficult, if not impossible, to demonstrate in a coherent, meaningful way. We have thus chosen to structure the volume along the life-cycle, which accounts for and allows us to lay out some of the complexity of human development.

The structure of this volume reflects the nature of the topic, with significant overlap between the parts to one degree or another. This overlap stems from analytical concepts, theories, and models that are not confined to one domain or age group; from the empirical evidence on human development, which reveals that different aspects of development span many ages; and perhaps most important, from the dynamic, self-perpetuating, and often self-limiting characteristics of human development. To minimize repetition, we have included cross-references. While individual chapters may be read in isolation, readers might find themselves opening other sections to get a more comprehensive picture of human development. For example, the effects of attachment-related issues, while often rooted in early infancy, have been shown to carry over into adulthood. Thus, while "forming a secure attachment" is a stage-salient developmental task in early childhood, it will reappear throughout the other chapters in different contexts and with different implications.

The book consists of three parts: introduction and framing; empirical evidence on how crises affect children and youth; and policy. Chapter 2 in part I provides a conceptual framework for analyzing how economic crisis affects young people's development, bringing together diverse concepts and theories. The intention is to uncover the ways in which families and individuals experience shocks. The conceptual framework builds a structure around *timing*, *context*, and *transmission mechanisms* of shocks. Following this logic, part II is divided into three chapters, each roughly corresponding to various stages of development: early childhood, middle childhood, and adolescence. Part III then applies the basic structure and principles developed in the conceptual framework to inform policy response to economic crisis.

Summary

Economic Crisis

A first challenge is to understand what constitutes "economic crisis." Economic policy research has focused on identifying the causes of the shock—such as business-cycle fluctuations, financial crises, terms-of-trade disruptions, or natural events—and on measuring the impact, for example, on economic growth rates, household consumption, and investment and on whether these different types of shocks have different consequences. Those who study human development are also interested in how individuals, families, and communities perceive shocks and their causes and implications. According to the underlying premise, individuals respond at least as much to their subjective experience of shocks as they do to more conventionally and objectively measured aggregate statistics.

In any event, the evidence does not provide enough information for a comprehensive typology of shocks with regard to how they affect child and youth development. More generally, shocks—as experienced by the household—can be distinguished by *cause*, such as financial crisis or natural disaster; by *severity*, that is, how many people are affected and how deeply; and by *perception*, that is, how these shocks are perceived or experienced by the people affected. Cause, severity, and perception are interrelated and ultimately influence how people, both as individuals and as communities, respond. For example, Argentina's dissolution of its currency board and banking system collapse in early 2002 led to massive popular protest and a widespread state of panic. People took to the streets with pots and pans, while supermarkets in poorer parts of town were looted (Schamis 2002). However, economic crisis does not always lead to political and social upheaval. Conversely, political and social crises do not require actual contraction, but may be the result of an actual or perceived accentuation of a broaden economic and social trend (Chauvel 2010).

Economists often ask how such crises affect the way individuals and households make decisions about investments in human capital. Of course, the most comprehensive solution would be to launch specific, in-depth longitudinal research to obtain comparable cross-country data, which would enable us to better understand the immense subtleties of households' behavior, including decisions about their children's school attendance and about their participation in the labor market. Given the costs and complexity of the task, this ideal analytical solution is unlikely to be launched on a large scale; that said, we argue in this volume that we can improve our comprehension of the impacts of shocks by achieving a more complete and nuanced understanding of human developmental processes.

The Evidence under a Developmental Lens

Human development, which spans fields from genetics to sociology, has been strongly influenced by Bronfenbrenner's bioecological model (1979, 1994), in which the developmental process is presented as an intricate mesh of interacting systems, actors, and processes, embedded in contexts. Human development is the result of continuous interactions among various levels of functioning, from the genetic, physiological, and neurological to the behavioral and environmental. The tools developed to look at these processes allow us to disentangle some of the enormous heterogeneity in risk, resilience, and response to crisis, as they highlight the importance of timing, context, and transmission mechanisms.

Timing. Different outcomes, systems, and interactions are of greater or lesser importance at different stages of development (Sroufe 1979; Aber and Jones 1997). For example, chapter 3 shows that children's development is especially vulnerable to shocks that affect their health and nutrition in utero and during the first 24 months of life. During this critical early period, children's cognitive, socioemotional, and sensory-motor skills rapidly emerge in coordination with the development of the brain and the formation of attachment bonds with primary caregivers. Exposure to shocks during this period can have severe long-term consequences, both for physiological and for behavioral and socioemotional development. For example, severe famine and malnutrition during gestation and the first two years of a child's life can lead to an array of physical and mental disorders and developmental delays. A wealth of evidence from the Dutch Hunger Winter of 1944 links extreme famine during gestation to a range of problems related to, for example, congenital anomalies of the nervous system, obesity, and mental health issues such as schizophrenia and major affective disorder (for a review, see Lumey et al. 2007). Insofar as economic crises affect the food and nutritional sufficiency of pregnant women and very young children, their health may be at great risk. But also maternal stress and depression during pregnancy and the first two years of a child's life have been linked, among other things, to low birth weight, failure to thrive in early years, and lower educational attainment in later life. In utero these outcomes can be caused by exposure to high levels of certain hormones, such as testosterone or the stress hormone cortisol, measured in the amniotic fluid (see, for example, Sarkar et al. 2008; Bergman et al. 2010). During early childhood, stress and depression of the primary caregiver, often the mother, may prevent the child from establishing a safe attachment or from receiving adequate stimulating interaction, hampering several developmental outcomes ranging from self-efficacy to conscientiousness, memory processing to healthy relationships with peers and other nonfamily people (Ainsworth 1967; Bowlby 1988; Kochanska 1995; Belsky, Spritz, and Crnic 1996; Cassidy 1988; Bee and Boyd 2010; Sroufe and Egeland 1991; for more detail, see chapter 3 on shocks during early childhood).

Thus, while the evidence does not abound, there is reason to believe that economic crisis is likely to affect young children's cognitive and socioemotional development. A study of the 1998–2000 crisis in Ecuador indicated significant decreases in vocabulary test scores in children 6–11 months and 18–29 months of age (Hidrobo 2011). These periods happen to coincide with particular spurts in brain development (see box 3.2 in chapter 3). In addition, studies of idiosyncratic shocks and poverty support these findings and highlight some of the causal mechanisms through which children are affected (Dearing, McCartney, and Taylor 2001; Duncan, Morris, and Rodrigues 2011; Duncan, Brooks-Gunn, and Klebanov 1994; Paxson and Schady 2007; Macours, Schady, and Vakis 2008; Fernald et al. 2011; Naudeau et al. 2011). Thus, it seems safe to conclude that children from conception to approximately 24 months of age are the most vulnerable to insults and that the greatest risks are related to health and nutrition inadequacies and mental health of caregivers.

Relatively more attention has been given to the long-term consequences of early childhood events. But during middle years, children develop basic skills and competencies, including the ability to learn and reason systematically and to initiate autonomous relationships with teachers and peers; these skills play a significant role in shaping their later success in school, work, and personal relationships. These competencies emerge as children begin to explore different settings beyond the household, including, most notably, formal schooling (Lerner 1998; Eccles 1999). Chapter 4 considers how an economic crisis could potentially disrupt children's educational outcomes. The evidence on aggregate economic shocks, while available only for middle- and high-income countries, demonstrates countercyclical effects on schooling: school enrollment and attendance seem to increase during economic downturns (Goldin 1999; Betts and McFarland 1995; Kane 1994; Eloundou-Enyegue and Davanzo 2003; Ferreira and Schady 2009). However, the literature on idiosyncratic economic and health shocks do show negative effects on children's education (Duryea, Lam, and Levison 2007; Case and Ardington 2006; Skoufias and Parker 2006; Lam, Ardington, and Liebbrandt 2011; Glick, Sahn, and Walker 2011). Disentangling the two effects poses some challenges. However, a more recent study seems to support the findings that aggregate shocks in and by themselves may exhibit countercyclical effects, while individual households affected by the crisis might still experience problems sending their children to school, especially in poorer households (Cunningham and Bustos-Salvagno 2011).

Either way, these studies shed little light on actual measures of development and the acquisition of skills and competencies. However, research suggests that cognitive skills—including literacy, numeracy, and the ability to solve abstract problems—do predict variance in labor market outcomes later on. The developmental literature provides additional nuance to our understanding of how an economic crisis may affect children's educational outcomes by linking economic deprivation and volatility to declines in children's actual cognitive skills. Economic crisis may limit the resources and time that parents have to invest in their children, resulting in a decline in children's literacy and math skills during middle childhood (Gershoff et al. 2007). In addition, lower socioeconomic status of the household is related to increased socioemotional and behavioral problems during middle childhood; poor socioemotional skills, in return, predict lower academic achievement and higher rates of internalizing and externalizing behavior during adolescence (Teo et al. 1996; Dishion, Capaldi, and Yoerger 1999).

Adolescence is a time when youth become more subjected to the world outside their family; they experiment and take risks while developing their identity. The significant biological and socioemotional changes during this stage of development make youth particularly vulnerable to depression and anxiety and susceptible to the influence of deviant peers and risky behavior (Lerner 1998). New capacities for thought and for moral commitment, self-understanding and definition, learning about one's sexuality, social skills, and physical abilities; negotiating relationships with parents, peers, and teachers; and embarking on the transition to work and thus adulthood, provide both opportunities and risks (Lerner 1993). Adverse experiences during this period can also have long-lasting consequences. For example, chapter 5 indicates that, on the one hand, the experience of entering the labor market during a recession can result in prolonged unemployment and lower lifetime earnings (Kahn 2010; Oreopoulos, von Watcher, and Heisz 2006; Stevens 2008; Burgess et al. 2003). On the other hand, in his acclaimed study of the Great Depression in the United States, Elder (1999) finds that the effect depended on the exact developmental stage of the adolescent at the time of the crisis, and that socially constructed gender roles led to marked differences in experiences and outcomes for girls and for boys. Working outside the household seems to have rewarded boys with greater respect and appreciation within the family and to have protected the son from possibly negative household influences. Conversely, daughters, who were more likely to work within the household producing goods that were previously bought in the market, had a harder time coping and often suffered negative consequences from exposure to unemployed and depressed fathers.

However, the evidence does not support the notion that young people leave school during crises to work and support the family. In general, studies that look at the short-term labor market impacts find declines in young people's employment (see, for example, Choudhry, Marelli, and Signorelli 2010; Duryea and Arends-Kuenning 2003; Schady 2004). Other studies find no or few effects on young people's labor supply (see, for example, Cunningham and Bustos-Salvagno 2011; McKenzie 2003). Yet again the 2008–09 recession caused youth unemployment to reach record highs in Eastern Europe and Central Asia (World Bank 2011a). Interestingly, though, Koettl, Oral, and Santos (2011) found that young workers were the first to be let go but were also the first to be rehired once the economies started recovering from the most recent financial crisis. Nevertheless, prolonged unemployment in the transition to work can have serious long-term implications, resulting in lower earnings, higher job turnover, higher rates of unemployment, and worse physical and mental health later in life (Crockett and Silbereisen 2000; Gregg and Tominey 2005; Bell and Blanchflower 2010; McLoyd et al. 2009).

There also seems to be more heterogeneity in the long term, depending on the person's ability to further her education during a period of harsh labor market conditions (Burgess et al. 2003). Given youth's greater awareness of their and their families socioeconomic situation, there is reason to worry about their mental health during economic crises; studies have shown an economic crisis to affect mental health in a myriad of ways (Das et al. 2007; Tangcharoensathien et al. 2000; Friedman and Thomas 2009; Hong, Knapp, and McGuire 2011). In addition, the ubiquity of teen pregnancies in many developing countries, and the risks to the unborn and during early childhood associated with mental health problems increase the need to pay attention to these issues. Above all, adolescence is a time of great vulnerability to external events that will affect the capacity of young people to renegotiate relationships, achieve autonomy, and develop their identity in an environment in which choices are already constrained. These external events will also change the context in which young people develop their perceptions and aspirations, the relevance and achievability of the goals they establish and the choices and investments needed to reach them.

Context. The impact of an economic shock changes along with the contexts in which the developing individual interacts. For example, the impact of an economic shock on education will vary by individual characteristics such as age and gender, microsystemic characteristics such as family and neighborhood, and macrosystemic factors such as employment opportunities and social cohesiveness as well as broader contextual factors such as levels of gross domestic product and growth rates. Contextual factors at all levels can buffer—or exacerbate—the impact of shocks, directly through institutional protections to minimize the exposure of households to shocks or instrumentally by providing tools and resources to help the family cope or adapt to changes.

Socioeconomic circumstances of their immediate context play an important role in how children develop and how shocks might affect them. Of course, wealthy households will weather economic crises in different ways and with presumably greater success than poorer households. There is a wealth of evidence on how poverty or socioeconomic status affects children at various stages, but the pathways may be enormously complex, ranging from the availability of prenatal and perinatal care, exposure to environmental toxins, and harsh and inconsistent parenting to lower teacher quality associated with living in poorer neighborhoods (see, for example, Duncan and Brooks-Gunn 1997; Brooks-Gunn, Duncan, and Aber 1997; McLoyd 1998). In addition, studies comparing temporary and chronic deprivation find different impacts, depending on the life stage of the child when experiencing this hardship (for accounts, see Elder 1999; McLoyd 1998; McLoyd et al. 2009).

The contexts of a developing person are constantly changing as the child progresses through the various stages of development. A young child's primary context will be within the family and with his or her primary caregiver, commonly the mother. At this stage, shocks experienced by the household affecting intrahousehold dynamics, or parental (in particular, maternal) stress and mental health, will have a greater effect on young children (see, for example, Corrales and Utter 2004; O'Brien et al. 2004; Campbell et al. 2004).

Nevertheless, parental stress and mental health also affect older children's cognitive and behavioral skills and socioemotional outcomes through similar pathways: marital conflict, depression, and resulting negative parenting (Gershoff et al. 2007). However, during middle childhood the young person spends increasing amounts of time outside the household, mainly at school, but also in community settings. While intrahousehold factors still greatly influence the child's development, the school environment becomes a socializing factor that also interacts with his home environment. Trouble at home can lead to behavioral problems in school, complicating teacher-child and peer relationships, and can negatively affect the learning process. And vice versa, problems in school may affect the child's behavior at home and his relationship with his parents.

Adolescents orient themselves increasingly toward peers and adults outside the immediate family, such as teachers, mentors, and possibly employers. For adolescents the impact of changes within the family may become less prominent as outside influences become stronger. However, as youth become more aware of their family's socioeconomic status, the stigma associated with poverty and welfare negatively influences their perceptions of self (see, for example, McLoyd et al. 2009). In addition, contextual factors specific to poor youth may affect their resilience or ability to adapt (see, for example, Crockett and Silbereisen 2000). Such factors may range from high-quality school settings to strong communities that provide the supporting environment in which young people can develop healthy identities and aspirations. Context also shapes social expectations about age-appropriate behavior and transitions, which may be challenged by the changes in the social, economic, and political environment during a crisis.

Therefore, the macropolicy environment will determine how domestic markets are affected by a global economic recession. Social safety nets can alleviate the impact on affected populations (see, for example, Galasso and Ravallion 2004). Around the world, people make use of sophisticated networks of informal insurance or mutual support and exchange to mitigate the effects of shocks. However, in crisis times such informal networks are often ineffective at insuring households (see, for example, Carter and Maluccio 2003; McKenzie 2003). In addition, people rely on cultural frameworks and repertoires, or scripts, to cope with and make meaning of their situation (see, for example, Hall and Lamont 2009; Sharone 2011; Chauvel 2010). For example, strong ethnic and cultural identity and a sense of belonging increased individual and community resilience among Mexican immigrant families in California during the great recession (Conger and Stockdale 2011). In sum, the historical, cultural, economic, political, and institutional context at various (system) levels may moderate the impact of shocks on the child's development.

Transmission mechanisms. A deeper understanding of the interactions and processes that drive human development also allows us to better identify transmission mechanisms (other than the fall in household income) through which a child may be affected. Economic crises are transmitted to households through changes in prices and markets for credit, goods and services, and labor. Households generally experience shocks in different ways, depending on their resources and their relationship to these markets. For example, farm households and urban working-class households will be differently affected by an increase in food or fuel prices. The causes of a shock—for example, a sovereign debt default or a currency crisis, together with the context and structure of the economy—will determine who will be more affected and how. For instance, evidence suggests that the recession of 2008–09 had a greater impact on middle-to-high-income countries and households (Dao and Loungani 2010). Nevertheless, such shocks often have spillover effects that will affect poorer countries and households: foreign direct investment, official development assistance, private remittances, and demand for developing-country exports can all fall in a crisis. Moreover, the mechanisms available to smooth consumption and investment will differ across households. Poorer households tend to rely on informal insurance mechanisms to smooth consumption, but these informal and community-based insurance systems can break down when many households are affected.

As box 4.1 (chapter 4) explores further, economic shocks can influence children's outcomes indirectly by shaping family practices, processes, and relationships. In a crisis, parents bear the burden of economic pressures, but their ability to cope with the stress of insufficient income has consequences for their interactions with their family. Worries about income loss or the inadequacy of household resources may be just as strong a transmission mechanism as the actual inability to provide for one's children (Conger and Conger 2008; Tubbs, Hughes, and Way 2011). Parents who experience economic pressure also have an increased risk of emotional problems (depression and anxiety, for example) and behavior problems (such as substance abuse), which in turn may lead to or exacerbate family conflict (Mistry et al. 2002; Conger and Conger 2008). Parents who experience severe conflict or emotional distress may be more likely to withdraw from or become hostile toward their children, which can adversely affect children's cognitive and socioemotional development (Gershoff et al. 2007). The consequences for the child can include early school leaving, early abandonment of the parental household, or adoption of self-destructive or costly antisocial behaviors that may last a lifetime. Understanding these processes allows us to identify the ways in which households are affected, in addition to the obvious drop in household income.

Transmission mechanisms will vary depending on the timing or age of the child and the context in which the child is embedded. It is useful to think along the lines of the salient developmental tasks pertaining to each stage of development and the dominant settings within which the child interacts. During early childhood, the family or household is the primary setting within which the child has face-to-face interactions. Chapter 3 shows how the child depends on the family to provide nutrition, safe attachment, and stimulation in order to master the stage-salient developmental tasks, establish secure attachment relationships, learn to actively explore and communicate, and develop the ability to regulate thoughts, behaviors, and emotions (Aber and Jones 1997). During this stage, the most important transmission mechanisms seem to be resources for food and other investments, the family dynamics and functioning, and the time and mental health of the primary caregivers. As pointed out earlier, a child's development is vulnerable to insults in utero, for example, from exposure to malnutrition or high levels of stress hormones caused by tension or pressures experienced by the mother. The infant depends on nurturing and stimulating care to form a safe attachment; stress or other mental health issues of the primary caregivers will inhibit these processes.

Chapter 4 finds that, as children increasingly interact with the wider world, especially school, three main transmission mechanisms are likely to affect their success at mastering the dominant developmental tasks of systematic reasoning and interpersonal negotiation and social problem solving: (1) parental stress and family functioning; (2) investments in learning and stimulation within the home; and (3) teachers, peers, and the learning environment in schools.

In general, the evidence does not show any significant impacts of aggregate economic shocks on schooling attendance or attainment. It is not true that crises always lead young people to leave school. In fact, studies from middle- and high-income countries indicate countercyclical effects of shocks on schooling: that is, economic crises seem to increase school enrollment (Ferreira and Schady 2009). This is likely due to the fact that in economic downturns, the opportunity cost of leaving the labor market to stay in school is lower.

However, schooling is but one indicator of human development. It may not accurately measure more subtle aspects of cognitive and behavioral development or, in other words, the competencies that ultimately matter for success in work and life. For example, economic pressure often increases parental stress and intrahousehold tensions, leading to the deterioration of parental stimulation and enforcement of rules and routines (Gershoff et al. 2007). These factors can inhibit the development of self-regulatory skills and social competence, decrease academic achievement, and increase the likelihood of adverse or even self-destructive behaviors during adolescence (see, for example, Teo et al. 1996; Dishion, Capaldi, and Yoerger 1999; Votruba-Drzal 2006).

However, given the importance of the school setting during middle childhood, one needs to look at how aggregate economic shocks might affect the supply of schooling. Aggregate economic shocks may reduce public spending on education, although children's academic performance is not highly correlated with a country's aggregate expenditures on education (Hanushek and Kimko 2000; Woessman 2001). On the other hand, shocks may disrupt learning by affecting the teaching environment and teacher-student relationships. Teachers may bring their own stress into the classroom, and students may exhibit more behavioral issues due to their home situation (Cohen, Raudenbush, and Ball 2003).

Young people become increasingly aware of their surroundings and are increasingly influenced by people and social processes outside the family. A young person will also be increasingly affected directly by shifts in the environment or changes caused, for example, by economic crisis (Crockett and Silbereisen 2000). Chapter 5 identifies two major transmission mechanisms through which crises can affect an adolescent's mastery of three particular stage-salient developmental tasks (establish autonomy; develop identity; establish competence for goal setting and achievement) and thus interfere with her transition to work and adulthood: (1) number and predictability employment opportunities and (2) parental employment and family dynamics.

Crises will alter the context within which young people develop their identity, set goals, plan strategically, and work to achieve them (Crockett and Silbereisen 2000). Similar to elderly workers, young people can have a harder time finding and keeping a job during economic downturns. The inability to find a job is likely to delay achieving financial independence and establishing autonomy. In addition, the degrees and qualifications needed to acquire a particular job may change due to shifts in both available employment opportunities and available education and skills-training programs. This may force a young person to reexamine previously formed identities and aspirations, and it may be difficult to adapt positively to the new environment and opportunities for healthy development and the transition to work. This process of identity formation begins in early adolescence, and such environmental shifts are likely to alter expectations about the future even for younger children. One goal of protective interventions must be to facilitate the establishment of identities that can weather and adapt to changing environments.

The family remains a strong socializing influence on adolescents; children adopt values, perceptions, and attitudes toward work and family life from their own family experiences. A parent's unemployment and cynical and pessimistic outlook about future employment prospects are likely to influence the child (McLoyd et al. 2011). Furthermore, unemployment can impair mental health and cause family tension, increase substance abuse, and lead to abusive home environments (Elder 1974).

With age the young person becomes more susceptible to influences outside the family. The young person's ability to integrate these influences successfully depends largely on his self-regulation skills and adaptive capacity. While research indicates that adolescents tend to engage with people who share their parents' values (Allison and Lerner 1993), economic crisis may change these patterns (Elder 1974). Moreover, exposure to positive extrafamilial adult role models can be particularly important for young people with limited family resources. These relationships can be a source of values and aspirations contributing to developing a productive future orientation (McLoyd et al. 2011). In addition, a parent's unemployment and a young person's own difficulties in transitioning to work may have an array of influences on identifying goals and the development of autonomy and identity.

Policy Options

Beyond traditional safety net programs, we have limited experience with programs and interventions that protect the development of children and youth during crisis, especially in developing countries. Given the enormous heterogeneity in contexts, policies, and individual responses to economic shocks, no policy response is universally applicable. The effectiveness of an intervention or suite of programs to protect and promote children's development during crisis will depend on the context and how design features and implementation strategy address this context. However, we can propose a set of principles that leads to a clearer diagnosis and to a mechanism for the identification of appropriate policies and programs. The key principles to be considered are nested points of entry, substitutability, and targeting. Note, however, that the evidence supporting some of the most important policies and interventions comes from noncrisis environments.

It is important to *break the transmission* of the shock to the developing child. In the first instance, this is accomplished by minimizing the exposure of the household to the shock, for example, by maintaining sound macroeconomic policies. Where that is insufficient, the next line of defense is to minimize the consequences of the shock to the household or to assist the household in recovering from the worst ravages of the shock through a social safety net program. However, as the evidence in this book emphasizes, even that may not be sufficient. Policies should not stop at the door of the household. By clarifying the mechanisms through which a shock can be transmitted to children, we open up a whole range of possible avenues for intervention, or *nested points of entry*, through which we can target interventions.

For example, cash transfer programs can effectively maintain consumption during economic crises. But it may also be necessary to help families deal with the psychosocial effects of unemployment or a significant reduction in wages. The crisis may be affecting them in subtle and unexpected ways, resulting in increased family conflict or mental health issues. They should be supported and encouraged to maintain effective and positive parenting behaviors and to sustain good relationships with their children in order to foster better socioemotional and cognitive outcomes.

Second, understanding the ways in which the development of children of different ages is embedded in different contexts and settings, and tracing how an economic shock may affect these settings differently, will inform the design of effective policies and interventions. Among the essential factors in policy design is to understand to what extent policies in one setting can *substitute* for the lack of positive stimulation, or, in other words, can compensate for negative impacts that occur in another setting. For example, we know that young children's socioemotional development may be particularly affected by intrafamilial conflict stemming, among others, from financial stress. However, it is costly to implement interventions targeted to individual families or family members. Instead, it may be possible to implement or augment existing socioemotional learning programs in schools in times of crisis to buffer against the potential negative consequences of family stress.

Finally, vulnerability to shocks is not merely a matter of income or employment. Broadening the definition of vulnerability beyond financial characteristics and understanding susceptibilities that differ by timing and context will enable more accurate *targeting* of policies during a crisis. Income-based targeting mechanisms may be complex and not sufficiently responsive to establish in a crisis. Crises demand rapid responses: safety nets must be rolled out quickly, and governments often resort to programs that can be self-targeted, such as public works programs that pay inframarginal wages, or the distribution of inferior commodities to ensure food security.[2] But public works programs may not be the most effective way to ensure child welfare and, as chapter 5 points out, may be largely inadequate to address the issues related to and consequences of prolonged unemployment among young people.

Furthermore, strict income-based targeting may miss large numbers of vulnerable children and young people who are at risk of suffering severe adverse long-term impacts but who do not satisfy stricter, single-dimensional targeting criteria. Building on the insights gained from incorporating approaches from other social sciences, policy makers may replace income-based targeting with programs aimed at particular age groups or groups that share other specific vulnerabilities. For example, unemployment of a parent can create stress in otherwise financially secure families, severely affecting a child's development, without pushing the family close to the poverty line. School-based programs involving all children may counter the negative effects of a stressful home situation by strengthening peer relationships. In addition, all young people may experience stresses caused by greater uncertainty in the transition to work. Training programs that are open to all those who experience difficulties can provide a supportive environment and the opportunity for acquiring technical skills, but can also foster networks and enhance behavioral and social skills that all youth, but particularly disadvantaged young people, need desperately.

Conclusions

Economic depression, banking crisis, or natural disaster, whether occurring locally, regionally, or worldwide, have the potential to disrupt and do permanent damage to the course of human development. This may be particularly costly to the youngest among us, both because of their lack of agency—that is, their dependency on adults to provide for and invest in them—and because of the critical developmental milestones to be achieved during those years. At stake is nothing less than the development of healthy, productive, and effective citizens. The attainment of good health, the skills needed to find and prosper in employment, and the ability to form nurturing and sustaining relationships are essential for shared growth and welfare. For children to perform these tasks well in times of relative stability requires that diverse aspects of the developmental processes—psychosocial as well as physiological—be nurtured and protected. To ensure that these tasks are performed well during times of economic volatility and upheaval requires that we identify how shocks affect developing children and that we use this information to design and target policies and interventions to best protect children and young people from lasting damage to their human capital.

Depending on the timing, duration, transmission mechanisms, and context of an economic shock, the consequences for children's physical, cognitive, and socioemotional development may be long lasting, costly, and in some cases irreversible. Happily, the research presented in this volume suggests that children at higher risk may exhibit greater sensitivity to context in general and may benefit more positively when exposed to especially enriching environments (Baltes 1997). In that case, the damages resulting from exposure to physical or emotional stress may not be permanent, if protective and corrective interventions can be identified, designed, and effectively implemented.

Notes

1. The MDGs are eight broad objectives, adopted by all 193 United Nations member states in 2000, intended to enhance human capability and well-being, including reducing poverty and improving health, education, gender equality, and environmental sustainability by 2015. See http://www.un.org /millenniumgoals/.

2. Note that this is inferior in the sense that those with lower incomes are more likely to consume it; this does not mean nutritionally inferior. For example, coarsely ground flours are often nutritionally superior to finely ground flours; yet the latter are generally preferred by consumers (Lundberg and Diskin 1995).

References

Aber, L., and S. Jones. 1997. "Indicators of Positive Development in Early Childhood: Improving Concepts and Measures." In *Indicators of Children's Well-being*, ed. R. Hauser, B. Brown, and W. Prosser, 395–427. New York: Russell Sage Foundation.

Ainsworth, M. D. S. 1967. *Infancy in Uganda: Infant Care and the Growth of Love.* Baltimore, MD: Johns Hopkins University Press.

Allison, K., and R. Lerner. 1993. "Adolescents and the Family." In *Early Adolescence: Perspectives on Research, Policy, and Intervention*, ed. R. Lerner, 1-17. Hillsdale, NJ: Erlbaum.

Baltes, Paul B. 1997. "On the Incomplete Architecture of Human Ontogeny: Selection, Optimization, and Compensation as Foundation of Development Theory." *American Psychologist* 32 (4): 366–80.

Bee, H., and D. Boyd. 2010. *The Developing Child.* 12th ed. Boston: Allyn and Bacon.

Bell, D., and D. Blanchflower. 2010. "Young People and Recession: A Lost Generation?" Dartmouth College Working Paper. Hanover, NH: Dartmouth College.

Belsky, J., B. Spritz, and K. Crnic. 1996. "Infant Attachment Security and Affective-Cognitive Information Processing at Age 3." *Psychological Science* 7 (2): 111–14.

Bergman, K., V. Glover, P. Sarkar, D. H. Abbott, and T. G. O'Connor. 2010. "In Utero Cortisol and Testosterone Exposure and Fear Reactivity in Infancy." *Hormones and Behavior* 57 (3): 306–12.

Betts, J., and L. McFarland. 1995. "Safe Port in a Storm: The Impact of Labor Market Conditions on Community College Enrollments." *Journal of Human Resources* 30 (4): 741–65.

Bowlby, J. 1988. *A Secure Base*. New York, NY: Basic Books.

Bronfenbrenner, U. 1979. *The Ecology of Human Development: Experiments by Nature and Design*. Cambridge, MA: Harvard University Press.

———. 1994. "Ecological Models of Human Development." In *International Encyclopedia of Education*. 2nd ed. Vol. 3. Oxford, UK: Elsevier.

Brooks-Gunn, J., G. Duncan, and J. L. Aber, eds. 1997. *Neighborhood Poverty: Context and Consequences for Children*. Vol. 1. New York: Russell Sage Foundation.

Burgess, S., C. Propper, H. Rees, and A. Shearer. 2003. "The Class of 1981: The Effects of Early Career Unemployment on Subsequent Unemployment Experiences." *Labour Economics* 10 (3): 291–309.

Campbell, S. B., C. A. Brownell, A. Hungerford, S. J. Spieker, R. Mohan, and J. S. Blessing. 2004. "The Course of Maternal Depressive Symptoms and Maternal Sensitivity as Predictors of Attachment Security at 36 Months." *Development and Psychopathology*, 16 (2): 231–52.

Carter, M. R., and J. Maluccio. 2003. "Social Capital and Coping with Economic Shocks: An Analysis of Stunting of South African Children." *World Development* 31 (7):1147–63.

Case, A., and C. Ardington. 2006. "The Impact of Parental Death on School Outcomes: Longitudinal Evidence from South Africa." *Demography* 43 (3): 401–20.

Cassidy, J. 1988. "Child-Mother Attachment and the Self in Six-Year-Olds." *Child Development* 59 (1): 121–34.

Chauvel, L. 2010. "The Long-Term Destabilization of Youth, Scarring Effects, and the Future of the Welfare Regime in Post-*Trente Glorieuses* France." *French Politics, Culture and Society* 28 (3): 74–96.

Cho, Y., and D. Newhouse. 2011. "How Did the Great Recession Affect Different Types of Workers? Evidence from 17 Middle-Income Countries." Policy Research Working Paper 5636, World Bank, Washington, DC.

Choudhry, M., E. Marelli, and M. Signorelli. 2010. "The Impact of Financial Crises on Youth Unemployment Rate." Working Paper 79, Department of Economics, Università di Perugia, Perugia, Italy.

Cohen, D., S. Raudenbush, and D. Ball. 2003. "Resources, Instruction, and Research." *Educational Evaluation and Policy Analysis* 25 (2): 119–42.

Conger, R. D., and K. J. Conger. 2008. "Understanding the Processes through Which Economic Hardship Influences Families and Children." In *Handbook of Families and Poverty*, ed. R. Crane and T. Heaton, 64– 81. Thousand Oaks, CA: Sage.

Conger, R., and G. D. Stockdale. 2011. "Response to the Great Recession: Mexican Origin Families and Children in California." Paper presented at the conference "Children and Youth in Crisis," World Bank and the Jacobs Foundation, May 5–6, Marbach, Germany.

Corrales, K., and S. Utter. 2004. "Failure to Thrive." In *Handbook of Pediatric Nutrition*, 2nd ed., ed. P. Samour, K. Helm, and C. Lang, 395–412. Sudbury, MA: Jones and Bartlett Publishers.

Crockett, L., and R. K. Silbereisen. 2000. *Negotiating Adolescence in Times of Social Change*. Cambridge, UK: Cambridge University Press.

Cunningham, W., and J. Bustos-Salvagno. 2011. "Shocks, Child Labor and School Dropouts in Argentina." Mimeo. World Bank, Washington, DC.

Dao, M., and P. Loungani. 2010. "The Human Cost of Recessions: Assessing It, Reducing It." Staff Position Note SPN/10/17. International Monetary Fund, Washington, DC.

Das, J., Q. Do, J. Friedman, D. McKenzie, and K. Scott. 2007. "Mental Health and Poverty in Developing Countries: Revisiting the Relationship." *Social Science and Medicine* 65: 467–80.

Dearing, E., K. McCartney, and B. Taylor. 2001. "Change in Family Income-to-Needs Matters More for Children with Less." *Child Development* 72 (6): 1779–93.

Dishion, T., D. Capaldi, and K. Yoerger. 1999. "Middle Childhood Antecedents to Progressions in Male Adolescent Substance Use: An Ecological Analysis of Risk and Protection." *Journal of Adolescent Research* 14 (2): 175–205.

Duncan, G., and J. Brooks-Gunn, eds. 1997. *Consequences of Growing up Poor*. New York: Russell Sage Foundation.

Duncan, G. J., J. Brooks-Gunn, and P. K. Klebanov. 1994. "Economic Deprivation and Early-Childhood Development." *Child Development* 65 (2): 296–318.

Duncan, G. J., P. A. Morris, and C. Rodrigues. 2011. "Does Money Really Matter? Estimating Impacts of Family Income on Young Children's Achievement with Data from Random-Assignment Experiments." *Developmental Psychology* 47 (5): 1263–79.

Duryea, S., and M. Arends-Kuenning. 2003. "School Attendance, Child Labor, and Local Labor Market Fluctuations in Urban Brazil." *World Development* 31 (7): 1165–78.

Duryea, S., D. Lam, and D. Levison. 2007. "Effects of Economic Shocks on Children's Employment and Schooling in Brazil." *Journal of Development Economics* 84 (1): 188–214.

Eccles, J. S. 1999. "The Development of Children Ages 6 to 14." *Future of Children: When School Is Out* 9 (2): 30–44.

Elder, G. H. 1974. *Children of the Great Depression: Social Change in Life Experience.* Chicago: University of Chicago Press.

Elder, G. 1999. *Children of the Great Depression: Social Change in Life Experience.* 25th anniversary ed. Boulder, CO: Westview Press.

Eloundou-Enyegue, P., and J. Davanzo. 2003. "Economic Downturns and Schooling Inequality, Cameroon, 1987–95." *Population Studies* 57 (2): 183–97.

Fasih, T., H. A. Patrinos, and M. N. Shafiq. 2009. The Impact of Financial and Macroeconomic Crises on Education and Labor Market Outcomes. Technical Report. Washington DC: World Bank.

Fernald, L., A. Weber, E. Galasso, and L. Ratsifandrihamanana. 2011. "Socio-economic Gradients and Child Development in a Very Low Income Population." *Developmental Science* 14 (4): 832–47.

Ferreira, F. H. G., and N. Schady. 2009. "Aggregate Economic Shocks, Child Schooling, and Child Health." *World Bank Research Observer* 24 (2): 147–81.

Friedman, J., and J. Sturdy. 2011. "The Influence of Economic Crisis on Early Childhood Development: A Review of Pathways and Measured Impact." In *No Small Matter: The Impact of Poverty, Shocks, and Human Capital Investments in Early Childhood Development,* ed. H. Alderman. Washington, DC: World Bank.

Friedman, J., and D. Thomas. 2009. "Psychological Health before, during, and after an Economic Crisis: Results from Indonesia, 1993–2000." *World Bank Economic Review* 23 (1): 57–76.

Galasso, E., and M. Ravallion. 2004. "Social Protection in a Crisis: Argentina's Plan Jefes y Jefas." *World Bank Economic Review* 18 (3): 367–99.

Gershoff, E., J. L. Aber, C. Raver, and M. C. Lennon. 2007. "Income Is Not Enough: Incorporating Material Hardship into Models of Income Associations with Parenting and Child Development." *Child Development* 78 (1): 70–95.

Glick P., D. E. Sahn, and T. F. Walker. 2011. "Household Shocks and Education Investment in Madagascar." Working Paper 240, Food and Nutrition Policy Program, Cornell University, Ithaca, NY.

Goldin, Claudia. 1999. "Egalitarianism and the Returns to Education during the Great Transformation of American Education." *Journal of Political Economy* 107 (6): S65–S94.

Gregg, P., and E. Tominey. 2005. "The Wage Scar from Male Youth Unemployment." *Labour Economics* 12 (4): 487–509.

Hall, P., and M. Lamont, eds. 2009. *Successful Societies: How Institutions and Culture Affect Health*. Cambridge, UK: Cambridge University Press.

Hanushek, E. A., and D. D. Kimko. 2000. "Schooling, Labor Force Quality, and the Growth of Nations." *American Economic Review* 90 (5): 1184–208.

Harper, C., N. Jones, A. McKay, and J. Epey. 2009. "Children in Times of Economic Crisis: Past Lessons, Future Policies." Background Note, Overseas Development Institute, London.

Hidrobo, M. 2011. "The Effect of Ecuador's 1998–2000 Economic Crisis on Child Health and Cognitive Development." University of California Berkeley, http://ecnr.berkeley.edu/vfs/PPs/Hidrobo-Mel/web/Hidrobo_JMP_1.16.11.pdf.

Hong, J., M. Knapp, and A. McGuire. 2011. "Income-related Inequalities in the Prevalence of Depression and Suicidal Behaviour: A 10-Year Trend following Economic Crisis." *World Psychiatry* 10 (1): 40–44.

Kahn, L. 2010. "The Long-Term Labor Market Consequences of Graduating from College in a Bad Economy." *Labour Economics* 17 (2): 303–16.

Kane, T. 1994. "College Entry by Blacks since 1970: The Role of College Costs, Family Background, and the Returns to Education." *Journal of Political Economy* 102 (5): 878–911.

Kochanska, G. 1995. "Children's Temperament, Mothers' Discipline, and Security of Attachment: Multiple Pathways to Emerging Internalization." *Child Development* 66 (3): 597–615.

Koettl, J., I. Oral, and I. Santos. 2011. "Employment Recovery in Europe and Central Asia." ECA Knowledge Brief, World Bank, Washington, DC.

Lam, D. A., C. Ardington, and M. Leibbrandt. 2011. "The Impact of Household Shocks on Adolescent School Outcomes in South Africa." Mimeo. University of Michigan.

Lerner, R. 1993. *Early Adolescence: Perspectives on Research, Policy, and Intervention*. Hillsdale, NJ: Erlbaum.

———. 1998. "Developmental Science, Developmental Systems, and Contemporary Theories of Human Development." In *Handbook of Child Psychology*, 6th ed., vol. 1, ed. R. Lerner. New York: Wiley.

Lumey, L. H., et al. 2007. "Cohort Profile: The Dutch Hunger Winter Families Study." *International Journal of Epidemiology* 36 (6): 1196–1204.

Lundberg, M., and P. Diskin. 1995. "Targeting Assistance to the Poor and Food Insecure." Technical Paper 9, U.S. Agency for International Development, Office of Sustainable Development, Washington, DC.

Macours, K., N. Schady, and R. Vakis. 2008. "Cash Transfers, Behavioral Changes, and Cognitive Development in Early Childhood: Evidence from a

Randomized Experiment." Policy Research Working Paper 4759, World Bank, Washington, DC.

McKenzie, D. J. 2003. "How Do Households Cope with Aggregate Shocks? Evidence from the Mexican Peso Crisis." *World Development* 31 (7): 1179–99.

McLoyd, V. 1998. "Socioeconomic Disadvantage and Child Development." *American Psychologist* 53 (2): 185–204.

McLoyd, V., R. Kaplan, K. Purtell, E. Bagley, C. Hardaway, and C. Smalls. 2009. "Poverty and Socioeconomic Disadvantage in Adolescence." In *Handbook of Adolescent Psychology*, 3rd ed., vol. 2, ed. R. Lerner and Laurence Steinberg, 444–91. Hoboken, NJ: Wiley.

McLoyd, V., R. Kaplan, M. Purtell, and A. Huston. 2011. "Assessing the Effects of a Work-Based Antipoverty Program for Parents on Youth's Future Orientation and Employment Experiences." Special issue, "Raising Healthy Children," *Child Development* 82 (1): 113–32.

Mistry, R., E. Vandewater, A. Huston, and V. McLoyd. 2002. "Economic Well-Being and Children's Social Adjustment: The Role of Family Process in an Ethnically Diverse Low-Income Sample." *Child Development* 73 (3): 935–51.

Naudeau, S., S. Martinez, P. Premand, and D. Filmer. 2011. "Cognitive Development among Young Children in Low-Income Countries." In *No Small Matter: The Impact of Poverty, Shocks, and Human Capital Investments in Early Childhood Development*, ed. H. Alderman, 9–50. Washington, DC: World Bank.

O'Brien, L. M., E. G. Heycock, M. Hanna, P. W. Jones, and J. L. Cox. 2004. "Postnatal Depression and Faltering Growth: A Community Study." Pt. 1. *Pediatrics* 113 (5): 1242–47.

Oreopoulos P., T. von Watcher, and A. Heisz. 2006. "The Short and Long-Term Career Effects of Graduating in a Recession: Hysteresis and Heterogeneity in the Market for College Graduates." Working Paper 12159, National Bureau of Economic Research, Cambridge, MA.

Paxson, C., and N. Schady. 2007. "Cognitive Development among Young Children in Ecuador: The Roles of Wealth, Health, and Parenting." *Journal of Human Resources* 42 (1): 49–84.

Reinhart, C., and K. Rogoff. 2009. *This Time is Different: Eight Centuries of Financial Folly*. Princeton, NJ: Princeton University Press.

Sarkar, P., K. Bergman, T. G. O'Connor, and V. Glover. 2008. "Maternal Antenatal Anxiety and Amniotic Fluid Cortisol and Testosterone: Possible Implications for Foetal Programming." *Journal of Neuroendocrinology* 20 (4): 489–96.

Schady, N. 2004. "Do Macroeconomic Crises Always Slow Human Capital Accumulation?" *World Bank Economic Review* 18 (2): 131–54.

Schamis, H. 2002. "Argentina: Crisis and Democratic Consolidation." *Journal of Democracy* 13 (2): 81–94.

Sharone, O. 2011. "Chemistry or Specs: Job Search Games, Playercentrality, and Subjective Responses to Unemployment." Working Paper, Sloan Business School, Massachusetts Institute of Technology, Cambridge, MA.

Skoufias, E., and S. Parker. 2006. "Job Loss and Family Adjustments in Work and Schooling during the Mexican Peso Crisis." *Journal of Population Economics* 19 (1): 163–81.

Sroufe, A. 1979. "The Coherence of Individual Development: Early Care, Attachment, and Subsequent Developmental Issues." *American Psychologist* 34 (10): 834–41.

Sroufe, L. A., and B. Egeland. 1991. "Illustrations of Person-Environment Interaction from a Longitudinal Study." In *Conceptualization and Measurement of Organism-Environment Interaction*, ed. T. D. Wachs and R. Plomin, 68–84. Washington, DC: American Psychological Association.

Stevens, K. 2008. "Adverse Economic Conditions at Labour Market Entry: Permanent Scars or Rapid Catch Up?" Job Market Paper, University of Sydney, Australia.

Tangcharoensathien, V., H. Piya, P. Siriwan, and K. Vijj. 2000. "Health Impacts of Rapid Economic Changes in Thailand." *Social Science and Medicine* 51 (6): 789–807.

Teo, A., E. Carlson, P. J. Mathieu, B. Egeland, and L. A. Sroufe. 1996. "A Prospective Longitudinal Study of Psychosocial Predictors of Achievement." *Journal of School Psychology* 34 (3): 285–306.

Tubbs, C., D. Hughes, and N. Way, N. 2011. "Disentangling Financial Strain: Pathways between a Change in Income and Parent-Adolescent Conflict during 'The Great Recession.'" Paper presented at the Center for Research on Culture, Development, and Education, New York University, conference "Children and Youth in Crisis," Marbach, Germany, May 5–6.

Votruba-Drzal, E. 2006. "Economic Disparities in Middle Childhood Development: Does Income Matter?" *Developmental Psychology* 42 (6): 1154–67.

Woessman, L. 2001. "New Evidence on the Missing Resource-Performance Link in Education." Kiel Working Paper 1051, Ifo Institute for Economic Research, Munich.

World Bank. 2009. *Averting a Human Crisis during the Global Downturn: Policy Options from the World Bank's Human Development Network*. Washington DC: World Bank.

———. 2011a. *The Jobs Crisis: Household and Government Responses to the Great Recession in Eastern Europe and Central Asia*. Washington, DC: World Bank.

———. 2011b. *Stepping Up Skills: For More Jobs and Higher Productivity*. Washington, DC: World Bank.

CHAPTER 2

A Conceptual Framework

Alice Wuermli, Rainer K. Silbereisen, Mattias Lundberg, Michèle Lamont, Jere R. Behrman, and Larry Aber[*]

Overview

This chapter has two main objectives: (1) to summarize the approaches taken by economics, developmental psychology, and sociology to understand the development and protection of human capital; and (2) to integrate these approaches into a comprehensive framework for analyzing the impact of aggregate economic shocks on human development during the critical formative years of a young person's life, between conception and about 25 years. Shocks matter during these years both because of the biological changes that take place (for example, during the first three years after conception and at the start of adolescence) and because young people begin to engage with social institutions and markets. Setbacks in either dimension of development can be prohibitively expensive or even impossible to reverse.

Empirical studies in economics have examined how negative shocks, including financial crises, can affect the development of human capital among children and youth. The shock is generally identified at the household level, for instance as a sudden and significant decrease in household income or the involuntary unemployment or bad health of a parent.

[*] Authors listed in reverse alphabetical order.

These shocks may originate in the community or the country, or they may have an international origin. They may be caused by severe weather, natural disasters, or unexpected large fluctuations in demand, supply, or prices. Whatever the cause, households must cope with a sudden drop in available resources. In some cases, the shock can also have significant impact on the need for services, especially health care, which increases the demands on resources at the same time.

Studies in economics of crises in low- and middle-income countries generally focus on school enrollment and attendance, labor market participation, and health-related outcomes such as child growth and mortality. This volume reviews these studies (see chapter 3, 4, and 5). The main message seems to be that there is enormous heterogeneity in the impact of shocks on children and youth. Few of these studies attempt to disentangle the sources of heterogeneity in outcomes beyond some readily available characteristics of individuals and households such as sex, age, demographic composition, and some socioeconomic indicators. In addition, given the data requirements, most of these studies are restricted to examining the short-run impact of shocks. From a policy perspective, however, it is of great interest to identify long-run implications of childhood and adolescent exposure to adversity (see, for example, Lumey and Stein 1997a, 1997b; Stein and Lumey 2000; Almond and Chay 2003; Almond 2006; Goldin 1999; Banerjee et al. 2007; Hoddinott et al. 2008, 2010; Behrman et al. 2009; Maluccio et al. 2009).

The failure to explain adequately the heterogeneity of outcomes and long-term impacts may also arise from the complexity of human development, embedded within an intricate web of subtle and interrelated systems and processes. Standard tools of microeconomics are largely inadequate to produce a comprehensive understanding of such. This chapter thus proposes a strong human development–centered approach allowing us to better understand the variety of short- and long-run impacts of shocks on child and youth development.

The framework developed in this chapter is an attempt to bring together economics with other social sciences—notably, developmental psychology, and sociology—in the study of the impact of economic shocks on young people's development. The economics discipline currently dominates the policy domain in international development. Incorporating research and methods from other social sciences will arguably yield a broader understanding and a more comprehensive set of analytical and policy tools to protect and enhance human development. These may prove especially important among countries that face economic crises, with widespread poverty, potential social unrest, and limited resources for constructive intervention.

The global development community has long understood that investments in human development, especially in job skills, are essential for higher productivity and growth. For example, the World Bank's recent publication *Stepping Up Skills for More Jobs and Higher Productivity* (World Bank 2011a) lays out a five-step development process for the acquisition of skills that will lead toward productivity and growth. That document also identifies economic crises and other shocks as potential threats to the skills development processes. However, it takes a narrow view of both the outcomes at risk and the pathways through which they can be affected. An interdisciplinary approach allows us to delve deeper into the human developmental processes. It enables us to identify the vulnerabilities and protective factors that characterize the crucial years of a young person's life and to understand the complex and interrelated mechanisms through which crises affect human development.

While yielding new insights and tools, combining different disciplinary perspectives has its challenges. The first is to ensure some consistency among divergent vocabularies and concepts. For example, the *Handbook of Child Psychology* and the *Handbook of Population and Family Economics* use different terms to refer to similar concepts, use the same terms for different concepts, or use terms that seem esoteric to other disciplines. We do our best to identify such jargon in advance and explain the terms in an attempt to minimize the confusion where possible (see also the glossary).

A further challenge in bridging disciplines stems from divergent implicit or explicit theoretical assumptions, models, methods, and data that underlie the empirical research. Traditional microeconomics is based on the principle that each person acts rationally in order to fulfill her objectives. This concept has little relevance in psychology and sociology, or at least is not of central importance. A primary objective of this chapter is to identify and discuss such differences in assumptions, models, methods, and data to avoid misunderstandings and misconceptions. To achieve this semantic, conceptual, and analytical clarity, we have made certain simplifications, sometimes omitting an element in one discipline or the other for the sake of intelligibility.

That said, this work is based partly on the important and substantive diversity in perspectives, methods, and understanding that derive from the different disciplines. We hope that this volume will provide an accessible guide and tool for researchers, policy makers, and practitioners to gain a broader understanding of how crises affect the developing child and to assist in the design of appropriate measures for the protection and promotion of human development.

Finally, in addition to serving an interdisciplinary audience, it is our objective to produce a volume that can address the concerns of policy makers and nongovernmental organizations that may not be interested in working through a highly technical document. We hope that we have attained a middle ground, which covers the fundamental and indispensable aspects in a way that adequately addresses the topic of child and youth development during economic crises.

This framework starts by establishing a common understanding of aggregate economic shocks. The section thereafter outlines the economics approach to human capital formation, following which we introduce concepts and theories from human developmental sciences. We then begin the process of integrating the two approaches to produce a comprehensive framework highlighting relevant transmission mechanisms to deepen our understanding of the impact of shocks on the developmental processes of children and youth. This interdisciplinary approach has implications for policy, which we elaborate on in the final section.

Given the length of the chapter, not every reader will need or feel the desire to read all the sections in equal detail. We encourage readers to make their own decision about which sections are of importance to further their understanding of the subject. Thus, economists are likely to skip the section on "The Economics of Human Capital," whereas human developmentalists will be prone to omit the section on "Human Development and a Bioecological Model." However, a rudimentary understanding of both approaches will be fundamental to further integration of approaches in research and policy.

Shocks, Crises, Business Cycles, Recessions, Depressions, and Busts

Terms such as *shock, crisis,* and *recession* are often used interchangeably and often refer to similar phenomena, without paying too much attention to their actual meanings. To highlight just one conceptual ambiguity, however, a *shock* can be a positive or a negative disturbance. Therefore, while a crisis or recession might be characterized as a negative shock, certainly not all shocks are negative; and even what presents itself as a negative shock for many in a society may be positive for a few in that it opens up new opportunities. A *crisis* is generally associated with large-scale social dislocation or disruption (see, for example, Elder 1999). *Recessions* and *depressions* are a particular type of negative shock or crisis associated with slow economic growth or contraction. For the purposes of this volume, we define negative shocks to the household as the inability to meet current consumption needs without a significant reorientation of resources.

Shocks can be distinguished by their direction (positive, negative), depth or intensity, duration, ubiquity or idiosyncrasy, frequency, and predictability. Households can experience negative shocks caused by a myriad of factors, ranging from the death of a household member to a currency crisis. Some shocks, such as unemployment, may be related both to individual characteristics and to shared, more aggregate events such as business cycles. Illness or death may hit one sole household because of unfortunate circumstances, or a large segment of the population can be affected by a pandemic or widespread natural disaster. Without examining other factors at the social, household, and individual level, there is no way to predict a priori what impact these shocks will have on the developmental processes of children and youth.

This study is concerned with the negative aggregate or systemic economic shocks that affect groups of households in a particular country or region or households of a particular type. These shocks occur in the wider economy, and are manifest to the household as changes in the terms of trade they face, or changes in demand or in the value of and returns to household assets. These shocks can include financial and credit market crises, declining prices for products sold, increased prices for items purchased, or business-cycle declines. While natural disasters including earthquakes, droughts, and floods and human crises such as wars and epidemic diseases are also aggregate in nature, they are not the central focus of this analysis. We do our best to draw clear distinctions where the data are available.

Some types of shocks may be repeated over time. Deaton (1997) finds that the ability of households to maintain consumption diminishes if there are repeated negative shocks in a short time period. Households can draw on assets to smooth consumption over the course of one drought; a succession of droughts, however, is more difficult to overcome, particularly if they occur close together. Systemic economic shocks are similar. Some degree of repetition makes it possible to learn from experience—to apply the lessons learned during one event to future events—thereby lessening their adverse consequences. Gertler and Gruber (2002), for example, find that households in Indonesia are better able to insure consumption against more frequent risks such as illness and idiosyncratic unemployment than against rare shocks such as death. Similarly, Rosenzweig and Wolpin (1985) find that older individuals in rural households in traditional agriculture provide insights into dealing with rarer shocks because they have experienced more such shocks in their longer lifetimes than have younger adults and can therefore provide intergenerational benefits.

It may be tempting to define a crisis by its *consequences:* that is, a crisis is a negative event for which the household is inadequately insured. But that begs the question of the relative efficacy of insurance practices across households, including the success of the household in minimizing exposure ex ante. Clearly, many households are affected by negative changes in prices or demand, but not all suffer equally in their ability to maintain a minimum level of consumption. In general, though—or at least for certain subpopulations, in particular the poor—systemic economic shocks tend to be large and widespread enough to disturb the performance of local consumption smoothing and (informal) insurance mechanisms.[1]

Identification and Measurement

While natural disasters or wars, for instance, and the causes thereof are comparatively easy to identify, economic crises, including financial crises, and their causes tend to be more ambiguous. In general, assets lose value suddenly and unpredictably in financial crises. These events can include banking panics, stock market crashes, and the bursting of other speculative bubbles (especially for commodities and quasi-fixed assets such as housing), currency crises, and sovereign defaults. Economic shocks in the sense of business-cycle movements are challenging to identify empirically. These are usually defined ex post as a function of manifest changes in aggregate economic growth rather than as a function of structural or policy factors that can be foreseen in advance.

Table 2.1 shows the frequency of negative shocks based on a number of alternative definitions, as well as shocks defined more conventionally as the three-year moving average of growth per capita. We include three measures of shocks: (1) shocks are those periods in which growth is greater than 5 percent or less than –5 percent; (2) shocks are those periods in which growth is outside the global mean plus or minus one standard deviation; (3) shocks are those periods in which growth is outside the country-specific mean plus or minus one standard deviation. For each measure of shocks, table 2.1 also includes the probability with which any country is likely to experience the shock; this probability is naively

Table 2.1 Global Incidence of Shocks, Selected Years, 1946–2010

	Number of episodes	Number of countries	Years	Mean number of episodes per country-year	Source
Economic shocks					
Growth <–5%	186	190	1960–2009	0.02	Penn World Tables 6.3
Growth > 5%	524	190	1960–2009	0.06	Penn World Tables 6.3
Growth < global mean – 1 sd	325	190	1960–2009	0.03	Penn World Tables 6.3
Growth > global mean + 1 sd	316	190	1960–2009	0.03	Penn World Tables 6.3
Growth < within-country mean – 1 sd	506	190	1960–2009	0.05	Penn World Tables 6.3
Growth > within-country mean + 1 sd	511	190	1960–2009	0.05	Penn World Tables 6.3
Financial shocks					
Banking crises	124	161	1976–2007	0.02	Laeven and Valencia (2008)
Currency crises	207	161	1972–2005	0.04	Laeven and Valencia (2008)
Debt crises	63	161	1976–2004	0.01	Laeven and Valencia (2008)
Social and political shocks					
Coups, attempted and successful	733	120	1946–2009	0.10	Center for Systemic Peace
More than 1,000 forcibly displaced people	134	175	1964–2008	0.02	U.S. Committee for Refugees and Immigrants
Major episodes of political violence	1,671	175	1947–2008	0.16	Center for Systemic Peace
Armed conflict	1,957	152	1946–2008	0.21	Peace Research Institute of Oslo
Political interregnum, interruption, or transition	382	175	1946–2009	0.03	Polity IV Project
Natural disasters					
Total	11,188	221	1960–2010	1.01	Center for Research on the Epidemiology of Disasters (CRED)
Number that are climate related	8,683	221	1960–2010	0.79	CRED

Source: Authors.
Note: sd = standard deviation.

defined as the total incidence of each type of crisis over the number of country-years in the dataset.

Growth-related shocks are defined as distinct episodes in which the phenomenon is observed, which can comprise multiple sequential years. For example, while there were only 186 separate country episodes in which the moving average of growth was less than –5 percent per year, there are 432 country-years.

It seems safe to conclude that natural disasters and social and political crises happen much more frequently than financial crises or large economic shocks in general. In addition, it is worth mentioning that large (>5 percent) positive shocks are almost three times as likely as large negative economic shocks (<–5 percent), whereas smaller positive and negative fluctuations seem to mirror each other, indicating business cycles rather than crises. Note that these numbers convey no information about what caused gross domestic product (GDP) to rise or fall. This is a combination of the economic structure, assets, policies, and integration into the world economy: for example, the impacts of a banking crisis and a weather shock on a primarily agricultural economy are likely to differ considerably. More important, there will be significant heterogeneity in the way that different segments of the population are affected by different shocks. Farm households are different from rural nonfarm households and even more different from urban households engaged in the service sector.

Similar shocks may be experienced and perceived differently across societies and across different groups within societies. These variations will partly be determined by the coping strategies available, and this in turn will partly determine how the shock affects them psychologically. For instance, the psychological impact of shocks will differ whether one believes that unemployment is a function of one's own characteristics or of events and circumstances beyond one's control. A recent comparative survey of Israel and the United States found that Israelis are more likely to perceive unemployment as structural, whereas Americans are more likely to blame the unemployed themselves. For middle-class Israelis, the experience of unemployment does not affect their core identity; middle-class professionals in the United States, however, interpret unemployment very differently, because their definition of self is more deeply tied to their work status (Sharone 2011). Expectations also color the experience of shocks. Poor families in Brazil may view the loss of a child as a terrible but commonplace event, while parents in societies with low infant mortality and low birth rates may experience that death as a more profound tragedy (Scheper-Hughes 1993). Context and history play an enormous role in the social and individual perception of and responses to shocks; the definitions of possible, appropriate, or optimal responses; and their impact on individual mental and physical health and social resilience (Hall and Lamont 2009; for more detail on social resilience, see box 6.2).

Whether an economic shock leads to a political and social crisis, as was the case for example in the 2001–02 financial crisis in Argentina, depends largely on how people perceive the changes and alternatives available to them. Importantly, political and social crises do not require actual economic contraction: a shock that merely lowers growth rates below what is expected, or that is combined with perceived changes in income distribution, may have significant social and political consequences. Among youth in France, for example, the most recent global crisis was perceived as an accentuation of a broader trend of economic and social decline (Chauvel 2010).

In sum, the profound shifts in the economic, political, and social structure that often accompany economic crises lend urgency to the topic of child and youth development. As pointed out previously, human development, or the formation of human capital, has been studied in an array of disciplines using a variety of indicators, methods, and sources of data. We thus turn to outline the dominant approaches in modern day social and behavioral sciences, starting with the economics of human capital and proceeding to the human developmental sciences.

The Economics of Human Capital

To economists, human development is the result of accumulated investments in growing children, including nutrition, education, stimulation, and care, in a supportive environment that allows the child to flourish. The microeconomic framework leads to empirically testable hypotheses about the determinants of human capital investments and the impact of shocks, policies, and environments on investment behavior and outcomes. We begin this chapter with the economic model of the production of human capital, which illustrates these determinants and outcomes and demonstrates how different human resource investments interact both contemporaneously and over time. We conclude this section with a framework for considering policies related to human capital investment and finally discuss the strengths and weaknesses of the standard economic approach.

Modeling Human Capital

Before we discuss the production of human capital, we describe the benefits of human capital; that is, the reason why a family (or a firm) might want to enhance the human capital of its members in the first place. Becker's Woytinsky Lecture (1967) provides a simple but useful and widely used framework to help think about these investments from the perspective of families or individuals at a particular point in time. It is important to note, however, that the investor (for example, the child's parents) may not be the sole beneficiary of the returns to these investments.[2] We will return to this agency problem later on. At this point, we will explore how private and societal resource management interacts through markets and policies to determine private human capital investments and the returns to those investments in the presence of shocks.

Economic models usually assume that families decide whether to invest in the human capital of their children in part because these investments are expected to yield payoffs today or in the future. The decision on how much to invest is based on their expectations of the net returns to the investments.[3] Other things equal, higher expected private benefits and lower expected private costs will encourage greater private investment. The optimum private investment is achieved at the point where the present discounted value of the expected marginal private benefit equals the present discounted value of the marginal private costs.[4,5] The value of of these marginal private costs and benefits can vary across households in the same environment and even across individuals in the same household. Age, sex, birth order, genetic predispositions, different levels of health and life expectancy, and other personal characteristics lead families to differential valuations of marginal returns and differential investment decisions, even across siblings within the same household. These differences are even greater across households, where the marginal private costs can differ considerably. For example, households differ in their access to credit, in their ability to ensure consumption in a crisis, or in the information to which they have access when making investment decisions.

The family produces outputs that it either sells or consumes, and it does so in a systematic way that transforms inputs into outputs. This systematic relationship between inputs and outputs can be described as a production function. A production function is a technical relation that gives the maximum output that can be produced with a given set of inputs by a firm (or by the household or other production unit). For example, the output might be a firm's production of wheelbarrows and the inputs might be labor, physical capital in the form of machine tools and buildings, and intermediate inputs such as steel, wood, plastic, and rubber. Or the output might be wheat, and the inputs might be seeds, soil, fertilizer, pesticides, water, and labor. Or the output might be child health, and the inputs might be nutrients, genetic predispositions, stimulation, parental time, environmental health conditions, and aspects of health care. The production function in itself does not say anything about whether the inputs actually used are the best combination of inputs, given the decision maker's objectives. But production functions are essential parts of economic models of behaviors related to human capital investments within the larger contexts of individuals' or families' objectives, the markets and policies they face, and the assets they have at the time that decisions related to human development are made.

We write the production function for the output (Q_f) of firm f to highlight the role of some attributes of worker i in firm f, including innate characteristics (G_{if}) and human capital that reflects previous human resource investments such as learning skills at home or in school (H_{if}) that might reflect past shocks, given similar attributes of other workers in the firm (L_f), capital stock of the firm (K_f), firm management capabilities and organization (M_f), and technological knowledge (T_f):

$$Q_f = Q(G_{if},\ H_{if},\ L_f,\ K_f,\ M_f,\ T_f).$$

All these variables can be vectors with multiple elements. Human capital, for example, can be interpreted to include education (whether from formal schooling, training, work experience, or on-the-job learning), physical and mental health, personality, and psychological states, and social relations—although the literature of empirical economics focuses primarily on the schooling and training components of education, with physical health a distant second.

The firm's production function (or that of the relevant production unit) is of key interest in determining, say, the impact on adult productivity of investments in children and youth and the shocks that in part determine such investments. Similarly, the productivity of a worker, the human capital that the adult worker possesses, is itself a function of the investments made in that worker when he or she was a child. It is useful to think of the stock of human capital as an outcome of a similar production function, which transformed inputs (education, nutrition, care, and stimulation) into outputs (human capital). And since human capital is multidimensional—encompassing, for example, both cognitive skills and self-discipline—one can imagine a multiplicity of production functions, each mapped to a specific outcome. These production functions reflect the cumulative impact of human capital investments from conception to the time of measurement and include the impact of any shocks or crises that affect the inputs invested or their effectiveness in producing human capital (see, for example, Todd and Wolpin 2003, 2007).

Dynamic and Life-Cycle Aspects of Human Capital Development

Since human capital production is an ongoing process, the examination of production functions may shed some light on how human capital investments at different stages of development can mitigate the impact of shocks over time.

Dynamic complementarities. According to Heckman (2006), human development exhibits increasing returns in the forms of dynamic complementarities and self-productivity. In other words, skills beget new skills, and capabilities foster future capabilities; new capabilities build on a foundation of capacities that were developed earlier. The downside to this is that it is often difficult to recover from early injuries. Later investments can complement previous ones, but may likely not substitute completely for earlier insults. Whether investments in the production of human capital are substitutes or complements is critical to the decision and the returns to investment. The hypothesis of limited substitutability between earlier and later investments has received recent empirical support (see, for example, Cunha and Heckman 2007; Cunha et al. 2006; Heckman 2006). It is clear that the returns to human capital investments in later adolescence depend critically on earlier investments and that remediation, while not impossible, is comparatively expensive (Knudsen et al. 2006).

Human capital investments in an individual over time can be viewed as a continuous sequence of investment decisions, each one reflecting not only factors (such as shocks) prevailing at that moment, but also expectations about the future, the outcomes of past decisions, and the experience of past crises. The decision to continue in postsecondary schooling, for example, is determined by the youth's innate capabilities; past investments in the youth's human capital (and thus the youth's current stock of human capital at the time of the postsecondary schooling decisions); current prices such as tuition and fees and the wage rates that reflect the cost of not working in order to attend school; and expectations about the future returns to postsecondary schooling. All such investments are made under uncertainty and in the presence of unanticipated past and current shocks, as well as future expectations.

Dynamic complementarity has significant implications for investment decisions taken by governments, firms, and families. If negative shocks reduce human capital investments, or adversely affect the level of human development in a person, the costs in terms of forgone human development and economic productivity may accumulate over time, since lower human capital investments today reduce the returns to any future investments. There is a present loss in the returns to past investments at the time of the crisis, and there is a future loss, relative to the higher level of skills and the higher returns that might have been achieved in the absence of the crisis. This is a public as well as a private calamity: both the society and the family lose the benefits from greater productivity and income in the long run. This path-dependence implies that a crisis can cause families and societies to underinvest in human capital, leading to lower growth, further reducing the returns to investment, and so on.

Critical periods. The notion of path dependence or dynamic complementarities takes on even greater importance if there are critical windows of opportunity for certain investments. If negative shocks reduce investments during sensitive periods in human development, the long-run costs of forgone human development and economic productivity may be even higher. As will be explored in more detail in the section "Human Development and a Bioecological Model," human development is marked by "stage-salient" tasks. If these tasks are not mastered by certain ages, they are costly to make up later in life, and their absence makes it even more difficult to master more complex skills. Cunha and Heckman (2007) review some of this evidence in both animal models and human development (see also Knudsen 2004).

Implications for Empirical Estimation of Human Capital Investments

The simple framework below systematizes six critical common-sense considerations for empirical investigations of the determinants and effects of human capital investments.

First, the marginal benefits and marginal costs of human capital investments in a particular individual differ, depending on the point of view from which they are evaluated:

- Because of externalities (that is, effects on others that are not transferred through markets, such as knowledge spillovers or congestion arising from overcrowding), or capital and insurance market imperfections, the social returns may differ from the private returns.

- Because there may be a difference between who makes the investment decision (for example, individual children's parents) and the individuals in whom the investment is made, differences in incentives for investments in one individual rather than another may result, for example, from traditional gender and birth-order roles in household responsibilities such as old-age care for parents.

Second, human capital investments are determined by many individual, family, community, market, and policy characteristics, only a subset of which are observed in datasets available for analyzing human capital determinants and effects. To identify correctly the impact of observed characteristics on human capital investments, we must control for the correlated unobserved characteristics. For example, children with better family backgrounds may have greater innate abilities of the types that increase economic success and may grow up in more supportive environments and attend higher-quality schools. In that case, if we observe only family incomes and parental schooling and not the children's abilities or the community and school characteristics, the usual research procedures and observational data are likely to overestimate the impact of family background on such investments.

Third, to identify the impact of human capital investments, we must also control for individual, family, and community characteristics that both determine the human capital investments and have direct effects on outcomes independently of their impact on investment decisions. Failing to make this distinction leads us to conflate the impact of the human capital investments with the effects of individual, family, and community characteristics that directly affect the outcomes of interest and are correlated with the human capital investments. For example, innate ability directly affects both the decision to invest in a child's schooling and the wages the child earns when he enters the labor market. In this case, it is difficult to separate the impact of education from the impact of the child's underlying ability, and naïve estimates are likely to be biased.

Fourth, estimated determinants and effects of human capital investments apply to a given macroeconomic, market, policy, social, and regulatory environment. The actual returns may change substantially with changes in that environment, such as those associated with improving domestic markets, opening up an economy to international trade, relaxing regulations on migration, or lessening discrimination in labor markets. As a result, evaluation of current and future human development programs and other policies based on historical data is difficult, unless the historical data allow us to identify the stable parameters in underlying structural relations that determine behavior (for example, production functions and preferences). Reduced-form estimators such as demand functions, which combine production and preference parameters and responses to current and expected future market changes, are likely to be unstable in the case of changing environments, policies, or prices.

Fifth, policy makers and outside analysts may find the impacts of changes in policies hard to predict. If families face a policy change, they can adjust all of their behaviors in response—with cross-effects on other outcomes, not only on the outcome to which the policy is directed. Subsidized school feeding programs, for example, are in effect an income subsidy to the family, which the family can divert in part at least to whatever use it wishes (more consumption of alcoholic beverages, for example, or new clothing for other family members) by cutting back on family provision of food to the recipient child.

Sixth, it is important to understand *when* the shock occurs in the course of a young person's life and what sort of investments were made in the past. Schooling history, for example, will affect the returns to the family's current investments in education and also the probability that the young person will be in school given external shocks. Past investments encourage current investments, by making current investments more productive, partly because previously mastered skills make the acquisition of further skills more efficient.

Estimation of demands for human capital investments sensitive to these considerations can help address a number of relevant questions, including what the impacts of shocks—past, present, or expected in the future—are on human capital investments and how such factors as household behaviors, social networks, markets, community characteristics, and policies may mitigate or exacerbate such effects. Good estimates of these relations are useful for the design of effective policies to protect human capital and minimize the impact of shocks. Challenges to obtaining good estimates include avoiding biases due to unobserved or omitted variables that are correlated with the outcome, measurement errors, and unrepresentative samples. In addition, estimates of the impact of policies on human capital outcomes are generally conditional on other variables, policies, or circumstances. To the extent that these also change, they will influence the impact of the policies being examined.

Framework for Policy Choices Related to Human Capital Investments

Policies determine an important part of the context in which individuals or families make decisions about human capital investments; what the pioneering developmental psychologist Bronfenbrenner (1979) calls the "macro-system." And policy changes can significantly alter the context in which individuals make human capital investments, effectively shifting the marginal benefits and marginal costs for private human capital investment decisions, thus changing the optimum level of these investments for individuals and families. In this way, policies can affect the total aggregate level of human capital, which determines the efficiency or productivity of citizens as workers, as well as its distribution across different people, families, and groups, who each make decisions in the face of different environments and contexts.

Efficiency and distribution. A situation is *efficient* (in terms of welfare) if no one person could be made better off without making someone else worse off.[6] Or, to turn this statement around, in a state of welfare inefficiency, at least some people could be made better off with the same resources and technologies without making anyone worse off. This concept of efficiency can refer either to the welfare of different individuals at the same point in time or to individuals at different points in time. Inefficiency may arise from "market failures" or "policy failures." Market failures may be caused by externalities (that is, contagious diseases or knowledge spillovers), increasing returns to scale over the relevant output range (so that private profit-maximizing prices do not reflect the true marginal social costs), or public goods (in which case at least some of the benefits to investing in an individual accrue to others who do not make the investment). Policy failures include restrictions on prices (for example, on wages, school tuition, and health services) so that they do not reflect social marginal costs, or restrictions on entry and exit in markets, especially in services. These restrictions can give rise to incentives to set prices different from social marginal costs and to socially inefficient levels of investment in human capital.

Distribution is a major policy motive distinct from efficiency. A very efficient economy might have a very undesirable distribution of resources. Society might want to ensure, for example, that everyone attains basic human development levels even at some cost in efficiency or productivity.

Choosing among policies. For many reasons, private decisions relating to human capital investments, including responses to shocks, may not be efficient within a particular market and policy environment. The most commonly cited sources of inefficiency are externalities (that is, effects transmitted other than through market prices), imperfect markets (for example, markets for human capital investments, insurance, and information), and coordination problems. Concerns also arise over distribution, most commonly the command over resources of the poorer and more vulnerable members of society. These have been among the stated motives for human development policies, although some policies purported to benefit the poor may primarily benefit middle- and upper-income families (for example, general subsidies for tertiary education).

The gain from making an inefficient market in human capital investment more efficient does not in itself point toward the best policy for inducing human capital investments at desirable levels.[7] The range of possible interventions and policies is large, including governmental fiats and regulations, governmental provision of or subsidies for human development services, price incentives in the market for human capital investments, price incentives in other markets, changing institutional arrangements in various markets, and more.

Three important considerations should guide choices among alternative policy changes:

- First, policies have *costs*—not only the direct public sector costs of implementation and monitoring but also private costs, including distortions introduced by policies that may encourage socially inefficient behavior. These include time costs for individuals and the distortionary costs of raising revenues to finance the fiscal expenditures necessary for policy formulation and implementation. In some cases, such costs are estimated to be considerable (see, for example, Devarajan, Squire, and Suthiwart-Narueput 1997). In fact, the costs may be so large that it is not desirable to attempt to offset some market failures by policies. But, if it is desirable to do so, a case can generally be made for instituting policy changes directed as specifically as possible to the distortion of concern because that lessens the distortion costs introduced by the policy. The less well focused the policies are, the more widespread and more substantial the distortion costs of the policies themselves are likely to be, in addition to any distortion costs from raising revenues to finance the policies.

- Second, significant *information problems* make it unclear exactly what effects policies have, particularly in a rapidly changing world. This factor is an argument in favor of policies that are as transparent as possible, such as price policies (through imposing taxes or subsidies). Furthermore, society has a strong rationale for subsidizing the collection and provision of more information—for example, about human development—because the private sector is not likely to provide the information optimally. Information has "public goods" characteristics so that the marginal cost of providing more information is near zero and possibly declining. As a result private providers cannot cover their production costs except by restricting the quantities provided and charging a price above the low marginal social costs.[8]

- Third, as noted above, distribution is a concern separate from efficiency. Moreover, there well may be *trade-offs* between policies that increase efficiency and those that promote distributional ends, for example, between increasing human capital for people who can achieve the greater productivity effects and increasing human capital for the poorest.[9] Although society might wish to ensure that everyone has basic access to human development resources, as noted earlier, it is also presumably desirable to ensure that everyone has this basic access at as little cost in productivity as possible.

  Possible complementarities between pursuing efficiency and pursuing distributional objects, however, may result in "win-win" policies. For instance, imperfections in capital, insurance, and information markets are more likely to affect human capital investments of poorer members of society than those of the better-off, so that making these markets more efficient may benefit primarily poorer people. There is some evidence, though not uniform, that inequality in itself causes health and developmental problems, particularly in those less well-off; in that case, reducing inequality by shifting resources to poorer people may make investments in health and human development more effective (see Marmot and Wilkinson 1999; Deaton 2003). But whether trade-offs or complementarities dominate efficiency and distributional policy motives, we should choose the most efficient policies as possible that still ensure that basic distributional targets are met, rather than ignoring efficiency considerations in pursuit of distributional goals.

Summary of the Economics Approach to Human Capital

The standard economic model of human capital has a number of strengths as a framework for investigating the impact of economic shocks on human development. These include a structure for establishing the optimum level of human capital investments and for analyzing how households make changes in investments in response to changes in policies and markets. These changes to behavior may imply that even short-run crises can have significant long-run consequences if there is limited substitutability between earlier and later investments in human capital development. The model also provides major criteria for policy evaluation, as well as to a number of challenges in empirical estimation, given important unobserved variables and other measurement problems. The model as usually applied, however, tends to abstract from the subtle and complex characteristics and interactions considered in the human development literature. For example, the role of personal traits such as perseverance and self-efficacy, the importance of school and teacher quality, and the characteristics of parenting have only recently been examined in empirical microeconomics. These factors have been at the core of the approach to which we turn in the next section; they complement and enrich the standard economic model and greatly expand our understanding of the processes involved in the development and protection of fundamental human capital.

Human Development and a Bioecological Model

Can we productively complement the standard economic model for how people make decisions about human capital investments and for how they respond and adapt to changes in their environment, for example, in a financial crisis? We now consider whether and how human developmental approaches can help enrich the analysis by more integration with the standard economic approaches.

Human Development: An Introduction

The literature from the human developmental sciences provides more comprehensive conceptual and operational definitions of human development than the economic literature typically does (see, for example, Gottlieb, Wahlsten, and Lickliter 1998; Lerner 1998; Baltes, Lindenberger, and Staudinger 1998). In essence, according to Thelen and Smith, "The theory of development is based on very general and content-independent principles that describe the behavior of complex physical and biological systems" (1998, 258). Thus, development can only be understood as (1) "the multiple, mutual, and continuous interaction of all the levels of the development system, from the molecular to the cultural"; and (2) "as nested processes that unfold over many time scales, from milliseconds to years" (Thelen and Smith 1998, 258). In other words, human development refers to change over time, and time is typically characterized as chronological age. Age is not the cause of development; it is just a frame of reference. More specifically, development comprises interactions among various levels of functioning, from the genetic, physiological, and neurological to the behavioral, social, and environmental. Human development is a permanent exchange among these levels. And the more mature the person, the more influence and control the person has over the organization of these interactions.

Human developmental science attributes the driving force of development to so-called *proximal processes*: stimulating, regular face-to-face interactions over extended periods of time with people, objects, or symbols, which promote the realization of the genetic potential for effective biological, psychological, and social development. For example, parents influence and shape their children through parenting behaviors, role modeling, and encouraging certain behaviors and activities for their children.

Bronfenbrenner's bioecological model (figure 2.1) is well suited to illustrate some important dimensions of these human developmental processes, as it captures the complexity of human development as an intricate web of interrelated systems and processes. A basic tenet of the bioecological systems' theories of development (Bronfenbrenner and Morris 2006) is that child and youth development is influenced by many different "contexts," "settings," or "ecologies" (for example, family, peers, schools, communities, sociocultural belief systems, policy regimes, and, of course, the economy). The model is able to account for multiple face-to-face environments, or *settings*, within the microsystem of a person (for example, family, school, peers); how relations between settings (mesosystem) can affect what happens within them (for example, interactions between school and family); and how settings within which the individuals have no direct presence (exo- and macrosystem) can affect settings in their microsystems (for example, how parents' experiences at their workplace affect their relationships within the family) (Bronfenbrenner 1979). Thus, this model allows the analysis of the lives of people, "living organisms whose biopsychological characteristics, both as a species and as individuals, have as much to do with their development as do the

Figure 2.1   A Bioecological Model of Human Development

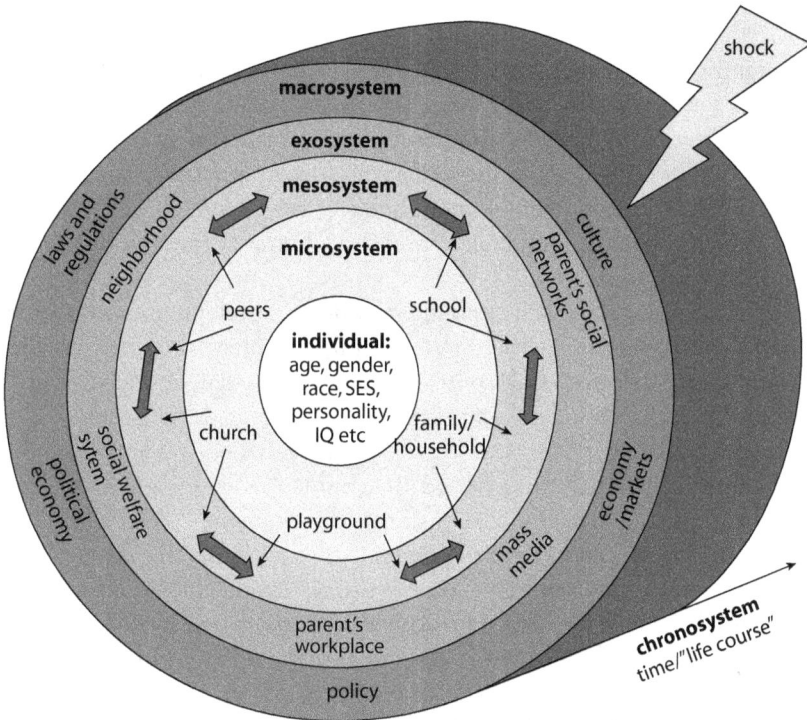

Source: Visual adaptation of Bronfenbrenner's bioecological model of child development (Bronfenbrenner 1979).
Note: SES = socioeconomic status.

environments in which they live their lives" (Bronfenbrenner 1995, 8). We will elaborate in more detail on the various systems and settings of this model later on.

A central question in scientific research on how ecologies influence development is how macrosystem contexts and events (for example, aggregate economic shocks) influence intermediate (exo- and mesosystem) contexts, which in turn influence the settings or contexts within the developing person's microsystem, settings within which the person has face-to-face interactions or proximal processes. Aggregate economic shocks are thought to affect the ecology of human development by hitting the macrosystem, as depicted in figure 2.1.

This model is integrative and interdisciplinary, drawing on and relating concepts and hypotheses from disciplines as diverse as biology, behavioral genetics and neurobiology, psychology, sociology, cultural anthropology, history, and economics—focusing on and highlighting processes and links that shape human development through the life course (Bronfenbrenner 1995). In particular, this model relates to the economic model of human capital investments outlined earlier in many, but not all, respects. It provides a complementary framework for understanding how shocks affect human development understood as complex systems of interactive processes between developing individuals and their surroundings. As such, bioecological developmental models have the potential to enrich or expand the standard economic approach to human capital outlined earlier in this chapter.

In what follows we will expound on human developmental processes and how these are nested within a complex set of systems and settings. "Domains," "processes," and "context" provide a convenient organizational structure for discussing the complex topic of human development.

Domains. It is widely understood that human development has many distinct and important dimensions, or domains (Alkire 2002). Fundamental domains of development are not generally hierarchical (one is not more important than others), irreducible (fundamental dimensions cannot be reduced to other dimensions), or incommensurable (they cannot be adequately compared to each other). Nonetheless, in the practical world of science, programs, and policies, some domains receive more attention than others. In the scientific study of child and youth development, three domains—physical, biological, and neuroanatomical development; cognitive, language, and academic development; and social, emotional, and behavioral development—have received much more attention than have moral, spiritual, and religious development or artistic and aesthetic development. The program and policy world parallels the scientific world in placing greater emphasis on children's physical, cognitive, and social-emotional development, roughly aligned with the domains of health, education, and social-emotional or psychosocial well-being.

Each of these three fundamental domains is a complex system of complex subsystems. These systems emerge and evolve over the course of human development and are complexly interrelated to other domains of human developmental systems and subsystems. The "organizational systems" perspective on human development focuses on these fundamental domains and strives to account for how advances or lags in one domain affect and are affected by advances or lags in other domains. For example, the evidence reveals that nutrients by themselves do not suffice to bring about even purely physical, biological, or neuroanatomical development and thus that development can be significantly delayed and even irreversibly compromised in the absence of other factors crucial to development, such as a secure attachment relationship and other proximal processes (Corrales and Utter 2005). The bioecological systems' perspective on human development examines how different contexts, settings, experiences, and events affect different domains of child and youth development.

The implications of multiple and interrelated domains of development for this study are clear. Examining the impacts both within the physical (health), cognitive (educational), and social-emotional (psychosocial well-being) domains and across these domains will likely enrich efforts to understand the impact of economic shocks on child and youth development.

Processes. Put very simply, children's development is the result of proximal processes; of participating in increasingly complex reciprocal interactions with people, objects, and symbols in their immediate environments (their microsystem contexts) over extended periods of time (represented by the chronosystem) (Bronfenbrenner 1994a). Thus, according to Bronfenbrenner's definition, "a microsystem is a pattern of activities, social roles, and interpersonal relations experienced by the developing person in a given face-to-face setting with particular physical, social, and symbolic features that invite, permit, or inhibit engagement in sustained, progressively more complex interaction with, and activity in, the immediate environment" (Bronfenbrenner 1994b, 39). Examples of settings within the microsystem are families, neighborhoods, day care centers, schools, playgrounds, and so on within which activities, roles,[10] and interpersonal relations set the stage for proximal processes as crucial mechanisms for human development.

The heterogeneity in individual outcomes thus stems from systematic variation in individuals' characteristics and environments and in the nature of the developmental outcomes under scrutiny, which jointly determine form, power, content, and direction of proximal processes (Bronfenbrenner 1994a). Thus, proximal processes determine the capacities of individuals to (1) differentiate perception and response; (2) direct and control their own behaviors; (3) cope successfully under stress; (4) acquire knowledge and skills; (5) establish and maintain mutually rewarding relationships; and (6) modify and construct their own physical, social, and symbolic environments (Bronfenbrenner 1994a). Proximal processes are thought to be the most important influences on children's development.

Of course, not only do microcontexts affect children and youth, but also children and youth affect their microcontexts. Children and youth and the mircocontexts transact (see Sameroff 2009 for a transactional model). Insecurely attached children are more emotionally demanding for stressed parents to care for, and children slowed in language development stimulate less verbal exchange with adults. Economic shocks are likely to have an impact on these transactional, bidirectional systems of influences between children or youth and their immediate environments. This view of human development as transactional places heavy design and data demands on studies of the underlying mechanisms or pathways of influence, including studies of the influence of economic shocks on child and youth development.

Context and the interplay of systems and settings. In the bioecological model, contextual effects are manifested in a complex interplay of the micro-, meso-, exo-, and macrosystems. The ways these systems interact and influence each other can contribute to an understanding of how shocks to the macrosystem, such as a financial crisis, can disrupt the developmental process as it is transmitted to various settings in a child's *microsystem*. Household socioeconomic status, neighborhood characteristics, and school environments, just to mention a few, will determine the quality, frequency, and intensity of proximal processes. For instance, there is a significant body of literature that looks at how household poverty and hardship affect child development (see, for example, Duncan and Brooks-Gunn 1997). Neighborhood and community contexts and their influence on children have also been studied extensively (see, for example, Brooks-Gunn, Duncan, and Aber 1997). For instance, although family socioeconomic status is correlated with well-being and human development, it is not clear if socioeconomic status *causes* variations in health and well-being or if personal characteristics and dispositions of individuals influence both their socioeconomic status and their future socioemotional well-being and behavior (Conger, Conger, and Martin 2010, 687; Mayer 1997). In addition, studies have started to unravel the pathways through which poverty affects child and youth development, ranging from the availability of quality prenatal and perinatal care, exposure to environmental toxins such as lead, less cognitive stimulation at home, harsh and inconsistent parenting, to lower teacher quality (McLoyd 1998). Furthermore, various studies have compared the implications of temporary versus chronic deprivation and how the impact differs according to life stage of the developing person (see, for accounts, Elder 1999; McLoyd 1998; McLoyd et al. 2009). In other words, a temporary drop in socioeconomic status during a crisis may have markedly different long-term implications depending on the age of the child.

A *mesosystem*, according to Bronfenbrenner, "comprises the linkages and processes taking place between two or more settings containing the developing person," such as the relations between home and school (1994b, 40). He notes that "it is formed or extended whenever the developing person moves into a new setting" (1979, 25). The main distinction between the meso- and the microsystem is that in the microsystem activities, social roles, and interpersonal relations are confined to one setting, whereas the mesosystem incorporates the interactions across the boundaries of at least two settings (Bronfenbrenner 1979, 209). The mesosystem is structured by institutions that have taken-for-granted rules for interaction and that shape expected behaviors with the help of shared norms. Institutions may be mutually reinforcing or in tensions with one another, as when the implicit rules for gaining status among peers are at odds with standards of behavior valued by schools and with rules facilitating educational achievement (Carter 2007; Warikoo 2010).

Settings in the mesosystem can enhance (or diminish) people's developmental potential when (1) a transition is made together with a group of others that they have engaged with in previous settings (versus alone) (for example, transition with a group of peers from kindergarten to school); (2) when roles and activities between two settings are compatible (or incompatible) and encourage (or discourage) trust, positive orientation, and consensus on goals, as well as a balance of power in favor of the developing person; (3) when the number of structurally different settings is increased (or decreased) and others are more (or less) mature or experienced; and (4) when cultural or subcultural contexts differ from each other[11] (Bronfenbrenner 1979, 209–23).

An *exosystem* refers to "the linkages and processes taking place between two or more settings, at least one of which does not contain the developing person, but in which events occur that indirectly influence processes within the immediate setting in which the developing person lives" (Bronfenbrenner 1994b). An example of such an exosystem setting would be the parent's workplace, in which the child does not interact directly, but which could indirectly, through parental stress, job loss, or the like, influence family dynamics and thus the developing child. Consequently, a causal sequence of at least two steps is required to qualify as an exosystem. The first step is to establish a connection between events in the external setting, or exosystem, which does not include the developing person, to processes in the microsystem, which does include the person, and, second, to link these processes to developmental changes in the developing person (Bronfenbrenner 1979). Important to note in this context is the ability of the child to influence parents just as much as parents influence the child, and this influence can reach far beyond the family into settings of the child's exosystem (Bronfenbrenner 1979).

Research to date has focused on three prominent exosystems that are particularly likely to influence the developmental processes of children and youth through their influence on the family, school, and peers: parents' workplaces, family social networks, and neighborhood-community contexts (Bronfenbrenner 1994b). To illustrate, Kohn's research (see, for example, Pearlin and Kohn 2009) demonstrated that the beliefs, standards, and expectations parents face at work, for example concerning their autonomy or dependency, is what they bring home and essentially expect the same from their children. As a result, parents who were always subdued at work have a tendency to subdue their children. This factor may help explain intergenerational transmission of values. Economic shocks can have a tremendous effect on exosystems, affecting not only the workplaces of parents but also the situations of those who do not have work. Several functions of work—such as organization of the day, income, and social status, among others—can be affected.

The *macrosystem* captures "the overarching pattern of micro-, meso-, and exosystems characteristic of a given culture or subculture, with particular reference to the belief systems, bodies of knowledge, material resources, customs, lifestyles, opportunity structures, hazards, and lifecourse options that are embedded in each of these broader systems" (Bronfenbrenner 1994b, 40). These include the laws and regulations, political economy, economic markets, and public policies of the societies within which the developing person is embedded. Incorporating the macrosystem takes the analysis beyond the identification of class, ethnic, and cultural differences in child-rearing practices and outcomes and incorporates the phenomena of aggregate economic shocks. Of particular interest are dynamic aspects of "ecological transitions," such as investigations of how social and economic changes affect children's and youths' development and how they adapt to such changes in the macrosystem. (We will return to these questions later on.)

While Bronfenbrenner refers mainly to cultural aspects of the macrosystem, a society's cultural frameworks, politics, and institutions are all closely interrelated and mutually reinforcing. Thus, the process of change can be induced through several channels or entities, the result of which will be a "complicated set of interlocking physical and social relations, patterns, and processes" (Martin, McCann, and Purcell 2003). Put another way, the macrosystem can be interpreted as "space" that Lefebvre defined as an "unavoidably social product created from a mix of legal, political, economic, and social practices and structures" (Lefebvre 1991). Individuals draw on these cultural tools that their environment puts at their disposal, or that they choose to make sense of challenges and imagine effective solutions. They also find strategies for action by observing the behaviors of those around them and the consequences of their actions.

The bioecological model is flexible enough to accommodate cross-national variations in the weight given to various aspects of human development influenced by the local culture (for instance, the greater emphasis on self-esteem, self-actualization, and individualization characteristic of the American upper-middle class; see Markus 2004). It also takes into consideration meso- and macrolevel conditions for collective human development, including shared myths and narratives that buttress the individual sense of self and capabilities (see, for example, Hall and Lamont 2009).

Similarly, the bioecological model is capable of capturing "experiences." Proximal processes and other interactions are "experienced by the developing person," which is meant to indicate "that the scientifically relevant features of any environment include not only its objective properties but also the way in which these properties are perceived by the persons in that environment" (Bronfenbrenner 1979, 22). Experiences in this sense are individual (and collective) constructs of the "objective," which determines an individual's (and a group's) capacity for making meaning and for self-representation (Hall and Lamont 2009). Experiences, while in part determined by the individual's personality, are embedded in local culture and customs; thus, understanding the cultural frameworks and narratives that shape the relationships and processes within and between settings and systems is crucial to recognizing factors that enhance or weaken the resilience of a developing person.

One example of the cultural or contextual variability in the meaning of experience comes from the empirical literature on the influence of parenting styles on the development of children's academic and social-emotional competencies. Early research indicated that authoritative parenting (which combines warmth with firm control) promoted greater child competence than did authoritarian (low warmth, very high control) or laissez-faire (low warmth, low control) parenting (for reviews, see Baumrind 1989, 1991). But subsequent research observed race, ethnic, and neighborhood differences in the influence of parenting styles on child competence. In a sample of African American and Latino-American parents living in dangerous inner-city neighborhoods, authoritarian parenting behaviors were associated with less adolescent delinquency than authoritative parenting behaviors (Florsheim, Tolan, and Gorman-Smith 1996). This pattern of findings has led child developmentalists to believe that "high control" parenting has greater adaptive value in more dangerous neighborhoods and may be "experienced" by children in a different way in those contexts (Furstenberg et al. 1999; Garcia-Coll et al. 1996; McLoyd 1990; Rodriguez and Walden 2010). (We will return to the subject of resilience and culture later.)

Finally, only recently have the theory, measures, and mathematical models been available to enable the rigorous empirical study of child and youth development in context. As pointed out previously, children and youth are embedded in and transact with each other in and across contexts. Consequently, the study of peer and other spillover effects in human developmental science has grown, as it has in the social sciences, although many of these studies do not convincingly control for what determines the individuals with whom one interacts. These advances are directly relevant to improving our understanding of the impact of economic shocks on child and youth development.

To reiterate, the human developmental process consequently depends on more than the available resources, prices, policies, and parental preferences for investments in their children. From a human development perspective, if we are to fully understand the effects of economic shocks on child and youth development, we must track the influence of economic (macro) shocks on exo- and mesosystems and in turn on children's microsystem contexts and the proximal processes—that is, the reciprocal interactions between children and immediate contexts—that are the drivers of human development.

Stage-Salient Human Developmental Tasks

When asking the question of how some event, such as a crisis, influences a young person's development, we need to have a common understanding of what the indicators of optimal development in a particular context should be. Some developmental outcomes may be more normative, or applicable across contexts, and others more context specific, reflecting cultural preferences and expectations. Nonetheless, positive child development has been conceptualized in a sequence of so-called stage-salient developmental tasks. According to Aber and Jones (1997, 398),

> Stage-salient developmental tasks are those newly emergent tasks which children must face (in particular social/cultural contexts) using their most recently developed capacities and which are critical to children's immediate and long-term adaptation. They represent the cutting edge of development where individual differences in the quality of adaptation and development are easily discerned.

A well-accepted description of stage-salient issues was developed by Sroufe (1979). For this volume, we have adapted and consolidated these for reasons of simplicity and cultural transferability. Table 2.2 shows the stage-salient developmental tasks by age as they are presented in chapters 3, 4, and 5.

Over the past two decades, it has become increasingly clear that variation over time in the emergence of stage-salient human development issues is based in part on both the developmental course of human brain development and on children's age-graded progression through settings in which they live (their microsystems). Thompson and Nelson (2001) summarize a wealth of evidence on the variation over time in brain cell migration (prenatally), myelination (over the first 10 years of life), and synaptogenesis (over the first 18–25 years of life)(see figure 2.2). Children's transactions with their ecologies both influence and are influenced by brain development in a highly predictable fashion (see for more detail box 3.2). Correlated with both the emergence of stage-salient issues and the stages of brain development are the increasing expansion and differentiation of the settings in their microsystem from family and parental care, to nonparental care, to school, to nonfamily, and to

Table 2.2   Stage-Salient Human Developmental Tasks, by Age

Age (in years)		Stage-salient developmental tasks
0–1	Early childhood	Establishing (secure) attachement relationships
1–3		Learning to explore and communicate
3–5		Learning to self-regulate thoughts, behaviors and emotions
6–12	Middle childhood	Learning and reasoning, developing interpersonal and social problem-solving skills
13+	Adolescence and emerging adulthood	Establishing autonomy (renegotiage relationships), forming identity, setting and achieving goals

Source: Authors.

Figure 2.2   The Developmental Course of Human Brain Development by Months, Years, and Decades

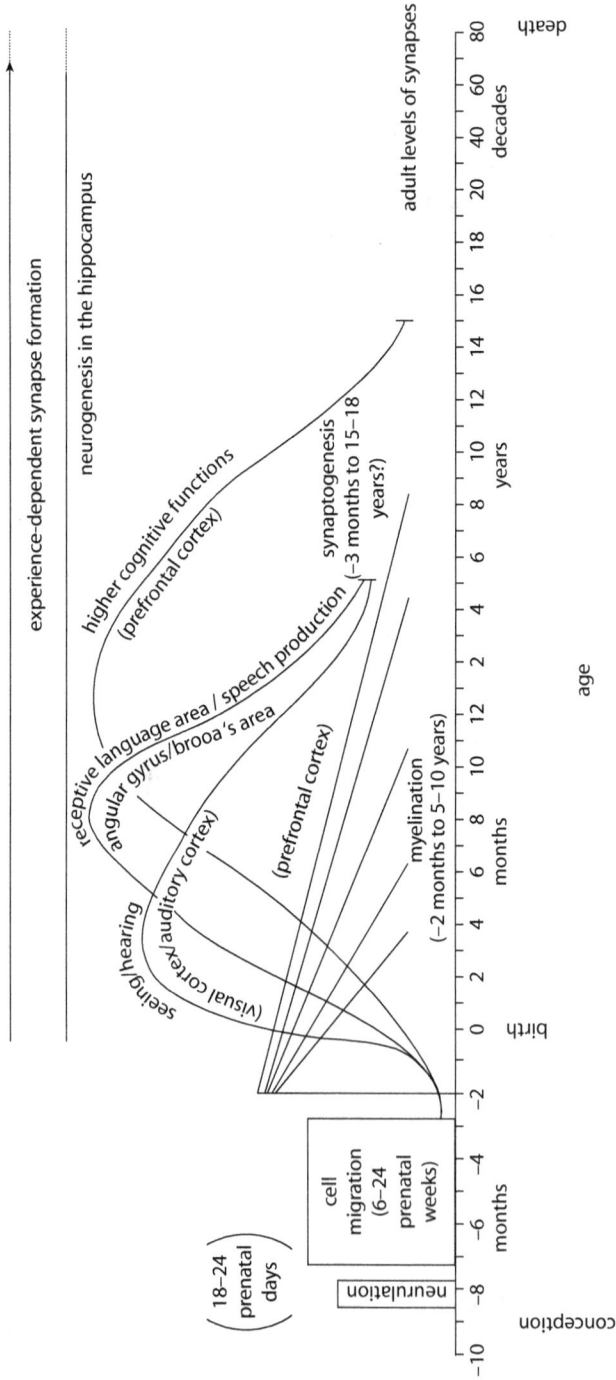

Source: Thompson and Nelson (2001).

Note: This graph illustrates the importance of prenatal events, such as the formation of the neural tube (neurulation) and cell migration; critical aspects of synapse formation and myelination beyond age three; and the formation of synapses based on experience, as well as neurogenesis in a key region of the hippocampus (the dentate gyrus), throughout much of life.

nonschool youth settings in communities and workplaces. This coordinated unfolding of stage-specific human developmental tasks, brain development, and settings explains why any serious risk, adversity, or threat (including economic shocks) is likely to have different impacts on children at different ages and stages of development.

In the bioecological model, the *chronosystem*, which refers crudely to the dimension of time, captures the sequence of these stage-salient human developmental tasks. The chronosystem captures both the age or life course of the developing person and the changes in the context over time. In addition, the interconnections between the various contexts are not static but change across historical periods of time. Adding this dimension allows us to (1) enrich the modeling of dynamics in economic behavior and decision making about human capital investments over the life course; and (2) map exogenous events, such as economic shocks, that might affect the context and therefore the development of children and youth along their life-course trajectory; highlight critical periods in the human developmental process; and thus identify those most vulnerable and in need of attention at a particular point in time. Thus, the chronosystem also incorporates, the idea of "path dependency": that is, what happens to people when economic shocks hit them depends on the stage of their life span and what transpired before. Thus, in his work *The Children of the Great Depression*, Elder (1998) finds evidence in support of the "life course" principles: (1) individuals' life courses are embedded in and shaped by historical times and places that determine their experiences throughout their lives; (2) impacts on human developmental processes depend on the point in time a succession of life transitions or events occur in a person's life; (3) the interdependence of people's lives leads to the expression of social and historical influences through this network of shared relationships; and (4) human agency enables individuals to construct their own life courses through choices and actions available within the constraints and opportunities of history and social circumstances. Each of these principles has implications for how to conceptualize and model the influences of aggregate economic shocks on child and youth development.

A shock can thus produce a dramatically heterogenous impacts within a group of people who differ only a little in their chronological age or in their stage of development (see, for example, Elder 1999).

Another example refers to the stage of cognitive development a child has attained when the shock occurs; the further along that child is in his or her cognitive development, the more possibilities he or she has for thinking about the good side of things. Bleak future prospects, however, may incur sadness or even depression. A divorce is a case in point. The family conditions that typically lead to divorce may differentially affect children according to how old they are during the period of family turmoil (Hetherington 1989). Recent research indicates that young children who experience a divorce have a greater risk of behavioral problems and anxiety than do children whose parents divorce during adolescence, in part because they may be less capable of accurately assessing the causes and repercussions of a divorce. Adolescents, however, face a greater risk of academic problems than younger children, perhaps because of the increasing importance and demands of the school context as children mature (Lansford et al. 2006).

The examples outlined in this section highlight the complex ways in which the chronosystem transacts with other stage-salient contexts to affect development. Many stage salient developmental tasks are very context specific, depending on perceptions and expectations of what a child should be capable of at what age. Thus, one will need to adapt the list of tasks in table 2.2 to account for contextual differences. Nevertheless, the use of stage-salient developmental milestones allows us to monitor progress and identify developmental delays and threats to healthy development. This is particularly useful when analyzing the impact of economic crisis on the developmental progress of children and youth and will allow us to identify particularly vulnerable groups of young people. Nevertheless, a great deal of heterogeneity in outcomes remains seemingly unexplained.

Heterogeneity, Resilience, and Differential Susceptibility

Over the past decades, interest has grown in the concept of *resilience* as a way to explain some of the heterogeneity in child development. Resilience has become a central topic, particularly when analyzing child development under adverse circumstances, such as poverty and economic crisis. Behavioral scientists made the important observation that some children seemed to develop "normally" under risky conditions. They expanded their research agenda to include the correlates and markers of good adaptation among young people at risk (genetic or environmental) and to uncover the processes and regulatory systems that produce these correlates and markers (Masten 2007). More recently, the focus has shifted to prevention, intervention, and policy to support children at risk (Masten and Obradovic 2006).

While the concept of resilience can and often is applied to any functional system, in developmental science the term most frequently refers to individuals (Masten and Obradovic 2006). It has also been applied to larger social systems, however, such as families, communities, or schools. In popular terms, a child is seen as being resilient when he or she is seemingly unaffected by a highly adverse situation, experience, or event. From a developmental perspective resilience is defined as positive adaptation or development in the face of past or current risk, adversity, or threat (see figure 2.3). This term refers both to positive adaptation to adverse changes in the environment—for example, school achievement in the face of poverty—and to "internal integration," such as psychological well-being in the face of a history of exposure to violence (Masten and Obradovic 2006). Resilience does *not* refer to variation in exposure to risk, adversity, or threat. Nor is it a simple, direct influence on positive adaptation or development (protective process).

Adaptation is multidimensional and developmental in nature. For example, success in the mastery of tasks in one developmental period forecasts future success, while success or failure in one or more domains can have cascading consequences leading to problems in other domains of adaptation. Thus, interventions to promote mastery of such tasks will decrease the incidence of developing behavioral and emotional problems and increase success in school and related areas (Masten and Obradovic 2006).

Figure 2.3   Distinction between Resilience and Risk Reduction and Protection

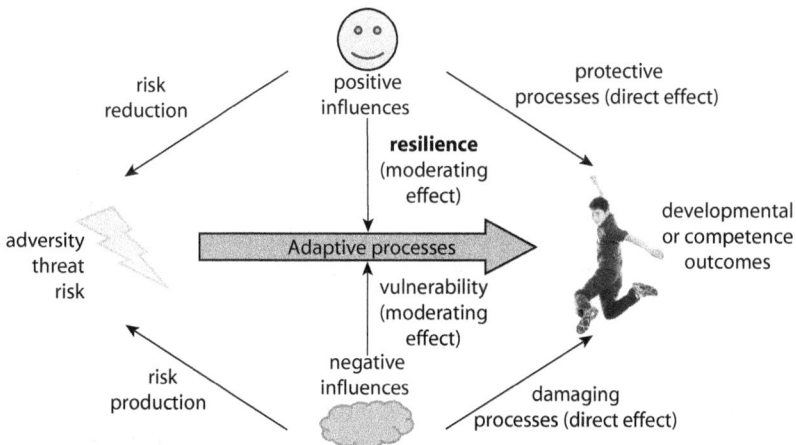

Source: Aber, personal communication.

Resilience factors and processes moderate the impact of risk, adversity, or threat to adaptation or development. A resilience perspective raises the question, Why do some children, youth, and families demonstrate positive adaptation or development in the face of aggregate economic shock while others do not? In general, cases of low risk and poor adaptation are much less common than cases of high risk and good adaptation, possibly "indicating the adaptive and self-righting bias of development in a species shaped by eons of natural and cultural selection" (Masten and Obradovic 2006, 20).

Prior theory and research have distinguished several sources of resilience along different dimensions of human ecology. These include (1) biological and genetic sources at the individual level (for example, Belsky et al. 2009; Bakermans-Kranenburg and Van Ijzendoorn 2007; Bakermans-Kranenburg and Van Ijzendoorn 2011; Rutter, Moffitt and Caspi 2006); (2) psychosocial sources at the relationship level (for example, Rutter 1987; Kim-Cohen et al. 2004); and (3) cultural, systems, and policy sources (for example, Wright and Masten 2005). In other words, resilience stems from processes at various levels of interaction in the bioecological model, from genes to the greater environment. Masten (2009) argues that sources of resilience are deeply rooted in fundamental biological, interpersonal, and sociocultural systems of human adaptation in the face of risk, adversity, or threat. Based on research in advanced economies (particularly the United States), she has identified a short list of resilience factors (see box 2.1).

More recent research on genetic and other physiological sources of heterogeneity has identified a phenomenon termed *differential susceptibility*. While not to be equated with the concept of resilience, it has unearthed novel insights into gene-environment interactions and how a genetic predisposition or other physiological characteristic renders some individuals more sensitive to environmental influences, both for better and for worse. Researchers have found compelling evidence that some individuals react more strongly to negative as well as positive influences, based on an underlying physiological predisposition (see, for example, Bakermans-Kranenburg and Van Ijzendoorn 2007; Bakermans-Kranenburg and Van Ijzendoorn 2011; Belsky et al. 2009; Belsky and Pluess 2009; Pluess and Belsky 2009; for more detail on differential susceptibility, see box 3.2). This lends reason to believe that economic crises may affect some individuals more than others and that the right policies may have a stronger positive effect on these same individuals.

As box 2.1 aptly shows, resilience is not only about individual genetic predisposition and psychological resilience but also about collective tools

Box 2.1

Short List of Resilience Factors, with Implicated Human Adaptive Systems

- Positive attachment bonds with caregivers (attachment; family)
- Positive relationships with other nurturing and competent adults (attachment)
- Intellectual skills (integrated cognitive systems of a human brain in good working order)
- Self-regulation skills (self-control systems and related executive functions of the human brain)
- Positive self-perceptions; self-efficacy (mastery motivation system)
- Faith, hope, and a sense of meaning in life (meaning-making systems of belief)
- Friends or romantic partners who are supportive and prosocial (attachment)
- Bonds to effective schools and other prosocial organizations (sociocultural systems)
- Communities with positive services and supports for families and children (sociocultural)
- Cultures that provide positive standards, rituals, relationships, and supports (sociocultural)

Source: Masten (2009).

for self-valuation. These tools are made available by the environment and linked to messages that institutions provide groups and individuals about their relative worth, status, and social contribution. For example, a study of Mexican immigrant families in California during the recent recession showed that strong ethnic and cultural identity and a sense of belonging increased resilience in individuals and communities (Conger and Stockdale 2011). Tools for producing and sustaining collective recognition or positive collective identity are key to developing resilience and have received particular recognition and attention in the sociological literature (for a more detailed account on social resilience, see box 6.2) but have also been recognized in the psychological and disaster response literature. The literature on cultural sociology, collective memory, and the media helps us better understand how management of social identity is enabled and constrained by various groups of actors, including nongovernmental organizations, governments, and social movements, among others (Lamont, Fleming, and Welburn, forthcoming). Adopting a historical perspective is crucial to understanding how a group makes sense of its past and defines its aspirations, challenges, and possible future trajectory, with possible impact on physical and mental health. We will return to this discussion later on when talking about the policy implications stemming from a deeper understanding of resilience in the face of risk, adversity, and threat.

Framework for Policy Choices Related to the Human Development Perspective

As noted earlier in this chapter, the standard economic model directs attention to the role of economic efficiency and distribution in guiding policy decisions. The human development model, by comparison, directs attention to the issues of mediation, heterogeneity of response, and non-market influences as guides to policy.

Transmission mechanisms (mediation). The bioecological model of human development emphasizes not only the macropolicy and the household but also the exo-, meso- and other microcontexts of child and youth development. In keeping with this perspective, a bioecological perspective asks how an aggregate macroeconomic shock affects households both directly and indirectly: that is, how the aggregate shock may affect other macrocontexts (cultural beliefs, for example), exocontexts (employment, education, and health systems, for example), and meso- and microcontexts (such as parent and youth workplaces, schools, and neighborhoods).

As much as possible, policy recommendations should be based on a solid empirical understanding of how aggregate shocks affect these mediating contexts that in turn affect child and youth development. Each malleable link in the transmission progress becomes a potential target for policy intervention.

Heterogeneity of response (moderation). The degree to which the macro-, exo-, meso-, and microsystem changes induced by shocks or policy shifts influence child and youth development depends on the extent to which they affect those critical proximal processes that drive development. As we have noted, these proximal processes are highly context and child specific, and difference in adaptive behavior to both shocks and policies vary widely. Consequently, a developmental perspective could influence policy by challenging the assumption that one size will fit all. It raises the potential value of tailoring policy to some extent on the basis of key sources of heterogeneity, or resilience, in response to both shocks and policies. The reality of the heterogeneity of adaptation suggests developing a range of policy responses that explicitly account for the predictable heterogeneity in child and youth contexts and proximal processes.

Nonmarket influences. Another way in which a human development perspective offers unique guidance to policy development and evaluation is by identifying and empirically testing the influence of nonmarket factors in explaining the impact of aggregate shocks on child and youth development. For example, the transition from adolescence to young adulthood is a period of rapid development of individual identity. Personal, social, and other identities are built in response to opportunities and challenges in youth environments. Thus, for example, developing an identity as a "worker" in a crisis period of high unemployment is very likely to be quite different from that during a stable period of low unemployment. The market affects identity development by making certain opportunities or growth paths available, and identity development influences labor market activities in the future; but identity development is a nonmarket process of child and youth development and determinant of how shocks affect development. Other key nonmarket influences, such as parental stress and mental illness, can also serve as a target for policy action in response to aggregate shocks. (We will illustrate how mediation, heterogeneity in adaptive behavior and nonmarket influences help guide policy decisions in chapter 6 of this volume.)

Summary of the Human Developmental Model

The human development model has several strengths as a framework for investigating the impact of aggregate economic shocks on human development. These include identifying a broader set of child and youth developmental outcomes that could be affected by shocks; using a life-stage approach to understand variation in the biological and brain sensitivity to shocks; identifying nonmarket influences and specifying multilevel transmission mechanisms through which shocks affect child and youth development. Based on these insights, the field of human development has built a rich history in systematic rigorous evaluations of experimental interventions designed to enhance human development in the face of adversity.

Empirical research based on these strengths holds considerable promise for identifying and testing new policy interventions on child and youth development (see Alderman 2011 for an example focused on early childhood policy efforts of the World Bank). In addition, it bears substantial potential to further our understanding of how conventional welfare and safety net programs affect recipient children. Further examples will be raised in the chapters of this book that review the empirical literature.

The human development model has serious limitations, however. The data and design demands necessary for empirically testing features of the model, while not insurmountable, are very high. In comparison to the economic model, the human development model has no framework for evaluating trade-offs among investment and policy options. Research in human development has advanced the methods of longitudinal research and statistical approaches to modeling growth and change. But too often developmentalists infer causality from temporal precedence. Fortunately, econometric and truly experimental approaches to causal inference are increasingly being adapted by developmentalists (see Duncan, Magnuson, and Ludwig 2004). The next section discusses how to move toward an integration of the economic and human development perspectives that is more than the sum of its parts.

Shocks, Transmission Mechanisms, and the Dynamics of Human Development

The two perspectives discussed here—the economic and the human developmental—clearly differ in some important respects. The usual representation of the standard human capital model, for example, does not incorporate specific measurable constructs at the multiple levels (micro-, meso-, macro-, and chronosystem) emphasized by the bioecological model, or the importance of interactions among these levels. The usual representation of the bioecological model does not incorporate roles of individual and family choices within a dynamic forward-looking framework, and raises a range of estimation issues for obtaining empirical knowledge and rationale for policy choices. But the two approaches are also complementary in important respects, which promises greater gains in understanding the impact of shocks on child and youth development through integrating the insights of both these approaches.

Economic models emphasize how individuals, families, firms, and other agents make decisions to achieve a set of goals, under constraints imposed by the relevant budgets, physical environments, production functions, networks, prices, and policies. Shocks affect decision making partly by altering the external conditions and constraints under which households operate as well as by changing the resources available to them. We must understand the mechanisms through which shocks are transmitted to the household—that is, which conditions and constraints change and how the value of household resources changes—to identify factors that exacerbate or mitigate the impact on the household. These transmission mechanisms influence the decision about human capital investments in children and youth. These mechanisms reflect both those factors exogenous to the household and those that are the consequence of previous decisions made by the household, for example, whether to invest in insurance measures. Beyond the household, these factors include decisions made by national governments, local social institutions, and even other households to moderate the transmission of shocks through the economy. For example, the local impact of natural disasters may be affected by previous investments in conservation made by one's neighbors; and the stability of informal mutual insurance schemes is partly the result of the investments made by the members of the local community.

The bioecological model depicts how the developmental processes of children and youth are affected by the settings within their microsystems and how those settings relate to each other (the mesosystem), and to factors in the exo- and macrosystems. Therefore, a negative shock, or a disruption within one of the systems or settings, could have potentially harmful (or potentially beneficial) effects on human development in different domains and at different points in the life cycle. Shocks that hit the macrosystem (for example, a recession) may transmit through children's exosystem (for example, their parents' workplace through parental unemployment), to their microsystem (such as their families and homes). The same shock may simultaneously severely curtail government spending, leading, for example, to a drop in resources for education, increased teacher absenteeism, and other changes that affect children's microsystems through other channels.

Transmission of Aggregate Economic Shocks

Aggregate economic shocks often emanate from fluctuations in international markets, and a country's *border policies* will have an important impact on the transmission of these shocks to the domestic economy. At one extreme, a perfectly closed border will isolate the domestic economy entirely from such shocks by prohibiting all international economic exchange. But this approach is unsustainable because of its impact on growth, and closed borders are likely to be porous in any event. Moreover, the movement of nominal prices and exchange rates through international trade and international flows of resources can absorb or reduce the impact of shocks experienced in the domestic economy due to fiscal policies, weather, and other factors. At the other extreme, global shocks enter the domestic economy unhindered by constraints on the movement of capital, goods, or factors of production. Most countries lie somewhere along the spectrum between these extremes.

In general, border policies temper the transmission of global shocks to the domestic economy. For example, a country might buffer its economy from fluctuations in the international commodity markets in which it sells a significant share of its exports by taxing export revenues when the relevant international commodity prices are high and investing the proceeds in assets that can be drawn upon when commodity prices are low. Such schemes are difficult to operate in part because of strong pressures to use the high-price "windfalls" immediately, but some countries (Chile, for example, with its copper) appear to have implemented such a strategy quite successfully. Another example is a policy strategy that restricts international financial capital movements, particularly large, short-term flows that can be huge in comparison with most individual economies.

Within the economy, shocks are transmitted to households through their effect on *markets and prices*, especially for credit, inputs and products, labor and employment, and household assets. Crises can change the demand for and the relative prices of the goods and services exchanged in markets. For example, a household can suffer both a drop in the demand for the goods it produces and a drop in the demand for its labor, as well as changes in the prices offered for these commodities. At the same time, the prices of goods consumed or used by the household in production can increase. In other words, the terms of trade—the relative value of what the household sells and what it purchases—can shift adversely. The net impact of relative price changes will be determined by the position of the household in the economy (whether it is engaged in traded or nontraded activities, whether it is a net buyer or a net seller of goods) and by the ease with which it can reallocate its resources in response to the price change. Such terms-of-trade shocks can be particularly devastating for countries that rely on the export of primary commodities (see, for example, Cogneau and Jedwab 2010 for Ghana).

Changes in terms of trade may be strictly exogenous to a trading country, for example, reflecting falling demand among trading partners, but such changes may also reflect domestic inflation and exchange rates. The devaluation and inflation that marked the Asian crisis of the late 1990s eroded real wages and savings and drove up the prices of imported food, fuel, and agricultural inputs. In some cases, governments also controlled food prices, which depressed the returns to agriculture (Knowles, Pernia, and Racelis 1999). In principle, devaluations will improve the terms of trade for people engaged in the production of tradable goods, as happened in Africa during the 1980s and 1990s (Sahn 1996). Again, for the household, the net impact will depend on its position in the economy, whether it produces tradable or nontradable goods and whether it is a net seller or buyer of specific goods.

Economic downturns and the reduced demand for goods and services lead to lower labor demand and lower labor income to the household, whether through layoffs, reductions in hours worked, or reduced wages (see, for example, Smith et al. 2002 for Indonesia; McKenzie 2004 for Argentina; Lustig 1998 for Mexico). Particularly hard hit were Eastern Europe and Central Asian countries (World Bank 2011b) and young workers (Cho and Newhouse 2011). Globally, young people make up about a quarter of the world's population but about half of its unemployed. Some young people can take many months or even years to find employment. Changes in labor demand can have serious long-term consequences for young people who are trying to negotiate the transition to employment. In Bosnia-Herzegovina, youths' difficult entry into the labor market led to lower earnings later in life (Fares and Tiongson 2007). Long spells of unemployment can discourage youth from remaining in the labor force and prevent them from obtaining the early experience, skills, and social capital they need to be successful in the labor market. Initial failure to find a job can lead to persistent joblessness, lower satisfaction, lower productivity, and lower lifetime earnings (World Bank 2006).

Public services for welfare and human capital (health, education, safety nets) can change as government revenues and budgets are altered by shocks. Lower current revenue can force a reduction in the public financing and provision of services and in the allocation of public resources across activities and investments. Social spending in Chile fell by 20 percent between 1981 and 1986, for example, and the poorest 40 percent of families were particularly hard hit (Bourguignon and Morrisson 1992). (See Knowles, Pernia, and Racelis 1999 for Thailand and Stalker 2000 for Indonesia.) Finally, severe shocks can affect the structure and functioning of social institutions—both those that mediate relationships across individuals within communities and those that might serve to safeguard households in the event of aggregate crises. Tighter international credit markets will constrain government borrowing to finance domestic spending, while tighter domestic credit markets will constrain households' responses to shocks, making it more difficult to ensure consumption by borrowing. Households are likely to compensate by disposing of assets or making other decisions that affect longer-term development and growth.

The significant increase in domestic social spending over the past decade has led to great improvements in social and welfare outcomes, but social spending also exhibits considerable volatility, especially among the poorest countries (Lewis and Verhoeven 2010). Fortunately, governments seem to have become more sophisticated in managing crises, protecting core social sector and safety net spending. Some evidence indicates that, although the growth of social spending fell during the most recent crisis, real levels of spending were maintained, especially in middle-income countries (Brumby and Verhoeven 2010). However, there are significant differences across countries and regions. Preliminary evidence from the most recent global recession suggests that social safety net programs, which were comparatively uncommon in previous crises, also played a considerable role in protecting people from the worst consequences of the crisis (World Bank 2009).

Aggregate shocks often affect all members of a household's risk-sharing networks, rendering traditional safety net arrangements ineffective. Carter and Maluccio (2003) find that households in South Africa are unable to insure against economic shocks when others in their community also suffer large losses. McKenzie (2003) finds that traditional informal mechanisms were largely ineffective in the face of income loss during the Mexican peso crisis of 1995. Economic hardship can disrupt bonds among households as well as larger social networks and erode social capital, especially if fault lines emerge between different ethnic, religious, or racial groups. Crisis increased religious and ethnic tensions and riots in Indonesia, for example, and eroded family and community ties in the countries of the former Soviet Union (Ferreira, Prennushi, and Ravallion 1999). Some evidence also suggests that as incomes fall and unemployment rises, crime and violence increase (Ferreira, Prennushi, and Ravallion 1999). Qualitative research conducted in Bangladesh, Indonesia, Jamaica, Kenya, and Zambia in early 2009 yielded reports of increased drug and alcohol abuse and crime, lower social participation, and greater tension among ethnic and social groups (Hossain 2009).

Whether shocks originate in international or in domestic markets, domestic policies can buffer such shocks through countercyclical revenue and expenditure policies, particularly ones directed at the more vulnerable members of society where vulnerability refers not only to poverty but also to salient life-cycle stages. In some cases (Chile, again, in part using copper revenues), governments have been able to provide fairly effective social safety nets to protect the more vulnerable members of society during economic shocks. The effectiveness of such policies, of course, depends on responses among both market and nonmarket institutions. The fewer rigidities there are in the markets (for example, policy-induced restrictions on hiring and firing labor and geographically segmented markets) and the greater the effectiveness of various forms of formal and informal insurance, the less likely a shock is to affect human capital investments among children and youth.

The adjustments to the shocks experienced at the microlevel, or adaptive behaviors in the household, can be modeled as if individuals are making choices in order to achieve some goals, subject to a number of factors that may be affected by shocks. For both individuals and households, these behaviors will have unanticipated consequences and will have both short- and long-run effects. Moreover, the decisions made by individuals and families in the face of a crisis are also influenced by any precautionary arrangements or other decisions that governments and households themselves had made ex ante to buffer future shocks. Governments, for example, could put in place strategies to buffer against fluctuations in commodity exports as noted above, or households could begin saving in good times so that they have resources to spend in bad times. These decisions interact, so that households may feel less compelled to self-insure if they are confident that the government will provide insurance for them. Similarly, governments will be less anxious to provide insurance if they know that households have themselves fairly well covered in the event of a shock.

Transmission within a Bioecological Systems Model
From a human capital investment point of view, policy makers are interested in household poverty because children are affected by the economic conditions of the household. Household resources are shared among household members, not necessarily equally, but in the pursuit of idiosyncratic objectives (see, for example, Manser and Brown 1980; McElroy and Horney 1981; Behrman, Pollak, and Taubman 1982; Thomas 1990, 1994; Brooks-Gunn, Duncan, and Maritato 1997). It is therefore important to understand the intrahousehold dynamics of the decision-making process.

It is often assumed that parents make the decisions about their children's human capital investments and that such decisions are thus subject to parental preferences. However, a child, especially the older he or she gets, has considerable influence over these investments or their realization, and the wishes of the growing child may not be consistent with the wishes of his or her parents. This problem of *agency* will yield significant variation in human capital investments across families and cultures, reflecting differences in preferences and the influence of individuals in household decision making.

Similarly, expectations of familial obligations across generations will influence parents' willingness to invest in their children. In the face of sudden changes in constraints, the household may protect human capital investments in one child over another, leading to, for example, systematic differences in educational investments for boys and girls. In many countries, traditional gender roles as well as expected gender-based differences in the returns to human capital investments heavily influence the division of resources among family, household, or kin members.[12] These differences in productivity may reflect differences in access to markets and other discriminatory practices and not inherent differences in ability. Thus, it is important to understand the mediating influence of social institutions, within and outside the market for human capital, both directly on the decision-making processes within households and on the impact of shocks on these decisions.

The bioecological, or human developmental approach, emphasizes transmission, or mediation of shocks through a broad range of social institutions, not merely through the economic resources available to the family for consumption and investment. Shocks also affect proximal processes within a developing person's microsystem through changes in the macro-, exo-, and mesosystems.

The household and proximal processes. Households make a wide range of adjustments in response to constraints caused by shocks, with consequences often unanticipated by policy makers. As noted earlier, economic models tend to emphasize decisions made in response to changing prices and resources, recognizing possible important externalities. Other disciplines emphasize other changes—such as the levels of stress, substance abuse, and violence in the presence of increased economic hardship and pressure—that are likely to affect the behavioral and emotional functioning of parents and consequently of child and youth development (Conger, Conger, and Martin 2010).

Studies of family stress, for example, find that poverty or economic hardship is not by itself the cause of "negative" development. Rather, worsening intrafamily relations, exacerbated by economic hardship, have negative effects on child development (for more detail see box 4.1). In other words, it is the engagement or disengagement of family members and their ability to cope with stress that create the link between exogenous shocks and psychosocial outcomes. For example, even if households are able to maintain income in the presence of a negative shock, child and youth development may be affected because of increased family stress,[13] which may be manifest in increased domestic violence, increased substance abuse, parental depression, or changes in family structure (such as divorce, the departure of some household members, or the incorporation into the household of additional people).

Human development is largely driven by family processes that actualize the genetic potential for effective physiological and psychological growth and functioning. Because shocks can cause significant disruption in the environments in which these proximal processes need to happen, they could, if the environment becomes too unstable, significantly reduce the effectiveness of those key processes, "with corresponding disruptive effects on psychological functioning" (Bronfenbrenner 1995). What follows are a few concrete examples of how shocks might influence intermediate systems, microsystems, and hence children's development:

- Economic crises can increase parental stress and depression. Depending on the timing and severity, an increase in a mother's stress and depression may reduce her sensitivity and responses to infant cues, which may in turn reduce the probability that the infant will develop a secure *attachment* relationship (see Campbell et al. 2004; Coyl, Roggman, and Newland 2002). This failure to develop a secure attachment during the early years of a child's life has been linked to myriad negative outcomes, such as decreased psychosocial well-being (for example, depression and anxiety; see Goodman and Gotlib 1999) and socioemotional development (such as self-esteem, social anxiety, antisocial behavior, self-efficacy; see Hammen et al. 1987), which may in turn affect educational achievement, labor market outcomes, and mental and physical health (see Heckman, Stixrud, and Urzua 2006).

- The same paths of influence, from macroeconomic shock to parental stress and depression, could reduce the frequency, complexity, and meaningfulness of verbal exchange between mothers and their very young children and could in turn slow growth in children's *language development*.

- Unemployment, often of the primary breadwinner (father), has also been shown to increase stress, frustration, and depression, which can increase parental *substance abuse, domestic violence, and family abandonment.* Substance abuse reduces parental attentiveness and often increases domestic violence. While the effect of parental inattentiveness or lack of sensitivity has been noted, studies have also documented the severe negative effects that domestic violence and family abandonment have on children (Holt, Buckley, and Whelan 2008).

- Households in which a primary earner loses a job may be tempted to add workers to substitute for the lost income (for Mexico, see, for example, Skoufias and Parker 2006). This decision can affect children within the household in different ways, depending on their age. Where traditional gender norms still predominate, small children may be left in the care of elder daughters (Benería and Roldan 1987) or in another child care arrangement. The effect that this separation from the primary caregiver can have on a very young child depends on the quality of care and stimulation the child receives from the alternative caregiver (Belsky et al. 2007). Either way, the influence parents have on the development of their child decreases with the amount of time the child spends in secondary care settings.

Developmental processes, life course, and the chronosystem. Household financial stress affects children's development differently at different ages (Bronfenbrenner 1979; Elder 1999; Elder and Caspi 1988). Furthermore, differences in historical contexts will have their own effects on developmental processes. In other words, the basic premise of the chronosystem is that from a developmental perspective, it matters at what point in a person's life course a shock happens; changing environments over time affect the developmental process differently; and the life stage and the changing environment interact in various ways. Shifts in the microsystem can affect proximal processes, and the long-term impact of these shifts depends on the life stage of the developing child. For example, when a shock decreases the availability of the primary caregiver during the first 6-12 months of a child's life, the child may be unable to form a safe attachment with possibly long-lasting consequences. If a shock happens, however, when the child is a little older, decreased availability of the primary caregiver may not have the same consequences.

In addition, the impact of proximal processes on children's neurocognitive and affective-behavioral functioning also depends on the stage of children's brain and neurophysiological development (see for more detail box 3.2 and Shonkoff et al. 2012). And severe nutritional deficiencies during gestation (see Tobi et al. 2009; Susser, Hoek, and Brown 1998; Susser et al. 1996 for studies of the Durch Hunger Winter) and the first 24–36 months of life have significant and substantial effects on a range of outcomes such as cognitive skills and wage rates and on the nutritional status of the next generation 30–40 years later (Hoddinott et al. 2008; Behrman et al. 2009; Maluccio et al. 2009), whereas nutritional deficiencies at a later stage do not seem to have the same lasting consequences.

To the extent that families are aware of this, decisions to invest and how to respond to crisis will be forward looking. Families may also have a sense of the importance of dynamic complementarities in investments: the idea that early investments increase the returns to investments later in life (Cunha et al. 2006; Cunha and Heckman 2007). Similarly, families may engage in precautionary savings in anticipation of expected future shocks, in order to smooth both consumption and human capital investments in their children. Whether households take precautionary actions depends not only on individual characteristics, such as subjective discount rates, but also on the extent to which formal and informal capital and insurance markets as well as social safety nets facilitate such smoothing. The dynamic nature of these investments means that it may take a long time to realize the returns on investment, and this increases the uncertainty of those returns. This uncertainty arises partly from the difficulty of predicting what the future labor market will be and partly from the basic agency problem caused by the intergenerational nature of these investments.

Transmission through other settings and systems. In addition to individuals and households, the functioning of other settings and systems affects the options and the human capital outcomes of interest through interactions, for example, with peers, and other spillover effects. The behavior of individuals in peer groups, communities, and schools and health and human services institutions directly influences human capital development in the microsystem. Entities more removed from children and youth, including social networks such as neighborhood, civic, and religious associations, may also provide a supportive environment.

How shocks affect settings in the exosystem or macrosystem differs greatly across contexts. For example, Paugam (1996) notes that negative shocks such as unemployment are more associated with a deterioration of social relationships (marital breakdown, lack of private support at work, and deterioration of familial relationships) in France, Germany, and the United Kingdom than in Denmark, Italy, and Spain. Much less is known about how negative shocks affect the deterioration of social relationships in low-income countries. The experience of shocks and their impact on social relationships is not monolithic and varies in part according to the meaning of community and representations of the reciprocal rights and duties that citizens and family members have in relation to one another. These may be mediated by a shared definition of community, based, for instance, on notions of autonomy and self-reliance or on a notion of solidarity, shared human dignity, blood ties, or kinship (Lamont 2000; Silver 1994). These societal scripts influence the impact of crises on individuals and on the social, symbolic, and material resources they believe they are entitled to and can draw on in times of vulnerability.

According to many social analysts (see, for example, Silbereisen, Ritchie, and Overmier 2010; Silbereisen and Tomasik 2010; Noack and Kracke 1997), we are in a period of accelerated change, socioculturally but also economically, particularly because of increased economic volatility. Nonetheless, regardless of how drastic the change, the fundamental institutions of a society are generally not affected much in the short run. For example, the transformation in Eastern and Central Europe did not change the fact that all the status hierarchies in these societies were built on a merit system based on credentials and accomplishments. Only the criteria for achieving such status changed (see, for example, Silbereisen and Wiesner 2000). The social status hierarchy based on experience, credentials, diplomas, seniority, and such represented a constant in spite of the changes in the political and economic systems. Put differently, a shock can create an imbalance or a mismatch between the roles and livelihoods people expected or desired to take on and the actual current situational imperative they perceive (Pinquart and Silbereisen 2004; Tomasik and Silbereisen 2009), inevitably shifting the equilibrium and requiring a whole range of adaptations, both behavioral and psychological. The household's experience of the aggregate shock is in part determined by the experience, behavior, and decisions of its neighbors. Human development occurs among communities of people whose behavior is mutually influential and which may serve to exacerbate shocks, if destructive behavior leads to further destructive behavior. For example, individuals may respond to negative shocks by increasing the depletion of commonly held network resources. However, shared experiences may lessen the impact, if a solution to the common governance problem is found and the shock induces a counterresponse and raises a sense of solidarity—for example, "in these hard times, let us all work together to support one another." Furthermore, the effects of unemployment on mental health are less severe if aggregate unemployment is high. This is referred to as the "social norm effect" (see, for example, Clark 2003). In the face of crises, people—especially adolescents—often seek support and encouragement from their peers and to try to make meaning of the situation. In the absence of healthy role models or peers, such newly formed relationships may have negative effects and lead to negative adaptive or deviant behavior.

Thus, it is helpful to think along the lines of the resilience factors presented in box 2.1 that may stem from biological, genetic, and social sources, as well as from interactions between genes and the environment (for more detail, see box 3.2). The success of potentially powerful adaptive systems, such as attachment or self-regulation, will depend on the context and the resources available in that context. Maintaining positive relationships with parents, teachers, or mentors or having a well-developed self-regulatory system will have a protective effect on the developing child. Adaptive success will depend on how successfully the developing child has mastered previous stage-salient tasks, especially the development of major adaptive systems, and on how supportive the environment is and what resources it provides. In addition, while the child's own adaptive system is of primary importance, the adaptive responses of people in his or her environment will also influence the resilience and development of the child.

For example, families and family life affect child development. However, intrafamilial interactions, between parents or among parents and children, are generally not measured or observable in most socioeconomic datasets. Education, however, influences family life; being better educated typically means that one has more resources of various kinds, including stronger conflict resolution strategies, wider future opportunities, and the like. Better-educated adults are generally better equipped with tools to help them manage a family and are also better equipped to minimize or mitigate the effect of hardship on internal family relations and consequently on children (see also Behrman et al. 1980; Behrman and Rosensweig 2002, 2004; Yoshikawa, Aber and Beardslee 2012; Gershoff et al. 2007).

Institutional and cultural resources also help buffer individuals and communities against shocks. These resources enable and constrain different responses or adaptive behaviors to shocks and make them more or less likely across contexts. For example, the predictable availability of comprehensive social services helps an individual choose from among a range of strategies to cope with unemployment or other forms of crisis. In addition, individuals will also respond to the targeting mechanisms used in the distribution of public support services: a means-tested program will engender a different perception of state assistance and its availability and behavior than a universal program.

Individual and collective interpretations or perceptions of events, such as economic crises and subsequent adaptations, are rooted in shared definitions of rights and mutual obligations in the community as well as in standards for cooperation and individualism. Awareness of a shared commitment to developing and managing common property and resources, such as a public housing complex, may also affect how individuals deal with collective violence or other forms of social disorder (Small 2004). Conversely, in communities with low expectations about collective governance, individuals experience more fear and perceive their environment as more threatening (Sampson 2006), and these perceptions will trigger responses different from those in close-knit communities with higher expectations.

Along the same line, the cultural frames through which the poor are construed, and how they perceive themselves, also influence how they understand their own plight and develop approaches for addressing their situation. These collective experiences and perceptions can vary across ethnic or racial groups. In other words, the same environment and event may be interpreted and constructed differently by different groups. In the United States, for instance, Latinos are also more prone to help one another find jobs than are African Americans, a phenomenon that has been linked to observations that African Americans have a comparatively stronger sense of self-reliance (Smith 2010), as well as the view that this has adverse effects on their ability to find jobs.

Different definitions of individual and collective goals and different interpretations of experience can lead to different perceptions of the range of choices and options available. For instance, in an environment where socioeconomic achievement is the sole measure of success, low-income populations are doomed to perceive themselves as losers. However, if their environment also values, for example, "morality" as a highly recognized basis for human worth, low socioeconomic status or unemployment may have markedly different psychological implications for the individual who perceives himself to be living up to high standards of morality (Lamont 2000). Along the same lines, if a group has historically been characterized by low socioeconomic achievement, expressive aspects of collective identity (history of struggle and resilience, cultural tradition, intellectual production, and the like) may be particularly valued and become a source of positive identification, pride, and strength. This response is tied to a shared definition of collective identity or to "symbolic communities" of "people like us." These factors have to be taken into account, as they provide recognition and support in a moment of crisis, a sense that one is not alone and that one's experience is understood and shared by others, and a belief that one can develop individual and collective strategies in response to problems. This collective identity may also lead to the development of distinctive skills or modes of coping by which the population can create a sense of achievement. In other words, cultural intimacy and support in time of crisis and vulnerability can play an important role in enhancing resilience.

Policy Implications of an Integrated Approach

So far, part I has reviewed the fundamentals of human developmental science and economic theory of human capital development and investment and explored how the impacts of systemic economic shocks can be better understood through an interdisciplinary framework combining the two approaches. The purpose of this exercise is to identify policies and interventions that best protect children and youth from the negative consequences that crises might bring. In addition, responses to shocks should not only mitigate the impact, "providing immediate and effective relief" (Skoufias 2003, 1088), but also be designed to alleviate poverty in the long run, reduce susceptibility to future crises, and halt the intergenerational perpetuation of poverty. Programs that protect households from the brunt of a crisis should include features that promote healthy child and youth development. For this, we must fully understand the *transmission mechanisms* or pathways through which shocks reach the developing person as outlined above. A drop in income does not necessarily affect a child, if it does not change the dynamics within and between settings of its microsystem. In other words, whether a drop in income will affect a child depends partly on how it affects proximal processes, such as interactions between parent and child, between teacher and child, or among peers.

The impact of shocks on systems and on young people will vary according to the *context* in which the shock occurs. The context is affected by political, economic, institutional, historical, and cultural factors that shape and are shaped by the policy environment. Social policy can then shield vulnerable populations from serious impacts through stabilizing incomes and consumption and maintaining public spending on services such as schools and health care. Social policy also influences collective resources, cultural frameworks, and repertoires that affect the ability of individuals to understand, adapt, and cope with the situation they find themselves in. For example, the impact of a transfer or social support program on the child will depend on who within the household receives the transfer. In some contexts, money in the hands of women rather than men is more likely to be spent on children (Benería and Roldan 1987; see also the papers in Haddad, Hoddinott, and Alderman 1997). In addition, certain design features and targeting strategies could also increase family tensions, when intra- as well as extrafamilial relations are altered and power distributions shift, or when receipt of the transfer is conditioned on some behavior that might be controversial within the household (see, for example, Greenberg, Dechausay, and Fraker 2011). Thus, the context can affect vulnerability and resilience (see box 2.1). Conger and Stockdale (2011) find in a sample of Mexican immigrant families in California that a strong ethnic and cultural identity and a sense of belonging contributed significantly to an individual's and a community's resilience during the recent recession.

Finally, the impact of the shock will depend on its *timing*, with regard both to the person's age and to the historical time. Contexts and vulnerabilities change over time, and the impact of the shock will differ according to the person's stage of development as well as the historical context in which a shock occurs.

This conceptual framework provides a set of principles that informs the design and implementation of interventions to achieve both efficiency and distributional goals in the face of an economic crisis. The insights gained by taking a human-developmentalist approach can—among other benefits—improve short-term outcomes, augment long-term outcomes, increase cost-effectiveness of crisis response, or improve political viability and postcrisis sustainability. This approach leads to three main overarching principles, or tools: nested points of entry, substitutability, and targeting.

Nested Points of Entry: Breaking Transmission

This chapter outlined how a systemic economic shock can transmit from the global or national level through various systems and settings and ultimately affect an individual child. The pathways through which a shock is transmitted to the individual child provide a number of possible options, or *nested points of entry*, for interventions aimed at breaking the transmission of the shock. For example, a fall in income can create stress within the family in domains other than consumption and subsistence. Unemployment is often accompanied by a loss of status and feelings of inadequacy and hopelessness, often resulting in depression and anxiety. Depression can lead to substance abuse, domestic tension, and violence, as well as to changes in family dynamics. Policies may aim at replacing lost income, providing employment, or a combination of both. However, such transfer or public works programs are often accompanied by unforeseen externalities, and design features will determine the impact they have on children's development (see, for example, Huston et al. 2005). As these changes in individuals and the family happen in subtle and unexpected ways, interventions to provide information and support as the family deals with the crisis can be as important as income transfers in helping families maintain effective and positive parenting behavior and healthy relationships among partners and children.

Alternatively, an intervention could deliver services directly to the child in support of the factors driving the developmental processes. For example, we know that parental stress can hinder the cognitive and socioemotional development of children through various channels as children attempt to cope with that stress. Thus, we might want to consider a mother-child intervention to help the mother cope with the stresses induced by a crisis and maintain positive parenting.

An adolescent on the verge of transitioning to work, in contrast, may be affected by economic shocks through nonfamily influences. For example, changes in labor market opportunities might clash with previously formed perceptions and aspirations about work, which could negatively affect a youth's future orientation (see, for example, Silbereisen 2000). An intervention might aim to provide guidance and resources to support the development of identity and future orientation during such difficult times.

Considering resilience factors as outlined earlier (see box 2.1) may prove helpful for policy makers, because they provide something like a menu of nested points of entry that could be targeted to help buffer children and youth from the adverse effects of aggregate shocks. Chapter 6 will provide some concrete examples of evidence-based interventions that have proved effective at fostering positive adaptation in the face of risk and adversity.

Substitutability

A solid understanding of how children are embedded in different contexts and settings at different ages and stages of development—and being able to recognize how these settings might be affected by a shock—enables us to identify a range of effective alternative policies, or *substitutes*,[14] in cases where the actual threat to development is difficult to address directly. For example, in some countries, social norms might restrict programs aimed at influencing parenting styles and interfamily dynamics; intervening in child-rearing practices may be perceived as an invasion of an exclusively private domain and thus politically and socially unacceptable. Alternatively, introducing special programs in schools may effectively reach young people and have positive impacts despite obstacles or confounding family difficulties. However, it must be noted that family responses may diminish the benefits of interventions delivered to the children. For example, the net impact of school feeding programs may be less than the value of the school food package if the household responds by giving the beneficiary child less food at home.

Of course, relevant settings are very much age and context specific. Applying a bioecological systems perspective as was discussed earlier in this chapter will guide the identification of alternative settings in which interventions might be introduced. For example, school-age children, and adolescents to an even greater extent, spend more and more of their time outside the family setting, providing a range of substitutes for family- or household-based interventions. It will be more challenging to reach the unborn and very young children who do not attend day care or out-of-school children and youth. Possible substitutes for those cases and ways in which to reach the "unreachable" are discussed in chapter 6.

The sources of resilience listed in box 2.1 can help us identify alternative settings for public action and thus a range of possible substitutes. It must be remembered that interventions in one setting can spill over into others. A program that directly affects schooling or health care provision, for example, will likely indirectly affect perceptions and behaviors within the family, such as those relating to parenting and other intrafamily relations; conversely, parenting practices and other family-related contextual variables will influence the impact of an intervention in school. In other words, settings, or contexts, interact, and this interaction may be more relevant than the main effect of any one context alone. For instance, research has demonstrated that the same parenting styles lead to different child development outcomes in safe as opposed to dangerous communities (see Florsheim, Tolan, and Gorman-Smith 1996; Brody and Flor 1998; Chao and Tseng 2002). Similarly, parenting styles may interact with ethnic differences in family socialization processes and actual or perceived educational and occupational discrimination (Steinberg, Dornbusch, and Brown 1992).

Targeting

Targeting of safety nets and other interventions relates to the questions raised earlier in this chapter in the section on efficiency and redistribution and usually focuses on some indicator of well-being, such as household income or some proxy for income. Targeting has direct and indirect costs, and it is not always the case that sharper targeting is preferable. More accurate targeting requires more information and more monitoring, and it may diminish support for programs among those who might benefit from looser targeting (see, for example, van de Walle and Nead 1995; Cornia and Stewart 1995; Sen 1995). Moreover, during times of crisis, effective safety net programs need to be rolled out quickly. The delays associated with identifying eligible people can be substantial (Sen 1995). Governments therefore often resort to self-targeted programs, in which participants self-select to take part, such as public works programs where the wage offered is no greater than the prevailing market wage or food programs in which the food distributed is considered inferior (by preferences and not nutritionally).

However, as observed earlier in this chapter, children and youth may be affected through channels other than household income. Targeting based strictly on income may therefore miss large numbers of vulnerable children and young people who are at risk of suffering severe adverse long-term effects but who do not satisfy conventionally defined or easily observable targeting criteria. Furthermore, self-targeted public works programs for parents may not be the most effective at ensuring healthy child and youth development (see, for example, Morris et al. 2001; Gennetian et al. 2004; McLoyd et al. 2011). Parental workfare programs are also unlikely to adequately address specific developmental issues and the consequences arising from prolonged unemployment spells of youth transitioning to work (see chapters 5 and 6).

Moreover, targeting based on some indicator of poverty may have significant psychological costs in self-respect and respect perceived from others (Sen 1995), which can influence a person's abilities and affect confidence and achievement. This can influence younger children indirectly, through parents' feelings of self-worth or empowerment, and older children or adolescents more directly, as they gain awareness of their family's situation (see, for example, McLoyd et al. 2011).

The developmental approach provides tools to address some of the political economy concerns of targeting. Programs can be designed for specific age groups (for example, infants, primary school children, and out-of-school adolescents); settings (for example, households, schools, or youth centers); levels of aggregation (for example, individual households or communities); or resilience factors (for example, children without extended family networks or with poor self-regulation skills). Universal programs targeted to particular age groups may be preferable to income-based targeting, if we know which age groups are especially vulnerable and why. For example, the unemployment of a parent in a middle-income family can create considerable stress without threatening subsistence and can significantly affect a child's development. However, transfers to families not under severe economic duress may be both ineffective and very expensive, and thus politically unjustifiable. In this case, targeting support services at a different setting could provide a viable alternative for protecting children in a crisis. For example, depending on its focus and content, school-based programs involving all children can help counter the negative effects of a stressful home situation. Furthermore, programs open to all youth experiencing difficulties can not only provide a supportive environment and opportunity to acquire skills but also foster networks and the behavioral or social skills that all youth need to make the transition to productive adulthood. Broadly targeted programs for youth can increase social cohesion and a sense of solidarity by uniting youth from different socioeconomic backgrounds, as well as reducing the stigma associated with participating in the program.

Alternatively, programs could target on a basis of selective or indicative prevention. Selective prevention is based on specific criteria associated with high risk of negative outcomes, whereas indicative prevention identifies subjects who already show early signs of behavioral or socioemotional problems. Selective preventative targeting, for example, may be based on indicators such as high-risk neighborhoods ("Moving to Opportunity"),[15] or high-risk single mothers ("Nurse Family Partnership").[16] Alternatively, or in addition, "Friends of the Children," a long-term mentoring program, for example, uses an indicative preventative approach that targets children with weak self-regulation skills identified by behavioral markers early on in day care or school settings.[17]

Concluding Remarks

This chapter presents a concerted effort at integrating the economic human capital approach with that from human developmental science to enhance our understanding of how aggregate economic crises, particularly in developing countries, affect children and youth. We developed a conceptual framework that enables us to improve our understanding of the empirical work and the policy choices reviewed in the remaining chapters.

The effectiveness of generating and interpreting new empirical work, and designing and testing new policy responses, will be the real tests of the utility of this framework. Under the assumption that most readers will be more familiar with the economic approach, we have focused relatively more on the human developmentalist perspective. However, we hope that those approaching this subject from either perspective (or neither) will have gained an appreciation of both, as well as an understanding of how they are complementary and can enhance the design of programs designed to protect and promote young people's development.

In sum, considerations of basic economic modeling lead to a richer interpretation of the Bronfenbrenner bioecological model by allowing for induced changes in behaviors of a number of entities. Some of these induced changes are proximal and some more distal from the point of view of human resource investments in children and youth. They include a multiplicity of adjustments with implications not only for immediate responses to the shocks but also for the dynamics of longer-run responses to actual or anticipated shocks (and with implications for targeting of policies).

Combined, the three principles—nested points of entry, substitutability, and targeting—provide a coherent framework for designing and implementing effective interventions to protect and promote young people's development during economic crises. Thus, this multilayered approach expands the set of possible policy interventions, for example, by presenting a more nuanced depiction of the experiences and relationships that shape children and youth and how those experiences are conditioned by the mental health of their parents. But more work remains for further integration in program design and implementation, as well as in empirical measurement and testing of combined approaches to achieve both faster recovery and enhanced well-being in times of crisis.

Notes

1. Of course, the consequences of all crises may be related to past economic policy. The impact of natural disasters, for example, depends strongly on the quality of previous investments, especially prior infrastructure development. This is in part why the 2010 earthquake in Haiti was much more devastating than the 2010 earthquake in Chile, even though the latter was one of the strongest earthquakes ever measured, 500–700 times more forceful than the devastating earthquake in Haiti, (<http://en.wikipedia.org/wiki/Richter_magnitude_scale>, accessed 12/27/2011.)

2. The investor may vary depending on the particular situation and the life-cycle stage of the individual in whom the investment is made. In some cases, for

example, the individual may be the investor, but in other cases it may be his or her family. In still other cases there may be implicit or explicit bargaining among family members—between spouses or between children and their parents—regarding investments in human capital. If there is such bargaining, the fall-back or "threat point" of the individuals involved may be critical because their bargaining power may depend on what their options are if they opt out of the family. Space precludes developing the implications of these bargaining possibilities in this chapter, but see Behrman (1997), Haddad, Hoddinott, and Alderman (1997), and Lundberg and Pollak (1996) and the references therein for more extensive discussion. To avoid awkward terminology, we refer to the investor as the family of the individual, but we try to be clear when it makes a difference who the investor is.

3. Becker (1967, 1975, 1993), Mincer (1974), and Schultz (1961, 1963) are the seminal papers in economics describing human capital investments. For a more detailed discussion of the links between economics and the life-span in developmental psychology, see Behrman (2003).

4. The net discounted present value of benefits is the sum of all the benefits that derive from an item or service, today and into the future; that is, this year's benefits, plus next year's benefits, plus the subsequent year's benefits, and so on. Future benefits are usually discounted to account for inflation, the opportunity cost of the resources used, and the observation that people generally prefer things that are closer in time over things that are farther in the future. The same principles hold for costs.

5. This analytical model is developed more formally and graphically in appendix A. The "present discounted value" of future outcomes adjusts for the fact that money received (or spent) today is more valuable than the same amount of money received (or spent) in the future because money received now can be reinvested and receive a return before money received at some point in the future. "Marginal" means additional. At the time of the investment decision, the relevant marginal benefits and costs are not known but are expected in the future.

6. This is not the same as engineering or scientific efficiency. An engine that is very efficient in the engineering sense, for example, may be very inefficient economically because it uses inputs that have better uses elsewhere.

7. If all other markets in the economy are *not* operating efficiently, policies that narrow the differences between private and social marginal incentives in the human capital investment market or in some segment of that market do not necessarily increase efficiency and productivity. And clearly in the real world there are many market failures so that some distortions may counterbalance others. But, in the absence of specific information to the contrary (such as on the existence of two counterbalancing distortions), a safe operating presumption is that lessening any one distortion between social and private incentives is likely to increase efficiency.

8. The relevant information includes not only information about the functioning of human capital investment markets and possible market failures but also serious evaluations of government policies that are related to human development and possible policy failures. Policies are the result of behaviors and are subject to estimation problems such as those mentioned earlier.

9. Most available studies on the positive relations between productivity (or wage) gains and human development–education interactions, however, may overstate the causal effect because of the failure to control for the selectivity of human development in the presence of important unobserved (by analysts) attributes such as ability and motivation.

10. A *role* is a set of behaviors and expectations pertinent to an individual in a particular setting and at a particular point during the life course, associated with a particular position in society, for example, the role of mother, baby, teacher, friend, and so forth (Bronfenbrenner 1979).

11. For more detail on the mesosystem, see Bronfenbrenner (1979); depicting the system in more detail would exceed the scope of this section.

12. Quisumbing (1994) and DeGraff and Bilsborrow (2003) show that Filipino parents tend to prefer educating girls over boys as they perceive greater returns to investing in girls' secondary education. This preference, they explain, seems to stem from the fact that migrating daughters provide greater financial support to their parents than their sons later on. More generally, while there once was a pattern of schooling boys on average more than girls, in recent years that pattern has been reversed among children enrolled in school in most countries, although there still persist smaller enrollment rates for girls than boys in a number of countries (Grant and Behrman 2010).

13. See, for example, the Family Stress Model by Conger, Conger, and Martin (2010).

14. We are not looking at intertemporal substitution or inability thereof, as in Almond and Currie (2011).

15. See http://portal.hud.gov/hudportal/HUD?src=/programdescription/mto.

16. See http://www.nursefamilypartnership.org/.

17. See http://www.friendsofthechildren.org/.

References

Aber, L., and S. Jones. 1997. "Indicators of Positive Development in Early Childhood: Improving Concepts and Measures." In *Indicators of Children's Well-being*, 395–408, ed. R. Hauser, B. Brown, and W. Prosser. New York: Russell Sage Foundation.

Alderman, H., ed. 2011. *No Small Matter: The Impact of Poverty, Shocks, and Human Capital Investments in Early Childhood Development*. Washington, DC: World Bank.

Alkire, S. 2002. "Dimensions of Human Development." *World Development* 30 (2): 191–205.

Almond, D. 2006. "Is the 1918 Influenza Pandemic Over? Long-Term Effects of *in Utero* Influenza Exposure in the Post-1940 U.S." *Journal of Political Economy* 114 (4): 672–712.

Almond, D., and K. Chay. 2003. *The Long-Run and Intergenerational Impact of Poor Infant Health: Evidence from Cohorts Born during the Civil Rights Era.* Mimeo. University of California Berkeley.

Almond, D., and J. Currie. 2011. "Killing Me Softly: The Fetal Origins Hypothesis." *Journal of Economic Perspectives* 25 (3): 153–72.

Bakermans-Kranenburg, M., and M. Van Ijzendoorn. 2007. "Genetic Vulnerability or Differential Susceptibility in Child Development: The Case of Attachment." *Journal of Child Psychology and Psychiatry* 48: 1160–73.

————.2011. "Differential Susceptibility to Rearing Environment Depending on Dopamine-Related Genes: New Evidence and a Meta-Analysis." *Development and Psychopathology* 23: 39–52.

Baltes, Paul B. 1997. "On the Incomplete Architecture of Human Ontogeny: Selection, Optimization, and Compensation as Foundation of Development Theory." *American Psychologist* 32 (4): 366–80.

Baltes, Paul B., Ulman Lindenberger, and Ursula M. Staudinger. 1998. "Life-Span Theory in Developmental Psychology." In *Handbook of Child Psychology*, 5th ed., vol. 1, ed. R. M. Lerner, *Theoretical Models of Human Development*, 1029–143. New York: Wiley.

Banerjee, A., E. Duflo, G. Poste-Vinay, and T. Watts. 2007. "Long Run Health Impacts of Income Shocks: Wine and Phylloxera in 19th Century France." NBER Working Paper, National Bureau of Economic Research, Cambridge, MA.

Baumrind, D. 1989. "Rearing Competent Children." In *Child Development Today and Tomorrow*, ed. W. Damon, 349–78. San Francisco: Jossey-Bass.

————. 1991. "Parenting Styles and Adolescent Development." In *The Encyclopedia of Adolescence*, ed. J. Brooks-Gunn, R. Lerner, and A. C. Petersen, 746–58. New York: Garland.

Becker, Gary S. 1967. "Human Capital and the Personal Distribution of Income: An Analytical Approach." University of Michigan, Ann Arbor, Woytinsky Lecture. Republished Becker (1975, 94–117).

————. 1975. *Human Capital.* 2nd ed. New York: National Bureau of Economic Research.

————. 1991. *A Treatise on the Family.* 2nd ed. Cambridge, MA: Harvard University Press.

————. 1993. "Nobel Lecture: The Economic Way of Looking at Behavior." *Journal of Political Economy* 101 (3): 385–409.

Behrman, Jere R. 1997. "Intrahousehold Distribution and the Family." In *Handbook of Population and Family Economics*, ed. Mark R. Rosenzweig and Oded Stark, 107–68. Amsterdam: North-Holland Publishing Company.

————. 2003. "Selection, Organization and Compensation in Economics: Resource Management." In *Understanding Human Development: Dialogues with Lifespan Psychology*, ed. Ursula M. Staudinger and Ulman Lindenberger, 125–55. Boston: Kluwer Academic Publishers.

Behrman, Jere R., Maria Cecilia Calderon, Samuel Preston, John Hoddinott, Reynaldo Martorell, and Aryeh D. Stein. 2009. "Nutritional Supplementation of Girls Influences the Growth of their Children: Prospective Study in Guatemala." *American Journal of Clinical Nutrition* 90 (November): 1372–79.

Behrman, Jere R., Andrew Foster, and Mark R. Rosenzweig. 1997. "The Dynamics of Agricultural Production and the Calorie-Income Relationship: Evidence from Pakistan." *Journal of Econometrics* 77 (1): 187–207.

Behrman, Jere R., Z. Hrubec, Paul Taubman, and T. J. Wales. 1980. *Socioeconomic Success: A Study of the Effects of Genetic Endowments, Family Environment and Schooling*. Amsterdam: North-Holland Publishing Company.

Behrman, Jere R., Robert A. Pollak, and Paul Taubman. 1982. "Parental Preferences and Provision for Progeny." *Journal of Political Economy* 90 (1): 52–73.

————. 1995. "The Wealth Model: Efficiency in Education and Equity in the Family." In *From Parent to Child: Intrahousehold Allocations and Intergenerational Relations in the United States*, ed. Jere R. Behrman, Robert A. Pollak, and Paul Taubman, 138–82. Chicago: University of Chicago Press.

Behrman, Jere R., and Mark R. Rosenzweig. 2002. "Does Increasing Women's Schooling Raise the Schooling of the Next Generation?" *American Economic Review* 92 (1): 323–34.

————. 2004. "Returns to Birthweight." *Review of Economics and Statistics* 86 (2): 586–601.

Behrman, Jere R., Mark R. Rosenzweig, and Paul Taubman. 1994. "Endowments and the Allocation of Schooling in the Family and in the Marriage Market: The Twins Experiment." *Journal of Political Economy* 102 (6): 1131–74.

Belsky, J., C. Jonassaint, M. Pluess, M. Stanton, B. Brummett, and R. Williams. 2009. "Vulnerability Genes or Plasticity Genes?: *Molecular Psychiatry* 14 (May): 746–54.

Belsky, J., D. L. Vandell, M. Burchinal, K. A. Clarke-Stewart, A. McCartney, and M. T. Owen. 2007. "Are There Long-Term Effects of Early Child Care?" *Child Development* 78 (2): 681–701.

Belsky, J., and M. Pluess. 2009. "The Nature (and Nurture?) of Plasticity in Early Human Development." *Perspectives on Psychological Science* 4 (4): 345–51.

Benería, L., and M. Roldán. 1987. *The Crossroads of Class and Gender: Industrial Homework, Subcontracting, and Household Dynamics in Mexico City*. Chicago: University of Chicago Press.

Bourguignon, F., and C. Morrisson. 1992. *Adjustment and Equity in Developing Countries*. Paris: OECD Development Studies Centre.

Bourguignon, F., and Christian Morrisson. 1993. *Adjustment and Equity in Developing Countries: A New Approach*. Paris: Organisation for Economic Co-operation and Development, Development Centre.

Brody, G. H., and D. Flor. 1998. "Maternal Resources, Parenting Practices, and Child Competence in Rural, Single-Parent African American Families." *Child Development* 69 (3): 803–16.

Bronfenbrenner, U. 1979. *The Ecology of Human Development: Experiments by Nature and Design*. Cambridge, MA: Harvard University Press.

———. 1994a. "Nature-Nurture Reconceptualized in Developmental Perspective: A Bioecological Model." *Psychological Review* 101 (4): 568–86.

———. 1994b. "Ecological Models of Human Development." In *International Encyclopedia of Education*. Vol. 3. 2nd ed. Oxford, UK: Elsevier.

———. 1995. "Developmental Ecology through Space and Time: A Future Perspective." In *Examining Lives in Context: Perspectives on the Ecology of Human Development*, ed. P. Moen, G. Elder, and K. Lusher, 619–47. Washington, DC: American Psychological Association.

Bronfrenbrenner, U., and P. A. Morris. 2006. "The Biological Model of Human Development." In *Handbook of Child Psychology*, 6th ed., vol. 1, *Theoretical Models of Human Development*, ed. W. Damon and R. M. Lerner, 793–828. New York: Wiley.

Brooks-Gunn, J., G. Duncan, and J. L. Aber, eds. 1997. *Neighborhood Poverty: Context and Consequences for Children*. Vol. 1. New York: Russell Sage Foundation.

Brooks-Gunn, J., G. Duncan, and N. Maritato. 1997. "Poor Families, Poor Outcomes: The Well-Being of Children and Youth." In *Consequences of Growing Up Poor*, ed. G. Duncan and J. Brooks-Gunn, 1-17. New York: Russell Sage Foundation.

Brumby, Jim, and Marijn Verhoeven, 2010. "Public Expenditure after the Global Financial Crisis." In *The Day after Tomorrow*, ed. O. Canuto and M. Giugale. Washington, DC: World Bank.

Campbell, S. B., C. A. Brownell, A. Hungerford, S. J. Spieker, R. Mohan, and J. Blessing. 2004. "The Course of Maternal Depressive Symptoms and Maternal Sensitivity as Predictors of Attachment Security at 36 Months." *Development and Psychopathology* 16 (2): 231–52.

Carter, Michael R., and John Maluccio. 2003. "Social Capital and Coping with Economic Shocks: An Analysis of Stunting of South African Children." *World Development* 31 (7):1147–63.

Carter, Prudence. 2007. *Keeping It Real: School Success beyond Black and White*. New York: Oxford University Press.

Chao, R. K., and V. Tseng. 2002. "Parenting of Asians." In *Social Conditions and Applied Parenting*, Vol. 4. *Handbook of Parenting*, 2nd ed., ed. M. Bornstein, 59–93. Mahwah, NJ: Erlbaum.

Chauvel, Louis. 2010. "The Long-Term Destabilization of Youth, Scarring Effects, and the Future of the Welfare Regime in Post-Trente Glorieuses France." *French Politics, Culture and Society* 28 (3): 74–96.

Cho, Y., and D. Newhouse. 2011. "How Did the Great Recession Affect Different Types of Workers? Evidence from 17 Middle-Income Countries." Policy Research Working Paper 5636, World Bank, Washington, DC.

Chiappori, Pierre-Andre. 1988. "Rational Household Labor Supply." *Econometrica* 56 (1): 63–89.

———. 1992. "Collective Labor Supply and Welfare." *Journal of Political Economy* 100 (3): 437–67.

Clark, A. 2003. "Unemployment as a Social Norm: Psychological Evidence from Panel Data." *Journal of Labor Economics* 21 (2): 323–51.

Cogneau, D., and R. Jedwab, 2010. *Commodity Price Shocks and Child Outcomes: The 1990 Cocoa Crisis in Côte d'Ivoire*. CEPREMAP Working Papers (Docweb) 1018. Paris: Centre Pour la Récherche Économique et ses Applications (CEPREMAP).

Conger, R., K. Conger, and M. Martin. 2010. "Socioeconomic Status, Family Processes, and Individual Development." *Journal of Marriage and Family* 72 (June): 685–704.

Conger, R. D., H. Song, G. E. Stockdale, E. Ferrer, K. F. Widaman, and A. M. Cauce. 2011. "Resilience and Vulnerability of Mexican Origin Youth and Their Families: A Test of a Culturally-Informed Model of Family Economic Stress." In *Adolescence and Beyond: Family Processes and Development*, ed. P. K. Kerig, M. S. Schulz, and S. T. Hauser. New York: Oxford University Press.

Conger, R., and G. E. Stockdale. 2011. "Response to the Great Recession: Mexican Origin Families and Children in California." An invited paper presented at the World Bank and Jacobs Foundation Conference on Children and Youth in Crisis, May 5–6, Marbach, Germany.

Cornia, G., and F. Stewart. 1995. "Two Errors of Targeting." In *Public Spending and the Poor*, ed. D. Van de Walle and K. Nead, 350–86. Baltimore: Johns Hopkins University Press.

Corrales, K., and S. Utter. 2005. "Growth Failure." In *Handbook of Pediatric Nutrition*, 3rd ed., ed. Patricia Queen Samour and Kathy King. Sudbury, MA: Jones and Bartlett Publishers.

Coyl, D., L. Roggman, and L. Newland. 2002. "Stress, Maternal Depression, and Negative Mother-Infant Interactions in Relation to Infant Attachment." *Infant Mental Health Journal* 23 (1/2): 145–63.

Crockett, L., and R. K. Silbereisen. 2000. *Negotiating Adolescence in Times of Social Change*. Cambridge, UK: Cambridge University Press.

Cunha, Flavio, and James J. Heckman. 2007. "The Technology of Skill Formation." *American Economic Review* 97 (2): 31–47.

Cunha, Flavio, James J. Heckman, Lance J. Lochner, and Dimitriy V. Masterov. 2006. "Interpreting the Evidence on Life Cycle Skill Formation." In *Handbook of the Economics of Education*, ed. E. Hanushek and F. Welch, 697–812. Amsterdam: North Holland.

Deaton, Angus. 1997. *The Analysis of Household Surveys*. Baltimore: John Hopkins University Press.

———. 2003. "Health, Inequality and Economic Development." *Journal of Economic Literature* 41 (March): 113–58.

DeGraff, D., and R. Bilsborrow. 2003. "Children's School Enrollment and Time at Work in the Philippines." *Journal of Developing Areas* 37 (1): 127–58.

Devarajan, S., L. Squire, and S. Suthiwart-Narueput. 1997. "Beyond Rate of Return: Reorienting Project Appraisal." *World Bank Research Observer* 12 (1): 35–46.

Dodge, K. 2011. "Context Matters in Child and Family Policy." *Child Development* 82 (1): 433–42.

Duncan, G., and J. Brooks-Gunn, eds. 1997. *Consequences of Growing up Poor*. New York: Russell Sage Foundation.

Duncan, G., K. Magnuson, and J. Ludwig. 2004. "The Endogeneity Problem in Developmental Studies." *Research in Human Development* 1 (1/2): 59–80.

Elder, G. 1998. "The Life Course as Developmental Theory." *Child Development* 69 (1): 1–12.

———. 1999. *Children of the Great Depression: Social Change in Life Experience*. 25th anniversary ed. Boulder, CO: Westview Press.

Elder, G., and A. Caspi. 1988. "Economic Stress in Lives: Developmental Perspectives." *Journal of Social Issues* 44 (4): 25–45.

Fares, J., and E. R. Tiongson. 2007. "Youth Unemployment, Labor Market Transitions, and Scarring: Evidence from Bosnia and Herzegovina, 2001–04." Policy Research Working Paper Series 4183. Washington, DC: World Bank.

Ferreira, Francisco H. G., and Ricardo Paes de Barrios. 1999. "The Slippery Slope: Explaining the Increase in Extreme Poverty in Urban Brazil, 1976–96." Policy Research Working Paper 2210, World Bank, Washington, DC.

Ferreira, F., G. Prennushi, and M. Ravallion. 1999. "Protecting the Poor from Macroeconomic Shocks." Policy Research Working Paper 2160, World Bank, Washington, DC.

Florsheim, P., P. H. Tolan, and D. Gorman-Smith. 1996. "Family Processes and Risk for Externalizing Behavior Problems among African American and Hispanic boys." *Journal of Consulting and Clinical Psychology* 64 (6): 1222–30.

Furstenburg, F. F., T. Cook, J. Eccles, G. H. Elder, and A. Sameroff. 1999. *Managing to Make It: Urban Families in High-risk Neighborhoods.* Chicago: University of Chicago Press.

Garcia-Coll, C., G. Lamberty, R. Jenkins, H. P. Mc Adoo, P. Crnic, B. H. Wasik, and H. Vázquez García. 1996. "An Integrative Model for the Study of Developmental Competencies in Minority Children." *Child Development* 67 (5): 1891–914.

Gennetian, L., G. Duncan, W. Knox, E. Clark-Kauffman, and A. London. 2004. "How Welfare Policies Affect Adolescents' School Outcomes: A Synthesis of Evidence from Experimental Studies." *Journal of Research on Adolescence* 14 (4): 399–423.

Gertler, P., and J. Gruber. 2002. "Insuring Consumption against Illness." *American Economic Review* 92 (1): 51–70.

Gershoff, E., J. L. Aber, C. Raver, and M. C. Lennon. 2007. "Income Is Not Enough: Incorporating Material Hardship into Models of Income Associations with Parenting and Child Development." *Child Development* 78 (1): 70–95.

Goldin, Claudia. 1999. "Egalitarianism and the Returns to Education during the Great Transformation of American Education." *Journal of Political Economy* 107 (6): S65–S94.

Goodman, S., and I. Gotlib. 1999. "Risk for Psychopathology in the Children of Depressed Mothers: A Developmental Model for Understanding Mechanisms of Transmission." *Psychological Review* 106 (July): 458–90.

Gottlieb, G., D. Wahlsten, and R. Lickliter. 1998. "The Significance of Biology for Human Development: A Developmental Psychobiological Systems View." *Handbook of Child Psychology*, 6th ed., vol. 1, ed. R. Lerner. New York: Wiley.

Grant, Monica J., and Jere R. Behrman. 2010. "Gender Gaps in Educational Attainment in Less Developed Countries."*Population and Development Review* 36 (1): 71–89.

Greenberg, D., N. Dechausay, and C. Fraker. 2011. "Learning Together: How Families Responded to Education Incentives in New York City's Conditional Cash Transfer Program." MDRC, http://www.mdrc.org/publications/594/full .pdf.

Greenough, W. T., and J. E. Black. 1992. "Induction of Brain Structure by Experience: Substrates for Cognitive Development." In *Developmental Behavior Neuroscience*, ed. M. R. Gunnar and C. A. Nelson, 155-200. Hillsdale, NJ: Erlbaum.

Haddad, Lawrence, John Hoddinott, and Harold Alderman, eds. 1997. *Intrahousehold Resource Allocation: Methods, Models, and Policy*, Baltimore, MD: The Johns Hopkins University Press for the International Food Policy Research Institute.

Hall, P., and M. Lamont, eds. 2009. *Successful Societies: How Institutions and Culture Affect Health*. Cambridge, UK: Cambridge University Press.

Hammen, C., D. Gordon, D. Burge, C. Adrian, C. Jaenicke, and G. Hirohito. 1987. "Communication Patterns of Mothers with Affective Disorders and Their Relationship to Children's Status and Social Functioning." In *Understanding Mental Disorder: The Contribution of Family Interaction Research*, ed. K. Hahlweg and M. J. Goldstein, 103–19. New York: Family Process Press.

Harding, David J. 2010. *Living the Drama: Community, Conflict, and Culture among Inner-City Boys.* Chicago: University of Chicago Press.

Heckman, James J. 2006. "Skill Formation and the Economics of Investing in Disadvantaged Children." *Science* 312 (30): 1900–02.

Heckman, J. J., J. Stixrud, and S. Urzua. 2006. "The Effects of Cognitive and Noncognitive Abilities on Labor Market Outcomes and Social Behavior." *Journal of Labor Economics* 24 (3): 411–82.

Heston, Alan, Robert Summers, and Bettina Aten. 2009. "Penn World Table Version 6.3." Center for International Comparisons of Production, Income and Prices, University of Pennsylvania.

Hetherington, E. M. 1989. "Coping with Family Transitions: Winners, Losers, and Survivors." *Child Development* 60 (1): 1–14.

Hoddinott, John, John A. Maluccio, Jere R Behrman, Rafael Flores and Reynaldo Martorell. 2008. "The Impact of Nutrition during Early Childhood on Income, Hours Worked, and Wages of Guatemalan Adults." *Lancet* 371(February): 411–16.

Hoddinott, John, John Maluccio, Jere R. Behrman, Reynaldo Martorell, Paul Melgar, Agnes R. Quisumbing, Manuel Ramirez-Zea, Aryeh D. Stein, and Kathryn M. Yount. 2010. "The Consequences of Early Childhood Growth Failure over the Life Course." Washington, DC: International Food Policy Research Institute.

Holt, S., H. Buckley, and S. Whelan. 2008. "The Impact of Exposure to Domestic Violence on Children and Young People: A Review of the Literature." *Child Abuse and Neglect* 32 (8): 797–810.

Hossain, Naomi. 2009. "Crime and Social Cohesion in the Time of Crisis: Early Evidence of Wider Impacts of Food, Fuel and Financial Shocks." *IDS Bulletin* 40 (5): 59–67.

Huston, A., G. Duncan, V. McLoyd, D. Crosby, M. Ripke, T. Weisner, and C. Eldred. 2005. "Impacts on Children of a Policy to Promote Employment and Reduce Poverty for Low-Income Parents: New Hope after Five Years." *Developmental Psychology* 41 (6): 902–18.

Kim-Cohen, J., T. E. Moffitt, A. Caspi, and A. Taylor. 2004. "Genetic and Environmental Processes in Young Children's Resilience and Vulnerability to Socioeconomic Deprivation." *Child Development* 75 (3): 651–58.

Knowles, J. C., E. M. Pernia, and M. Racelis. 1999. "Social Consequences of the Financial Crisis in Asia." Economic Staff Paper 60, Asian Development Bank, Manila.

Knudsen, E. I. 2004. "Sensitive Periods in the Development of the Brain and Behavior." *Journal of Cognitive Neuroscience* 16 (1): 1412–25.

Knudsen, E. I., J. J. Heckman, J. Cameron, and J. P. Shonkoff. 2006. "Economic, Neurobiological, and Behavioral Perspectives on Building America's Future Workforce." *Proceedings of the National Academy of Sciences* 103 (27): 10155–62.

Laeven, Luc, and Fabien Valencia. 2008. "Systemic Banking Crises: A New Database." Working Paper 08/224, International Monetary Fund, Washington, DC.

Lamont, Michele. 2000. *The Dignity of Working Men: Morality and the Boundaries of Race, Class, and Immigration.* Cambridge, MA: Harvard University Press.

Lamont, M., C. Fleming, and J. Welburn. Forthcoming. "Response to Discrimination and Social Resilience under Neo-Liberalism: The Case of Brazil, Israel, and the United States." In *Social Resilience in the Neo-Liberal Era*, ed. P. A. Hall and M. Lamont. Cambridge, UK: Cambridge University Press.

Lamont, Michele, and Nissim Mizrachi, eds. 2012. "Responses to Stigmatization in Comparative Perspective: Brazil, Canada, France, Israel, South Africa, Sweden and the United States." Special issue of *Ethnic and Racial Studies* 35 (3).

Lansford, J. E., P. S. Malone, D. R. Castellino, K. A. Dodge, G. S. Pettit, and J. E. Bates. 2006. "Trajectories of Internalizing, Externalizing, and Grades for Children Who Have and Have Not Experienced Their Parents' Divorce or Separation." *Journal of Family Psychology* 20 (2): 292–301.

Lefebvre, H. 1991. *The Production of Space.* Hoboken, NJ: Blackwell Publishing.

Lerner, R. 1998. "Developmental Science, Developmental Systems, and Contemporary Theories of Human Development." In *Handbook of Child Psychology*, 6th ed., vol. 1, ed. R. Lerner. New York: Wiley.

Lewis, M., and M. Verhoeven. 2010. "Financial Crises and Social Spending." *World Economics* 11(4): 79–110.

Li, Hongbin, Mark Rosenzweig, and Junsen Zhang. 2010. "Altruism, Favoritism, and Guilt in the Allocation of Family Resources: Sophie's Choice in Mao's Mass Send Down Movement." *Journal of Political Economy* 118 (1): 1–38.

Lumey, L. H., and A. D. Stein. 1997a. "*In Utero* Exposure to Famine and Subsequent Fertility: The Dutch Famine Birth Cohort Study." *American Journal of Public Health* 87 (12):1962–66.

———. 1997b. "Offspring Birth Weights after Maternal Intrauterine Undernutrition: A Comparison within Sibships." *American Journal of Epidemiology* 146 (10): 810–19.

Lundberg, Shelly, and Robert A. Pollak. 1993. "Separate Spheres Bargaining and the Marriage Market." *Journal of Political Economy* 6 (101): 988–1010.

———. 1996. "Bargaining and Distribution in Marriage." *Journal of Economic Perspectives* 10 (4): 139–58.

Lustig, N. C. 1998. *Mexico: The Remaking of an Economy*, 2nd ed. Washington, DC: Brookings Institution Press.

Maluccio, John A., John Hoddinott, Jere R. Behrman, Agnes Quisumbing, Reynaldo Martorell, and Aryeh D. Stein. 2009. "The Impact of Nutrition during Early Childhood on Education among Guatemalan Adults." *Economic Journal* 119 (April): 734–63.

Manser, Marilyn, and Murray Brown. 1980. "Marriage and Household Decision-making: A Bargaining Analysis." *International Economic Review* 21(1): 31–44.

Markus, Hazel R. 2004. "Culture and Personality: Brief for an Arranged Marriage." *Journal of Research in Personality* 38: 75–83.

Marmot, Michael, and Richard Wilkinson. 1999. *The Social Determinants of Health*. Oxford, UK: Oxford University Press.

Martin, D., E. McCann, and M. Purcell. 2003. "Space, Scale, Governance, and Representation: Contemporary Geographical Perspectives on Urban Politics and Policy." *Journal of Urban Affairs* 25 (2): 113–21.

Masten A. 2007. "Resilience in Developing Systems: Progress and Promise as the Fourth Wave Rises." *Development and Psychopathology* 19: 921–30.

———. 2009. "Ordinary Magic: Lessons from Research on Resilience in Human Development." *Education Canada* 49 (3): 28–32.

Masten, A., and J. Obradovic. 2006. "Competence and Resilience in Development." *Annals New York Academy of Sciences* 1094: 13–27.

Mayer, S. 1997. *What Money Can't Buy: Family Income and Children's Life Chances.* Cambridge, MA: Harvard University Press.

McElroy, Marjorie B., and M. J. Horney. 1981. "Nash-Bargained Household Decisions: Toward a Generalization of the Theory of Demand." *International Economic Review* 22 (2): 333–47.

McKenzie, David J. 2003. "How Do Households Cope with Aggregate Shocks? Evidence from the Mexican Peso Crisis." *World Development* 31(7): 1179–99.

McKenzie, D. 2004. "Aggregate Shocks and Urban Labor Market Responses: Evidence from Argentina's Financial Crisis." *Economic Development and Cultural Change* 52 (4): 719–58.

McLoyd, V. C. 1990. "The Impact of Economic Hardship on Black Families and Children: Psychological Distress, Parenting, and Socioemotional Development." *Child Development* 61 (2): 311–46.

———. 1998. "Socioeconomic Disadvantage and Child Development." *American Psychologist* 53 (2): 185–204.

McLoyd, V., R. Kaplan, K. Purtell, E. Bagley, C. Hardaway, and C. Smalls. 2009. "Poverty and Socioeconomic Disadvantage in Adolescence." *Handbook of Adolescent Psychology*, 3rd ed., vol. 2, ed. R. Lerner and L. Steinberg. Hoboken, NJ: Wiley.

McLoyd, V., R. Kaplan, M. Purtell, and A. Huston. 2011. "Assessing the Effects of a Work-Based Antipoverty Program for Parents on Youth's Future Orientation and Employment Experiences." Special issue, "Raising Healthy Children," *Child Development* 82 (1): 113–32.

Mincer, Jacob B. 1974. *Schooling, Experience, and Earnings.* New York: National Bureau of Economic Research.

Morris, P., A. Huston, G. Duncan, D. Crosby, and J. Bos. 2001. *How Welfare and Work Policies Affect Children: A Synthesis of Research.* New York: MDRC.

Noack, P., and B. Kracke 1997. "Social Change and Adolescent Well-Being: Healthy Country, Healthy Teens." In *Health Risks and Developmental Transitions during Adolescence*, ed. J. Schulenberg, J. Maggs, and K. Hurrelmann. Cambridge, UK: Cambridge University Press.

Paugam, Serge. 1996. "Poverty and Social Disqualification: A Comparative Analysis of Cumulative Social Disadvantages in Europe." *Journal of European Social Policy* 6 (4): 287–303.

Pearlin, L., and M. Kohn 2009. "Social Class, Occupation, and Parental Values: A Cross-National Study." In *Class and Personality in Society*, ed. A. Grey, 161–84. New Brunswick, NJ: Transaction Publishers.

Pinquart, M., and R. K. Silbereisen. 2004. "Human Development in Times of Social Change: Theoretical Considerations and Research Needs." *International Journal of Behavioral Development* 28 (4): 289–98.

Pluess, M., and J. Belsky. 2009. "Differential Susceptibility to Rearing Experience: The Case of Childcare." *Journal of Child Psychology and Psychiatry* 50 (4): 396–404.

Quisumbing, Agnes R. 1994. "Intergenerational Transfers in Philippine Rice Villages: Gender Differences in Traditional Inheritance Customs." *Journal of Development Economics* 43 (2): 167–96.

Ratha, D. 2009. "Dollars without Borders." *Foreign Affairs*, October 16, http://www.foreignaffairs.com/articles/65448/dilip-ratha/dollars-without-borders.

Reinhart, C., and K. Rogoff. 2008. "Banking Crises: An Equal Opportunity Menace." NBER Working Paper, National Bureau of Economic Research, Cambridge, MA.

Rodriguez, M. L., and N. J. Walden. 2010. "Socializing Relationships." In *Adolescence: Development during a Global Era*, ed. D. P. Swanson, C. M. Edwards, and M. B. Spencer, 299–340. Burlington, MA: Academic Press.

Rosen, Eva. 2010. "Heterogeneity in the Construction of Disorder: Blacks, Puerto Ricans and Mexicans in Chicago." Department of Sociology, Harvard University.

Rosenzweig, Mark R., and Kenneth J. Wolpin. 1985. "Specific Experience, Household Structure, and Intergenerational Transfers: Farm Family Land and Labor Arrangements in Developing Countries." *Quarterly Journal of Economics* 100 (Supplement): 961–87.

Rutter, M. 1987. "Psychosocial Resilience and Protective Mechanisms." *American Journal of Orthopsychiatry* 57 (3): 316–31.

Rutter, M., T. E. Moffitt, and A. Caspi. 2006. "Gene-Environment Interplay and Psychopathology: Multiple Varieties but Real Effects." *Journal of Child Psychology and Psychiatry* 47 (3/4): 226–61.

Sahn, D. 1996. *Economic Reform and the Poor in Africa*. New York: Oxford University Press.

Sameroff, A., ed. 2009. *The Transactional Model of Development: How Children and Contexts Shape Each Other*. Washington, DC: American Psychological Association.

Sampson, Robert J. 2006. "Collective Efficacy Theory: Lessons Learned and Directions for Future Inquiry." In *Advances in Criminological Theory*. Vol. 15, *Taking Stock: The Status of Criminological Theory*, ed. Francis T. Cullen, John Paul Wright, and Kristie R. Blevins, 149–67. New Brunswick: Transaction Publishers.

Scheper-Hughes, Nancy. 1993. *Death without Weeping: The Violence of Everyday Life in Brazil*. Berkeley, CA: University of California Press.

Schultz, Theodore W. 1961. "Investment in Human Capital." *American Economic Review* 51(1): 1–17.

————. 1963. *The Economic Value of Education*. New York: Columbia University Press.

Schofield, T., M. Martin, K. Conger, T. Neppl, M. Donnellan, and R. Conger. 2011. "Intergenerational Transmission of Adaptive Functioning: A Test of the Interactionist Model of SES and Human Development." *Child Development* 82 (1): 33–47.

Sen, A. 1995. "The Political Economy of Targeting." In ed., D. Van de Walle and K. Nead. *Public Spending and the Poor*. Baltimore, MD: Johns Hopkins University Press.

Sharone, Ofer. 2011. "Chemistry or Specs: Job Search Games, Player Centrality, and Subjective Responses to Unemployment." Working Paper, Sloan Business School, Massachusetts Institute of Technology, Cambridge, MA.

Shonkoff, J. P, A. S. Garner, THE COMMITTEE ON PSYCHOSOCIAL ASPECTS OF CHILD AND FAMILY HEALTH, COMMITTEE ON EARLY CHILDHOOD, ADOPTION, AND DEPENDENT CARE, AND SECTION ON DEVELOPMENTAL AND BEHAVIORAL PEDIATRICS, B. S. Siegel, M. I. Dobbins, M. F. Earls, L. McGuinn, J. Pascoe, and D. L. Wood. 2012. "The Lifelong Effects of Early Childhood Adversity and Toxic Stress." *Pediatrics* 129 (1): e232–e246.

Silbereisen, R. K. 2000. "German Unification and Adolescents' Developmental Timetables: Continuities and Discontinuities." In *Negotiating Adolescence in Times of Social Change*, ed. L. Crockett and R. Silbereisen. Cambridge, UK: Cambridge University Press.

Silbereisen, R. K., P. Ritchie, and B. Overmier. 2010. "Psychology at the Vortex of Convergence and Divergence: The Case of Social Change. In *World Social Science Report: Knowledge Divides*, 213–17. UNESCO International Social Science Council.

Silbereisen, R. K., and M. Tomasik. 2010. "Human Behavior in Response to Social Change: A Guide to the Special Section." *European Psychologist* 15 (4): 243–45.

Silbereisen, R. K., and M. Wiesner. 2000. "Cohort Change in Adolescent Developmental Timetables after German Unification: Trends and Possible Reasons." In *Motivational Psychology of Human Development: Developing Motivation and Motivating Development*, ed. J. Heckhausen. New York: Elsevier Science.

Silver, Hilary. 1994. "Social Exclusion and Social Solidarity: Three Paradigms." *International Labour Review* 133 (5-6): 531–78.

Skoufias, E. 2003. "Economic Crises and Natural Disasters: Coping Strategies and Policy Implications." *World Development* 31 (7): 1087–102.

Skoufias, E., and S. Parker. 2006. "Job Loss and Family Adjustments in Work and Schooling during the Mexican Peso Crisis." *Journal of Population Economics* 19(1): 163–81.

Small, Mario Luis. 2004. *Villa Victoria: The Transformation of Social Capital in a Boston Barrio.* Chicago: University of Chicago Press.

Smith, J. P., D. Thomas, E. Frankenberg, K. Beegle, and G. Teruel. 2002. "Wages, Employment, and Economic Shocks: Evidence from Indonesia." *Journal of Population Economics* 15 (1): 161–93.

Smith, Sandra Susan. 2010. "A Test of Sincerity: How Black and Latino Service Workers Make Decisions about Making Referrals." *Annals of the American Academy of Political and Social Sciences* 629 (May): 30–52.

Sroufe, A. 1979. "The Coherence of Individual Development: Early Care, Attachment, and Subsequent Developmental Issues." *American Psychologist* 34 (10): 834–41.

Stalker, Peter. 2000. *Beyond Krismon: The Social Legacy of Indonesia's Financial Crisis.* UNICEF Innocenti Research Centre, Italy.

Stein A. D., and L. H. Lumey. 2000. "The Association of Maternal and Offspring Birth Weights under Conditions Affecting Maternal Prenatal Famine Exposure: The Dutch Famine Birth Cohort Study." *Human Biology* 72 (4): 641–54.

Steinberg, L., S. Dornbusch, and B. Brown. 1992. "Ethnic Differences in Adolescent Achievement: An Ecological Perspective." *American Psychologist* 47 (6): 723–29.

Susser, E., H. Hoek, and A. Brown. 1998. "Neurodevelopmental Disorders after Prenatal Famine: The Story of the Dutch Famine Study." *American Journal of Epidemiology* 147 (3): 213–16.

Susser, E., R. Neugebauer, H. W. Hoek, S. Lin, D. Labovity, and J. M. Gorman. 1996. "Schizophrenia after Prenatal Famine: Further Evidence." *Archives of General Psychiatry* 53 (1): 25–31.

te Velde, D., et al. 2010. "The Global Financial Crisis and Developing Countries." Working Paper 316, Overseas Development Institute, London.

Thelen, E., and L. Smith. 1998. "Dynamic Systems Theories." In *Handbook of Child Psychology*, 6th ed., vol. 1, ed. R. Lerner. New York: Wiley.

Thomas, Duncan. 1990. "Intrahousehold Resource Allocation: An Inferential Approach." *Journal of Human Resources* 25 (4): 635–64.

———. 1994. "Like Father, Like Son; Like Mother, Like Daughter: Parental Resources and Child Height." *Journal of Human Resources* 29 (4): 950–89.

Thompson, R. A., and C. A. Nelson. 2001. "Developmental Science and the Media: Early Brain Development." *American Psychologist* 56 (1): 5–15.

Tobi, E. W., L. H. Lumey, R. P. Talens, D. Kremer, H. Putter, A. D. Stein, P. E. Sagboom, and B. T. Heijmans. 2009. "DNA Methylation Differences after Exposure to Prenatal Famine Are Common and Timing- and Sex-Specific." *Human Molecular Genetics* 18 (21): 4046–53.

Todd, Petra E., and Kenneth I. Wolpin. 2003. "On the Specification and Estimation of the Production Function for Cognitive Achievement." *Economic Journal* 118 (February): F3–33.

———. 2007. "The Production of Cognitive Achievement in Children: Home, School and Racial Test Score Gaps." *Journal of Human Capital* 1 (Winter): 91–136.

Tomasik, M. J., and R. K. Silbereisen. 2009. "Demands of Social Change as a Function of the Political Context, Institutional Filters, and Psychosocial Resources." *Social Indicators Research* 94(1): 13–28.

Van de Walle, D., and K. Nead, eds. 1995. *Public Spending and the Poor.* Baltimore, MD: Johns Hopkins University Press.

Warikoo, Natasha. 2010. *Balancing Act: Youth Culture in the Global City.* Berkeley, CA: University of California Press.

World Bank. 2006. *World Development Report 2007: Development and the Next Generation.* Washington, DC: World Bank.

World Bank. 2009. *Averting a Human Crisis during the Global Downturn: Policy Options from the World Bank's Human Development Network.* Washington, DC: World Bank.

World Bank. 2011a. *Stepping Up Skills: For More Jobs and Higher Productivity.* Washington, DC: World Bank.

———. 2011b. *The Jobs Crisis: Household and Government Responses to the Great Recession in Eastern Europe and Central Asia.* Washington, DC: World Bank.

Wright, M., and A. Masten. 2005. "Resilience Processes in Development: Fostering Positive Adaptation in the Context of Adversity." In *Handbook of Resilience in Children,* ed. S. Goldstein & R. B. Brooks, 17–37. Berlin: Springer Science + Business Media.

Yoshikawa, H., J. L. Aber, and W. R. Beardslee. 2012. "The Effects of Poverty on the Mental, Emotional and Behavioral Health of Children and Youth: Implications for Prevention." *American Psychologist* 67 (4): 272–84.

PART II

The Empirical Evidence of the Impact of Economic Crises on Children and Youth

CHAPTER 3

Aggregate Economic Shocks in Utero and during Early Childhood

Development in utero and early childhood has been touted as of utmost importance for later-life outcomes, and investments in early childhood are said to increase the returns to investments in human capital later in life (see, for example, Cunha et al. 2006; Cunha and Heckman 2007; Maluccio et al. 2009; Behrman and Rosenzweig 2004). Insults to early development through economic crisis, poverty, or disease can therefore be associated with high costs in the long run (see, for example, Alderman 2011; Almond 2006; Almond and Chay 2003; Almond and Currie 2011). It is thus of great interest to understand how aggregate economic shocks affect the development of young children from conception to approximately five years of age. This chapter applies the conceptual framework developed in chapter 2 to the review of the empirical literature of how economic crisis affects early childhood development. This chapter begins by introducing the basic premises and stage-salient developmental tasks of early childhood. In what follows, the authors present the empirical evidence from a range of disciplines to establish a more comprehensive understanding of how economic crisis affects young children's development and conclude with the main messages.

Early Childhood Development: An Introduction
Carly Tubbs and Dana Charles McCoy

The period from conception to approximately five years is one of profound and rapid change in the life course of a developing person (see box 3.1 for a short overview on prenatal health and development). The relatively helpless infant who relies on her caregivers to meet all her basic needs soon becomes the wobbly toddler attempting her first steps, before becoming a confident child demanding to walk to her first day of school by herself. The growth that occurs during this period of early childhood cuts across multiple domains—biological, cognitive, and emotional—and their interrelatedness makes separating them a rather futile exercise. Nevertheless, in practice, researchers often concentrate on one domain at a time, and much of the research in economics conducted in developing countries has focused primarily on early childhood health indicators.

Health and nutrition, dealt with in more detail later in this chapter, are clearly central to early stages of development. They provide the basis for, and interact with, the processes that support mastery of certain stage-salient developmental tasks that are crucial to children's intermediate and long-term success. Achievement of these stage-salient tasks involves the simultaneous development of cognitive, socioemotional, and physical skills, all of which occur in concert with the maturation of the brain and the nervous and other biological systems (see the conceptual framework in part I and box 3.2 in this chapter for further elaboration). During infancy and early childhood, these tasks include establishing (secure) attachment relationships with primary caregivers (from birth to approximately one year), learning to actively explore and communicate about their worlds (approximately one to three years old), and developing the ability to regulate their thoughts, behaviors, and emotions (approximately three to five years old) (Aber and Jones 1997). As indicated in chapter 2, success in one task influences the probability of success in other tasks. For example, secure attachment relationships facilitate active exploration of the environment and vice versa. Furthermore, if such tasks are not mastered during early childhood, children find it difficult to "catch up" later in life, and mastering more complex developmental tasks at later stages becomes increasingly challenging (see, for example, Roisman et al. 2004).

Accomplishing these tasks involves transactions, or processes, between all levels of a child's world, from cells and neurons, to caretakers and the larger cultural milieu (see the bioecological model described in chapter 2).[1] Many of the processes—including developing a secure attachment to primary

Box 3.1

Prenatal Health and Development

Children's health and development begin with mothers' reproductive health and behavior. The prenatal period is divided into three stages: (1) the germinal stage (zero to two weeks after conception), during which time a sperm cell combines with an egg cell to form a zygote; (2) the embryonic stage (two weeks to two months after conception), during which time all the major organs form; and (3) the fetal stage (two months after conception to birth), during which time bones and muscles form, the brain increases rapidly in size, and the respiratory and digestive systems begin to function independently. While prenatal development is generally remarkably predictable and regular, it is vulnerable to disruption by a number of factors, including environmental factors such as poor nutrition; use of cigarettes, alcohol, or other drugs; maternal illness and exposure to toxins; and especially toxic stress. For example, there is a wealth of evidence on in utero exposure to severe famine during the Dutch Hunger Winter (1944–45; for more detail see this chapter; see also Lumey et al. 2007). But also maternal stress during pregnancy can expose the unborn to high levels of certain hormones, such as testosterone or the stress hormone cortisol; this has been linked, among other things, to low birth weight and lower educational attainment in later life (see, for example, Sarkar et al. 2008; Bergman et al. 2010). The outcome of prenatal exposure to such factors depends on the timing of exposure; given that most organ systems develop during the embryonic stage, the first eight weeks after conception are the period of greatest vulnerability. But exposure during later gestation has also been linked to negative outcomes.

As elaborated in this chapter, to the extent that an economic crisis results in a decrease in access to adequate health care and nutrition for expectant mothers and to an increase in maternal stress, children's prenatal development may be at risk, with long-term consequences.

Source: Prepared by Carly Tubbs.

caregiver(s) and acquiring language skills—are universal. However, many of these processes also depend on interactions that occur between children and their caregivers. Who these caregivers are, how they respond to the child, what their goals and motivations are, and what their immediate environments look like vary according to the cultural context and the settings in which the child is embedded.

Establishing (Secure) Attachment Relationships

Armed primarily with crying and fussing to demand attention, infants have to rely on their caregivers for protection, nourishment, and emotional and cognitive stimulation. Thus the most important task during the first year of life is for infants and the people who care for them to establish close and effective ("secure") emotional bonds, or attachments. These attachments provide young children with a secure base from which to explore the novel and, at times, stressful world (Ainsworth 1967; Bowlby 1988). They also facilitate the development of self-efficacy and competency by demonstrating to children that others will respond to their needs (Carson and Parke 1996). Research indicates that across cultures, young children have two main types of attachments to their caregivers: secure and insecure (for more details on manifestations of attachment styles, see Ainsworth et al. 1978). Consistent, available, reliable, and affectionate caregivers enable a secure attachment to develop (Ainsworth et al. 1978). Inconsistent (that is, at times overbearing, at other times unavailable), unreliable, abusive, or neglectful caregiving is likely to result in insecure attachment styles (van Doesum et al. 2008). Children then use these early attachment relationships to construct working models to interpret experiences with other people and as guidelines for future relationships and interactions (Bee and Boyd 2010). Secure attachment relationships in early childhood are associated with better socioemotional outcomes in later childhood and even adulthood; children with secure attachment styles tend to have more positive, supportive relationships with teachers and peers as they grow up (Sroufe and Egeland 1991), a more holistic self-concept (Cassidy 1988), better memory processing (Belsky, Spritz, and Crnic 1996), and greater conscientiousness (Kochanska 1995).

However, characteristics of the child, the caregiver, and the context can make consistently responsive parenting difficult to achieve. For example, parents may have a harder time always responding sensitively to infants with a difficult and fussy temperament or to infants that seem constantly in distress due to, for example, colic symptoms. In addition, challenging emotional and family circumstances such as depression, stress, and marital conflict can disrupt responsive parenting (Belsky and Isabella 1988). To the extent that an economic crisis increases parental depression and marital conflict—as posited by the Family Stress Model (see box 4.1)—children's ability to form secure attachment relationships may be at risk. In reference to the bioecological model in chapter 2, this suggests one pathway at one level—also known as a nested point of entry—through which an economic crisis may have an impact on early childhood development.

Learning to Explore and Communicate

As infants establish attachments with their primary caregivers (and increase their ability to locomote by crawling and walking), between ages one and three they are well positioned to go out into the world to explore their environment. Indeed, from the moment of birth, children are active participants in the development of their knowledge, constructing their own understandings with support from parents, siblings, peers, and other adults. Before the age of five, children typically learn how to communicate through language, how to count or quantify objects, how to take into account the perspective of others, how to distinguish cause from effect, and how to solve problems (Shonkoff and Phillips 2000). Most of these cognitive processes begin to emerge well before the age of three. Delays in cognitive and linguistic development in early childhood are associated with negative academic outcomes in the short term (such as lower academic achievement in elementary and high school, increased probability of repeating a grade, and higher likelihood of dropping out of school early) and negative economic outcomes in the long term (lawbreaking, unemployment, and reliance on welfare, for example) (Feinstein 2003; Naudeau et al. 2010; Schweinhart, Barnes, and Weikart 1993). Such delays may also inhibit development in later stage-salient developmental tasks, such as establishing peer relationships (Guralnick et al. 1996).

Children can develop some cognitive and linguistic skills with relatively little environmental support beyond that necessary for normal brain development, suggesting some sort of genetic blueprint for cognitive development (for a more detailed discussion of neurological and genetic processes, see box 3.2). However, children's experiences and environments play a key role in shaping certain aspects of their cognitive and linguistic skills, including "the extent of their vocabulary, language proficiency, understanding of number concepts . . . and executive functioning" (Shonkoff and Phillips 2000, 162). Researchers have paid particular attention to the extent to which early learning environments, including adult-child interactions and the quality of resources, enhance these aspects of cognitive development, finding them to be important predictors of preschool-aged children's test scores (Smith, Brooks-Gunn, and Klebanov 1997). Yet it is important to remember that these early learning environments vary substantially by culture (for more details, see Rogoff 2003). For example, in some cultures young children are readily exposed

Box 3.2

Biological and Environmental Transactions in Children's Development

From ancient philosophers to modern scientists, people have long been fascinated by how much influence "nature" (biological bases such as genes and neurons) has on human development compared to "nurture" (environmental factors such as parenting and culture). Many have tended to view nature and nurture as dichotomous and, at times, as opposing forces that independently shape development: hence the common phrase "nature *versus* nurture." Yet scientific advancements over the past 30 years in developmental behavioral genetics, molecular genetics, neuroscience, and developmental psychology have led to the definitive conclusion that nature and nurture are inherently inseparable.

From the moment of conception to the moment of death, transactions continuously occur among myriad hierarchical levels of biological and environmental systems—from genes nested in cells, to cells nested in organs, to organs nested in persons, to persons nested in families and other social relationships, to families nested in communities, to communities nested in cultures—resulting in the extreme heterogeneity in human behaviors observed around the world. While scientists are just beginning to map out and understand these infinitely complex processes, at this juncture cutting-edge research on two biological-environmental transactional processes stands out as particularly important in understanding how children develop and, consequently, how an economic crisis may affect children's development. Research on *neuroplasticity* examines how structures and functions of the brain and nervous system may change in response to experience across the lifespan. Research on *differential susceptibility* to the environment, meanwhile, more broadly identifies the genetic and neurobiological processes that underlie individuals' reactivity to the environment, resulting in the wide variability in children's outcomes when exposed to either adverse or advantageous environments.

Brain Development and Neuroplasticity

The rapid advances in children's cognitive, physical, and socioemotional development that take place between conception and adulthood occur in concert with the developing brain. Early childhood in particular is a crucial period for brain development; many of the cognitive and linguistic skills that children develop during infancy and toddlerhood correspond to growth spurts in the brain that

(continued next page)

Box 3.2 *(continued)*

occur between birth and 5 months and at 8, 12, 20, and 48 months of age (Fischer and Rose 1994). One of the main processes that contribute to such spurts in brain growth is termed *synaptogenesis;* it is the process through which connections, known as synapses, are formed between neurons in the brain that allow neurons to communicate with each other through chemicals called neurotransmitters (Johnson 2005). However, children do not retain all the neuronal connections that are formed during childhood. Instead, each burst of synaptogenesis is followed by a period of *pruning*, during which connections that are less active or efficient are lost. Researchers think that many bursts of synapse formation proceed according to a built-in genetic outline but that pruning appears to be largely dependent on experience (Greenough, Black, and Wallace 1987). In other words, pruning follows the old dictum of "use it or lose it," and, as such, is an example of *neuroplasticity*, the ability of the brain to change in response to experience (Nelson, de Haan, and Thomas 2006). For example, children who are deprived of visual sensory stimulation, such as through blindness in one eye, retain less complex neurological networks in the visual cortex than do children who receive such stimulation (Gordon 1995).

Two types of experiences seem to affect brain development: experience-expectant synaptogenesis and experience-dependent synaptogenesis (Greenough and Black 1992). Experience-expectant synaptogenesis involves environmental inputs such as auditory and visual stimulation and nutrition adequate to normal brain development across the human species in all environments. Deprivation of these "expected" experiences can cause deficits in brain development that become increasingly hard to reverse over time. In experience-dependent synaptogenesis, unique experiences such as secondary language inputs or soccer practice optimize children's adaptation to specific environments. As opposed to experience-expectant synaptogenesis, in which brain development across humans is based on certain common basic experiences, in experience-dependent synaptogenesis individual differences in brain development arise "depending" on the unique experiences encountered during the life course.

Indeed, while brain development is particularly sensitive to environmental inputs in the earliest years of life, the brain does possess a certain degree of plasticity throughout the life course (Nelson, de Haan, and Thomas 2006). Moreover, not all areas of the brain develop at the same rate at the same time; in fact, the

(continued next page)

Box 3.2 *(continued)*

maturation of brain regions associated with particular skills corresponds largely to the developmental stage at which those skills become increasingly salient and observable. For instance, both synaptogenesis and pruning in the visual cortex are finalized by the time children reach toddlerhood. In contrast, synaptogenesis in the prefrontal cortex (the area of the brain associated with executive functioning and higher-level cognitive development) occurs mainly during early childhood, while growth of white matter and further pruning in the same region do not finish until late adolescence (Huttenlocher and Dabholkar 1997) or early adulthood (Giedd et al. 1999; Schmithorst and Yuan 2010). The relationship between neuroplasticity of particular brain regions and developmental stage is also complicated by the fact that because the brain is so plastic during early childhood, brain development is both highly susceptible to environmental insults *and* more easily able to rebound from such insults during this period. For example, an otherwise healthy adolescent who endures a period of malnutrition will be less vulnerable to brain damage than an infant who does not receive adequate nutrition. An adolescent who encounters such severe malnutrition that he develops brain damage, however, will rebound much more slowly than an infant (Bee and Boyd 2009).

Differential Susceptibility to the Environment

As discussed in chapter 2, children exhibit remarkable heterogeneity in their responses to adversarial or stressful environments such as poverty, family conflict, or neighborhood violence: some children develop cognitive, socioemotional, and physical health problems, while other children do not (see, for example, Luthar 2006). Children show a similar pattern of response to supportive environments such as contingent parenting or high-quality educational instruction: some flourish, while others do not (see Quas, Bauer, and Boyce 2004; Bakermans-Kranenburg and van Ijzendoorn 2011). Interestingly, a growing body of research suggests that individuals most at risk in adversarial environments also may be the most likely to benefit from supportive environments. This finding has led researchers to develop the theory of *differential susceptibility* to the environment, according to which certain individuals display heightened susceptibility to both positive *and* negative environmental influences (Ellis et al. 2011). In other words, individuals who are less susceptible to the environment will function similarly across contexts, regardless of how supportive or stressful the environment; individuals who are susceptible to

(continued next page)

Box 3.2 *(continued)*

the environment have a wide range of reactions and functioning, depending on the contexts in which they are embedded (Manuck 2009).

Moreover, theory and research indicate that individuals' susceptibility to the environment is grounded in neurobiological processes that arise from genetic and epigenetic variation and give rise to observable behavioral markers (see Bakermans-Kranenburg and van Ijzendoorn 2006; Belsky and Pluess 2009). Several implications follow. First, individuals' neurobiological susceptibility to the environment underlies "many reliable interactions between features of persons and features of environments in guiding human development and functioning" (Ellis et al. 2011, 13). In this way, neurobiological susceptibility to the environment moderates the relationship between environmental factors and developmental outcomes.

Second, children's neurobiological susceptibility to the environment may be increased by early exposure to either stressful or highly supportive environments (Boyce and Ellis 2005). When presented with stressful environments, developing such susceptibility may be adaptive in that it allows children to better identify and respond to dangers in the environment. While the consequences of the adaptations—including fearful and defensive behaviors such as insecure attachments—may be perceived as maladaptive within a Western developmental psychopathological framework, from an evolutionary perspective such risky behaviors may ensure immediate survival, at a long-term cost (Ellis et al. 2011).

Finally, recent evidence suggests that genetic, neural, neuroendocrine, and behavioral differences may exist in individuals who display neurobiological susceptibility to the environment. Below, we give a few illustrative examples of how these factors may moderate the association between environmental factors and developmental outcomes:

• *Genetic moderation.* Alternative forms of a gene that occur at a given locus are called alleles, polymorphisms of the gene governing the expression of this particular gene. For children with a particular allele, the seven-repeat D4 (DRD4) allele, maternal insensitivity during infancy predicted children's externalizing behaviors two years later; for children without the allele, there was no association between maternal insensitivity during infancy and children's later externalizing behaviors. Interestingly, children with the DRD4 allele showed the most externalizing behavior when their mothers were rated highly insensitive but the

(continued next page)

Box 3.2 (continued)

least externalizing behavior when their mothers were judged highly sensitive (Bakersmans-Kranenburg and van IJzendoorn 2006).

- *Neuroendocrine moderation.* The parasympathetic nervous system (PSNS) is responsible for the "rest-and-digestive" activities that occur when the body is at rest. In families characterized by high stress and conflict, children showing low parasympathetic nervous system reactivity evidenced greater improvements in academic competence over the course of the kindergarten year than children with highly reactive parasympathetic nervous systems. However, the opposite was true in low-stress and low-conflict families: children with high PSNS reactivity showed more improvement in academic competence than children with low reactivity (Obradović et al. 2010).

- *Behavioral moderation.* When infants with "difficult" temperaments and more negative emotionality were exposed to low-quality child care settings, they were more prone to develop behavior problems in kindergarten than infants with "easy" temperaments who experienced similar low-quality child care settings. However, difficult infants exposed to high-quality child care settings evidenced fewer behavior problems in kindergarten than their easy-temperament peers did (Belsky and Pluess 2009).

Source: Prepared by Carly Tubbs.

to and will quickly learn multiple languages (de Houwer 1995); however, children's retention of the language as they age depends on a number of environmental factors, such as whether relatives, peers, schools, and the broader culture use and value that language.

Children's development of an ability to communicate and reason is fairly resilient: that is, it may take more to compromise these processes than certain other processes. Even if their ability to communicate and reason is endangered, children can often recover when exposed to better learning environments (Shonkoff and Phillips 2000). One of the major risk factors to both healthy brain development and supportive early learning environments, however, is poverty. Families who live in poverty may not be able to afford adequate nutrition, a situation associated with decreased cognitive abilities during early childhood (Morgan and Winick 1985; Nokes, van den Bosch, and Bundy 1998). We will elaborate in more detail on the effects of nutritional deficiencies later in this chapter. In addition, young children raised in impoverished environments may also receive less cognitive stimulation and have less access to learning resources (Miller and Davis 1997). Thus poverty due to an economic crisis can affect cognitive development through these two channels.

Learning to Self-Regulate Thoughts, Behaviors, and Emotions

Between the ages of about three and five years old, children experience dramatic growth in their ability to self-regulate thoughts, behaviors, and emotions. During this time, children slowly move from "other" regulation characteristic of infancy and toddlerhood, whereby important figures in their lives provide the necessary emotional or behavioral support to help them maintain or bring them back to an adaptive baseline state (Sameroff 2010), to self-regulation, or the ability to more independently modulate and control thoughts, actions, and feelings to meet a particular goal. These self-regulatory processes occur across multiple domains and include cognitive processes such as planning, rule following, and focusing; behavioral processes such as impulse control and activity reduction; and emotional processes such as management of excitement or anger. Indeed, well-regulated children tend to be better able to focus and sustain their attention during cognitively challenging tasks; more capable of inhibiting emotionally laden, aggressive behaviors; and better equipped to form more positive and supportive relationships with their teachers and peers (Barkley 1997; Gross and Oliver 2003).

Children's success in developing these self-regulation strategies depends on a number of factors that range from microlevel biological predispositions to high-level social influences, many of which interact with one another across time. For example, naturally fussy, overly active, or withdrawn children may elicit negative reactions from their caregivers, thereby compromising attachment relationships, reducing positive modeling of self-regulation strategies, and increasing the likelihood that their challenging behaviors will persist or increase over time. Negative life events and persistent environmental challenges have also been shown to have critical implications for children's self-regulatory development. For example, research has shown that exposure to poverty—particularly when it is chronic and severe—may have both indirect and direct effects on children's self-regulatory development (Raver et al., forthcoming). Exposure to economic adversity can increase family conflict while simultaneously reducing the availability of resources that provide the support, stability, and cognitive stimulation necessary for self-regulation. Thus, because a crisis can affect parenting behavior and responsiveness, it is likely to affect the processes supporting early development of a capacity to self-regulate.

As noted earlier, most of the evidence on how macroeconomic shocks affect early childhood development focuses on health and nutrition indicators. Partly this attention is due to the challenges associated with measuring other outcomes, particularly in other cultural contexts. We now turn to the question of how crises affect health and nutrition during early childhood.

Shocks, Health, and Nutrition during Early Childhood
Sarah Baird, Kathleen Beegle, and Jed Friedman

Adequate health and nutrition during early childhood are critical inputs for human development and subsequent adult outcomes. A growing body of research shows that investments in early childhood play a disproportionate role in the production of adult human capital (Bärnighausen et al. 2008; Horton, Alderman, and Rivera 2008; Currie and Thomas 1999; Case and Paxson 2008; Case, Fertig, and Paxson 2005). In Guatemala, for example, poor children who participated in a nutrition intervention scored higher on cognitive tests and earned higher wages (Hoddinott et al. 2008; Maluccio et al. 2009). Shorter children become shorter adults who also tend to have lower educational outcomes (Behrman and Rosenzweig 2004), lower earnings (Strauss and Thomas 1998), and, among women, worse schooling outcomes (Maccini and Yang 2009).

Along with improving adult outcomes, investments in child health and nutrition could play a role in breaking the intergenerational cycle of poverty, since not only do healthier children have improved cognitive and noncognitive skills and grow up to be more productive, but also evidence suggests that parental education and skill are subsequently related to improved survival, health, nutrition, cognition, and education of the next generation (Helmers and Patnam 2010; Lam and Duryea 1999; Psacharopoulos 1989; Rosenzweig and Wolpin 1994). Stunted mothers may have a higher probability of having low-birth-weight babies, thus perpetuating the economic consequences of low birth weight across generations (Alderman and Behrman 2006). And as was indicated in the introduction to early childhood development, investments in child health, and thus investments in later-life outcomes, begin in utero. Exposure to severe famine in utero can lead to a range of developmental issues (Lumey et al. 2007).

For a better understanding of the critical role of health in early childhood development, it is useful to know which factors drive successful cognitive development and skill acquisition. Walker et al. (2007) identify four key risk factors that may inhibit development in the domains out-lined earlier in the introduction to early childhood development and thus affect readiness for school and subsequent school performance. Each of these risk factors affects at least 20 percent of children in developing countries: stunting (31 percent of children under age five), iron deficiency (23–33 percent of children under age four), iodine deficiency (35 percent of the population worldwide), and inadequate cognitive stimulation. Additional risk factors include intrauterine growth restriction (11 percent of births) and maternal depression (17 percent prevalence). These risk factors are obviously related to nutrition and to physical and behavioral health, either of the mother or of the child. Sufficient nutritional and caloric intake alone may not suffice for children's healthy development. This phenomenon, also referred to as "failure to thrive," is related to developmental failures or delays stemming from lack of or inadequate environmental or maternal stimulation despite adequate caloric and nutritional intake (Corrales and Utter 2004; O'Brien et al. 2004).

One of the major risk factors to children's development is poverty. Poverty is associated with worse physical health, psychosocial health, and cognitive outcomes observed in children (Bradley and Corwyn 2002; Sameroff et al. 1993). In the long run, childhood poverty is inversely related to working memory in adults,[2] driven by, among other pathways, elevated chronic stress during childhood (Evans and Schamberg 2009). Increased exposure to poverty during childhood leads to damaged stress-regulatory mechanisms in adolescents, making it harder to navigate the demands of the environment and leading to a life-course trajectory of bad health outcomes (Evans and Kim 2007; Evans 2003; see also box 3.2 on neurological development). It is likely that this burden grows during times of crisis, given the associated increases in poverty and food insecurity. According to an analysis of one extreme outcome, that of lifespan, evidence from individuals born in the Netherlands between 1812 and 1912 finds that the total mean lifetime of those born in a recession decreases by about 5 percent compared to individuals born in a boom (van den Berg, Lindeboom, and Portrait 2006).

Although abundant evidence points to the role low income plays in child health and development, short-run cyclical changes in income may not necessarily lead to worse outcomes. On the one hand, as described by Ferreira and Schady (2009), negative shocks (income declines) may reduce household consumption of nutritious foods, may lower expenditures on other inputs into child health, including preventative and curative health care utilization, and may involve serious disruptions of public health services, leading to procyclical outcomes. On the other hand, since aggregate shocks depress wages, women may opt out of the workforce and spend more time caring for children, which is associated with improved child health. As a result, child health may be countercyclical to macroeconomic crises. Ferreira and Schady (2009) find that the question of counter- versus procyclicality may depend on the level of development measured in gross domestic product (GDP) per capita income in the country under scrutiny—where in wealthier countries child health improves in times of crisis, while in poorer countries it declines. Finally, the composition of women giving birth may change. For example, Dehejia and Lleras-Muney (2004) find that less-educated single Black mothers in the United States are less likely to have babies during a recession. Therefore, changes may come about in the average characteristics of birth cohorts, which in turn determine long-run human capital measures.

The Effects of Shocks on Health and Nutrition

Based on the above findings, a major concern is how financial crises might affect (surviving) children through lower quantity and quality of nutritional intake resulting from increased food insecurity and lower household income during their early years of development. The literature specifically linking the impact of financial crises with nutrition, while growing, is still limited. We will explore the existing evidence on the impact of economic crises on birth weight, stunting, and other nutritional outcomes. Because these outcomes usually entail aggregate economic shocks as well, we will also draw on evidence from natural disasters and conflict, recognizing the limitations of generalizing these results to economic crises per se.

Low birth weight and other intrauterine developmental deficiencies. Low birth weight, defined as less than 2,500 grams at birth, affects more than 11 million children in developing countries each year (Alderman and Behrman 2006). The main causes of low birth weight include premature birth, particularly in developed countries, and intrauterine growth retardation in developing countries (Villar and Belizan 1982).[3] The proximate determinants of low birth weight are many—including stress and anxiety, high maternal blood pressure and acute infections in the case of premature births, maternal undernutrition, anemia, malaria, and acute and chronic infections in the case of intrauterine growth retardation (Alderman and Behrman 2006). Low birth weight is a significant determinant of infant mortality (McCormick 1985) and reduced developmental outcomes (Gardner et al. 2003; Gorman and Pollitt 1992; Grantham-McGregor et al. 1998; Walker et al. 2004). Moreover, children with low birth weight associated with intrauterine growth retardation tend not to catch up (Alderman and Behrman 2006). Some evidence also suggests that low birth weight leads to higher susceptibility to high blood pressure and cholesterol, among other conditions (Barker 1998). As discussed earlier, poor child health and cognition resulting from low birth weight then affects subsequent school attainment and income in adulthood.

The evidence from the developed world, specifically the United States, suggests that the incidence of low-birth-weight babies declines during a recession, similar to the countercyclical child survival results that will be discussed later. This decline is due both to a changing composition of women giving birth and to behavior change, such as decreased smoking and drinking and more prenatal care visits (Dehejia and Lleres-Muney 2004).

The evidence on the impact of economic crises on birth weight in developing countries comes largely from Argentina, where the 1999–2001 recession and consequent 2001–02 economic collapse resulted in a 17 percent drop in GDP from 2000 to 2002. Cruces, Gluzmann, and Lopez Calva (2010) use data over the 1993–2006 period and leverage regional variation in GDP and health outcomes to estimate a low-birth-weight-to-GDP elasticity. The authors estimate an elasticity of 0.25 cases of low birth weight per 1,000 births for every percentage point decline in GDP per capita. Applying this estimate to the growth shortfall from the 2007–09 crisis in Argentina, the authors project an increase in the rate of low-weight births from 68.1 to 70.1 per 1,000. Interestingly, the authors' estimates find no significant impact from an increase in GDP on low birth weight, suggesting an asymmetric relation between changes in low-birth-weight prevalence and changes in aggregate income. Similarly, Bozzoli and Quintana-Domeque (2010) find evidence that the birth weight of infants born to low-educated mothers is sensitive to macroeconomic fluctuations during both the first and the third trimester of pregnancy, while children of high-educated mothers are affected only by shocks in the first trimester of pregnancy. According to their interpretation of the results, low-educated women, who face credit constraints, may suffer from both nutritional deprivation and maternal stress, while high-educated women are affected only by stress.

There is additional evidence on the impact of nonfinancial shocks on birth weight. Burlando (2010) combines data from 350 household surveys, as well as 20,000 birth records covering a multiyear period, to demonstrate that income loss associated with a month-long power outage in Tanzania resulted in reductions in birth weights of infants born seven to nine months later. The author observes a reduction in birth weight of, on average, 75 grams for children exposed to the blackout in the first six weeks of their mothers' pregnancy as well as those conceived within a month of the end of the blackout. Having ruled out other channels, the author proposes reduced maternal nutritional intake resulting from the temporary income shock as the main cause for this reduced birth weight. Evidence from the Dutch Hunger Winter suggests that birth weight declined by 300 grams for children exposed to maternal undernutrition during the third trimester (Lumey et al. 2007). Looking at a more common shock, fasting during Ramadan, Almond and Mazumder (2011) find that prenatal exposure to Ramadan among Arab mothers in Michigan during 1989–2007 resulted in babies with lower birth weights. The authors also find, using census data from Uganda and Iraq, a strong association between in utero exposure to Ramadan and the likelihood of being disabled as an adult.

Low birth weight is not the only indication of developmental problems in early life. The Dutch Hunger Winter of 1944–45, when food became increasingly scarce as a result of World War II, provides a unique natural experiment for investigating some of the long-term consequences of intrauterine exposure to acute nutritional deprivation. While intrauterine exposure to famine is not clearly linked to lower cognitive outcomes at age 18, a significant body of literature links exposure to other outcomes. These studies indicate that prenatal exposure to famine commonly leads to persistent changes in DNA methylation, or biochemical processes, that may result in a range of later-life outcomes depending on the timing of exposure during gestation and the sex of the fetus (Tobi et al. 2009). The cohorts conceived during the peak of the Dutch famine show increased rates of congenital anomalies of the nervous system, including spina bifida, hydrocephalus, and cerebral palsy (Susser, Hoek, and Brown 1998). In addition, researchers found increased prevalence of schizophrenia in this cohort, in earlier studies only in women (Susser and Lin 1992) but in later, more complete studies also in men (Susser et al. 1996). These findings were replicated in a study of the Chinese famine of 1959–61, which shows that the mortality-adjusted relative risk of developing schizophrenia among those born during the famine was around two years of age compared to those born in nonfamine years (St. Clair et al. 2005). Looking at cohorts conceived at the peak of the

Dutch famine, Neugebauer, Hoek, and Susser (1999) found a relationship between exposure to severe maternal nutritional deficiency during the first and second trimester and the development of antisocial personality disorder in men during young adulthood. Brown et al. (2000) found increases in major affective disorder in subjects exposed to famine in the second trimester and significant increases for those exposed during their third trimester. Lumey and Stein (1997) found an increase in perinatal deaths of children born to women exposed to the famine during their third trimester. Other studies found lower birth weight in children exposed during the third trimester and higher birth weight if exposed during the first and second trimester (for an overview of the studies, see Lumey et al. 2007).

Stunting. Childhood stunting, an indicator of chronic malnutrition reflecting both in utero and in vivo malnutrition, is calculated by comparing the height-for-age of a child with a reference population of well-nourished and healthy children, summarized by a "z-score." A child is considered stunted if his or her height-for-age z-score is below –2 (more than two standard deviations from the mean of healthy children). Stunted children have a demonstrated increased risk of poorer cognitive outcomes, including poor school performance and decreased scores on cognitive function tests (Berkman et al. 2002; Mendez and Adair 1999). Stunted children fail to acquire skills at normal rates compared with nonstunted children (Grantham-McGregor et al. 1997). As discussed earlier, stunting also translates into lower education and lower adult earnings. For this reason, the impacts of aggregate economic shocks during early childhood on stunting may have severe consequences for a person's development over the life course.

Turning first to financial crises, Paxson and Schady (2004) use data from the Demographic and Health Surveys (DHS) from 1992, 1996, and 2000 to estimate the impact of the 1988–92 Peruvian financial crisis (where per capita GDP dropped by 30 percent) on child nutritional status. They find that children born at the beginning of the crisis and observed at four years of age in 1992 had significantly lower height (approximately 0.25 z-scores lower) than the same-aged peers in 1996 and 2000 who exhibited no differences from each other.[4] Maluccio (2005) examines the impact of the Nicaraguan crisis in coffee prices in 2000–02 (where coffee prices declined over 50 percent) on stunting and finds a decline in the height-for-age z-score of 0.15 standard deviations for children 6–48 months. In contrast, Strauss et al. (2004) find no negative consequences from the 1997 Indonesian financial crisis (that led to the local currency being worth 20 percent of its previous value) on stunting when comparing a panel of children measured in 1997 and then in 2000. Similarly, in their study of economic crisis in Russia (where real GDP collapsed by 30 percent), Stillman and Thomas (2004) find no effect on child stunting. A number of factors could drive these differences in impact, including the magnitude of the crisis, the precrisis level of nutrition, and the extent to which health expenditures collapsed.

Other studies examine the impact of natural disasters and conflict on stunting. These results are applicable to the study of the effect of financial crises insofar as the impacts come through a loss in income as opposed to the direct impact of the natural disaster or conflict on health through, for example, changes in the disease environment or decreases in food availability. Using panel data from households in rural Zimbabwe, Hoddinott and Kinsey (2001) estimate the impact of an extreme crisis, the 1994–95 drought, on childhood stunting. The authors use data from households first interviewed in 1983–84, interviewed again in 1987, and then annually from 1992 to 1997. This approach enables a comparison of height-for-age between children in similar age cohorts in years of average rainfall (measured in 1993 and 1994) with those in drought years (measured in 1995 and 1996). The analysis finds that children aged 12–24 months lost 1.5–2.0 centimeters of growth, with no impact on older children (for whom growth trajectories had mostly been established). Their evidence further suggests that the drought had an impact only on children residing in poorer households (who presumably had lower precrisis nutritional levels), which were arguably less able to buffer income shortfalls with asset sales. This result is particularly pertinent to the impact of financial crises on stunting, since it suggests a clear link to income. The nutritional effects of the drought for those affected also persisted to the end of the study period, indicating a lack of "catch-up" growth.

In a similar analysis, Alderman, Hoddinott, and Kinsey (2006) examined the effects on stunting of both the 1982–84 drought and the pre-1980 civil war in Zimbabwe. Using data on children's nutritional status as preschoolers and the nutritional status of their siblings at a comparable age, the authors find that the Zimbabwean civil war resulted in a reduction in the child height-for-age z-score of 0.5, while the 1982–84 drought shock resulted in a reduction of 0.6. Perhaps most important, the authors find that these impacts are persistent: individuals stunted as children remain stunted as adults and have worse schooling outcomes.

Finally, two additional studies have potentially important ramifications for policy responses. Yamano, Alderman, and Christiaensen (2005) use 1995–96 national survey data in Ethiopia to assess the impact of food aid programs on stunting in the presence of crop damage resulting from droughts, insect attacks, and crop disease. The authors find that a 10 percent increase in crop damage corresponds to a 0.12-centimeter reduction in growth over a six-month period for children 6–24 months old. When food aid is controlled for in the analysis, it is a significant positive predictor of child growth in height; however, the crop damage corresponds to a 0.17-centimeter reduction in child height, indicating the partially protective effects of such aid. Similar to other findings, no significant impact of crop damage is observed for growth in children 25–50 months old, highlighting the vulnerability of the younger age group (under 24 months) to shocks. Evidence from Maccini and Yang (2009) suggests that higher rainfall during the first year of life in Indonesia results in height gains for women, with no effect for men.

Other health outcomes. Beyond birth weight and stunting, a number of other nutritional outcomes might be affected by financial crises. These include being underweight, having micronutrient deficiencies, and suffering from behavioral and mental health issues. It is important to note that whereas stunting is a long-run outcome (since a child's height cannot change quickly), underweight status can change in the short run and may be more sensitive to financial crises.

Although underweight is a short-term indicator, it is still an important outcome because it contributes significantly to both morbidity and mortality among children (Fishman et al. 2004). Pongou, Salomon, and Ezzati (2006) use pooled cross-sectional Cameroon DHS data from 1991 and 1998 to estimate the combined effect of economic crisis and subsequent government adjustment programs (which reduced public expenditures) on underweight status (weight-for-age z-scores two standard deviations or more below the mean) of children under age three. The authors find that underweight status for children under age three increased from 16 percent in 1991 to 23 percent in 1998. The authors also find that declines in economic status and health care accessibility were both correlated with an increase in underweight children in urban areas. In rural areas, reductions in health access, but not economic status, were correlated with an increase in underweight children, and children born into poor households suffered the largest increases in underweight status. In both urban and rural areas, children of educated mothers were the most protected from adverse changes. With reference to the conceptual framework, such results suggest that poverty serves as a vulnerability factor while mother's education acts as a resilience factor.

Similarly, evidence from Russia suggests that although total caloric intake did not decrease during the crisis, the weight-for-height z-score declined 0.11 points, possibly because of a change in the quality of food consumption, such as a drop in the consumption of fruit and vegetables (Stillman and Thomas 2004). In contrast, there is no evidence that the Indonesian financial crisis of 1997–98 affected weight-for-age (Waters, Saadah, and Pradhan 2003; Block et al. 2004). Evidence for the same period, however, found slight decreases in women's body mass index (Frankenberg, Thomas, and Beegle 1999), a result that suggests within-household coping strategies in which women and perhaps other adults served as a buffer for children during the shock period.

A handful of studies have documented the impact of the 1997 Indonesian crisis on other health outcomes that can be ultimately linked to child development, including micronutritional deficiencies and general access to health care. Using nutritional surveillance data from rural central Java, Block et al. (2004) estimate the impact of Indonesia's 1997–98 drought and financial crisis on child health. Along with finding a large and long-lasting impact on being underweight (z-score less than –2) the authors also find a significant decline in micronutrient status. The effects on mean hemoglobin concentration from December 1996 to July 1998 show a decrease of 6.1 percent. With larger impacts on hemoglobin concentration in children born or conceived during the crisis, maternal malnutrition during gestation appears to be an additional pathway for increased risk of iron deficiency in children. This conclusion is validated through observed decreases in household consumption of eggs, dark green leafy vegetables, and cooking oil. The only other evidence on child anemia and crisis also derives from the 1997 crisis in Indonesia. Strauss et al. (2004) and Frankenberg, Thomas, and Beegle (1999) find no change in hemoglobin levels in children or mothers, although their research might not have been able to identify the impacts observed in Block et al. (2004) because of the infrequency of data collection.[5]

Shocks and Infant Mortality

A substantial literature explores the impact of economic shocks, particularly financial crises, on infant and early childhood mortality. Initial evidence, derived largely from developed economies, concluded that the likelihood of infant survival, like many health indicators, actually *improves* during recessions (see, for example, Dehejia and Lleras-Muney 2004). Researchers have proposed a variety of transmission mechanisms to explain why economic recessions lead to improved child health in developed countries, including reductions in air pollution (Chay and Greenstone 2003), reductions in health-damaging behaviors such as smoking and drinking, and increases in the probability that mothers engage in time-intensive activities such as exercise and prenatal care (Ruhm 2000; Ruhm and Black 2002).

Country-level studies from the developing world have shown a less definitive pattern. Sharp economic downturns were associated with increases in infant mortality in Mexico (Cutler et al. 2002), Peru (Paxson and Schady 2005), and India (Bhalotra 2010),[6] but not in Argentina (Rucci 2004) or in countries of the former Soviet Union (Brainerd 1998; Brainerd and Cutler 2005; Shkolnikov et al. 1998). Although evidence from the 1998 financial crisis in Indonesia is inconclusive, it generally suggests small effects on infant mortality (Rukumnuaykit 2003; Frankenberg, Thomas, and Beegle 1999; Strauss et al. 2004). Echoing the results from the United States, Miller and Urdinola (2010) find that regions hit by negative coffee price shocks saw improvements in child survival in Colombia. Finally, a handful of cross-country studies of the relationship between income and infant mortality in developing countries also finds mixed results (Pritchett and Summers 1996; Jamison, Sandbu, and Wang 2004; Deaton 2006).

One recent comprehensive study of developing countries identified a clear link between aggregate economic contractions of sufficient magnitude and increases in the likelihood of mortality in the first year of life. Baird, Friedman, and Schady (2011) pool all available Demographic and Health Surveys from 59 developing countries around the world to construct a dataset of 1.7 million live births over the years 1975–2003. The authors identify a large negative association between infant mortality in a given year and their measure of crisis—deviations of per capita GDP from trend. A 1 percent decrease in per capita GDP from trend results in an increase in infant mortality of between 0.24 and 0.40 deaths per 1,000 children born. On average, the country-specific year-on-year decrease in infant mortality in their data is 2.5 deaths per 1,000 live births; thus a 1 percent shortfall in per capita GDP from expected trends results in an increase in infant mortality of between 10 and 15 percent of the average annual mortality decline (and a crisis on the order of 7–10 percentage points of GDP completely erases the expected gains in infant survival).

Furthermore, Baird, Friedman, and Schady (2011) identify important heterogeneity within this average relationship between infant mortality and economic crisis. The mortality of children born to rural and less-educated women is more sensitive to economic shocks, a finding that suggests both that the poor are disproportionately affected during most economic crises and that maternal education and urban service systems may be "resilience factors." The mortality of girls is also significantly more sensitive to aggregate economic shocks than that of boys. This gender differential exists even in regions such as Sub-Saharan Africa that are not particularly known for son preference and indicates a behavioral dimension in which households may conserve resources to better protect young sons at the expense of daughters (Filmer, Friedman, and Schady 2009). Finally, the relationship between economic shocks and infant mortality is decidedly nonlinear. For small departures from trend (noncrisis years), little relation is seen between the infant mortality rate and GDP. However, as the magnitude of the economic shock increases, an increase in the mortality of female infants is particularly apparent.

Even though the gender difference in mortality response to crises observed in many regions suggests a behavioral dimension related to declines in household income, little evidence is available to illuminate the causal pathway by which economic shocks are translated into elevated mortality. Baird, Friedman, and Schady (2011) analyze birth timing to reveal that the economic conditions around the time of birth (a three-month window) appear to be most determinative of survival in the first year of life. However, the pathways by which shocks in this vulnerable period translate into increased likelihood of death are still not clear. Christian (2010) argues for the importance of maintaining adequate nutrition during crisis periods to avert increases in child mortality and morbidity but does not present evidence that poor nutrition is a dominant cause of elevated mortality. A decline in the quality or quantity of public health services during periods of crisis is another potential mechanism, and Ferreira and Schady (2009) contrast the experiences of Indonesia and Peru to indicate the likely importance of maintaining critical health services.

According to emerging findings, the inverse relationship between economic crisis and infant survival is weaker in middle- and upper-middle-income developing countries, perhaps indicating a transition zone where the countercyclicality of the infant mortality rate and aggregate income in low-income countries shifts to the procyclicality observed in high-income countries (see, for example, Schady and Smitz 2010). Currently, however, in much of the developing world, the risks to infant survival are still present. Friedman and Schady (2009) estimate that the 2008 global financial crisis led to 35,000–50,000 excess infant deaths in Sub-Saharan Africa the following year.

Economic Crises and Early Childhood Cognitive and Socioemotional Development
Carly Tubbs

The development of cognitive and socioemotional skills during early childhood lays the foundation for children's lifelong success in a variety of contexts, including school, work, and personal relationships. Delays in cognitive or socioemotional development, however, can begin early in life and accumulate quickly, leaving children who experience such delays to play a game of "catch up" for years to come.

Unfortunately, very little is known about how economic crises affect the development of cognitive and socioemotional skills during early childhood. Indeed, we are aware of only one study to date that has estimated the impact of an aggregate economic shock on cognitive outcomes during early childhood (Hidrobo 2011); we could find no such study linking an aggregate shock to early childhood socioemotional outcomes. However, psychologists and sociologists have amassed a wealth of rigorous evidence on the risk factors to early childhood cognitive and socioemotional development and outcomes in the context of economic disadvantage. Such evidence comes in part from studies examining the consequences of idiosyncratic economic shocks to the household in the context of broader macroeconomic stability (for example, Dearing, McCartney, and Taylor 2001, as well as from studies on the effects of persistent poverty such as Duncan, Brooks-Gunn, and Klebanov 1994) on early childhood development. By inferring that an economic crisis would make such events more widespread or severe, we can thus begin to form a picture of the consequences for early childhood cognitive and socioemotional development.

We should also keep in mind that the processes described in this box that shape children's cognitive and socioemotional development are also strongly interrelated with young children's physical health. As mentioned earlier, the failure to thrive is a phenomenon in which a young child fails to grow physically despite sufficient food and nutrition. Failure to thrive is often associated with a depressed or otherwise neglectful or abusive primary caregiver who does not provide healthy emotional and cognitive stimulation.

The evidence on early childhood cognitive and socioemotional skills stems mostly from countries in the Organisation for Economic Co-operation and Development (OECD). Given the implications for developmental processes of the demographic and cultural differences between (and within) countries, our ability to draw conclusions across contexts is severely limited. However, we hope that by focusing attention on these issues, we spur economists and developmental scientists alike to engage in research that broadens the scope of our understanding of how macroeconomic crises affect the cognitive and socioemotional development (as well as the physical health) of young children around the world.

The Pathways through Which Financial Crises Affect Children's Cognitive and Socioemotional Outcomes

Because the household is the context in which children spend a majority of their time during early childhood, an economic crisis will affect young children's cognitive and socioemotional development largely to the extent that their families are affected by the crisis. A drop in household income or the unemployment of the household head may affect young children's outcomes through two mediating pathways: resources for investments and family dynamics and functioning.

First, an economic crisis may influence caregivers' decisions about how to invest money or time in a variety of resources, including nutritious foods, cognitively stimulating materials and opportunities, and activities with their offspring, all of which affect cognitive development in early childhood (Mayer 1997; Gershoff et al. 2007). The impact of crises on families' abilities to invest in adequate nutrition during gestation and the first few years of life—and the long-lasting effects on the brain and cognitive development in particular—was discussed earlier in this chapter (see also Morgan and Winick 1985).

Second, caregivers' stress, typically manifested as marital conflict or depression and anxiety, places children at risk for social, emotional, and behavioral problems throughout all stages of childhood (Conger and Donnellan 2007). However, the effect of caregiver stress on children's outcomes differs according to timing (that is, early childhood versus adolescence). During early childhood, unreliable interactions with primary caregivers increase the chances that children will develop insecure attachment relationships and difficulties with self-regulation, thereby increasing the likelihood of socioemotional problems ranging from aggression and hyperactivity to anxiety and fearfulness (Campbell et al. 2004; Maughan et al. 2007). Moreover, caregiver stress may indirectly place young children at risk for delays in cognitive development by reducing caregivers' responsiveness and engagement in cognitively stimulating activities (Bornstein and Tamis-LeMonda 1989; Gershoff et al. 2007).

These two pathways—caregiver stress and resources for investment—may also interact to influence children's outcomes during an economic crisis. If caretakers lose their jobs, they may actually spend more time at home with their children; according to the first pathway, this extra time resource should have positive implications for children's cognitive development. However, if caretakers are stressed about their situation, the second pathway posits that this extra time may end up having a negative effect on their children's socioemotional outcomes (Elder and Caspi 1988). Alternately, these two pathways may interact in an additive manner. For instance, during an economic crisis parents may experience additional stress due to the fact that they are unable to provide adequate nutrition for their children and their children are going hungry (Hossain and McGregor 2011).

Empirical Evidence and Inferences for Cognitive and Socioemotional Outcomes

Evidence from many different types of studies across diverse disciplines suggests that young children's *cognitive* development is at risk during an economic crisis. To our knowledge, Hidrobo (2011) conducted the only study to date that has specifically estimated the impact of a negative aggregate economic shock on cognitive outcomes during early childhood. Leveraging variation in children's length of exposure to the 1998–2000 economic crisis in Ecuador, Hidrobo employed a mother-and-child-fixed-effects model to demonstrate that one year of exposure to the crisis between birth and five years of age significantly decreased vocabulary test scores by an average of 2.4 points. The author observes that this drop constitutes a 3 percent reduction in vocabulary test scores compared to baseline for every year of exposure to the crisis. Moreover, the effect of exposure to the crisis varied according to the timing of exposure: exposure to the crisis had a significant negative impact on children's vocabulary scores only when children were exposed between the ages of 6 and 11 months and 18 and 29 months. Interestingly, these ages coincide with the periods when children undergo rapid neurological and cognitive changes in their linguistic abilities.

Idiosyncratic shocks, such as a drop in household income, also negatively affect cognitive development during early childhood. However, this impact may depend on the household economic context at the time of the shock. For example, Dearing, McCartney, and Taylor (2001) find that a decrease in families' income-to-needs ratio was associated with significant decreases in children's school readiness and receptive language skills, but only for families living below the poverty line at the time of the income loss. Studies examining the impact of welfare-to-work randomized experiments in the United States also provide evidence that changes in income affect low-income children's cognitive development in early childhood. Using an instrumental variables approach, Duncan, Morris, and Rodrigues (2011) estimate that a US$1,000 increase in a low-income household's annual income, occurring when children are between the ages of two and five years, boosts children's cognitive achievement by 6 percent of a standard deviation.

Evidence from both OECD and developing countries (including Cambodia, Ecuador, Madagascar, Mozambique, and Nicaragua) indicates that poverty in and of itself is associated with children's cognitive delays during early childhood (Duncan, Brooks-Gunn, and Klebanov 1994; Paxson and Schady 2007; Macours, Schady, and Vakis 2008; Fernald et al. 2011; Naudeau et al. 2011). In accordance with the pattern noted above in studies of idiosyncratic shocks, evidence from Cambodia and Mozambique (Naudeau et al. 2011), as well as from Ecuador, Madagascar, and Nicaragua (Paxson and Schady 2007; Macours, Shady, and Vakis 2008; Fernald et al. 2011), indicates that children from the very lowest income quintiles have the highest risk of experiencing cognitive delays. Moreover, the magnitude of these delays increases as children approach the age of school entry. For example, although the linguistic abilities of young children around the world typically increase rapidly between the ages of three and five, Naudeau et al. (2011) provide evidence that five-year-olds living in poverty in Cambodia and Mozambique have only marginally better language understanding than their three-year-old counterparts.

As discussed above, such developmental delays stem in part from caretakers' investments, both financial and time, in cognitively stimulating materials and activities (see, for example, Smith, Brooks-Gunn, and Klebanov 1997; Baharudin and Luster 1998). The studies cited above provide evidence that an idiosyncratic shock or poverty may reduce parents' ability to invest such time and money, leading to cognitive developmental delays. For example, Votruba-Drzal (2003) find that the log of one dollar decrease in mean household income since birth is associated with a third of a standard deviation decrease in cognitive stimulation in the home at ages three and four. Naudeau et al. (2011) found that the poverty level was indirectly associated with young children's cognitive outcomes partially through parental investment in cognitively stimulating materials and parental language stimulation.

As for *socioemotional* outcomes, unfortunately no studies to date have explicitly examined how an aggregate economic shock affects young children's socioemotional development, while only a few studies have looked at such outcomes during an idiosyncratic household shock. For example, according to Dearing, McCartney, and Taylor's (2001) findings, a decrease in families' income-to-needs ratio when children were aged 15–36 months was associated with significantly lower positive social behaviors (including sociable, empathic, and cooperative behaviors) when those children were 36 months. Studies examining the impact of poverty in early childhood have found that children who had spent any time in poverty—whether short or long term—had higher levels of internalizing (for example, depression and anxiety) and externalizing (for example, aggression and impulsivity) behaviors than children who had never experienced poverty (Duncan, Brooks-Gunn, and Klebanov 1994). Taken together, these results suggest that young children may be more at risk of developing socioemotional problems during an economic crisis.

Some studies have identified important factors that may moderate and mediate the association between an idiosyncratic economic shock or poverty and young children's socioemotional outcomes. In their seminal study of the Great Depression, Elder and Caspi (1988) found markedly different socioemotional outcomes by gender. Boys who grew up in deprived households were less likely to be hopeful and confident, while girls evidenced no such negative effects. Elder and Caspi (1988) offer several explanations for this observed gender difference: (1) girls may have been protected by close mother-daughter relationships; (2) boys may have been more exposed to family conflict and stress; and (3) boys are more sensitive to environmental stress during early childhood than girls (Rutter 1982). These findings highlight that interactions with caregivers are one of the most important mechanisms influencing young children's socioemotional development. Numerous studies have found that an idiosyncratic household shock increases parents' risk of emotional distress and depression (see, for example, Prause, Dooley, and Huh 2009; Elder et al. 1992; Mistry et al. 2002). In turn, depressed mothers show less responsiveness and more irritability in their interactions with their infants, while infants of depressed mothers tend to be fussier and less positive than children of nondepressed mothers (Field et al. 1985; Cohn et al. 1990). In turn, these interactions have been found to predict young children's subsequent internalizing and externalizing behavior problems (Maughan et al. 2007).

While the evidence on some of the mechanisms outlined above is compelling, we should be cautious in making inferences about the link between aggregate economic shocks and young children's socioemotional outcomes, given that the majority of studies to date have been conducted in the United States. Norms for what constitute typical socioemotional development and parenting behavior, goals, and values vary across and within countries and contexts.

Conclusions

Because the health and development of young children may be at risk during times of crisis, this topic is a key area for policy. The subject area is particularly important, given the long-term effects of nutritional deficiencies, insecure attachments, and inadequate stimulation during early childhood on income and on mental and physical health later in life.

A significant number of studies confirms that birth weight and infant mortality fluctuate with aggregate GDP, while the findings on micronutrient deficiencies are less clear. According to the evidence, serious challenges related to health and nutrition in utero arise when fetuses are exposed to critical food or nutritional shortages. The studies of the Dutch Hunger Winter highlight the severe long-term consequences of exposure to harsh famine during gestation, ranging from congenital anomalies of the nervous system to schizophrenia and obesity. Thus, insofar as an economic crisis leads to a household experiencing famine, this problem is serious. Other than the inferences we can draw from our knowledge of the long-term consequences of economic crisis on health, we know little about how aggregate economic shocks affect cognitive and socioemotional development during early childhood. One study of the 1998–2000 crisis in Ecuador shows significant decreases in vocabulary tests scores. Studies of idiosyncratic shocks and poverty also find negative impacts on cognitive and socioemotional development.

Augmenting evidence-based theory with this review of the literature can enhance our understanding of the potential impacts of economic crisis on early childhood development and provide guidance for effective social interventions. Let us recall the three principles from the conceptual framework developed in chapter 2: transmission mechanisms, timing, and context.

Given that the family is the primary setting in which a child interacts, two dominant *mechanisms* for transmitting the effects of crisis need to be considered: (1) resources for food and other investments; and (2) family dynamics and functioning, including parental and maternal time and mental health. More specifically, the child will be affected to the extent that these factors affect nutrition and health, their ability to form early safe attachments to their primary caregiver(s), and the stimulation they receive. The evidence presented earlier clearly shows that lack of adequate nutrition is likely to have severe consequences in the long run as it affects neurological development. While studies on health and nutrition outcomes and infant mortality are relatively straightforward and the indicators more universally applicable, other measures of cognitive and, in particular, socioemotional development may be more difficult, especially in a cross-cultural context. Nevertheless, a large body of literature from noncrisis contexts indicates that the fetus and the infant are also affected by family functioning, in particular maternal stress and depression. And stress and mental health issues tend to increase during a crisis (for more detail, see chapter 2). Thus, during an economic crisis a mother may have less time to interact with her child and provide stimulation and also to be less patient. In addition, mental health issues may render her emotionally unavailable and inhibit a healthy, secure attachment to form. A child is also likely to be affected if exposed to high levels of cortisol and other hormones in utero.

The evidence reviewed in this chapter also suggests a *timing* aspect; studies that specifically look at and compare age cohorts detect ages or stages when children appear to be particularly vulnerable to shocks. For example, the studies of the Dutch Hunger Winter present compelling evidence that famine during gestation can have severe consequences in later life. Outcomes differed depending on the trimester during which the famine occurred. However, attention to adequate nutrition during gestation is called for in all cases. In addition, the first two years seem critical in setting the trajectory for future growth. While elevated levels of cortisol of the mother affect the child only in utero, stress more likely affects infants in how it affects the mother-child relationship. A study in Ecuador was able to establish a relationship between crisis and cognitive development particularly for children 6–11 and 18–29 months, which coincide with particular spurts in brain development (see box 3.2).

Even in the face of these age-related regularities, a great deal of heterogeneity remains, due, at least in part, to the *context*. For example, the evidence shows great variation in the impact of aggregate shocks on health and development by socioeconomic status. These differences may stem from income loss or resource constraints alone or on the associated stress and anxiety experienced. For example, the studies reviewed indicate that stunting is more common in poor households and that infant mortality is more likely in poor and rural households. While lack of food or nutrition will lead to stunting, aggregate economic shocks will not in all contexts lead to inadequate food or nutrition. For example, the study of Argentina found that poor women were affected by both income loss and stress, whereas nonpoor women suffered only from stress. While stress in itself can affect a young child's development starting in utero, interventions likely need to be adjusted to different target groups. For example, a food transfer program is unlikely to have the desired effect on the nonpoor child, whereas it might be crucial to covering the nutritional needs of the poor child. Stress will also be affected by the social resources available to people and households, and some of these social resources may influence the coping strategies that households employ (for a more detailed account on social resources and social resilience, see box 6.2). In addition, crisis-induced changes in the context, such as prices, may vary. In Indonesia, for example, researchers observed a decrease in the consumption of eggs, which led to an iron deficiency in young children. Such specific local factors need to be considered if we are to understand the likely impacts.

All in all, the evidence presented here suggests that children—in utero until about 24 months, especially in the poorest families—are the most vulnerable to the effects of economic crises on health, cognitive, and socioemotional outcomes. The good news, however, is that young children's development is susceptible to positive as well as to negative influences. In other words, if economic crises can derail young children's development, research indicates that both naturally occurring and policy-induced positive changes, including increases in income, can significantly improve young children's cognitive and socioemotional development (Dearing, McCartney, and Taylor 2001; Duncan, Morris, and Rodrigues 2011). The interdependence between domains of development—or the interplay between nutrition and health, secure attachment, and stimulation, all of which contribute to and drive cognitive and socioemotional development—calls for interventions that do not necessarily focus only on the child alone but also on the health and functioning of the entire family

(Aber 2012). In particular, efforts should be made to identify pregnant women as early as possible and provide the necessary support to prevent significant insults to development in utero. Chapter 6 of this volume will present suggestions and examples of interventions to ensure healthy development in utero and the first few years of life.

Notes

1. For the reader who is interested in a more comprehensive guide to early childhood development, see Shonkoff and Phillips (2000) and Gardner and Kosmitzki (2008).

2. Working memory is the temporary storage mechanism that enables us to hold a small amount of information active over a short interval and to manipulate it.

3. See Alderman and Behrman (2006) for a full review of the economic costs of low birth weight.

4. The lack of data on stunting for the precrisis period renders this finding suggestive but not definitive.

5. There is also some evidence impact of natural disasters on weight-for-height. Jensen (2000) using data from Côte d'Ivoire finds that children exposed to drought conditions are 3.1–3.8 percentage points more likely to have low weight-for-height and were less likely to consult a health practitioner when ill.

6. Note that Bhalotra (2010) finds no impact in urban areas, more consistent with results from the developed world.

References

Aber, J. L. 2012. "Poor and Low Family Incomes, Infant/Toddler Development and the Prospects for Change: Back to the Future." In *The Implications of Developmental Health Science for Infant/Toddler Care and Poverty*, ed. S. Odom, E. Pungello, and N. Gardner-Neblett. New York: Guilford Publications, Inc.

Aber, L., and S. Jones. 1997. "Indicators of Positive Development in Early Childhood: Improving Concepts and Measures." In *Indicators of Children's Well-being*, ed. R. Hauser, B. Brown, and W. Prosser, 395–427. New York: Russell Sage Foundation.

Ainsworth, M. D. S. 1967. *Infancy in Uganda: Infant Care and the Growth of Love.* Baltimore, MD: Johns Hopkins University Press.

Ainsworth, M. D. S., M. Blehar, E. Waters, and S. Wall. 1978. *Patterns of Attachment.* Hillsdale, NJ: Erlbaum.

Alderman, H., ed. 2011. *No Small Matter: The Impact of Poverty, Shocks, and Human Capital Investments in Early Childhood Development.* Washington, DC: World Bank.

Alderman, H., and J. Behrman. 2006. "Reducing the Incidence of Low Birth Weight in Low-Income Countries Has Substantial Economic Benefits." *World Bank Research Observer* 21 (1): 25–48.

Alderman, H., J. Hoddinott, and B. Kinsey. 2006. "Long-Term Consequences of Early Childhood Malnutrition." *Oxford Economic Papers* 58 (3): 450–74.

Almond, D. 2006. "Is the 1918 Influenza Pandemic Over? Long-Term Effects of *in Utero* Influenza Exposure in the Post-1940 U.S." *Journal of Political Economy* 114 (4): 672–712.

Almond, D., and K. Chay. 2003. *The Long-Run and Intergenerational Impact of Poor Infant Health: Evidence from Cohorts Born during the Civil Rights Era.* Mimeo, University of California Berkeley.

Almond, D., and J. Currie. 2011. "Killing Me Softly: The Fetal Origins Hypothesis." *Journal of Economic Perspectives* 25 (3): 153–72.

Almond, D., and B. Mazumder. 2011. "Health Capital and the Prenatal Environment: The Effect of Ramadan Observance during Pregnancy." *American Economic Journal: Applied Economics* 3(4): 56–85.

Baharudin, R., and T. Luster. 1998. "Factors Related to the Quality of the Home Environment." *Journal of Family Issues* 19 (4): 375–403.

Baird, S., J. de Hoop, and B. Ozler. 2011. "Income Shocks and Adolescent Mental Health." Policy Research Working Paper 5644, World Bank, Washington, DC.

Baird, S., J. Friedman, and N. Schady. 2011. "Aggregate Income Shocks and Infant Mortality in the Developing World." *Review of Economics and Statistics* 93 (3): 847–56.

Bakermans-Kranenburg, M. J., and M. J. van Ijzendoorn. 2006. "Gene-Environment Interaction of the Dopamine D4 Receptor (DRD4) and Observed Maternal Insensitivity Predicting Externalizing Behavior in Preschoolers." *Developmental Psychobiology* 48 (5): 406–9.

Bakermans-Kranenburg, M., and M. van Ijzendoorn. 2011. "Differential Susceptibility to Rearing Environment Depending on Dopamine-Related Genes: New Evidence and a Meta-Analysis." *Development and Psychopathology* 23 (1): 39–52.

Barker, D. J. P. 1998. *Mothers, Babies and Health in Later Life.* 2nd ed. Edinburgh: Churchill Livingstone.

Barkley, R. A. 1997. "Behavioral Inhibition, Sustained Attention, and Executive Functions: Constructing a Unifying Theory of ADHD." *Psychological Bulletin* 121 (1): 65–94.

Bärnighausen, T., D. E. Bloom, D. Canning, A. Friedman, O. Levine, J. O'Brien, L. Privor-Dumm, and D. Walker. 2008. *The Economic Case for Expanding Vaccination Coverage of Children Best Practice Paper: New Advice from Copenhagen Consensus 08.* Copenhagen Consensus Center: Copenhagen.

Bee, H., and D. Boyd. 2009. *The Developing Child.* 12th ed. Boston: Allyn & Bacon.

Behrman, Jere, and Mark Rosenzweig. 2004. "Returns to Birthweight." *Review of Economics and Statistics* 86 (2): 586–601.

Belsky, J., and R. Isabella. 1988. "Maternal, Infant, and Social-Contextual Determinants of Attachment Security." In *Clinical Implications of Attachment*, ed. J. Belsky and T. Nezworski, 41–94. Hillsdale, NJ: Erlbaum.

Belsky, J., and M. Pluess. 2009. "Beyond Diathesis-Stress: Differential Susceptibility to Environmental Influence." *Psychological Bulletin* 135 (6): 885–908.

Belsky, J., B. Spritz, and K. Crnic. 1996. "Infant Attachment Security and Affective-Cognitive Information Processing at Age 3." *Psychological Science* 7 (2): 111–14.

Bergman, K., V. Glover, P. Sarkar, D. H. Abbott, and T. G. O'Connor. 2010. "In Utero Cortisol and Testosterone Exposure and Fear Reactivity in Infancy." *Hormones and Behavior* 57 (3): 306–12.

Berkman, D. S., A. G. Lescano, R. H. Gilman, S. L. Lopez, and M. M. Black. 2002. "Effects of Stunting, Diarrhoeal Disease, and Parasitic Infection during Infancy on Cognition in Late Childhood: A Follow-Up Study." *Lancet* 359 (9306): 564–71.

Bhalotra, S. 2010. "Fatal Fluctuations? Cyclicality in Infant Mortality in India." *Journal of Development Economics* 93 (1): 7–19.

Block, S. A., L. Keiss, H. Keller, S. Kosen, R. Moench-Pfanner, M. W. Bloem, and C. P. Timmer. 2004. "Macro Shocks and Micro (Scopic) Outcomes: Child Nutrition during Indonesia's Crisis." *Economics and Human Biology* 2 (1): 21–44.

Bornstein, M., and C. Tamis-LeMonda. 1989. "Maternal Responsiveness and Cognitive Development in Children." *New Directions for Child and Adolescent Development* 1989 (43): 49–61.

Bowlby, J. 1988. *A Secure Base.* New York, NY: Basic Books.

Boyce, W. T., and B. J. Ellis. 2005. "Biological Sensitivity to Context: I. An Evolutionary–Developmental Theory of the Origins and Functions of Stress Reactivity." *Development and Psychopathology* 17 (2): 271–301.

Bozzoli, C., and C. Quintana-Domeque. 2010. *The Weight of the Crisis: Evidence from Newborns in Argentina.* IZA Discussion Papers 5294. Institute for the Study of Labor, Bonn.

Bradley, R. H., and R. F. Corwyn. 2002. "Socioeconomic Status and Child Development." *Annual Review of Psychology* 53: 371–99.

Brainerd, Elizabeth. 1998. "Market Reform and Mortality in Transition Economies." *World Development* 26 (11): 2013–27.

Brainerd, Elizabeth, and David Cutler. 2005. "Autopsy of an Empire: Understanding Mortality in Russia and the Former Soviet Union." *Journal of Economic Perspectives* 19 (1): 107–30.

Brown, A., J. van Os, C. Driessens, H. Hoek, and E. Susser. 2000. "Further Evidence of Relation between Prenatal Famine and Major Affective Disorder." *American Journal of Psychiatry* 157 (2): 190–95.

Burlando, A. 2010. "When the Lights Go Out: Permanent Health Effects of Transitory Shocks." Boston University, Boston.

Campbell, S. B., C. A. Brownell, A. Hungerford, S. J. Spieker, R. Mohan, and J. S. Blessing. 2004. "The Course of Maternal Depressive Symptoms and Maternal Sensitivity as Predictors of Attachment Security at 36 Months." *Development and Psychopathology* 16 (2):231–52.

Carson, J., and R. D. Parke. 1996. "Reciprocal Negative Affect in Parent-Child Interactions and Children's Peer Competency." *Child Development* 67 (5): 2217–26.

Case, Anne, Angela Fertig, and Christina Paxson. 2005. "The Lasting Impact of Childhood Health and Circumstance." *Journal of Health Economics* 24 (2): 365–89.

Case, A., and C. Paxson. 2008. "Stature and Status: Height, Ability, and Labor Market Outcomes." *Journal of Political Economy* 116 (3): 499–532.

Cassidy, J. 1988. "Child-Mother Attachment and the Self in Six-Year-Olds." *Child Development* 59 (1): 121–34.

Chay, K. Y., and M. Greenstone. 2003. "The Impact of Air Pollution on Infant Mortality: Evidence from Geographic Variation in Pollution Shocks Induced by a Recession." *Quarterly Journal of Economics* 118 (3): 1121–67.

Christian, P. 2010. "Impact of the Economic Crisis and Increase in Food Prices on Child Mortality: Exploring Nutritional Pathways." *Journal of Nutrition* 140 (1): 177S–81S.

Cohn, J. F., S. Campbell, R. Matias, and J. Hopkins. 1990. "Face-to-Face Interactions of Postpartum Depressed and Nondepressed Mother-Infant Pairs." *Developmental Psychology* 26 (1): 15–23.

Conger, R. D., and R. D. Donnellan. 2007. "An Interactionist Perspective on the Socioeconomic Context of Human Development." *Annual Review of Psychology* 58: 175–99.

Corrales, K., and S. Utter. 2004. "Failure to Thrive." In *Handbook of Pediatric Nutrition*, 2nd ed., ed. P. Samour, K. Helm, and C. Lang, 395-412. Sudbury, MA: Jones and Bartlett Publishers.

Cruces, G., P. Gluzmann, and L. F. Lopez Calva. 2010. "Permanent Effects of Economic Crisis on Household Welfare: Evidence and Projections from Argentina's Downturn." Paper prepared for UNDP-RB-LAC project "The Effects of the Economic Crisis on the Well-Being of Households in Latin America and the Caribbean."

Cunha, Flavio, and James J. Heckman. 2007. "The Technology of Skill Formation." *American Economic Review* 97 (2): 31–47.

Cunha, Flavio, James J. Heckman, Lance J. Lochner, and Dimitriy V. Masterov. 2006. "Interpreting the Evidence on Life Cycle Skill Formation." In *Handbook of the Economics of Education*, ed. E. Hanushek and F. Welch, 697–812. Amsterdam: North Holland.

Currie, J., and D. Thomas. 1999. "Early Test Scores, Socioeconomic Status, and Future Outcomes." Working Paper 6943, National Bureau of Economic Research, Cambridge, MA.

Cutler, D. M., F. Knaul, R. Lozano, O. Mendez, and B. Zurita. 2002. "Financial Crisis, Health Outcomes, and Ageing: Mexico in the 1980s and 1990s." *Journal of Public Economics* 84 (2): 279–303.

Dearing, E., K. McCartney, and B. Taylor. 2001. "Change in Family Income-to-Needs Matters More for Children with Less." *Child Development* 72 (6): 1779–93.

———. 2006. "Within-Child Associations between Family Income and Externalizing and Internalizing Problems." *Developmental Psychology* 42 (2): 237–52.

Deaton, Angus. 2006. "Global Patterns of Income and Health: Facts, Interpretations, and Policies." WIDER Annual Lecture, Helsinki, September 29.

Dehejia, R., and A. Lleras-Muney. 2004. "Booms, Busts, and Babies' Health." *Quarterly Journal of Economics* 119 (3): 1091–130.

Duncan, G. J., J. Brooks-Gunn, and P. K. Klebanov. 1994. "Economic Deprivation and Early-Childhood Development." *Child Development* 65 (2): 296–318.

Duncan, G. J., P. A. Morris, and C. Rodrigues. 2011. "Does Money Really Matter? Estimating Impacts of Family Income on Young Children's Achievement with Data from Random-Assignment Experiments." *Developmental Psychology* 47 (5): 1263–79.

Elder, G. H., Jr., and A. Caspi. 1988. "Economic Stress in Lives: Developmental Perspectives." *Journal of Social Issues* 44 (4): 25–45.

Elder, G. H., Jr., R. D. Conger, E. M. Foster, and M Ardelt. 1992. "Families under Economic Pressure." *Journal of Family Issues* 13 (1): 5–37.

Elder, G. H., Jr., T. Nguyen, and A. Caspi. 1985. "Linking Family Hardship to Children's Lives." *Child Development* 56 (2): 361–75.

Ellis, B., W. T. Boyce, J. Belsky, M. J. Bakermans-Kranenburg, and M. H. van IJzendoorn. 2011. "Differential Susceptibility to the Environment: An Evolutionary-Neurodevelopmental Theory." *Development and Psychopathology* 23 (1): 7–28.

Evans, G. W. 2003. "A Multimethodological Analysis of Cumulative Risk and Allostatic Load among Rural Children." *Developmental Psychology* 39 (5): 924–33.

Evans, G. W., & P. Kim. 2007. "Childhood Poverty and Health: Cumulative Risk Exposure and Stress Dysregulation." *Psychological Science* 18 (11): 953–57.

Evans, G. W., and M. A. Schamberg. 2009. "Childhood Poverty, Chronic Stress, and Adult Working Memory." *Proceedings of the National Academy of Sciences* 106 (16): 6545–49.

Feinstein, L. 2003. "Inequality in the Early Cognitive Development of Children in the 1970 Cohort." *Economica* 70 (277):73–97.

Fernald, L., A. Weber, E. Galasso, and L. Ratsifandrihamanana. 2011. "Socio-economic Gradients and Child Development in a Very Low Income Population." *Developmental Science* 14 (4): 832–47.

Ferreira, F. H. G., and N. Schady. 2009. "Aggregate Economic Shocks, Child Schooling, and Child Health." *World Bank Research Observer* 24 (2): 147–81.

Field, T., D. Sandberg, R. Garcia, N. Vega-Lahr, S. Goldstein, and L. Guy. 1985. "Pregnancy Problems, Postpartum Depression, and Early Mother–Infant Interactions." *Developmental Psychology* 21: 1152–56.

Filmer, D., J. Friedman, and N. Schady. 2009. "Development, Modernization, and Childbearing: The Role of Family Sex Composition." *World Bank Economic Review* 23(3): 371–98.

Fischer, K., and S. Rose. 1994. "Dynamic Development of Coordination of Components in Brain and Behavior: A Framework for Theory and Research." In *Human Behavior and the Developing Brain*, ed. K. Fischer and G. Dawson, 3–66. New York: Guilford.

Fishman, Steven M., Laura E. Caulfield, Mercedes de Onis, Monika Blossner, Adnan A. Hyder, Luke Mullany, and Robert E. Black. 2004. "Childhood and Maternal Underweight." In Vol. 1 of *Comparative Quantification of Health Risks: Global and Regional Burden of Disease Attributable to Selected Major Risk Factors*, ed. Majid Ezzati, Alan D. Lopez, Anthony Rogers, and Christopher J. L. Murray, 39-162. Geneva: World Health Organization.

Frankenberg, E., D. Thomas, and K. Beegle. 1999. "The Real Costs of Indonesia's Economic Crisis: Preliminary Findings from the Indonesia Family Life Surveys." Working Paper 99-04, RAND Corporation, Santa Monica, CA.

Friedman, J., and N. Schady. 2009. "How Many More Infants Are Likely to Die in Africa as a Result of the Global Financial Crisis?" Policy Research Working Paper 5023, World Bank, Washington, DC.

Gardner, H., and C. Kosmitzki. 2008. *Lives across Cultures: Cross-Cultural Human Development*. New York, NY: Pearson Education.

Gardner, J. M., S. P. Walker, C. A. Powell, and S. Grantham-McGregor. 2003. "A Randomized Controlled Trial of a Home-Visiting Intervention on Cognition and Behavior in Term Low Birth Weight Infants." *Journal of Pediatrics* 143 (5): 634–39.

Gershoff, E., J. L. Aber, C. Raver, C., and M. C. Lennon. 2007. "Income Is Not Enough: Incorporating Material Hardship into Models of Income Associations with Parenting and Child Development." *Child Development* 78 (1): 70–95.

Giedd, J., J. Blumenthal, N. Jeffries, F. Castellanos, H. Liu, A. Zijdenbos, T. Paus, A. Evans, and J. Rapoport. 1999. "Brain Development during Childhood and Adolescence: A Longitudinal MRI Study." *Nature Neuroscience* 2 (10): 861–63.

Gordon, N. 1995. "Apoptosis (Programmed Cell Death) and Other Reasons for Elimination of Neurons and Axons." *Brain and Development* 17 (1): 73–77.

Gorman, K. S., and E. Pollitt. 1992. "Relationship between Weight and Body Proportionality at Birth, Growth during the First Year of Life, and Cognitive Development at 36, 48, and 60 Months." *Infant Behavior and Development* 15 (3): 279–96.

Grantham-McGregor, S. M., P. I. Lira, A. Ashworth, S. S. Morris, and A. M. Assuncao. 1998. "The Development of Low Birth Weight Term Infants and the Effects of the Environment in Northeast Brazil." *Journal of Pediatrics* 132 (4): 661–66.

Grantham-McGregor, S., C. Walker, S. Chang, and C. Powell. 1997. "Effects of Early Childhood Supplementation with and without Stimulation on Later Development in Stunted Jamaican Children." *American Journal of Clinical Nutrition* 66 (2): 247–53.

Greenough, W. T., and J. E. Black. 1992. "Induction of Brain Structure by Experience: Substrates for Cognitive Development." In *Developmental Behavioral Neuroscience* (Minnesota Symposium on Child Psychology, Vol. 24), ed. M. R. Gunnar and C. A. Nelson, 155–200. Hillsdale, NJ: Erlbaum.

Greenough, W. T., J. E. Black, and C. S. Wallace. 1987. "Experience and Brain Development." *Child Development* 58 (3): 539–59.

Gross, J. J., and J. P. Oliver. 2003. "Individual Differences in Two Emotion Regulation Processes: Implications for Affect, Relationships, and Well-Being." *Journal of Personality and Social Psychology* 85 (2): 348–62.

Guralnick, M. J., R. Connor, M. Hammond, J. M. Gottman, and K. Kinnish. 1996. "The Peer Relations of Preschool Children with Communication Disorders." *Child Development* 67 (2): 471–89.

Helmers, C., and M. Patnam. 2010. "The Formation and Evolution of Childhood Skill Acquisition: Evidence from India." *Journal of Development Finance* 95 (2): 252–66.

Hidrobo, M. 2011. "The Effect of Ecuador's 1998–2000 Economic Crisis on Child Health and Cognitive Development." University of Berkeley, http://ecnr .berkeley.edu/vfs/PPs/Hidrobo-Mel/web/Hidrobo_JMP_1.16.11.pdf.

Hoddinott, J., and B. Kinsey. 2001. "Child Growth in the Time of Drought." *Oxford Bulletin of Economics and Statistics* 63 (4): 409–36.

Hoddinott, John, John A. Maluccio, Jere Behrman, Rafael Flores, and Reynaldo Martorell. 2008. "Effect of a Nutrition Intervention during Early Childhood on Economic Productivity in Guatemalan Adults." *Lancet* 371 (9610): 411–16.

Horton, S., H. Alderman, and J. A. Rivera. 2008. "The Challenge of Hunger and Malnutrition." Copenhagen Consensus 2008 Challenge Paper, Copenhagen Consensus Center, Copenhagen.

Hossain, N., and J. A. McGregor. 2011. "'A Lost Generation'? Impacts of Complex Compound Crises on Children and Young People." *Development Policy Review* 29 (5): 565–84.

Houwer, de, A. 1995. "Bilingual Language Acquisition." In *The Handbook of Child Language*, ed. P. Fletcher, 219–50. Oxford, UK: Blackwell.

Huttenlocher, P. R., and A. S. Dabholkar. 1997. "Regional Differences in Synaptogenesis in the Human Cerebral Cortex." *Journal of Comparative Neurology* 387 (2): 167–78.

Jamison, Dean T., Martin E. Sandbu, and Jia Wang. 2004. "Why Has Infant Mortality Decreased at Such Different Rates in Different Countries?" Working Paper 21, Disease Control Priorities Project, http://www.dcp2.org /main/Home.html.

Jensen, Robert. 2000. "Agricultural Volatility and Investments in Children." *American Economic Review* 90 (2): 399–404.

Johnson, M. 2005. "Developmental Neuroscience, Psychophysiology, and Genetics." In *Developmental Science: An Advanced Textbook*, 5th ed., ed. M. Bornstein and M. Lamb, 187–222. Hillsdale, NJ: Erlbaum.

Kochanska, G. 1995. "Children's Temperament, Mothers' Discipline, and Security of Attachment: Multiple Pathways to Emerging Internalization." *Child Development* 66 (3): 597–615.

Lam, D., and S. Duryea. 1999. "Effects of Schooling on Fertility, Labor Supply, and Investments in Children, with Evidence from Brazil." *Journal of Human Resources* 34 (1): 160–92.

Lieberman, S., M. Juwono, and P. Marzoeki. 2001. "Government Health Expenditures in Indonesia through December 2000: An Update." East Asia and the Pacific Region Watching Brief 6, World Bank, Washington, DC.

Lumey, L. H., and A. D. Stein. 1997. "In Utero Exposure to Famine and Subsequent Fertility: The Dutch Famine Birth Cohort Study." *American Journal of Public Health* 87 (12): 1962–66.

Lumey, L. H., A. D. Stein, H. S. Kahn, K. M. Van der Pal-de Bruin, G. J. Blauw, P. A. Zybert, and E. S. Susser. 2007. "Cohort Profile: The Dutch Hunger Winter Families Study." *International Journal of Epidemiology* 36 (6): 1196–204.

Luthar, S. S. 2006. "Resilience in Development: A Synthesis of Research across Five Decades." In *Risk, Disorder, and Adaptation.* Vol. 3 of *Developmental Psychopathology,* 2nd ed., ed. D. Cicchetti and D. J. Cohen, 739–95. Hoboken, NJ: Wiley.

Maccini, Sharon, and Dean Yang. 2009. "Under the Weather: Health, Schooling, and Economic Consequences of Early-Life Rainfall." *American Economic Review* 99 (3): 1006–26

Macours, K., N. Schady, and R. Vakis. 2008. "Cash Transfers, Behavioral Changes, and Cognitive Development in Early Childhood: Evidence from a Randomized Experiment." Policy Research Working Paper 4759, World Bank, Washington, DC.

Maluccio, John. 2005. "Coping with the Coffee Crisis in Central America: The Role of the Nicaraguan Red de Protección Social." FCND Discussion Paper 188, International Food Policy Research Institute, Washington, DC.

Maluccio, John A., John Hoddinott, Jere R. Behrman, Agnes Quisumbing, Reynaldo Martorell, and Aryeh D. Stein. 2009. "The Impact of Nutrition during Early Childhood on Education among Guatemalan Adults." *Economic Journal* 119 (April): 734–63.

Manuck, S. B. 2009. "The Reaction Norm in Gene × Environment Interaction." *Molecular Psychiatry* 15 (9): 881–82.

Maughan, A., D. Cicchetti, S. Toth, and F. Rogosch. 2007. "Early Occurring Maternal Depression and Maternal Negativity in Predicting Young Children's Emotion Regulation and Socioemotional Difficulties." *Journal of Abnormal Child Psychology* 35 (5): 685–703.

Mayer, S. E. 1997. *What Money Can't Buy: Family Income and Children's Life Chances.* Cambridge, MA: Harvard University Press.

McCormick, M. C. 1985. "The Contribution of Low Birth Weight to Infant Mortality and Childhood Morbidity." *New England Journal of Medicine* 312 (2): 82–90.

Mendez, M. A., and L. S. Adair. 1999. "Severity and Timing of Stunting in the First Two Years of Life Affect Performance on Cognitive Tests in Late Childhood." *Journal of Nutrition* 129 (8): 1555–62.

Miller, P. J., and D. Davis. 1997. "Poverty History, Marital History, and Quality of Children's Home Environments." *Journal of Marriage and the Family* 59 (4): 996–1007.

Miller, G., and B. P. Urdinola. 2010. "Cyclicality, Mortality, and the Value of Time: The Case of Coffee Price Fluctuations and Child Survival in Colombia." *Journal of Political Economy* 118 (1): 113–55.

Mistry, R., E. Vandewater, A. Huston, and V. McLoyd. 2002. "Economic Well-Being and Children's Social Adjustment: The Role of Family Process in an Ethnically Diverse Low-Income Sample." *Child Development* 73 (3): 935–51.

Morgan, B. L. G., and M. Winick. 1985. "Pathologic Effects of Malnutrition on the Central Nervous System." In *Nutritional Pathology: Pathobiochemistry of Dietary Imbalances,* ed. H. Sidransky, 161–206. New York, NY: Dekker.

Naudeau, S., N. Kataoka, A. Valerio, M. J. Neuman, and L. K. Elder. 2010. *Investing in Young Children: An Early Childhood Development Guide for Policy Dialogue and Project Preparation.* Washington, DC: World Bank.

Naudeau, S., S. Martinez, P. Premand, and D. Filmer. 2011. "Cognitive Development among Young Children in Low-Income Countries." In *No Small Matter: The Impact of Poverty, Shocks, and Human Capital Investments in Early Childhood Development,* ed. H. Alderman, 9–50. Washington, DC: World Bank.

Neugebauer, R., H. W. Hoek, and E. Susser. 1999. "Prenatal Exposure to Wartime Famine and Development of Antisocial Personality Disorder in Early Adulthood." *American Medical Association* 281(5): 455–62.

Nelson, C., M. de Haan, and K. Thomas. 2006. *Neuroscience of Cognitive Development: The Role of Experience and the Developing Brain.* New York: Wiley.

Nokes, C., C. van den Bosch, and D. Bundy. 1998. *The Effects of Iron Deficiency and Anemia on Mental and Motor Performance, Educational Achievement, and Behavior in Children.* Washington, DC: International Nutritional Anemia Consulting Group.

Obradović, J., N. R. Bush, J. Stamperdahl, N. E. Adler, and W. T. Boyce. 2010. "Biological Sensitivity to Context: The Interactive Effects of Stress Reactivity and Family Adversity on Socio-emotional Behavior and School Readiness." *Child Development* 81 (1): 270–89.

O'Brien, L. M., E. G. Heycock, M. Hanna, P. W. Jones, and J. L. Cox. 2004. "Postnatal Depression and Faltering Growth: A Community Study." Pt. 1. *Pediatrics* 113 (5): 1242–47.

Paxson, C., and N. Schady. 2004. "Child Health and the 1988–92 Economic Crisis in Peru." World Bank Policy Research Working Paper 3260, World Bank, Washington, DC.

———. 2005. "Child Health and Economic Crisis in Peru." *World Bank Economic Review* 19 (2): 203–33.

———. 2007. "Cognitive Development among Young Children in Ecuador: The Roles of Wealth, Health, and Parenting." *Journal of Human Resources* 42 (1): 49–84.

Pongou, R., J. A. Salomon, and M. Ezzati. 2006. "Health Impacts of Macroeconomic Crises and Policies: Determinants of Variation in Childhood Malnutrition Trends in Cameroon." *International Journal of Epidemiology* 35 (3): 648–56.

Prause, J., D. Dooley, and J. Huh. 2009. "Income Volatility and Psychological Depression." *American Journal of Community Psychology* 43 (1): 57–70.

Pritchett, Lant, and Lawrence H. Summers. 1996. "Wealthier Is Healthier." *Journal of Human Resources* 31 (4): 841–68.

Psacharopoulos, G. 1989. "The Determinants of Early Age Human Capital Formation: Evidence from Brazil." *Economic Development and Cultural Change* 37 (4): 683–708.

Quas, J. A., A. Bauer, and W. T. Boyce. 2004. "Physiological Reactivity, Social Support, and Memory in Early Childhood." *Child Development* 75 (3): 797–814.

Raver, C. C., C. Blair, M. Willoughby, and Family Life Project Key Investigators. Forthcoming. "Poverty as a Predictor of 4-Year-Olds' Executive Function: New Perspectives on Models of Differential Susceptibility." *Developmental Psychology*.

Rogoff, B. 2003. *The Cultural Nature of Human Development*. New York: Oxford University Press.

Roisman, G., A. Masten, D. Coatsworth, and A. Tellegen. 2004. "Salient and Emerging Developmental Tasks in the Transition to Adulthood." *Child Development* 75 (1): 123–33.

Rosenzweig, M. R., and K. I. Wolpin. 1994. "Are There Increasing Returns to the Intergenerational Production of Human Capital? Maternal Schooling and Child Intellectual Achievement." *Journal of Human Resources* 29 (2): 670–93.

Rucci, Graciana. 2004. "The Role of Macroeconomic Crisis on Births and Infant Health: The Argentine Case." Unpublished manuscript, University of California, Los Angeles.

Ruhm, C. 2000. "Are Recessions Good for Your Health?" *Quarterly Journal of Economics* 115 (2): 617–50.

Ruhm, C., and W. Black. 2002. "Does Drinking Really Decrease during Bad Times?" *Journal of Health Economics* 21 (4): 659–78.

Rukumnuaykit, Pungpond. 2003. "Crises and Health Outcomes: The Impacts of Economic and Drought/Smoke Crises on Infant Mortality and Birthweight in Indonesia." Unpublished manuscript, Michigan State University, East Lansing.

Rutter, M. 1982. "Epidemiological-Longitudinal Approaches to the study of Development." In *The Concept of Development*, ed. W. A. Collins, 105-144. Hillsdale, NJ: Erlbaum.

Sameroff, A. 2010. "A Unified Theory of Development: A Dialectic Integration of Nature and Nurture." *Child Development* 81 (1): 6–22.

Sameroff, A. J., R. Seifer, A. Baldwin, and C. Baldwin. 1993. "Stability of Intelligence from Preschool to Adolescence: The Influence of Social and Family Risk Factors." *Child Development* 64 (1): 80–97.

Sarkar, P., K. Bergman, T. G. O'Connor, and V. Glover. 2008. "Maternal Antenatal Anxiety and Amniotic Fluid Cortisol and Testosterone: Possible Implications for Foetal Programming." *Journal of Neuroendocrinology* 20 (4): 489–96.

Schady, Norbert, and Marc-Francois Smitz. 2010. "Aggregate Economic Shocks and Infant Mortality: New Evidence for Middle-Income Countries." *Economics Letters* 108 (2): 145–48.

Schmithorst, V., and W. Yuan. 2010. "White Matter Development during Adolescence as Shown by Diffusion MRI." *Brain and Cognition* 72 (1): 16–25.

Schweinhart, L. J., H. V. Barnes, and D. P. Weikart. 1993. *Significant Benefits: The High/Scope Perry Preschool Study through Age 27*. Monographs of the High Scope Educational Research Foundation Series, no. 10. Ypsilanti, MI: High/Scope Press.

Shkolnikov, Vladimir, Giovanni Cornia, David Leon, and France Mesle. 1998. "Causes of the Russian Mortality Crisis: Evidence and Interpretations." *World Development* 26 (11): 1995–2011.

Shonkoff, J. P., and D. Phillips, eds. 2000. *From Neurons to Neighborhoods: The Science of Early Childhood Development*. Washington, DC: National Academy Press.

Smith, J. R., J. Brooks-Gunn, and P. Klebanov. 1997. "The Consequences of Living in Poverty for Young Children's Cognitive and Verbal Ability and Early School Achievement." In *Consequences of Growing Up Poor*, ed. G. J. Duncan, and J. Brooks-Gunn 132–89. New York: Russell Sage Foundation.

Sroufe, L. A., and B. Egeland. 1991. "Illustrations of Person-Environment Interaction from a Longitudinal Study." In *Conceptualization and Measurement of Organism-Environment Interaction*, ed. T. D. Wachs and R. Plomin, 68–84. Washington, DC: American Psychological Association.

St. Clair, D., M. Xu, P. Wang, Y. Yu, Y. Fang, F. Zhang, X. Zheng, N. Gu, G. Feng, P. Sham, and L. He. 2005. "Rates of Adult Schizophrenia Following Prenatal Exposure to the Chinese Famine of 1959–1961." *Journal of the American Medical Association* 294 (5): 557–62.

Stillman, Steven, and Duncan Thomas. 2004. "The Effect of Economic Crises on Nutritional Status: Evidence from Russia." Discussion Paper 1092, Institute for the Study of Labor (IZA), Bonn.

Strauss, J., K. Beegle, A. Dwiyanto, Y. Herawati, D. Pattinasarany, E. Satriawan, B. Sikoki, Sukamdi, and F. Witoelar. 2004. *Indonesian Living Standards before and after the Financial Crisis*. Santa Monica, CA: RAND Corporation.

Strauss, John, and Duncan Thomas. 1998. "Health, Nutrition, and Economic Development." *Journal of Economic Literature* 36 (2): 766–817.

Susser, E., H. Hoek, and A. Brown. 1998. "Neurodevelopmental Disorders after Prenatal Famine: The Story of the Dutch Famine Study." *American Journal of Epidemiology* 147 (3): 213–16.

Susser, E. S., and S. P. Lin. 1992. "Schizophrenia after Prenatal Exposure to the Dutch Hunger Winter of 1944–1945." *Archives of General Psychiatry* 49 (12): 983–88.

Susser, E., R. Neugebauer, H. W. Hoek, S. Lin, D. Labovity, and J. M. Gorman. 1996. "Schizophrenia after Prenatal Famine: Further Evidence." *Archives of General Psychiatry* 53 (1): 25–31.

Tobi, E. W., L. H. Lumey, R, P. Talens, D. Kremer, H. Putter, A. D. Stein, P. E. Sagboom, and B. T. Heijmans. 2009. "DNA Methylation Differences after Exposure to Prenatal Famine Are Common and Timing- and Sex-Specific." *Human Molecular Genetics* 18 (21): 4046–53.

van den Berg, Gerard J., Maarten Lindeboom, and France Portrait. 2006. "Economic Conditions Early in Life and Individual Mortality." *American Economic Review* 96 (1): 290–302.

van Doesum, K., J. Riksen-Walraven, C. Hosman, and C. Hoefnagels. 2008. "A Randomized Controlled Trial of a Home-Visiting Intervention aimed at Preventing Relationship Problems in Depressed Mothers and Their Infants." *Child Development* 79 (3): 547–61.

Villar, J., and J. Belizan. 1982. "The Relative Contribution of Prematurity and Fetal Growth Retardation to Low Birth Weight in Developing and Developed Societies." *American Journal of Obstetrics and Gynecology* 143 (7): 793.

Votruba-Drzal, E. 2003. "Income Changes and Cognitive Stimulation in Young Children's Home Learning Environments." *Journal of Marriage and the Family* 65 (2): 341–55.

Walker, S. P., S. M. Chang, C. A. Powell, and S. M. Grantham-McGregor. 2004. "Psychosocial Intervention Improves the Development of Term Low Birth-Weight Infants." *Journal of Nutrition* 134 (6): 1417–23.

Walker, S. P., T. D. Wachs, J. M. Gardner, B. Lozoff, G. A. Wasserman, E. Pollitt, and J. A. Carter. 2007. "Child Development: Risk Factors for Adverse Outcomes in Developing Countries." *Lancet* 369 (9556): 145–57.

Waters, H., F. Saadah, and M. Pradhan. 2003. "The Impact of the 1997–98 East Asian Economic Crisis on Health and Health Care in Indonesia." *Health Policy and Planning* 18 (2): 172–81.

Yamano, Takashi, Harold Alderman, and Luc Christiaensen. 2005. "Child Growth, Shocks, and Food Aid in Rural Ethiopia." *American Journal of Agricultural Economics* 87 (2): 273–88.

CHAPTER 4

Aggregate Economic Shocks during Middle Childhood

Susan Parker and Carly Tubbs

Middle childhood has received significantly less attention in the academic literature than early childhood. Much of the research in economics from developing countries looks at schooling—in particular, school enrollment, attendance, or dropout rate. Very little is known from this body of literature about socioemotional, behavioral, or underlying cognitive development, especially during crisis times. Based on the conceptual framework (chapter 2), this chapter reviews the empirical evidence from various disciplines on how aggregate economic shocks affect development during middle childhood This chapter begins with an introduction to development during middle childhood and then reviews the existing evidence linking crises to schooling indicators. We then endeavor to advance our understanding of the observed heterogeneity in short-, medium-, and, in particular, long-term outcomes by incorporating concepts and evidence from developmental science.

Middle Childhood Development: An Introduction

Because early childhood is a period of both extreme growth and extreme vulnerability, researchers, practitioners, and policy makers alike have traditionally focused more attention on early childhood than on other times in children's development. However, during middle childhood (approximately 6–12 years old), children develop many of the basic skills and competencies that will shape their current and future success in school, work, and personal relationships (Lerner 1998). Physical health and development, of course, remain an important domain; and, in particular, exposing children to work settings that put their physical health and development at risk is of major concern. Literature from diverse fields of study, however, tends to focus on children's cognitive, behavioral, and socioemotional development during middle childhood.

Two developmental tasks that build on the physical, cognitive, and socioemotional capacities attained during early childhood become particularly salient during middle childhood: (1) the ability to learn and reason systematically about increasingly complex problems and circumstances and (2) the development of interpersonal negotiation and social problem-solving skills (Aber and Jones 1997; Eccles 1999; Collins, Madsen, and Susman-Stillman 2008). These developmental tasks emerge as children encounter different settings outside the family unit—most commonly formal schooling and peer group settings but, particularly in developing countries, work settings as well—that become key factors in shaping their development (Harkness and Super 1983).

Learning and Reasoning

Based on the myriad cognitive, socioemotional, and biological advances of early childhood, children's cognitive abilities during middle childhood expand in three significant ways. First, children learn how to reason more abstractly about objects and events, developing the skills to solve complex problems systematically. Second, they begin to engage in planful behavior, which includes setting goals, organizing tasks in service of those goals, and monitoring their behaviors and mental processes. Finally, children have the increased opportunity and capacity to acquire new knowledge and to use this knowledge in solving problems, reasoning abstractly, and setting goals (Collins, Madsen, and Susman-Stillman 2008).

These cognitive skills emerge gradually in concert with changes in children's roles and responsibilities, which vary substantially according to the cultural context in which they are embedded (Gardner and Kosmitzki 2008). For instance, in many countries around the world, middle childhood corresponds to the age at which children enter a formal educational system. These systems prepare children for eventual responsibilities in their societies by promoting the mastery of cognitive skills through structured curriculums and interactions with nonfamilial adults and peers.

However, children also develop complex cognitive skills through informal learning that takes place as they acquire additional responsibilities within family, community, or work contexts. In turn, the development of these middle-childhood cognitive skills is important for success in a variety of settings: children's cognitive skills during middle childhood are associated with their short-term (Silliphant 1983; Cohen, Bronson, and Casey 1995) and long-term school achievement (Alexander, Entwisle, and Horsey 1997; Jimerson et al. 2000); and they predict later life outcomes such as employment and risk-taking behaviors (Heckman, Stixrud, and Urzua 2006).

Children's cognitive development at this stage depends on a number of factors along multiple dimensions that reciprocally interact with each other over time. These factors include genetic influences and brain development, children's self-regulatory and interpersonal skills, parental involvement and investment, supportive peer and teacher relationships, and neighborhood and school structures, to name only a few. Although it is difficult to disentangle how all these factors interact to shape children's cognitive development, to the extent that an economic crisis affects any of these factors, children's cognitive development during middle childhood may be at risk.

Developing Interpersonal and Social Problem-Solving Skills

Advances in children's cognitive abilities during middle childhood coincide with their increased social understanding and competency: that is, their ability to understand and negotiate relationships with themselves and others, to make sense of life events, and to reason about abstract social norms. Such competency develops as children experience qualitative changes in their social-cognitive abilities. Specifically, during middle childhood children learn to take into account the perspective of others, to interpret social behaviors and cues, and to compare themselves to others (McHale, Dariotis, and Kauh 2003). Along with an emergent sense of self, these social skills contribute to their self-awareness and to their ability to understand and evaluate themselves (Harter 1999).

Children's burgeoning social competencies both result from and encourage further participation in increasingly complex social interactions with an expanding array of people, including teachers, same- and different-age peers, and neighbors. Because the type of people children encounter, the nature of the relationships they form with those people, and the competencies that promote the establishment of such relationships vary according to the cultural and historical contexts, it is impossible to draw broad conclusions about how, exactly, such competencies and relationships form (Gardner and Kosmitzki 2008). However, children's social competencies across a variety of settings have important implications for their development. In the school context, children who are less socially competent in middle childhood have more negative and conflictual relationships with teachers, which in turn predict trajectories of behavioral and academic problems into adolescence (Birch and Ladd 1998; Hamre and Pianta 2001). In the peer context, children who exhibit fewer social skills tend to be less accepted by their peers; in turn, peer rejection predicts children's internalizing (for example, anxiety or depression) and externalizing (for example, aggression or delinquency) behaviors, as well as their school adjustment and school achievement motivation (Ladd 1999). Finally, in the work context, middle-childhood social competency has been found to significantly predict work competency in early adulthood, even adjusting for the quality of early family functioning and adolescent friendships (Collins and van Dulmen 2006).

Family environments are one of the major factors determining the development of children's social understanding and competency, particularly during early and middle childhood. For example, children who had secure relationships with their caregivers in early childhood tend to exhibit better social skills with peers during middle childhood than those who were insecurely attached (Parke and Ladd 1992). As discussed in chapter 3, children are more likely to form insecure attachments in early childhood when their caregivers are depressed, a condition an economic crisis may make more likely. This example illustrates what is referred to as a "developmental cascade" (Masten and Cicchetti 2010). That is, an economic crisis that occurs during early childhood may have effects that cascade into middle childhood and beyond. Unfortunately, there is little empirical evidence on how an economic shock during middle childhood may affect the development of children's social competency.

In sum, family and school remain the two dominant and most studied settings in which children acquire important cognitive and socioemotional competencies during middle childhood. As the conceptual framework describes in chapter 2, these settings are linked, and their interactions constitute a mesosystem: family dynamics influence children's schooling experience and vice versa. While developmental lags might originate in early childhood—for example, through insecure attachment—middle childhood also offers an opportunity for "corrective" intervention as children spend, under most circumstances, a large part of their time in school settings. Thus, while ultimately we are interested in cognitive and socioemotional development, understanding schooling decisions is equally important. We thus turn to the evidence first on schooling decisions and then on actual developmental outcomes.

Economic Crisis and Schooling during Middle Childhood

While the main focus of this volume is on the impact of aggregate economic shocks, we include idiosyncratic economic shocks as well as natural disasters to supplement the rather scarce evidence from systemic economic shocks and to learn some important lessons from the effects of aggregate shocks in general. In economic terms, the distinction between aggregate and idiosyncratic shocks is important, as is discussed in the conceptual framework with regard to the failure of informal insurance networks when large segments of society are affected simultaneously and systematically. A large literature begun by Townsend (1994) studies the extent to which households apparently have access to at least partial informal insurance that they use to smooth the effects of shocks. We touch on the question of informal insurance in our examination of why, for example, households do not withdraw children from school when a household head becomes unemployed. While keeping a child in school during a crisis suggests that the household has other means of smoothing consumption, there are many other factors that influence the decision about children's schooling.

As noted earlier, the outcomes of interest in many of these studies are school enrollment and attendance, dropout, or grade progression. Other studies look at educational disparities or changes in inequalities (Eloundou-Enyegue and Davanzo 2003). Enrollment or attendance may be weak proxies for learning outcomes, which might be better measured, for instance, by standardized achievement tests. In addition, later life outcomes depend not only on cognitive development but also on socioemotional and behavioral development as was outlined earlier (for example, Heckman, Stixrud, and Urzua 2006). We thus proceed to a review of the developmental literature to shed light on the processes underlying some of the observed outcomes in enrollment and progression. In other words, we would like to understand more clearly how or why families may choose to pull their children out of school or why a parent's job loss may ultimately affect children's cognitive outcomes above and beyond a shock to household income.

Because children at this age encounter settings outside the family unit—most commonly, formal schooling—changes wrought by an economic crisis in both family and school contexts are likely to affect them. We have thus chosen to focus on these two main settings, family and school, elaborating in each section on the pathways through which an economic shock may affect children's cognitive and socioemotional development.

The Family Context: Household Dynamics and Educational Decisions

Given the particular characteristics of this stage of development, whether or not children stay in school or go to work during an economic crisis depends largely on how the crisis affects the family. Economic models tend to focus on how a crisis affects wage rates or employment patterns, which may or may not result in a decrease in household income. Once an economic crisis has affected a household, however, both economic and psychosocial models of family and household processes can be employed to explain how the household copes with and adjusts to the new circumstances; these adjustments and coping strategies then have implications for children's outcomes. For example, economic models often look at how households adjust their consumption patterns given a set of constraints and contextual factors. More specifically, with regard to decisions affecting education or human capital investment, changes in the macroeconomic conditions are likely to change the factors that determine income and substitution effects (for more detail on income and substitution effects and measurement of aggregate economic shocks, see annex 4A). The income effects stem from the reduction in household resources due to falling wage rates or unexpected job loss, whereas the substitution effect stems from lower opportunity costs, given, for example, tight labor markets.

Thus, in response to a drop in market wage rates, a household might increase its labor supply as it attempts to counter the resulting fall in income. On the expenditure side, the income effect may also lead a household to cut costs where possible. For instance, education is associated with present costs, both direct (in the form of school fees, books, uniforms, and transportation) and indirect (opportunity costs, often measured in the income forgone while spending time in school, traveling to and from, and studying). Hence, a household may decide to reduce expenditures on school supplies and, in the worst case, to pull its children out of school. The substitution effect reflects the opportunity costs of education and is often proxied by wage rates, which may fall in a crisis and lead to a decrease in labor supply or an increase in schooling. The overall net effect of macroeconomic crises on schooling is then ambiguous and subject to empirical investigation.

However, what economic studies of such schooling decisions often fail to capture are the underlying processes leading to the observed outcomes, for instance, the stresses brought about by economic hardship and how such changes alter family dynamics. In addition, despite these apparently objective determinants, concepts of what is needed or what constitutes a standard of living are subjective. They vary across historical time and place, across social groups, and even across individuals within a family (Shmink 1984). Across individuals, perceptions of what is needed or adequate may vary based on personality characteristics (optimism versus pessimism, for example), personal values (such as individual ideas of what is desirable), aspiration or expectation levels (the standard of living an individual aspires to or expects to attain, for instance), or social comparisons (the standard of living of others in one's social group). At the same time, all these individual characteristics may be reciprocally influenced by wider social norms (Campbell, Converse, and Rodgers 1976; Danes and Rettig 1993a). Then, as part of a household unit, individuals must negotiate their own perceptions and goals with those of other involved decision makers. The prevailing decision may be based on relative agreement between household members or it may reflect conflict across power differentials, such as generations and sexes (Shmink 1984; Danes and Rettig 1993b). In the latter case, individual preferences may diverge so far that the single utility function represented in unitary models of household decision making does not suffice (Arthur 1982). In fact, substantial empirical evidence rejects the unitary household model (Doss 1996; Chiappori et al. 1993) and supports intrahousehold bargaining models in a myriad of contexts (see, for example, Carter and Katz 1997; McElroy and Horney 1981; Horney and McElroy 1988; Chiappori 1992; Browning et al. 1994). Such models provide insights into how households arrive at decisions about investments in human capital (see Strauss and Thomas 2005).

Unfortunately, there is a dearth of empirical information about the processes by which individuals within households negotiate diverse perceptions about current economic conditions and aspirations about future economic well-being, both of which shape the decisions that are made in the bargaining process. The few studies that do exist are largely cross-sectional in nature and do not allow us to disentangle the sequencing of such processes. However, according to one study of rural families in the U.S. Midwest during the agricultural crisis of the 1980s, individual perceptions of whether objective economic constraints are enough to meet their subjective needs are associated with individuals' perceptions of control over the situation. Those who perceived themselves as having no control over their economic situation—as may happen in a widespread economic crisis—were more likely to perceive their objective economic resources as inadequate (Danes and Rettig 1993a). In a follow-up study, individuals who perceived their economic resources as inadequate were more likely to take action to decrease their household expenditures and increase their household production activities but less likely to spend time analyzing their economic situation, to seek information about their financial situation, or to plan for their future (Rettig, Leichtentritt, and Danes 1999). The evidence suggests that when individuals perceive their resources as inadequate to meet their needs, they may feel pressured to decrease their household expenditures (for example, by pulling their children out of school) with or without being fully aware of the long-term consequences of these decisions.

Thus, psychological models of household economic processes focus on how resource constraints affect individual behaviors and beliefs by shaping family relationships and practices. The most prominent model in the psychological and sociological literature is the Family Stress Model (Conger and Elder 1994), which was derived from data collected to explain the linkages among idiosyncratic household economic shocks, family processes, and child outcomes in U.S. families who experienced the Great Depression of the 1930s and the farm crisis of the 1980s. In the context of our analysis, the Family Stress Model does not directly provide information on aggregate economic crises. Nevertheless, the Family Stress Model can provide information on how economic pressure within families—a condition that may be made more likely by an aggregate economic shock—may then have a variety of consequences for both parents' and children's future well-being (for more information see box 4.1).

The Short-Term Impacts of Economic Crisis on Schooling

Aggregate economic shocks and children's schooling. Ferreira and Schady (2009) recently reviewed the literature on the impact of aggregate shocks on children's schooling and health. After a brief review of their findings, we describe some additional studies, including literature on idiosyncratic shocks, that focus on the concrete transmission mechanisms through which children's schooling is affected.

Box 4.1

Parenting in a Cultural Context and the Family Stress Model

Across cultures, the family is one of the primary components of children's microsystems. While decades of research have documented the important role that parenting plays in the development of children's cognitive, socioemotional, and behavioral competencies, much of this research has been based on middle-class, European-American families in the United States (Spencer and McLoyd 1990). However, according to the bioecological model of human development described in the conceptual framework in chapter 2, parenting beliefs and practices will be influenced by—and also influence—the sociocultural contexts in which families are embedded (Bronfenbrenner and Morris 2006). As such, parenting beliefs and practices—and their associations with children's outcomes—are subject to individual, group (for example, a gender or neighborhood group), cultural, and historical variation (Super and Harkness 1994). Parenting beliefs and practices may also be shaped by economic hardships, with important implications for children's well-being (Conger and Donnellan 2007).

Parenting Styles and Children's Outcomes

According to Baumrind's (1971) influential typology of parent-child interactions, three different styles of interactions are likely to vary across families and to influence children's development significantly. *Authoritative* parenting involves high levels of warmth and responsiveness, clarity and consistency in setting and enforcing rules and limits, and open communication between parents and children. *Authoritarian* parents, in contrast, tend to be highly controlling, demanding, and critical of their children, emphasizing obedience and respect for authority, with little warmth or responsiveness to their children's needs. *Permissive* parenting is characterized by high levels of warmth and responsiveness but little effort at discipline or rule setting. Maccoby and Martin (1983) subsequently amended this typology to include *neglectful* parenting, in which parents show little involvement on any dimension of parenting: low levels of warmth or responsiveness and little effort at setting expectations or rules.

The available literature indicates that compared to children with *authoritarian, permissive, or neglectful* parents, children in families with *authoritative* parents tend to have higher grades in elementary school, high school, and college; to have better relationships with peers; and to evidence fewer internalizing and

(continued next page)

Box 4.1 *(continued)*

externalizing behaviors (see, for example, Dornbusch et al. 1987; Fuligni and Eccles 1993; Steinberg et al. 1994; Wintre and Yaffe 2000; Steinberg 2001). In contrast, children with *authoritarian* parents fare less well in school, evidence less social competency with peers, and have a higher risk of internalizing problems (Baumrind 1991; Maccoby and Martin 1983; Barber and Harmon 2002). Finally, children with *permissive* or *neglectful* parents demonstrate more aggressiveness and antisocial behaviors and tend to have worse relationships with peers (Maccoby and Martin 1983; Steinberg et al. 1994; Pittman and Chase-Lansdale 2001).

Parenting Styles in a Cultural Context
These parenting styles were developed using primarily European-American middle-class samples. Thus, while these parenting styles may provide a helpful heuristic in certain contexts, research suggests that this taxonomy fails to adequately reflect the societal and cultural norms in which parent-child interactions are embedded. It may mischaracterize the quality and implications of such interactions in at least two ways. First, research indicates that the associations between parenting styles and children's outcomes vary according to the ethnic-racial, socioeconomic, and neighborhood context. For example, Florsheim, Tolan, and Gorman-Smith (1998) found that authoritarian parenting among urban African and Latino American male adolescents was associated with fewer risky and delinquent behaviors than authoritative parenting, the opposite of the pattern observed among European-American parent-child interactions. The authors and others suggest that strict and harsh authoritarian parenting may serve a protective function in the context of the dangers and risks to which urban, inner-city youth may be exposed (Brody and Flor 1998). Others contest the inherent validity of these parenting styles when applied across cultures and contexts. For example, Chao and Tseng (2002) note that strict and demanding authoritative parenting in Chinese-American families is seen as an indicator of concern and caring and, as such, as an indicator of warmth. None of Baumrind's typologies captures this style of parenting, which Chao (1994) describes as more akin to "training."

The Family Stress Model and Parenting
In the context of an economic hardship, parents may make a range of adjustments to their parenting behaviors. The Family Stress Model (FSM) (Conger and

(continued next page)

Box 4.1 *(continued)*

A number of studies, using data collected during the Great Depression and the Iowa farm crisis of the 1980s, explain how resource constraints alter family practices and interactions, such as parenting, and ultimately affect children's development (see, for example, Conger and Elder 1994; Conger et al. 1994; and Elder et al. 1992). The FSM proposes that when an economic hardship hits the household, families may face more difficulties making ends meet. They may no longer be able to pay their bills, buy adequate food, or afford to pay for housing. According to the FSM, these are "the experiences that give psychological meaning to economic hardship experiences" (Conger and Conger 2002; Conger et al. 1994). For example, parents may have different perceptions of and feelings about the difficulties they are experiencing; one person may be extremely worried about being behind on the rent, while another person may be calmer. Given that parents are typically responsible for paying bills and making fiscal decisions in families, parents—not children—bear the direct brunt of these economic pressures.

Parents who experience economic pressure have an increased risk of emotional problems like depression and anxiety and behavior problems like substance abuse (Mistry et al. 2002; Conger and Conger 2008), both of which may lead to or exacerbate marital conflict (Vinokur, Price, and Caplan 1996). In turn, parents who experience substantial marital conflict or emotional distress may be less likely to demonstrate consistent and warm parenting toward their children. For example, they may show less affection toward or involvement with their children, and they may be more hostile, punitive, and inconsistent in disciplining them. Such practices then put children's cognitive and socioemotional development at risk (for a review, see Conger and Donnellan 2007). Support for this model, suggesting the power of economic hardships to alter family practices and interactions, has been found across and within countries around the world, in nationally representative U.S. samples (Gershoff et al. 2007) and in African American (Conger et al. 2002), Latino American (Formoso et al. 2007), and Asian American (Benner and Kim 2010) samples, as well as samples from Turkey (Aytaç and Rankin 2009), the Czech Republic (Hraba, Lorenz, and Pechacova 2000), Finland (Kinnunen and Pulkkinen 1998), and the Republic of Korea (Kwon et al. 2003). Taken together, these studies provide compelling evidence for adequately incorporating family dynamics into interventions and policy responses during economic crisis.

Note: Prepared by Carly Tubbs.

Ferreira and Schady (2009) review a number of studies for Latin America, including studies for Brazil, Costa Rica, Mexico, Nicaragua, and Peru. They conclude that in four of these five Latin American countries (the exception is Costa Rica), school enrollment was countercyclical; that is, the effect of the economic crises was to increase school enrollment. Outside of Latin America, they review studies of three other countries—Côte d'Ivoire, Indonesia, and Malawi[1]—all of which are generally much poorer contexts than Latin America. These countries show procyclical effects of the macroeconomic crisis, with school enrollment falling during the economic crisis in all three countries, although the overall effects are small in Indonesia and relatively larger in Côte d'Ivoire and Malawi. The authors hypothesize that in poorer environments economic crises are more likely to result in drops in school enrollment: that is, the income effect is larger than the substitution effect, whereas in less poor environments, impacts of the economic crisis are countercyclical, with the substitution effect dominating the income effect.

The results for Costa Rica and Nicaragua do not quite fit into this general pattern, however, with Costa Rica showing decreases in school enrollment during the economic crisis in spite of higher income levels and Nicaragua showing countercyclical effects in spite of income levels similar to Côte d'Ivoire and Malawi. Nevertheless, for the Costa Rican study, a number of household-level variables are included in the regression for schooling enrollment that are likely to capture idiosyncratic effects of the household crisis not measured in other studies. In particular, the Costa Rican study includes variables measuring the potential youth wages (capturing opportunity costs) as well as variables measuring the employment of the household head and household income. Thus, the effect of the year dummies, which is used to model the effect of the aggregate shocks, measures the effect of the aggregate shock net of the household unemployment and income changes associated with the aggregate shock. In that sense, this study is not entirely comparable with the others.

Ferreira and Schady (2009) include three studies of the United States in their review: Goldin (1999), Betts and McFarland (1995), and Kane (1994). While they look at older age groups, these studies might nevertheless provide insights into the behaviors and decisions about education during economic downturns. Betts and McFarland (1995) look at community college enrollment behavior, degree attainment, and financial data between the late 1960s and the mid-1980s, using the U.S. Department of Education's Higher Education General Information Survey/Integrated Postsecondary Education Data System, an annual census of postsecondary institutions, combined with labor market data from the March Supplements of the Current Population Survey for the population aged 18–65. According to their findings, community college enrollment shows a strong countercyclical response to the unemployment rate. Similarly, Goldin (1999) looks at high school enrollment during the Great Depression and finds that high school enrollment and graduation rates increased significantly as manufacturing jobs for young people fell. The significant reduction in jobs in general but in manufacturing in particular along with the National Industrial Recovery Act, which prohibited the hiring of youth in manufacturing, encouraged youth to remain in school.

These studies show that in the United States the evidence indicates strong countercyclical behavior between work and education for youth, on average. Deteriorating labor market conditions decrease the opportunity costs of education, leading to higher enrollment rates or graduation rates. However, subpopulations may show different behavior. Kane (1994) looks at college entry behavior since 1973 of African Americans 18 to 19 years old, using cross-sectional data from the yearly Current Population Survey on school enrollment, family income, and educational attainment. He finds substantial growth in enrollment of young African Americans during the 1973–75 recession, indicating countercyclicality, while the 1981–83 recession appears to have had a procyclical impact, resulting in a decline in enrollment rates.

Eloundou-Enyegue and Davanzo (2003) look at the economic downturn in Cameroon from 1987 to 1995, using schooling histories of 2,249 pupils. Collected in 1995, the data consisted of interviews with 812 women in both rural and urban communities in Cameroon's central province. They adjust for a long-term trend, using the logarithm of number of years since 1970. They control, among other things, for family socioeconomic status, measured in household amenities, size, and birth order. They estimate the probability that a child will drop out at the beginning of or during the year. Their main interest pertains to schooling inequalities by sex, residence, socioeconomic status, and family size. They conclude that some, but not all, types of inequalities worsened during the downturn. Inequalities between sex and family size increased; the crisis had no impact, however, on the educational inequality between rural and urban children, nor between wealthier and poorer households. They claim to find evidence that boys' education was favored over girls', while larger families seemed to have had resource constraints, which had a negative impact on children's education.

Idiosyncratic economic shocks and children's schooling. We now turn to studies of idiosyncratic shocks, focusing on economic shocks. By idiosyncratic shocks, we refer to shocks that affect only a fraction of households; the impacts of the shocks are identified by comparing households in which a shock occurs and households in which a shock does not occur. These studies, while generally having more plausible identification strategies based on less restrictive assumptions than studies of aggregate economic shocks, are still subject to criticism that the household shock variables may themselves be endogenous. For instance, households that are better able to smooth consumption and protect the human capital investment of their children may be more likely to incur longer unemployment spells than those less able to smooth consumption; thus the variable measuring unemployment shocks is not exogenous to variables such as children's schooling. Most studies deal with this particular criticism by focusing on variables measuring involuntary or unexpected unemployment due to, say, firings, although even individuals who are fired may have some idea in advance, which may affect their behavior on variables including their children's schooling. Similar issues arise in studies of health shocks—for example, of omitted variables that might affect both parental death or illness and children's schooling. A number of studies do carry out some tests of exogeneity of the shock variable (Duryea, Lam, and Levison 2007; Case and Ardington 2006); we describe these efforts below.

Duryea, Lam, and Levison (2007) use data from Brazilian cities over almost two decades to analyze the response of children's schooling and work to involuntary male job loss. Using short panel surveys, they relate involuntary job loss in the first four months of their panel to the probability that a child advances to the next grade in the year following the shock. According to their findings, a child is less likely to advance to the next grade when the male head of household becomes unemployed. They find, however, no significant differences in the effects of shocks on poorer households as opposed to wealthier households, proxied by the education level of the household head.

Duryea, Lam, and Levison (2007) also test to see whether unobserved heterogeneity variables affect both the propensity of the household head to have spells of unemployment and the schooling and work of children. In other words, unobserved characteristics of the household could be driving both unemployment spells, rendering them somewhat anticipated, and children's school and work behavior. Thus, unemployment shocks that happen in months following the observance of a change in child activities would be correlated with these changes in child activities.

Specifically, they test whether shocks that occur after month four of the survey "affect" child activities observed in months one to four. If shocks are unanticipated, there should be no correlation between ex post unemployment shocks and previous time allocation of the child. Their results suggest that, in general, the "future" shock variables are not picking up unobserved household characteristics associated with both unemployment of the household head and child outcomes. Leaving the labor force, however, does seem to be significantly affecting children's advancement to the next grade.

Skoufias and Parker (2006) use a similar strategy to Duryea, Lam, and Levison (2007) to measure children's schooling response to unexpected unemployment spells of household heads during the 1994–95 period, a time when Mexico experienced a sharp economic downturn and unemployment spells were more common. Using longitudinal data over a 12-month period, they analyze the extent to which a household head's loss of employment affects future schooling outcomes of adolescents aged 12–19. They find some evidence that female attendance is negatively affected by unemployment of the household head but find no evidence that grade progression is affected by this lower school attendance. They also study whether the children of poorer households, as measured by position in the wage distribution, are more likely to show negative effects of the economic crisis than their less poor counterparts. Nevertheless, no significant differences in estimated impacts between these groups were found.

A study with a very similar setup is one by Lam, Ardington, and Liebbrandt (2011), which analyzes longitudinal data in South Africa over the three-year period from 2002 to 2005. For youth in eighth or ninth grade at the beginning of the sample period, they analyze how a spell of unemployment in the household affects the probability that the child will complete three grades over this three-year period. According to their findings, a child in a household that suffered an economic shock was 15 percentage points less likely to complete three grades, with no significant differences in the size of the impact by race.

Glick, Sahn, and Walker (2011) constructed hazard models of entry and exit to school, using retrospective information on timing of household shocks and schooling transitions for the case of Madagascar. For household income shocks, they find no significant impact on dropout rate or on enrollment for their sample.

Finally, Cunningham and Bustos-Salvagno (2011) studied the Argentine case, also using the Permanent Survey of Households (Encuesta

Permanente de Hogares) for 1995–2007 to look at schooling and work decisions of girls and boys at both 12–15 and 16–17 years of age. They differentiate between the aggregate shock and the idiosyncratic shocks (mother's and father's unexpected job loss). Using bivariate and panel estimates, they conclude that the aggregate economic shock affected only the decisions of young girls (ages 12–15) whether to participate in the labor force and the decisions of poor young girls whether to drop out of school. The idiosyncratic shock to the household, however, affects girls and older boys, but they find no differences between poor and nonpoor households. In particular, younger girls are more sensitive to a father's job loss, while older girls and boys are more responsive to a mother's job loss. These effects of the idiosyncratic shocks seem to be amplified during crisis.

Idiosyncratic health shocks and children's schooling. We now turn to the studies of health shocks. Available studies derive largely from African countries, because of the lower life expectancy and high numbers of children losing one or both parents to contagious diseases and epidemics, in particular, HIV/AIDS. Several studies—including Gertler, Levine, and Ames (2004), Case and Ardington (2006), and Glick, Sahn, and Walker (2011)—address the impact of parental death on children's schooling. Both Gertler, Levine, and Ames (2004) and Case and Ardington (2006) use longitudinal data to link the timing of parental death to subsequent child performance in school. Glick, Sahn, and Walker (2011) construct retrospective information to connect the timing of parental death with schooling outcomes. In all three studies, parental death is associated with inferior schooling outcomes, including lower enrollment and years of completed schooling. For the case of South Africa, Case and Ardington's evidence suggests that maternal death is harmful for children's schooling and that paternal death does not appear to have significant effects on their schooling. According to their findings, families in which a father died over the sample period tended to have children who were already doing worse in school than those in families where a father did not die over the sample period, but the impact of paternal death did not worsen this disadvantage.

Case, Paxson, and Ableidinger (2004) use the Demographic Health Surveys to study orphanhood and children's schooling for 10 African countries. They estimate the impact of orphanhood by comparing orphaned and nonorphaned children who reside within the same household, a type of household fixed estimator. They find that orphans generally have worse schooling outcomes than nonorphans.

Natural disasters and children's schooling. Natural disasters can also have an impact on children's schooling. Many studies in this literature focus on the agricultural impacts—for example, the effects of drought on schooling—where the main consequence is a substantial loss of income to the family through the reduction of crop income on schooling. These studies could technically be classified as an aggregate shock (that is, all households within a certain area are affected), but many of the studies tend to take a more idiosyncratic approach by focusing on households where an unexpected loss to income occurs. In nonagricultural families, for instance, the impacts of a drought are presumably smaller. As opposed to aggregate economic shocks, which affect household welfare through a number of different mechanisms, the main impact of natural disasters is to affect household welfare through the destruction of household assets like the stock of crops, animals, housing, or the like. Skoufias (2003) provides a summary of how natural disaster may affect household welfare, the ways in which risks may be managed, and public policy responses.

In their pioneering article, Jacoby and Skoufias (1997) analyze the response of household investment in child schooling to both idiosyncratic and aggregate shocks to agricultural income due to unexpected changes in rainfall in three villages in rural India. They decompose idiosyncratic changes in income to those based on expected versus unexpected changes, where unexpected changes derive from unexpected deviations in rainfall. Their results show that both aggregate and idiosyncratic shocks appear to affect children's school enrollment negatively. Although the results vary somewhat by village, evidence in at least one village suggests that the negative effect of the aggregate shock on children's schooling enrollment is larger than the negative effect of the idiosyncratic shock. This result is intuitive, given that aggregate shocks are presumably more difficult to insure against than idiosyncratic shocks.

Jensen (2000) compares children's schooling in agricultural communities subject to droughts with those in communities not subject to drought in Côte d'Ivoire. The identifying assumption is that trends in schooling in both types of communities would have been similar in the absence of the rainfall shocks. Using data before and after the drought, he shows that school enrollment for children aged 7–15 declined by about a third to a half for communities affected by the drought, very large effects by any measure.

Baez, de la Fuente, and Santos (2010) studied the effects of Hurricane Mitch—the most severe Atlantic hurricane in 1998, causing death and destruction in Central America—on a number of children's welfare variables, including school enrollment. They use variation in the severity of the hurricane, based on its path, to identify the impact of the hurricane on children's outcomes. Using Living Standard Measurement Survey data from before and after Hurricane Mitch, they estimate the impacts on children's outcomes by comparing children in municipalities affected by Mitch with those in municipalities not affected by Mitch. Interestingly, whereas Hurricane Mitch did affect a number of child outcomes, including nutrition, it did not affect overall school enrollment. However, child labor did increase significantly with Hurricane Mitch; in particular, the percentage of children both attending school and working doubled.

Yamauchi, Yohannes, and Quisumbing (2009) analyze the impact of natural disasters in three poor countries—Bangladesh, Ethiopia, and Malawi. They focus on the impact of floods in Bangladesh and droughts in Ethiopia and Malawi. Using panel data in all three cases, they are for the most part able to construct pre- and postdisaster data, although timing of the various rounds is not ideal. In Bangladesh, for example, baseline data were collected just after the 1998 flood. The results show some evidence of the negative effects of shocks on children's grades of schooling. The authors also focus on the role of what they term "biological human capital" prior to the shock, measured empirically by height-for-age, and show that this variable helps reduce the negative effect of the shock of the natural disaster on children's schooling.

While relatively few studies have looked at the specific effects of natural disasters on children's schooling, existing studies are consistent with the conclusion that natural disasters do affect investment in children's schooling, at least in the immediate aftermath. Further research is needed to study the extent to which these short-run impacts continue into the longer term or whether the effects of these adverse shocks decline over time.

Summary. On balance, it is noteworthy that nearly all the studies of idiosyncratic economic and health shocks show some significant and negative effects, with the exception of Glick, Sahn, and Walker in the Madagascar study (2011), which shows only some negative effects of health shocks. Thus, while there are relatively few studies in this area, the overall evidence is more consistent in demonstrating negative shocks than the aggregate shock studies summarized in Ferreira and Schady (2009).

One might expect, however, that the potential negative effect of economic shocks on schooling indicators would be larger for poorer households, which may have fewer alternative mechanisms for dealing with negative shocks. Several studies test this hypothesis by interacting the shock variable with household characteristics associated with poverty (for instance, schooling of the household head). In general, though, the interactions are not statistically significant, suggesting that the negative effects of shocks do not differ by socioeconomic status. This finding is worthy of further analysis; available studies have carried out relatively simple explorations, such as dividing samples into two groups at the median of the educational level of the household head, perhaps because these studies have thus far not been able to fully disentangle the actual transmission mechanisms. According to the general assumption, parental death and illness lead to financial problems, and these financial problems are the principal channel through which children's educational outcomes are affected. However, while poor households may be more likely to experience certain shocks, the shock might affect the outcome variables through different mechanisms, such as household stress, loss of attachment figure, or the like (see, for example, Goodman and Gotlib 1999 and Hammen et al. 1987 on the negative consequences of the lack of a secure attachment relationship and Heckman, Stixrud, and Urzua 2006 on how that can affect educational outcomes).

Notably, studies of health shocks also point to the significant and substantial negative effects of parental illness and death on children's schooling, particularly maternal death. On the one hand, this outcome could reflect the greater likelihood of mothers' investing in their children's human capital (Benería and Roldán 1987). On the other hand, evidence from the field of human development indicates that children's success and achievements in school and learning are highly vulnerable to disruptions in family relations and stress, as was laid out in the conceptual framework as well as in the earlier discussion of attachment aspects.

This body of evidence on short-term outcomes presented thus far provides little information on long-term outcomes or on actual developmental outcomes. The next sections aim to shed light on how some of these adjustments might affect developmental outcomes, in the short as well as in the long run.

The Long-Term Impacts of Economic Crisis on Cognitive and Socioemotional Developmental Outcomes

The Family Context

One way of better understanding actual developmental outcomes is to identify the long-term implications of shocks during childhood. While the available evidence on long-term outcomes is extremely limited, it is nevertheless very informative. For example, Goldin (1999) explores the long-term outcomes of cohorts that were children and youth during the Great Depression. Although these cohorts were slightly older than age groups in the majority of studies reviewed earlier, they provide interesting insight into educational decisions affecting young people facing the decision to stay in school or leave. According to Goldin (1999), the Great Depression led to a rise in high school enrollment and graduation rates as manufacturing jobs decreased, significantly improving the later-life outcomes of these students. Another way of addressing longer-term outcomes is to analyze cognitive and socioemotional outcomes. We thus turn our attention to studies that look specifically at such outcomes. As was the case with studies of early childhood cognitive and socioemotional outcomes, most studies look at developed countries and are thus limited in their applicability to developing country contexts. Nonetheless, these studies highlight some of the transmission mechanisms that may be relevant in any case.

Cognitive Outcomes

We have thus far been able to establish a relationship between an idiosyncratic household economic shock, in some cases an aggregate shock, and a negative impact on children's rates of school enrollment, attendance, and grade progression. However, these variables largely capture only how frequently or for how long children go to school and may therefore be weak proxies for children's actual learning or cognitive skills. Moreover, research indicates that such skills—including literacy, numeracy, and the ability to solve abstract problems—predict variance in later labor market outcomes (Heckman, Stixrud, and Urzua 2006). Psychological research employing the Family Stress Model (see box 4.1) has provided evidence on how poverty—a condition that may be made more likely by an aggregate economic shock—may ultimately affect cognitive skills during middle childhood.

For instance, Gershoff et al. (2007) estimate the pathways through which income and economic pressure[2] are associated with children's cognitive skills (including math, reading, and general knowledge) in a nationally representative sample of U.S. kindergarten children. The researchers controlled for family education, marital status, parental work status, household size, and race and ethnicity, all of which are correlated with both family income and children's cognitive skills. With these adjustments, Gershoff et al. found that income was primarily associated with parental stress through economic pressure. That is, the more economic pressure a family experienced, the greater the marital conflict, symptoms of depression, and parenting stress parents reported. This finding is important, because it suggests that income is significant largely to the extent that it affects parents' experiences of economic pressure. Applying this finding to an idiosyncratic shock framework suggests that when faced with the loss of a job or income, some resourceful families will still be able to make ends meet, while other families—who experience the same level of income loss—will experience heightened economic pressure and greater stress. In turn, parents who experienced more stress reported less positive parenting behavior (including less cognitive stimulation and weak and inconsistent enforcement of rules and routines), which was associated with lower cognitive skills. Parents with lower incomes and more economic pressure also reported less parental investment (including lower investments in cognitively stimulating materials and involvement in school and extracurricular activities), which was strongly related to poorer cognitive outcomes in their children.

However, the literature also indicates that the timing and context of an economic shock may be important in determining children's cognitive outcomes (Dearing, McCartney, and Taylor 2001). Although Gershoff et al. (2007) found a link between income, parenting processes, and cognitive outcomes among a nationally representative sample of kindergarten children (mean age = 6.25), other research based on a sample of older children (mean age = 8.5) failed to find associations among income, home environment, and children's cognitive skills (Votruba-Drzal 2006). This variation in the data suggests the possibility of an especially important window of development during which children's cognitive skills are most responsive to change, both negative and positive. This possibility is consistent with Duncan et al.'s (1998) findings that family economic conditions during children's earliest years have the greatest impact on the development of their cognitive skills. Interestingly, Pungello et al. (1996) did find a significant association between income during middle childhood and academic achievement during adolescence.

Socioemotional and Behavioral Outcomes

While economists have tended to focus mostly on cognitive outcomes in children, recent research has begun to study the impact of behavioral and socioemotional outcomes[3]—including self-confidence, social skills, emotional stability—on labor market outcomes (Heckman, Stixrud, and Urzua 2006). Aside from labor market outcomes, positive

socioemotional skills (cooperation, for example, and self-regulation) during middle childhood reliably predict academic achievement well into
adolescence, even controlling for prior cognitive ability (Teo et al. 1996).
Indeed, large-scale intervention trials targeting children's socioemotional
learning have found later childhood improvements in scores on standardized tests of math achievement (Brown et al. 2004). Conversely,
negative socioemotional problems (difficulty regulating emotion, for
example, or misperceptions of social cues) during middle childhood have
been associated with increases in both internalizing (depression and
anxiety) and externalizing (substance abuse and delinquency) behaviors
in adolescence (Dishion, Capaldi, and Yoerger 1999).

A large body of research based on the Family Stress Model suggests
that an idiosyncratic household shock will ultimately affect children's
socioemotional outcomes through increases in parents' economic pressure and subsequent negative parenting behaviors. In the Gershoff et al.
(2007) study mentioned earlier, for example, parents who experienced
greater economic pressure reported greater stress, which in turn was associated with more negative parenting behaviors. Children of parents who
engaged in harsh or punitive parenting had more difficulties with self-
regulation and were more likely to report internalizing mental health
problems. Moreover, teachers rated these children as having less social
competence and more problems acting out. Although Votruba-Drzal
(2006) failed to find a link between income, home environment, and
children's cognitive skills among a sample of slightly older children, she
did find that lower household income during middle childhood was associated with an increase in behavior problems in middle childhood above
and beyond the effect of income during early childhood. Both studies
point to the conclusion that middle childhood may be a critical period for
the development of socioemotional outcomes, which a shock to the
household could disrupt.

Moreover, some evidence suggests that an idiosyncratic household
economic shock would differentially disrupt the socioemotional development of boys and girls. For example, in Elder's studies of the Great
Depression (1974), fathers' emotional instability in the wake of large
decreases in household income was associated with harsher and more
inconsistent discipline of children; these disciplinary practices predicted
emotional difficulties in later childhood among girls but not boys.
According to Elder, this difference may have been due to the fact that girls
endured more of the discipline because they were physically in the home
more, while boys were outside the home working, as was traditional in the

United States at the time. Thus, dominant social roles and expectations at the time are likely to be a significant source of heterogeneity in children's socioemotional outcomes during an economic crisis.

Children at this age do not generally engage only within the household setting; as explained in the introduction to this chapter, during middle childhood, children encounter a variety of settings—including school settings and work settings—that may also contribute to their well-being during an economic crisis (see box 4.2 for an account of child labor during crisis).

Box 4.2

Economic Crisis and Child Labor

According to the definition of the International Labour Organization/International Programme on the Elimination of Child Labour,[a] not all forms of child labor should be targeted for elimination, and this distinction is crucial to exploring the link between financial crisis and child labor outcomes.[b] Some forms of child labor can, in fact, be positive when that labor contributes to child development and the household's welfare. With regard to on developmental processes, child labor is a concern when it exposes children to physically harmful tasks, including repetitive or arduous work; to dangerous tools or machinery or to toxins; denies children positive stimulation by limiting exposure to diverse settings (school and playground, for example), tasks (such as play or study), and interactions (with teachers, peers, parents, and siblings, among others); or exposes the child to situations and experiences (such as drugs, violence, or prostitution) that exceed his or her ability to cope. Any such stressors commonly lead to a variety of internalizing behavior (disturbances in emotion or mood such as depression or anxiety) or externalizing behavior (such as aggression, substance abuse, or delinquency).

There are many misconceptions about how children work. First, while poverty is often the main driver of child labor, it is not the only factor. In some cases, in fact, a wealth paradox has been observed; that is, in certain instances children work more in wealthier, land-owning households (see, for example, Bhalotra and Heady 2003). Other factors, such as preferences, insurance failures, land and labor markets, and household specialization, which are all very context specific, also explain why children work. Second, as shown through numerous surveys and studies, most working children are in agriculture, outside of traded sectors, and are rarely involved in the cash economy. Edmonds and Pavcnik (2005) report that participation in

(continued next page)

Box 4.2 *(continued)*

unpaid family services is three times more prevalent than participation in economic activity among children 5–14 in the 36 countries of their study. More important perhaps, the work they do may not deprive them of education. In fact, Edmonds (2007) finds that at the aggregate for children younger than 10, working children are more likely to attend school than nonworking children. Certainly, we should be most worried about child labor, in particular, its worst forms, where children are enslaved, separated from their families, or abandoned altogether. Yet, few empirical studies of child labor include the most extreme forms. Rather, the evidence tends to focus on the more common activities of children's work.

How Do Financial Crises Transmit and Affect Children's Work in Theory?
Several important implications follow from the patterns of child labor and from looking for potential impacts of financial crisis on children's work. First, children are most likely to be affected by the crisis through the effects on their family, since children who work are spending most of their time contributing to the family farm or business or providing unpaid household services to their family. Therefore, a drop in household income or a reallocation of labor among adult family members engaged in market work may change the workload of children in the household.

Second, child market (wage) employment opportunities will be affected by a crisis through shifts in demand for child labor and changes in relative prices. It seems reasonable to suppose that most financial crises will affect traded sectors, because traded sectors will be more vulnerable to problems related to the currency and to events emanating outside a given country. Changes in the industrial mix of employment might easily increase or decrease children's market work through the resulting change in demand for unskilled labor. However, as noted, the share of child workers in market employment is generally small. (An exception might be if agricultural trade is significantly affected and if children are involved in the household's production of agricultural traded goods.) Thus, while an economic crisis, such as the recent recession, will primarily affect formal or traded sectors of employment directly, these shifts may have spillover or ripple effects leading to changes in the informal and low-skill sectors that provide inputs to the formal sector and are more likely to employ children. And to the extent that a crisis might shift production into the household and children work more within the household, children might spend more time working.

(continued next page)

Box 4.2 *(continued)*

Third, shocks that affect the financial sector may cause liquidity problems as credit markets contract. A financial crisis may increase child labor because illiquidity induces families to send their children to work when incomes drop in the absence of credit or insurance options.

Finally, while crises may change returns to education, the impact of this is ambiguous. For instance, crisis-induced budgetary constraints may lead to a deterioration in the quality of the educational system, lowering the returns to time spent in school. Economic restructuring, however, may lead to reallocation of resources to higher-skill activities, increasing the returns to education. If labor markets are tight, though, the opportunity cost of education might fall, leading to an increase in the time spent at school and studying instead of working, even if returns to schooling do not change.

Child Labor and Financial Crisis: Evidence and Inferences

Few studies look at child labor during aggregate economic downturns, and those that do often make use of labor force surveys that usually have, at best, a lower-bound age cutoff of 12 years. Thus, we have even less information on younger children. Overall, these studies do not provide sufficiently compelling evidence to suggest that the number of children working rises significantly because of financial crisis.

Most economists would argue that an economic crisis would reduce the demand for child workers. Goldin (1999) finds evidence consistent with this view in her study of U.S. secondary school enrollment during the Great Depression. Schady (2004) finds similar evidence in his examination of schooling responses to Peru's 1988–92 macroeconomic crisis. He finds that schooling attainment increased among cohorts educated during the crisis and argues that the number of children combining work with school declined. On the other hand, Manacorda and Rosati (2010) look explicitly at the relationship between local labor demand and child labor and find that children 10–12 years old in Brazil work less when the local unemployment rates are lower and work more when local unemployment rates are higher.

On the reciprocal side, some evidence indicates that children work more during economic booms. In Northeast Brazil, for example, Kruger (2007) finds that children work more and go to school less when the value of coffee exports is temporarily high. As she sees it, families take advantage of higher wages in the

(continued next page)

Box 4.2 *(continued)*

local labor market by sending their children to work. This is consistent with the inverse story that child labor goes down in a crisis.

A gender dimension might be another factor in the response of child work to crises. In his study of the Great Depression, Elder (1999) finds a clear gender distinction in the kind of work children were expected to do. Teenage boys were more likely to support the family through market work, while girls were used at home to produce goods for consumption. While the children in this study were somewhat older than the age groups we focus on when talking about child labor, the analysis finds significant differences in the long-term impacts by the age of the child during the worst years of the Great Depression. In other words, specific transitions between stages of development and the historical, social, and political context in which these transitions are embedded will significantly shape the future of individuals.

Conclusions

Many countervailing forces can increase and decrease demand for children's labor in an economic crisis. On the one hand, a broad crisis may decrease employment opportunities open to children and thereby decrease the incidence and intensity of children's work. On the other hand, a crisis-induced change in industrial structure could increase children's work. Similarly, a shift in adult labor in the household or an increase in household production for its own consumption may increase the workload for children in nonmarket activities but decrease the incidence of paid employment and some of the worst forms of child labor. Thus the effects of an economic crisis on the incidence and intensity of children's work in general— including its worst forms more specifically—is an empirical question on which we have little evidence.

Beyond the potential for a crisis to change children's work, the developmental impacts of that work are unclear in general and during times of economic crisis. Elder (1974), for example, finds that the exposure that boys had through their market work, such as social networks and relationships with adults other than their parents, had a positive effect on their self-esteem, confidence, and interpersonal skills and increased their status and power within their families. Girls, however, by the nature of their involvement and responsibilities within the household, experienced quite the opposite regarding their self-perceptions and their power and status within the household. In addition, they were more exposed to the

(continued next page)

Box 4.2 *(continued)*

effects of parental stress and were at risk of falling victim to domestic abuse, as unemployed fathers were likely to develop emotional disorders and resort to substance abuse. Levison's (2000) observations coincide with Elder's in that children from diverse countries and contexts often prefer paid work, work outside the home, and working for nonfamily members. In other words, children prefer work that results in status, respect, and appreciation.

Thus, at the heart of policy debates about child labor are two big questions, What is in the best interest of the child? and What are the consequences of child labor? The answer to both will vary greatly depending on context. While not in equal amounts, some programs have been shown to decrease the time spent working while increasing education (see, for example, Ravallion and Wodon 2000; Edmonds and Schady 2009). On the other hand, work in moderation for children—respecting age minimums and hours—is acknowledged by the ILO itself as acceptable and potentially a contributor to the intergenerational transfer of skills.[c]

Source: Prepared by Kathleen Beegle and Alice Wuermli; based on a background paper by Eric Edmonds and Alice Wuermli.
a. For a more detailed definition and discussion of child labor, including the worst forms of child labor, see http://www.ilo.org/ipec/facts/lang--en/index.htm.
b. See, for example, Elder (1974).
c. See, for example, http://www.ilo.org/wcmsp5/groups/public/---ed_emp/documents/publication /wcms_165305.pdf.

The School Context

Around the world, children spend a good deal of their time in school. It follows that school contexts—like family contexts—are important environments that interact with children's development to shape their futures. However, while the psychological and sociological literature has, in recent years, developed an understanding of the pathways through which an economic shock may affect children's cognitive and socioemotional development within families, little is known about how school contexts may shape children's outcomes during an economic crisis.

To shed some light on these processes, we begin by positing that an aggregate economic shock may reduce public expenditures on education. Interestingly, research in times of relative economic stability has shown that children's academic performance is not highly correlated with countries' aggregate expenditures on education, even when adjusting for family background differences (Hanushek and Kimko

2000; Woessman 2001). While such analyses are prone to a variety of problems—particularly that they might be biased by the omission of other variables—the variation in the resources available across countries is so large that an effect should be apparent even in crude comparisons (Hanushek 2003). Within the psychological literature, Cohen, Raudenbush, and Ball (2003) come to a similar conclusion. Although conventional wisdom assumes that increases in public expenditures on education and corresponding increases in educational resources—including physical resources such as textbooks and buildings and human resources such as teacher qualifications—would translate into educational quality and improved outcomes, lack of consistent empirical findings from studies in the United States has prompted considerable debate over the topic. Cohen, Raudenbush, and Ball (2003) believe that conventional resources may be necessary but not sufficient: that is, while a certain level of conventional resources is necessary, those resources count largely to the extent that they are used in instructing. Put differently by Cohen, Raudenbush, and Ball, "Their effects all depend on teachers' and students' personal resources: their knowledge, skill, and will" (2003, 128). Of course, some conventional resources such as textbooks may be put to use more easily than others, while social norms dictate which resources are most noticed and put to use. But Cohen, Raudenbush, and Ball insist that the "chief means by which actors can influence the use [of resources] is by focusing their attention and improving their capabilities as users" (2003, 128).

If this is the case, an aggregate economic shock may be important for children's outcomes to the extent that it disrupts teachers' and students' use of conventional resources: to the extent that it disrupts coordinating instruction, managing classroom environments, and utilizing institutional supports. For example, a cut in teachers' salaries during an aggregate economic shock may have an effect on children's learning because it may force teachers to take on other paid work, leaving them tired and unable to communicate effectively during instructional periods. At the same time, if children are acting out in classrooms because of increased stress at home (as suggested by the Family Stress Model), teachers may have a harder time managing the classroom and providing quality instructional time. The problem may be further compounded if class sizes are increased as a way of saving resources. This scenario illustrates the multiple and complex ways in which physical, human, and economic resources may interact with social processes in a school setting to influence children's outcomes during an economic shock.

Conclusions

Not surprisingly, studies of idiosyncratic household shocks have somewhat different findings from those based on aggregate economic shocks. The studies of idiosyncratic household economic and health shocks are nearly universal in showing that children are negatively affected by these shocks. While available only for middle- and high-income countries, the studies based on aggregate economic shocks suggest that economic crises demonstrate countercyclical effects on school enrollment. In other words, economic crises are associated with increases in school enrollment. None of the idiosyncratic studies reviewed here are consistent with such a finding.

As argued by Ferreira and Schady (2009), the outcomes of aggregate economic crises reflect both income and substitution effects, whereas income effects strongly dominate in household-level idiosyncratic shocks. However, as noted earlier, macroeconomic crises tend to affect a number of different variables, including unemployment, real wages, prices, and spending on public education. Studies of aggregate shocks have not been able to distinguish the different effects of changes in these diverse economic variables and are therefore less useful to suggest specific policy recommendations.

Little of the evidence from economics sheds light on other measures of development or gains in fundamental competencies. Incorporating knowledge from the human developmental sciences can provide insights into other aspects of education, especially cognitive and other developmental outcomes, during middle childhood. In particular, these studies provide more information about the long-term impacts of economic shocks. For example, lower income during middle childhood is associated with increased socioemotional and behavioral problems. Poor socioemotional skills during middle childhood predict lower academic achievement, as well as more adverse internalizing and externalizing behaviors well into adolescence.

Developmental psychology further identifies key processes that help explain some of the observed heterogeneity in children's outcomes—both cognitive and socioemotional—during an economic shock. Given children's participation in school settings during middle childhood, we focus on three principal transmission mechanisms through which a child's development can be affected: (1) parental stress and family functioning; (2) investments in learning and stimulation within the home; and (3) teachers, peers, and the learning environment in schools. The literature finds that economic shocks are likely to lead to increased parental stress, which has a negative impact on parenting and leads to less cognitive stimulation and weak enforcement of rules and routines. These outcomes in turn affect children's capacity to self-regulate, increase internalizing problems, and lower social competence. Economic shocks may also decrease a household's ability to invest in cognitively stimulating resources and activities. Aggregate economic crises can also lead to a reduction in public spending on schools. Reduced funding for schools may affect children through its impact on the teaching environment and teacher-student relationships. For example, teachers may also be experiencing stress, which may lead to inconsistent instruction or to teacher absenteeism. If class sizes are increased, classroom dynamics may be disrupted.

However, family and schools are not the only settings through which an aggregate economic shock may be transmitted to children. During middle childhood, children may spend time at work, with peers, and in child care or activity settings, all of which can be affected by economic shocks. For example, during an economic shock communities may not have the resources to maintain local facilities, which may have implications for how and where children spend their time. Moreover, to the extent that children are affected by the changes wrought by an idiosyncratic household shock in their homes, they will bring these experiences with them to school, to their relationships with peers, and beyond.

In his numerous studies of children during the Great Depression, Elder emphasizes the importance of contextual factors and how these differ depending on the timing or age of the child when exposed to adversity. While much of the literature highlights the importance of investments in early childhood, there is also a relationship between family income during middle childhood and adolescent educational outcomes. Middle childhood is a crucial time for developing social and emotional competencies, and shocks will affect children's socioemotional and behavioral development and lead to difficulties later on.

In addition to the changes in the context depending on the age of the child when the economic shock occurs, other contextual factors will moderate the impact of crises on development. For example, Goldin (1999) examines a wealth of contextual factors that may have been as important as, or even more important than, the decrease in work opportunities. For example, homogenous communities—measured in lower income inequality, less ethnic and religious diversity, and greater stability—had higher rates of high school enrollment and graduation. In addition, considering that half the population of the United States was rural as late as 1920, the school bus was of great importance in expanding high school enrollment across the country, as was a 1910 campaign intended to convince youth and their parents of the benefits of graduating from high school.

Social norms and socioeconomic background can also mediate the impact of shocks. For example, if girls are more likely to stay home and work in the household, they may be more exposed to parental stress or harsh parenting. Similarly, children from poor households may be more affected than children from nonpoor households. While the relationship might be moderated through other factors, such as parental mental health or community support, this aspect is nevertheless important to the targeting of interventions. Incorporating this knowledge on transmission mechanisms, timing, and context into our analysis will greatly influence our policy choices. Chapter 6 will go into greater detail on policy.

Notes

1. Côte d'Ivoire and Malawi did not have economic crises but weather-related shocks.
2. Gershoff et al. (2007) actually use the term *material hardship* to refer to the difficulties in making ends meet (for example, residential instability, food insecurity, inadequacy of medical care) experienced by families with insufficient income. However, given the high degree of conceptual overlap between *material hardship* and *economic pressure*, to maintain consistency and avoid confusion we will continue to use the term *economic pressure*.
3. These skills are sometimes referred to as "noncognitive" skills or outcomes; we prefer not to use this term as we find it misleading to the extent that these skills are results of cognitive processes.

References

Aber, L., and S. Jones. 1997. "Indicators of Positive Development in Early Childhood: Improving Concepts and Measures." In *Indicators of Children's Well-Being*, ed. R. Hauser, B. Brown, and W. Prosser, 395–427. New York: Russell Sage.

Alexander, K., D. Entwisle, and C. Horsey. 1997. "From First Grade Forward: Early Foundations of High School Dropout." *Sociology of Education* 70 (2): 87–107.

Arthur, W. B. 1982. "Review of Gary S. Becker's 'A Treatise on the Family.'" *Population and Development Review* 8: 393–97.

Aytaç, I. A., and B. H. Rankin. 2009. "Economic Crisis and Marital Problems in Turkey: Testing the Family Stress Model." *Journal of Marriage and Family* 71 (3): 756–67.

Baez, Javier E., Alejandro de la Fuente, and Indhira Santos. 2010. "Do Natural Disasters Affect Human Capital? An Assessment Based on Existing Empirical Evidence." IZA Discussion Papers 5164, IZA (Institute for the Study of Labor), Bonn.

Barber, B. K., and E. L. Harmon, eds. 2002. *Violating the Self: Parental Psychological Control of Children and Adolescents.* Washington, DC: American Psychological Association.

Baumrind, D. 1971. "Current Patterns of Parental Authority." *Developmental Psychology* 4 (1): 1–103.

———. 1991. "The Influence of Parenting Style on Adolescent Competence and Substance Use." *Journal of Early Adolescence* 11 (1): 56–95.

Benería, L., and M. Roldán. 1987. *The Crossroads of Class and Gender: Industrial Homework, Subcontracting, and Household Dynamics in Mexico City.* Chicago: University of Chicago Press.

Benner, A., and S. Y. Kim. 2010. "Understanding Chinese American Adolescents' Developmental Outcomes: Insights from the Family Stress Model." *Journal of Research on Adolescence* 20 (1): 1–12.

Betts, J., and L. McFarland. 1995. "Safe Port in a Storm: The Impact of Labor Market Conditions on Community College Enrollments." *Journal of Human Resources* 30 (4): 741–65.

Bhalotra, S., and C. Heady. 2003. "Child Farm Labor: The Wealth Paradox." *World Bank Economic Review* 17 (2): 197–227.

Birch, S. H., and G. W. Ladd. 1998. "Children's Interpersonal Behaviors and the Teacher–Child Relationship." *Developmental Psychology* 34 (5): 934–46.

Brody, G. H., and D. Flor. 1998. "Maternal Resources, Parenting Practices, and Child Competence in Rural, Single-Parent African American Families." *Child Development* 69 (3): 803–16.

Bronfenbrenner, U., and P. A. Morris. 2006. "The Biological Model of Human Development." In *Theoretical Models of Human Development.* Vol. 1 of *Handbook of Child Psychology,* 6th ed., ed. W. Damon and R. M. Lerner, 793–828. New York: Wiley.

Brown, J. L., T. Roderick, L. Lantieri, and J. L. Aber. 2004. "The Resolving Conflict Creatively Program: A School-Based Social and Emotional Learning Program." In *Building Academic Success on Social and Emotional Learning: What Does the Research Say,* ed. J. E. Zins, R. P. Weissberg, M. Wang, and H. J. Walberg, 151–69. New York: Teachers College Press.

Browning, M., F. Bourguignon, P. A. Chiappori, and V. Lechene. 1994. "Income and Outcomes: A Structural Model of Intrahousehold Allocation." *Journal of Political Economy* 102 (6): 1067–96.

Campbell, A., P. Converse, and W. Rodgers. 1976. *The Quality of American Life: Perceptions, Evaluations, and Satisfactions.* New York: Russell Sage.

Carter, M., and E. Katz. 1997. "Separate Spheres and the Conjugal Contract: Understanding the Impact of Gender-Biased Development." In *Intrahousehold Resource Allocation in Developing Countries: Models, Methods, and Policy,* ed. L. Haddad, J. Hoddinott, and H. Alderman, 95–111. Baltimore: Johns Hopkins University Press.

Case, Anne, and Cally Ardington. 2006. "The Impact of Parental Death on School Outcomes: Longitudinal Evidence from South Africa." *Demography* 43 (3): 401–20.

Case, Anne, Christina Paxson, and Josepha Ableidinger. 2004. "Orphans in Africa: Parental Death, Poverty, and School Enrollment." *Demography* 41 (3): 483–508.

Chao, R. K. 1994. "Beyond Parental Control and Authoritarian Parenting Style: Understanding Chinese Parenting through the Cultural Notion of Training." *Child Development* 65 (4): 1111–19.

Chao, R. K., and V. Tseng. 2002. "Parenting of Asians." In *Social Conditions and Applied Parenting,* Vol. 4 of *Handbook of Parenting,* 2nd ed., ed. M. Bornstein, 59–93. Mahwah, NJ: Erlbaum.

Chiappori, P. A. 1992. "Collective Labor Supply and Welfare." *Journal of Political Economy* 100 (3): 437–67.

Chiappori, P. A., L. Haddad, J. Hoddinott, and R. Kanbur. 1993. "Unitary versus Collective Models of the Household: Time to Shift the Burden of Proof?" Policy Research Working Paper 1217. World Bank, Washington, DC.

Cohen, D., S. Raudenbush, and D. Ball. 2003. "Resources, Instruction, and Research." *Educational Evaluation and Policy Analysis* 25 (2): 119–42.

Cohen, G., M. Bronson, and M. B. Casey. 1995. "Planning as a Factor in School Achievement." *Journal of Applied Developmental Psychology* 16 (3): 405–28.

Collins, W. A., S. Madsen, and A. Susman-Stillman. 2008. "Parenting during Middle Childhood." In *Children and Parenting.* Vol. 1 of *Handbook of Parenting,* ed. M. Bornstein, 73–102. Mahwah, NJ: Erlbaum.

Collins, W. A., and M. van Dulmen. 2006. "The Significance of Middle Childhood Peer Competence for Work and Relationships in Early Adulthood." In *Developmental Contexts in Middle Childhood: Bridges to Adolescence and Adulthood,* ed. A. Huston and M. Ripke, 23–40. New York: Cambridge University Press.

Conger, R. D., and K. J. Conger. 2002. "Resilience in Midwestern Families: Selected Findings from the First Decade of a Prospective, Longitudinal Study." *Journal of Marriage and the Family* 64 (2): 361–73.

———. 2008. "Understanding the Processes through Which Economic Hardship Influences Families and Children." In *Handbook of Families and Poverty*, ed. R. Crane and T. Heaton, 64– 81. Thousand Oaks, CA: Sage.

Conger, R. D., and R. D. Donnellan. 2007. "An Interactionist Perspective on the Socioeconomic Context of Human Development." *Annual Review of Psychology* 58: 175–99.

Conger, R. D., and G. H. Elder. 1994. *Families in Troubled Times: Adapting to Change in Rural America*. New York: Aldine de Gruyter.

Conger, R. D., and G. H. Elder, with F. O. Lorenz, R. L. Simons, and L. B. Whitbeck. 1994. *Families in Troubled times: Adapting to Change in Rural America*. Hillsdale, NJ: Aldine.

Conger, R. D., X. Ge, G. Elder, F. Lorenz, and R. Simons. 1994. "Economic Stress, Coercive Family Process, and Developmental Problems of Adolescents." *Child Development* 65 (2): 541–61.

Conger, R. D., L. E. Wallace, Y. Sun, R. L. Simons, V. C. McLoyd, and G. H. Brody. 2002. "Economic Pressure in African American Families: A Replication and Extension of the Family Stress Model." *Developmental Psychology* 38 (2): 179–93.

Cunningham, W., and J. Bustos-Salvagno. 2011. "Youth Employment Transitions in Latin America." Policy Research Working Paper, World Bank, Washington, DC.

Danes, S., and K. Rettig. 1993a. "The Role of Perception in the Intention to Change the Family Financial Situation." *Journal of Family and Economic Issues* 14 (4): 365–89.

———. 1993b. "Farm Wives' Business and Household Decision Involvement in Times of Economic Stress." *Home Economics Research Journal* 21 (3): 307–33.

Dearing, E., K. McCartney, and B. Taylor. 2001. "Change in Family Income-to-Needs Matters More for Children with Less." *Child Development* 72 (6): 1779–93.

Dishion, T., D. Capaldi, and K. Yoerger. 1999. "Middle Childhood Antecedents to Progressions in Male Adolescent Substance Use: An Ecological Analysis of Risk and Protection." *Journal of Adolescent Research* 14 (2): 175–205.

Dornbusch, S. M., P. L. Ritter, P. H. Liederman, D. F. Roberts, and M. J. Fraleigh. 1987. "The Relation of Parenting Style to Adolescent School Performance." *Child Development* 58 (5): 1244–57.

Doss, C. 1996. "Women's Bargaining Power in Household Economic Decisions: Evidence form Ghana." Staff Paper Series, University of Minnesota, St. Paul.

Duncan, G. J., J. Brooks-Gunn, W. J. Yeung, and J. R. Smith. 1998. "How Much Does Childhood Poverty Affect the Life Chances of Children?" *American Sociological Review* 63 (3): 406–423.

Duryea, S., D. Lam, and D. Levison. 2007. "Effects of Economic Shocks on Children's Employment and Schooling in Brazil." *Journal of Development Economics* 84 (1): 188–214.

Eccles, J. S. 1999. "The Development of Children Ages 6 to 14." *Future of Children: When School Is Out* 9 (2): 30–44.

Edmonds, E. 2007. "Child Labor." In *Handbook of Development Economics*, ed. T. P. Schultz and J. Strauss, 3607–710. Amsterdam: Elsevier Science.

Edmonds, Eric, and Nina Pavcnik. 2005. "The Effect of Trade Liberalization on Child Labor: Evidence from Vietnam." *Journal of International Economics* 65 (2): 401–41.

Edmonds, E., and N. Schady. 2009. "Poverty Alleviation and Child Labor." Working Paper 15345, National Bureau of Economic Research, Cambridge, MA.

Elder, G. H. 1974. *Children of the Great Depression: Social Change in Life Experience.* Chicago: University of Chicago Press.

Elder, G. 1999. *Children of the Great Depression: Social Change in Life Experience,* 25th anniversary ed. Boulder, CO: Westview Press.

Elder, G. H., Jr., R. D. Conger, M. Foster, and M. Ardelt. 1992. "Families under Economic Pressure." *Journal of Family Issues* 31 (1): 5–37.

Eloundou-Enyegue, P., and J. Davanzo. 2003. "Economic Downturns and Schooling Inequality, Cameroon, 1987–95." *Population Studies* 57 (2): 183–97.

Ferreira, Francisco H. G., and Norbert Schady. 2009. "Aggregate Economic Shocks, Child Schooling and Child Health." *World Bank Research Observer* 24 (2): 147–81.

Florsheim, P., P. Tolan, and D. Gorman-Smith. 1998. "Family Relationships, Parenting Practices, the Availability of Male Family Members, and the Behavior of Inner-City Boys in Single-Mother and Two-Parent Families." *Child Development* 69 (5): 1437–47.

Formoso, D., N. A. Gonzales, M. Barrerra Jr., and L. E. Dumka. 2007. "Interparental Relations, Maternal Employment, and Fathering in Mexican American Families." *Journal of Marriage and Family* 69 (1): 26–39.

Fuligni, A. J., and J. S. Eccles. 1993. "Perceived Parent-Child Relationships and Early Adolescents' Orientation toward Peers." *Developmental Psychology* 29 (4): 622–32.

Gardner, H., and C. Kosmitzki. 2008. *Lives across Cultures: Cross-Cultural Human Development.* New York: Pearson Education.

Gershoff, E., J. L. Aber, C. Raver, and M. C. Lennon. 2007. "Income Is Not Enough: Incorporating Material Hardship into Models of Income Associations with Parenting and Child Development." *Child Development* 78 (1): 70–95.

Gertler, P., D. Levine, and M. Ames. 2004. "Schooling and Parental Death." *Review of Economics and Statistics* 86 (1): 211–25.

Glick P., D. E. Sahn, and T. F. Walker. 2011. "Household Shocks and Education Investment in Madagascar." Working Paper 240, Cornell Food and Nutrition Policy Program, Ithaca, NY.

Goldin, C. 1999. "Egalitarianism and the Returns to Education during the Great Transformation of American Education." *Journal of Political Economy* 107 (6): S65–S94.

Goodman, S., and I. Gotlib. 1999. "Risk for Psychopathology in the Children of Depressed Mothers: A Developmental Model for Understanding Mechanisms of Transmission." *Psychological Review* 106 (July): 458–90.

Guo, G., and K. M. Harris. 2000. "The Mechanisms Mediating the Effect of Poverty on Children's Intellectual Development." *Demography* 37 (4): 431–47.

Hammen, C., D. Gordon, D. Burge, C. Adrian, C. Jaenicke, and G. Hirohito. 1987. "Communication Patterns of Mothers with Affective Disorders and Their Relationship to Children's Status and Social Functioning." In *Understanding Mental Disorder: The Contribution of Family Interaction Research*, ed. K. Hahlweg and M. J. Goldstein, 103–19. New York: Family Process Press.

Hamre, B. K., and R. C. Pianta. 2001. "Early Teacher-Child Relationships and the Trajectory of Children's School Outcomes through Eighth Grade." *Child Development* 72 (2): 625–38.

Hanushek, E. A. 2003. "The Failure of Input-Based Schooling Policies." *Economic Journal* 113 (485): 64–98.

Hanushek, E. A., and D. D. Kimko. 2000. "Schooling, Labor Force Quality, and the Growth of Nations." *American Economic Review* 90 (5): 1184–208.

Harkness, S., and C. Super. 1983. "The Cultural Construction of Child Development: A Framework for the Socialization of Affect." *Ethos* 11 (4): 221–31.

Harter, S. 1999. *The Construction of the Self: A Developmental Perspective.* New York: Guilford Press.

Heckman, J., J. Stixrud, and S. Urzua. 2006. "The Effects of Cognitive and Noncognitive Abilities on Labor Market Outcomes and Social Behaviors." *Journal of Labor Economics* 24 (3): 411–82.

Horney, M. J., and M. B. McElroy. 1988. "The Household Allocation Problem: Empirical Results from a Bargaining Model." In *Research in Population Economics* 6: 679–94.

Hraba, J., F. O. Lorenz, and Z. Pechacova. 2000. "Family Stress during the Czech Transformation." *Journal of Marriage and the Family* 62 (2): 520–31.

Jacoby, J., and E. Skoufias. 1997. "Risk, Financial Markets, and Human Capital in a Developing Country." *Review of Economic Studies* 64 (3): 311–35.

Jensen, R. 2000. "Agricultural Volatility and Investments in Children." *American Economic Review* 90 (May): 399–404.

Jimerson, S., B. Egeland, A. Sroufe, and B. Carlson. 2000. "A Prospective Longitudinal Study of High School Drop Outs Examining Multiple Predictors across Development." *Journal of School Psychology* 38 (6): 525–49.

Kane, T. 1994. "College Entry by Blacks since 1970: The Role of College Costs, Family Background, and the Returns to Education." *Journal of Political Economy* 102 (5): 878–911.

Kinnunen, U., and L. Pulkkinen. 1998. "Linking Economic Stress to Marital Quality among Finnish Marital Couples: Mediator Effects." *Journal of Family Issues* 19 (6):705–20.

Kruger, Diana. 2007. "Coffee Production Effects on Child Labor and Schooling in Rural Brazil." *Journal of Development Economics* 82 (2): 448–63.

Kwon, H., M. A. Rueter, M. Lee, S. Koh, and S. W. Ok. 2003. "Marital Relationships Following the Korean Economic Crisis: Applying the Family Stress Model." *Journal of Marriage and Family* 65 (2): 316–25.

Ladd, G. W. 1999. "Peer Relationships and Social Competence during Early and Middle Childhood." *Annual Review of Psychology* 50: 333–59.

Lam, D. A., C. Ardington, and M. Leibbrandt. 2011. "The Impact of Household Shocks on Adolescent School Outcomes in South Africa." Mimeo. University of Michigan.

Lerner, R. M. 1998. "Theories of Human Development: Contemporary Perspectives." In *Theoretical Models of Human Development.* Vol. 1 of *Handbook of Child Psychology.* 5th ed., ed. W. Damon and R. M. Lerner, 1–24. New York: Wiley.

Levison, D. 2000. "Children as Economic Agents." *Feminist Economics* 6 (1): 125–34.

Maccoby, E. E., and J. A. Martin. 1983. "Socialization in the Context of the Family: Parent-Child Interaction." In *Socialization, Personality, and Social Development.* Vol. 4 of *Handbook of Child Psychology,* 4th ed., ed. P. H. Mussenand and E. M. Hetherington, 1–101. New York: Wiley.

Manacorda, M., and F. Rosati. 2010. "Local Labor Demand and Child Work." *Research in Labor Economics* 31: 321–54.

Masten, A. S., and D. Cicchetti, D. 2010. "Developmental Cascades." *Development and Psychopathology,* 22 (3): 491-495.

McElroy, M., and M. J. Horney. 1981. "Nash-Bargained Decisions: Toward a Generalization of the Theory of Demand." *International Economic Review* 22 (2): 333–40.

McHale, S. M., J. K. Dariotis, and T. J. Kauh. 2003. "Social Development and Social Relationships in Middle Childhood." In *Developmental Psychology*. Vol. 6 of *Handbook of Psychology*, ed. A. Easterbrooks and R. M. Lerner, 241–65. New York: Wiley.

Mistry, R., E. Vandewater, A. Huston, and V. McLoyd. 2002. "Economic Well-Being and Children's Social Adjustment: The Role of Family Process in an Ethnically Diverse Low-Income Sample." *Child Development* 73 (3): 935–51.

Parke, R. D., and G. W. Ladd. 1992. *Family-Peer Relationships: Modes of Linkage.* Hillsdale, NJ: Erlbaum.

Pittman, L., and P. Chase-Lansdale. 2001. "African American Adolescent Girls in Impoverished Communities: Parenting Style and Adolescent Outcomes." *Journal of Research on Adolescence* 11 (2): 199–244.

Pungello, E. P., J. B. Kupersmidt, M. R. Burchinal, and C. J. Patterson. 1996. "Environmental Risk Factors and Children's Achievement from Middle Childhood to Early Adolescence." *Developmental Psychology* 32 (4): 755–67.

Ravallion, M., and Q. Wodon. 2000. "Does Child Labour Displace Schooling? Evidence on Behavioural Responses to an Enrollment Subsidy." *Economic Journal* 110 (462):158–75.

Rettig, K., R. Leichtentritt, and S. Danes. 1999. "The Effects of Resources, Decision Making, and Decision Implementing on Perceived Family Well-Being in Adjusting to an Economic Stressor." *Journal of Family and Economic Issues* 20 (1): 5–34.

Schady, N. 2004. "Do Macroeconomic Crises Always Slow Human Capital Accumulation?" *World Bank Economic Review* 18 (2): 131–54.

Shmink, M. 1984. "Household Economic Strategies: Review and Research Agenda." *Latin American Research Review* 19 (3): 87–101.

Silliphant, V. M. 1983. "Kindergarten Reasoning and Achievement in Grades K-3." *Psychology in the Schools* 20 (3): 289–94.

Skoufias, E. 2003. "Economic Crises and Natural Disasters: Coping Strategies and Policy Implications." *World Development* 31 (7): 1087–102.

Skoufias, E., and S. Parker. 2006. "Job Loss and Family Adjustments in Work and Schooling during the Mexican Peso Crisis." *Journal of Population Economics* 19 (1): 163–81.

Smith, J. P., D. Thomas, E. Frankenberg, K. Beegle, and G. Teruel. 2002. "Wages, Employment, and Economic Shocks: Evidence from Indonesia." *Journal of Population Economics* 15 (1): 161–93.

Spencer, M. B., and V. C. McLoyd, eds. 1990. *Child Development: Special Issue on Minority Children* 61 (2): 263–589.

Steinberg, L. 2001. "We Know Some Things: Parent-Adolescent Relationships in Retrospect and Prospect." *Journal of Research on Adolescence* 11 (1): 1–19.

Steinberg, L., S. D. Lamborn, N. Darling, N. S. Mounts, and S. M. Dornbusch. 1994. "Over-Time Changes in Adjustment and Competence among Adolescents from Authoritative, Authoritarian, Indulgent, and Neglectful Families." *Child Development* 65 (3): 754–70.

Strauss, J., and D. Thomas. 2005. "Human Resources: Empirical Modeling of Household and Family Decisions." In *Handbook of Development Economics*, Vol. III, Pt. 1, ed. J. Behrman and T. N. Srinivasan, chap. 34. Oxford, UK: Elsevier.

Super, C. M., and S. Harkness. 1994. "The Developmental Niche." In *Psychology and Culture*, ed. W. J. Lonner and R. Malpass, 95–99. Boston: Allyn & Bacon.

Teo, A., E. Carlson, P. J. Mathieu, B. Egeland, and L. A. Sroufe. 1996. "A Prospective Longitudinal Study of Psychosocial Predictors of Achievement." *Journal of School Psychology* 34 (3): 285–306.

Thomas, D., K. Beegle, E. Frankenberg, B. Sikoki, J. Strauss, and G. Teruel. 2004. "Education in a Crisis." *Journal of Development Economics* 74 (1): 53–85.

Townsend, R. 1994. "Risk and Insurance in Village India." *Econometrica* 62 (3): 539–91.

Vinokur, A. D., R. H. Price, and R. D. Caplan. 1996. "Hard Times and Hurtful Partners: How Financial Strain Affects Depression and Relationship Satisfaction of Unemployed Persons and Their Spouses." *Journal of Personality and Social Psychology* 71 (1): 166–79.

Votruba-Drzal, E. 2006. "Economic Disparities in Middle Childhood Development: Does Income Matter?" *Developmental Psychology* 42 (6): 1154–67.

Wintre, M. G., and M. Yaffe. 2000. "First-Year Students' Adjustment to University Life as a Function of Relationships with Parents." *Journal of Adolescent Research* 15 (1): 9–37.

Woessman, L. 2001. "New Evidence on the Missing Resource-Performance Link in Education." Kiel Working Paper 1051, Kiel Institute of World Economics, Kiel, Germany.

Yamauchi, Futoshi, Yisehac Yohannes, and Agnes R. Quisumbing. 2009. "Natural Disasters, Self-Insurance, and Human Capital Investment: Evidence from Bangladesh, Ethiopia and Malawi." Policy Research Working Paper, World Bank, Washington, DC.

CHAPTER 5

Aggregate Economic Shocks during Adolescence: Transitions, Mental Health, and Behaviors

Previous chapters have repeatedly mentioned the importance of investments in early childhood. According to the most recent data, however, investments during adolescence are also critically important for adult outcomes. Failing to sustain these investments may reverse the beneficial impacts of investments in earlier life. Experiences in adolescence can still significantly affect brain development. For example, Ramsden et al. (2011) used MRI scans of adolescent brains to show that significant positive and negative changes in IQ test scores over a four-year period were correlated with changes in the brain structure. Adolescence is also a time of several deep-reaching transitions; at some point in time, a young person is usually expected to leave school, find employment, and start a family. In this sense, today's youth become tomorrow's adults: workers, parents, and citizens. Profound shifts in the context, for example, caused by economic crisis can disrupt these transitions. A better understanding of development during this stage is clearly warranted. This chapter reviews the empirical literature on how economic crisis affects youth's development through the conceptual framework developed in chapter 2. After a brief introduction to adolescent development in a global context, the chapter proceeds to review the evidence on how aggregate economic shocks affect youth employment, mental health, and risky behavior; it concludes with the main messages.

Adolescent Development: An Introduction
Alice Wuermli

Adolescence is marked by profound physical, emotional, and social transitions. Puberty kicks off the physical transition to adulthood with hormonal changes, bringing about alterations in physical appearance. Social, emotional, and cognitive transitions and changes in social expectations accompany the visible transformation. A young person is eventually expected to transition to work, become financially independent, and start a family, which often marks the completion of the transition to adulthood. However, development during adolescence does not always follow such a normative pattern. As children become more and more autonomous with age, they develop the ability to negotiate their lives and become active agents in their own development. In addition, because the developmental tasks are culturally specific, they can vary a great deal and are subject to an ever-shifting social, political, and economic context. In particular, social expectations of *when* certain transitions take place vary significantly. Much of the literature stems from the "Western" world and is thus not necessarily applicable to other cultures and contexts. The challenge here lies in identifying parameters of adolescent development that are more generally applicable and adaptable to a greater age range and historical time and space.

In developing countries, governments, international agencies, and nongovernmental organizations are often concerned with young people's transition to work. Prolonged unemployment or inactivity is often believed to lead to high costs related to risky behavior, crime, and violence and is perceived as a potential source of civil unrest, as we have observed with the Arab Spring movement across the Middle East. In a crisis context, when unemployment is likely to increase, these concerns move to the forefront. For this reason, this chapter focuses on young people's transition to work and their mental health, particularly the tasks to be mastered during adolescence, and risk and supportive factors that directly affect task mastery or moderate the impact of crises on development during this important life stage.

Roisman et al. (2004) regard "work" as an emerging task, rather than as a stage-salient task. In other words, work is an indicator of a healthy adaptation to adult life, while academic success and healthy peer relationships are salient tasks of adolescence. According to their study, mastery of the salient tasks of adolescence is a better predictor of success in emerging tasks than earlier success in emerging tasks themselves are, such as work and romantic relationships (Roisman et al. 2004). Thus, youth who have not yet mastered the age-appropriate salient tasks are likely to encounter more difficulty at emerging tasks, such as work; such difficulties are likely to lead to cascading effects, also referred to as ripple or spillover effects (see, for example, Masten and Cicchetti 2010).

As noted earlier, the problem with applying these indicators of the mastery of salient tasks and successful transition to adult life to our analysis of developing countries is that they reflect dominant developmental patterns in modern industrialized societies, which are characterized by a prolonged exploratory transition or stage of emerging adulthood. Settling into "stable adult roles and responsibilities" often does not happen until people are well into their 20s in the United States and other Western countries (Roisman et al. 2004). From a developmental perspective, the timing of these transitions will change their nature. For example, entering a marital relationship at the age of 12 as opposed to 25 will have markedly different implications. In particular, marriage at 12 implies that several transitions are likely to occur at once: puberty (menarche), leaving school, and leaving the parents' house to join the husband's house. These simultaneous transitions indicate a whole different level of stress, at an age where the self-regulatory capacity is not yet fully developed. The sequence of salient and emerging tasks is also often far from ideal, with parenthood forcing young people prematurely into adult roles. Should a 16-year-old adolescent who drops out of school to support a family therefore be treated as an adult because he has "mastered" an emerging task, fatherhood, and is now in need of some sort of financial assistance, for example, through a workfare program? Or should he be treated as a youth who has not yet mastered salient tasks, such as educational achievement? While there may be arguments on both sides, in all likelihood the young person probably will not yet have developed many of the skills and characteristics, in short the *competencies*, necessary to participate successfully in the world of work.

The specific competencies needed for a successful transition to the world of work are obviously country and context specific, but generally they fall into three major categories: cognitive, behavioral, and socioemotional. These categories are nonlinear, multidimensional, nonhierarchical, and strongly interrelated. Socioemotional difficulties, like depression or anxiety, can inhibit cognitive functioning; cognitive deficiencies can affect behavioral competencies, such as impulse control and the like. In some instances, assigning an indicator to one particular category, given the significant overlap and interactions, is difficult. However, these three categories serve as a useful organizational framework for thinking about the competencies needed to master the transition to work.

As outlined in the conceptual framework, in the face of adversity (loss of a parent, separation from family, high unemployment rates, war, recession, or social upheaval, for example) young people need a range of resources for positive adaptation. Positive adaptation, successful transition, or mastery of stage-salient developmental tasks, in the face of risk and adversity, is referred to as *resilience*. (For more detail, see chapter 2.) Resilience is built and strengthened through mediators and protective factors at the individual as well as at the social level. These factors range from physical health and intelligence to family and peer relationships, social connectedness, and the availability of cultural frameworks and repertoires for making meaning. Such resources set in motion cognitive processes for self-regulation, given socially acceptable and widely promoted aspirations and behaviors (for example, see Roisman et al. 2004; Masten 2007, 2009).

Crockett and Silbereisen (2000) identify mediating processes or factors that support positive adaptation to changes in context—for example, those brought about by an economic crisis—within which young people are expected to transition. More specifically, Crockett and Silbereisen refer to several cognitive mechanisms through which young people shape their development as active agents, including personal goals, identity, efficacy beliefs, and "planful" competence (see, for example, Brandstädter 1992; Clausen 1991).

Abstracting slightly, both for simplicity and for cross-cultural relevance, we identify three broad categories of salient developmental tasks that guide a young person's transition to the world of work: *autonomy and relatedness, identity,* and *goal setting and achievement.* These processes, which do not happen independently from each other, are marked by their interdependence with the categories and competencies referred to earlier. These three categories also represent roughly the three innate psychological needs identified by self-determination theory—competence, autonomy, and relatedness—that enhance or undermine intrinsic motivation, self-regulation, and well-being and seem to be relatively normative to human nature (Ryan and Deci 2000).

Autonomy and Relatedness

In adolescence, development becomes more self directed, given young people's greater cognitive and behavioral capabilities for exerting agency over the trajectory of their developmental path and for influencing their environment (Crockett and Silbereisen 2000). While achieving increasing autonomy becomes particularly salient during adolescence (see McLoyd et al. 2009), the young person does not disconnect from all social relations. Humans are social beings, and autonomy and relatedness are two poles on a continuum along which most people find themselves. Depending on the cultural context, individuals are somewhere between the two poles. Far from being static, this autonomy-relatedness dialectic (or dynamic) exhibits a great deal of plasticity and undergoes changes throughout the life course.

The processes leading to increased autonomy should be seen as dynamic interactions in which young people renegotiate their relationships with parents, peers, teachers, and other adults within a changing social context. When children are young, the strongest socializing influence is the family, particularly the parents, but the developing person becomes more and more exposed to other settings, such as school and peers, and eventually to nonschool adult settings like the workplace. These other settings take a dominant role in the process of socialization and are thus increasingly influential. While these processes signify change, many features of child-family relations show significant continuity (Lerner 1993). Probably one of the most important and challenging tasks for adolescents is to balance autonomy with a good relationship with their parents. Economic crisis can increase parents' stress and have an impact on these relationships.

Clearly, relationships other than those with parents, such as peers, teachers, and other adult role models, can have positive or negative influences, depending on the quality and scope of the relationship. While research has shown that adolescents tend to affiliate with people who have values similar to those of their parents (Allison and Lerner 1993), these extrafamilial relationships can nevertheless strongly influence and shape a person's identity, aspirations, and behavior, in both good and bad ways. Economic crisis in this context may have either positive or negative effects, as it can change the patterns of intrafamily relationships as well as exposure to extrafamilial influences (see, for example, Elder 1974).

Identity

In the process of negotiating autonomy and relatedness, adolescents embark on a journey of defining themselves as individuals in relation to their environment. Identity is reinforced by the choice of peers, educational achievements, and vocational aspirations, determining their future orientation.[1] In other words, the formation of preferences and aspirations is linked to "finding one's niche in society and acquiring a sense of self as existing through time" (Crockett and Silbereisen 2000).

According to Erickson (1959), the development of vocational or occupational identity occurs through adolescence and early adulthood, with adjustments according to external contexts and personal circumstances. Because the vocational hope and the development of occupational identity are shaped in part by labor market conditions, the age of entry into the labor market can be considered developmental in nature as well as economic. Economic crisis can change the context within which young people develop their identity by altering the landscape of, or the qualifying requirements for, vocational opportunities. Crisis may also render previous achievements fundamental to a person's identity irrelevant for operating successfully in a changed economic, social, and political context (Crockett and Silbereisen 2000). Even if young people are not seeking employment during the crisis or experiencing unemployment within the family, they are forming critical expectations for their future based on their increasing awareness of the world around them. Thus, during an aggregate shock, they face the challenge of updating previous expectations with the new realities. This conflict between expectations and reality can lead to what has been termed "cognitive dissonance" (Festinger 1957), broadly defined by an uncomfortable psychological state generally triggering adaptive behaviors to reduce the conflicting information.

Goal Setting and Achievement

Defining goals during adolescence becomes important, because it shapes subsequent development (Crockett and Silbereisen 2000). The goals themselves are culturally embedded. In other words, "adolescents are thought to perceive social expectations and to define tasks for themselves based on these expectations" (Crockett and Silbereisen 2000, 6). The process of pursuing these goals reflects individual interests, aspirations, and competencies, actual and perceived options and opportunities, and the ability to plan strategically. The ability to plan strategically, in turn, continues to be affected by advances in brain development during adolescence, especially development of the prefrontal cortex.

Thus, the processes that form identity in a dyadic relationship between autonomy and relatedness will greatly influence a young person's goal setting and achievement capabilities and involve skills ranging from, for example, self-regulation to efficacy beliefs, and other behavioral skills and characteristics. But what skills and characteristics are in demand is very context specific, and systemic shocks may shift these parameters. For example, societywide shifts toward more service sector jobs and away from manual labor jobs will increase the demand for such personal and social skills as communication, conflict management, conscientiousness, and willingness to take risks (Crockett and Silbereisen 2000). But such shifts can clash with previously formed identities, and positive adaptation could pose significant challenges and jeopardize healthy development and the transition to work.

To summarize the above, compared to earlier stages of development, the effects of economic crises during adolescence may differ, due to different meaning and consequences, pathways of influence, and moderating influences (McLoyd et al. 2009). As young people develop abstract thought, cognitive processing skills, social perspective-taking abilities, and capacity for empathy (all in concert with continued development of the prefrontal cortex), their awareness of how economic shocks affect their socioeconomic situation increases. Hence, their own perceptions of financial strain may be a more important pathway than an actual drop in household income through which economic crises affect their psychosocial adjustment (McLoyd et al. 2009). In addition, adolescents may become more aware of the stigma associated with poverty as they are exposed to the socializing attitudes about the causes of poverty (McLoyd et al. 2009), which invariably influence their self-esteem, identity, future orientation, and efficacy beliefs. Knowing that adolescents who experience economic pressures are at increased risk of mental health problems and knowing the implications of mental health issues for school achievement and successful transition to work, we will take a closer look at how economic crisis affects the psychosocial well-being of adolescents after reviewing the literature on labor force participation.

Economic Crisis and School-to-Work Transition
Suzanne Duryea

That youth may suffer the "labor market" burden of financial crises has been a longstanding concern. U.S. President Franklin Roosevelt declared in 1935, "I have determined that we shall do something for the Nation's unemployed youth, because we can ill afford to lose the skill and energy of these young men and women" (Roosevelt 1935). Evidence is accumulating that unemployment while young can cause permanent scars rather than temporary blemishes, and the potential for long-term damage is much greater in recessions (Ellwood 1982; Bell and Blanchflower 2010). Youth may be more vulnerable than older cohorts because they hold a disproportionate share of temporary jobs whose contracts offer less protection, as well as because they are experiencing critical developmental processes during this time. Effects may vary intertemporally and across countries and demographic groups. This chapter focuses primarily on existing literature to synthesize the short- and long-term effects of aggregate shocks on youth ages 15–24. While the lion's share of the chapter will focus on aggregate economic shocks, we will also explore the impacts of idiosyncratic shocks on youth employment outcomes.

The limitations of normatively interpreting the contemporaneous effects of aggregate shocks on the behavior of youth should be carefully considered. Unlike outcomes such as school dropout and malnutrition, no clear normative implications of declines in youth employment rates or increases in youth unemployment rates are associated with crises. Considering other jointly determined behavior such as school attendance is beyond the scope of this chapter. Some studies on adolescent schooling were highlighted in chapter 4. This chapter will focus on the larger picture of whether youth entering the labor market during a crisis are at risk of permanent impacts that effect long-term productivity. With that aim in mind, we examine the literature on the long-term developmental consequences of entering the labor market during a crisis.

Although the empirical analysis forming the bulk of the evidence base for the chapter comes from economics, the potential channels of influence consider a wider interdisciplinary scope, integrating important theories from sociology and neuroscience in addition to standard economics. This broader perspective also informs the discussion of the policy implications (see chapter 6): the policies implemented during a crisis should not focus on short-term economic behavior at the expense of the long-term developmental well-being of young people. As much as possible, the chapter attempts to disaggregate findings by age groups, gender, and the developmental stage of the country. Clearly, the long-term developmental impacts of entering the labor market during an extremely poor economic period will differ according to whether an individual experiences the crisis at age 15, 20, or 24.

Numerous transmission channels can lead to differences in how young people experience changes in the short-term labor market due to an economic crisis. During bad economic times, firms are likely to respond to reduced aggregate demand with hiring freezes, layoffs, or firing workers whose labor contracts make them the least costly to fire. Such actions are likely to have a disproportionate impact on young workers, who are less likely to have contracts with strong job protections. For example, when the temporary contracts commonly held by youth are allowed to run out, they may have difficulty finding other work opportunities (Scarpetta,

Sonnet, and Manfredi 2010). Both the downturn in hiring and the upturn in layoffs and firings contribute to higher unemployment in the short term and lower employment overall, with younger workers more likely to face disproportionate effects than older workers. On the more positive side, some employers may recognize that an economic downturn can provide an opportunity to ramp up activities such as apprenticeships for youth, putting some of the excess capacity of the adult workforce to use in training activities (Scarpetta, Sonnet, and Manfredi 2010).

Within the family, the trade-off between family income lost during a crisis and poor opportunities for finding good jobs leads to ambiguous welfare effects. The income effect during a crisis refers to young people's efforts to enter the labor market to compensate for income losses by other family members, whereas the substitution effect refers to the lower opportunity cost of not working since earning opportunities are lower. If the substitution effect dominates, then youth will not replace lost family income. Of particular concern is whether at younger ages the income effect may dominate the substitution effect and force youth to shift their time from school investments to the labor market to help their families through difficult economic times. Additional forces at play within the household can potentially influence the labor market experience of youth. For example, if unemployed or underemployed adults create greater household burdens, young people, particularly girls, may face additional domestic chores and engage less with the labor market.

We should also consider important psychological channels of influence. According to the Family Stress Model (see box 4.2), the anxiety experienced by parents during an economic crisis, associated with the threat or realization of income and asset loss, is transmitted to children through the parents' emotions and behavior. This model, based on family behavior observed during the Great Depression in the United States, has been refined based on research on families in rural America since the 1980s and tested in a number of countries (see box 4.1). As parents become more emotionally distressed, their parenting may turn harsh and inconsistent, deteriorating in ways that have negative developmental impacts (Conger et al. 1992; Conger and Elder 1994). Research has also established that adolescents who perceive economic stress within their families have lower self-expectations for the future (Flanagan 1988; Larson 1984). According to Galambos and Silbereisen (1987), parental income loss in Germany is associated with pessimistic outlooks by parents and, in turn, lower expectations of their adolescent daughters for job success.

Furthermore, crisis may directly affect adolescents' socioemotional well-being and the development of (vocational) identity, as noted earlier. In addition, adolescents are expected to develop self-regulation and planning skills. These skills have been shown to be highly rewarded by employers (Cunha, Heckman, and Lochner 2006). While it is not clear precisely how aggregate shocks can disrupt the development of these skills, the neurological research implies that promoting and protecting these investments during a crisis are of relatively more importance in early adolescence than in the late 20s (for more detail on neurological development see box 2.1).

These short-term channels form the basis for long-term impacts, as expectations are permanently shifted and some youth become "permanently discouraged" from engaging with the labor market. For example, if the aggregate shock has "scarred" a young person, he or she will have lower productivity in the labor market for many years as a result of a persistent lack of adequate matches with employers. Likewise, youth who have reacted to the crisis by becoming "permanently discouraged workers" are likely to have low rates of participation in the labor force well into the future. Researchers, for example, commonly regard the youth population in Japan, who faced a long 10-year recession over the 1990s, as permanently affected by the crisis (Scarpetta, Sonnet, and Manfredi 2010).

The overall long-term implications are also ambiguous, because youth may have responded to the crisis by shifting time away from compensated activities into educational activities such as school, internships, or vocational training. Under certain scenarios, employment may fall in the short term as unemployment rises, but 15 years later that generation might be doing well because it invested in training and education during the crisis. Under other scenarios, the same pattern in the short term may be consistent with declines in employment and wage profiles in the long term. We will first explore the literature on the short-term effects before moving to the long-term effects. The literature considers a variety of labor market outcomes, including labor market participation, employment, and unemployment. Only a few studies look directly at how a crisis affects hours worked in the labor market.[2]

The Short-Term Impacts of Crises on Young People's Labor market participation

Aggregate economic shocks. A number of studies examine the short-term effects of crises using cross-country, cross-time estimations for different subsets of countries. In a global analysis for 70 countries covering the period 1980–2000, Choudhry, Marelli, and Signorelli (2010) find that youth ages 15–24 are more affected by financial crises than older age groups, based on cross-country, cross-time regressions that include fixed effects for countries. According to their study, employment decreases and unemployment increases disproportionately for youth during a financial crisis, with young women more affected than young men. They do not find significant effects, however, for the low-income countries included in their study. Consistent with the Choudhry, Marelli, and Signorelli (2010), Bell and Blanchflower (2010) explore the 2008–09 crisis in the United Kingdom and the United States, finding again that young people ages 16–24 are more affected than older age groups. They find that for the United States the less educated and minority youth are more affected and that minority youth are most affected in the United Kingdom.

Verick (2009) examines trends in the unemployment rate for youth and older workers in relation to the five big crises of Finland (1991), Japan (1992), Norway (1987), Spain (1977), and Sweden (1991), as well as crises of smaller magnitudes in Mexico and Turkey.[3] In this descriptive analysis, he finds that youth are more vulnerable than adults to rising unemployment during and immediately after a crisis, with peak unemployment rates reached earlier for youth than for adults.

Cho and Newhouse (2011) examine the effect of the 2008–09 crisis on a broad variety of labor market outcomes using repeated household surveys for 17 middle-income countries. They explore whether the behavior for specific groups during the crisis is a deviation from precrisis trends. Although they find that youth in general are more affected by crises than older age groups, this finding does not hold across the sample. For example, among the five Latin American countries included in their sample, youth are not more sensitive than the older age group in the cases of Brazil, Costa Rica, and Mexico in employment-to-population trends, whereas Argentina and Chile follow the more general pattern. They apply decompositions to find that the relatively larger declines in employment for youth are driven mainly by larger across-the-board declines in employment within sector rather than by shifts across sectors. Cho and Newhouse do not find observed declines in wages associated with the crisis, speculating that rigid labor market rules may be preventing wages from adjusting.

A rather large literature also focuses on particular countries and attempts to isolate the effect of a shock on the labor outcomes of youth. This literature often concentrates on a smaller age range of younger children, given that a common concern is that the economic crisis may be driving youth away from schooling into paid work activities if the income effect dominates. The evidence from this literature is largely consistent with the more general findings that during an aggregate shock, youth employment declines. For example, Duryea and Arends-Kuenning (2003) find that youth employment for 14–16-year-olds in Brazil decreases with large declines in economic conditions. Their analysis examines 12 years of data for 18 or 25 urban areas of Brazil, with deep crisis years defined as 1983 and 1992. While employment is found to drop during large declines in economic conditions, the declines in employment are not as large during the deep crisis years, suggesting that the depth of the crisis may increase the relative power of the income effect.

Using a similar identification strategy, Lopez Boo (2010) finds comparable results for 13–18-year-olds in Argentina, with employment falling during the 2002 crisis. Other studies have examined Argentina (Cunningham and Bustos-Salvagno 2011), El Salvador (Duryea and Morales 2011), Indonesia (Thomas et al. 2002), Mexico (McKenzie 2003), and Peru (Schady 2004). Schady examines employment outcomes over three household surveys for Peru and finds that the employment rates for 12–17-year-olds were lowest during the economic crisis. In their study of Greater Buenos Aires, Cunningham and Bustos-Salvagno (2011) find no effect of the aggregate shock on the labor supply of three out of four groups (girls and boys ages 12–15 and ages 16–17). Although McKenzie's study for Mexico is not primarily centered on children or youth, his findings on the labor supply are similar to those of three out of four groups unaffected by the aggregate shock.[4]

With a few important exceptions, the available evidence on the 2008–09 economic crisis and previous crises generally shows that employment for youth declines during bad economic times. This suggests that the drop in expected earnings and opportunity cost of their time does not lead to dropping out of school to join the labor market.

However, a more severe crisis may force young people out of school. For example, Duryea and Morales (2011) explore the effect of an early phase of the 2008–09 global financial crisis on employment for youth ages 10–16 in El Salvador. The case of El Salvador was specifically selected to explore impacts associated with a deep crisis in the context of restricted fiscal space. The quarterly growth rate of the index of economic activity in El Salvador turned negative for both the third and the fourth quarters of 2008, following steady growth rates of 5 percent for 2006 and 2007 (Central Bank 2009), and the percentage of households reporting the receipt of remittances dropped from 23 percent in 2007 to 17 percent in

2008. A higher percentage of respondents from El Salvador in a regional public opinion poll perceived the crisis to be severer in nature than in 21 other countries in the region (Seligson and Zechmeister 2010). For their sample of boys ages 10–16, the authors find that the initial phase of the crisis was associated with a five-percentage-point increase in employment and a corresponding decline in school attendance for both sexes. In this case, the acute drop in income outweighed the discouraging effect of lower expected earnings, and drove young people out of school.

Exploring the implications of a positive aggregate shock is also informative. Atkin (2009a) finds that when a new factory opens in Mexico, providing employment opportunities for the sample of women ages 16–29, employment in manufacturing increases and schooling outcomes fall. In a related study, Atkin finds that for every 10 jobs created, one student drops out of school at grade 9 rather than continuing to complete high school at grade 12 (2009b).

A report on the impacts of the 2008–09 recession in Eastern Europe and Central Asia indicates that youth unemployment reached record highs as labor market conditions deteriorated during the crisis (World Bank 2011). Interestingly though, Koettl, Oral, and Santos (2011) find that while young workers were the first to be let go, they were also the first to be rehired once the recovery set in.

Idiosyncratic economic shocks. We can also explore the short-term effects of idiosyncratic shocks on youth employment. We consider this literature separately, since economic theory implies that households are more likely to find resources to buffer shocks if their extended families and neighbors are not hit contemporaneously. In other words, if one house is damaged by a lightning strike, the family can ask neighbors and nonresident family members for help. If the house is similarly damaged through a villagewide hurricane, however, the neighbors and nonresident family members will be in similar situations and less able to provide assistance.

Cunningham and Maloney (2000) follow households over five consecutive quarters using the Mexico National Urban Employment Survey over 1987–97. They find weak evidence that parental job loss causes children to leave school and enter employment, with some evidence that girls are more affected than boys. Using this same panel data from Mexico during the tequila crisis, Skoufias and Parker (2006) investigate whether idiosyncratic labor market shocks—proxied by unemployment of the male household head—affect the labor force participation of spouse and children. They find no evidence that the labor force participation of youth ages 12–19 is influenced by the job loss of the household head and no evidence that the youth's response differs by the poverty level of the family.

Based on the variation occurring in the exchange rate of remittances as a result of the Asian financial crisis, Yang (2006) finds that unanticipated reductions in remittances are associated with increases in hours worked by 10–17-year-olds. Because the remitting family members were differentially affected by the Asian crisis depending on their location, the crisis had heterogeneous impacts on remittance flows.

Duryea, Lam, and Levison (2007) exploit pooled panel data in Brazil, covering 1982–99, to explore the effect of unemployment of the household head on the employment and schooling outcomes of youth ages 10–16. They find that over a four-month period young people are significantly more likely to enter the labor force if the household head enters into unemployment over that period, with boys responding slightly more than girls. The probability of labor force participation is predicted to increase by approximately 50 percent for 16-year-old girls and 57 percent for 16-year-old boys. The consensus in the literature is that idiosyncratic shocks have the potential to increase the labor force participation of youth, possibly at the cost of schooling.

The Long-Term Impacts of Crises on Young People's Labor Market Participation

Early encounters with weak labor markets may shape labor market trajectories over many years, as both psychological expectations and experience profiles are formed (see, for example, Crockett and Silbereisen 2000). Various authors have documented that employment in countries in the Organisation for Economic Co-operation and Development (OECD) is more sensitive to crisis and severe downturns for young people than for older age groups, with youth failing to catch up when the economy rebounds (Scarpetta, Sonnet, and Manfredi 2010; Verick 2009). Other studies have tried to capture effects over 15–20 years. Developed countries have a rich literature examining longitudinal data that allow the long-term labor market trajectories to be explored in relation to the timing of the crisis. Many of these studies explore the effect of "entering" the labor market at a particular age, whether the individual experiences the crisis at the critical years of 15–17 or experiences the crisis just after high school or college graduation. Some empirical analyses are also available for a handful of developing countries.

For example, using longitudinal data for the United States, Kahn (2010) finds a persistent negative wage effect of graduating from college during an economic downturn. She finds an initial wage loss of 6–7 percent per a one-percentage-point increase in the state unemployment rate, with this effect declining in magnitude by approximately a quarter of a percentage point each year after college graduation. However, even 15 years after college graduation, the wage loss is still significant at 2.5 percent.

Using longitudinal data for Canada, Oreopoulos, von Watcher, and Heisz (2006) examine the long-term effects of graduating from college during a recession. On average, a two standard-deviation increase in the unemployment rate (roughly comparing the difference between those exiting college in a bust versus boom) leads to an initial wage gap of about 10 percent. Wage losses after five years fall to approximately half the difference and then fade to zero after 10 years. By exploiting matched data across individuals and firms, the authors are able to show that labor market conditions at the time of college graduation affect the quality of matches and job mobility, with lower-skilled graduates less able to switch into firms with higher productivity.[5]

Stevens (2008) follows a sample of German workers over a 19-year period to examine the long-term effects of initial labor market conditions. She argues that unemployment rates at the time of labor market entry can be considered as exogenous, because education is a predetermined variable given the tracking into different programs that happens before ages 16–18 in the German educational system. Her study is also notable for its ability to track individuals over the long panel and for examining the long-term effect on wages in addition to employment and unemployment. For less educated males, she finds that entering the labor market during a time of higher unemployment rates has a negative effect on wages.

Burgess et al. (2003) exploit repeated cross-sections of British labor force surveys (1981–97) to examine the long-term effects of initial unemployment, measured as the unemployment of the birth cohort at ages 16–18. Although Burgess et al. are motivated by the deep crisis of the 1980s, their identification strategy exploits all the intercohort business-cycle variation. They find that higher aggregate unemployment at the time of entry has mixed effects. For low-skilled individuals, they find a persistent effect and significantly higher unemployment rates (approximately one percentage point), with effects lasting between 15 and 20 years. Higher-skilled individuals, however, fare better in the long run from adverse initial labor market conditions, probably because, when faced with those poor conditions, they take advantage of the opportunity to invest further in their education. Their results are robust to controlling for cohort size and for estimating employment rather than unemployment.

For Norway, Raaum and Roed (2006) find that a severe economic slump that occurs when young people are 16–19-years-old may raise their adult unemployment rates at ages 25–38 by one to two percentage points. Using the population registry for 1993–2000 to trace individuals born between 1961 and 1974 as well as merged information on labor market and demographic characteristics, they are able to carefully explore the role of family background because they have information on the education of the parents of all individuals. They find that people with high predicted education, as based on parents' education and other family characteristics, also suffer long-term consequences from entering the labor market during bad economic times.

While longitudinal data covering 15–20 years of employment experiences are usually not available for developing countries, some countries do have consistent series of household surveys to which the Burgess et al. (2003) analysis can be applied. Table 5.1 shows the results for six countries for which this similar analysis has been conducted: Argentina, Brazil, Chile, Germany, Norway, and the United Kingdom. Although there is some cross-country heterogeneity in the samples and results, the table shows some commonalities. First, the results for Argentina, Germany, Norway, and the United Kingdom all show the significant negative effects of entering the labor market during poor economic conditions for less-educated males. The effects are not always found to be significantly negative, but only for one group were they found to be positive (highly educated males in the United Kingdom). The duration of effects as shown in table 5.2 was not explored for all countries but was found to be similar in Argentina and the United Kingdom, where the effects on employment faded after about 15 years. Overall, this evidence seems to point toward important negative and persistent effects of severe economic downturns on long-term employment trajectories.

Other studies have analyzed the long-term implications of unemployment experienced in early years (see Mroz and Savage 2006 for the United States; Gregg 2001 for the United Kingdom). While some of these studies find moderate effects on the employment and unemployment trajectories, a strong consensus on the long-term effects on wages has formed. For example, Gregg and Tominey (2005) find that unemployment at age 22 is associated with a 10 percent loss in wages two decades later. Moreover, a series of studies finds that unemployment experienced at early ages is associated later in life with illness, stress, depression, and lower life expectancy (see summary in Bell and Blanchflower 2010).

Table 5.1   Long-Term Effect on Employment of Entering the Labor Market during Poor Economic Conditions in Six Countries: Argentina (1980–2010), Brazil (1978–2002), Chile (1957–2005), Germany (1975–2001), Norway (1993–2000), and the United Kingdom (1981–97)

5.1a   Less-Educated and Highly Educated Males and Females in High-Income Countries

	Less-educated males	Less-educated females	Highly educated males	Highly educated females
Germany	–	n.a.	n.a.	n.a.
Norway	–	–	–	–
United Kingdom	–	–	+	0

5.1b   All Males and Females and Less-Educated and Highly Educated Males and Females in Middle-Income Countries

	All males	All females	Less-educated (males and females)	Highly-educated (males and females)
Argentina	0	0	–	–
Brazil	0	0	0	0
Chile	–	–	0	–

Sources: United Kingdom (Burgess et al. 2003 based on data for 1981–97), Germany (Stevens 2008 based on data for 1975–2001), Norway (Raaum and Roed 2006 based on data for 1993–2000), Argentina (author's calculations based on 1980–2010 with no data available for 1981, 1983, 1984), Chile (Fares and Montenegro 2011 based on data for 1957–2005), and Brazil (Fares and Montenegro 2011 based on data for 1978–2002 with no data available for years 1980, 1991, 1994 and 2000).

Note: The studies did not analyze the same skill and gender categorizations. Only Argentina was fully comparable. – indicates a significant negative effect was measured at least a 90% level of significance; + indicates a significant positive effect was measured at least a 90% level of significance; 0 indicates no significant effect was measured; n.a. indicates that this group was not tested.

Table 5.2   Estimated Duration of Adverse Effects on Employment of Entering the Labor Market during Poor Economic Conditions for Argentina and the United Kingdom (number of years effects persist)

		Less-educated males	Less-educated females	Less-educated (males and females)	Highly educated (males and females)
High income	United Kingdom	18	18	n.a.	n.a.
Middle income	Argentina	16	16	16	16

Sources: United Kingdom (Burgess et al. 2003 based on data for 1981–97), Argentina (author's calculations based on 1980–2010 with no data available for 1981, 1983, and 1984).

Note: n.a. = not tested.

Significant evidence indicates the relationship between unemployment and mental health issues (McLoyd et al. 2009). Psychological studies have found that difficulty in the labor market often leads to hopelessness and low self-esteem (Bowman 1990) with these adverse effects particularly pronounced in young people who are in the process of forming occupational identities. It seems pertinent to this analysis to look more closely at mental health during adolescence.

Economic Crisis and Adolescent Mental Health
Sarah Baird, Kathleen Beegle, and Jed Friedman

Just as difficulties in the labor market can cause mental health issues, mental health and behavioral issues can also cause problems in the labor market.

Mental Health among Adolescents

Mental health disorders are the major contributor to the disease burden among young people ages 12–24. Specifically, 20–25 percent of youth will suffer from a mental disorder in any given year (Patel et al. 2007). In a review of 11 epidemiological community studies from developed and developing countries, Patel et al. (2007) show that the point prevalence rate (the proportion of people in a population who have a disease or condition at a particular time) of mental disorders among adolescents range from 8 percent in the Netherlands to 27 percent in Australia. Beyond being a concern in their own right, mental health problems during youth can also lead to lower educational gains, substance abuse, violence, and risky sexual behavior (see, for example, Currie and Stabile 2006; Eisenberg and Golberstein 2009; Fletcher 2008, 2010; Fletcher and Wolfe 2008; Kessler et al. 1995; Patel et al. 2007; Prince et al. 2007; Stein and Kean 2000). Mental disorders also place a substantial burden on mortality among this age group. In India, for example, a study found that suicide accounted for a quarter of deaths in boys and between half and three-quarters of deaths in girls ages 10–19 years (Aaron et al. 2004). These adverse health and developmental effects can in turn have a long-term impact on socioeconomic outcomes and thus result in a reinforcing cycle of poverty and poor mental health (Patel and Kleinman 2003).

In general, adolescence may be a time when exposure to stress may have particularly strong long-term outcomes. The stress-vulnerability model suggests that exposure to stressful events during adolescence is associated with increased risky decision making (Fishbein et al. 2006; see also the section on risky behavior later in this chapter). Moreover, a negative shock to the household may have long-lasting effects on the mental health of adolescents (McLoyd et al. 2009) and long-term implications for physical health (Evans et al. 2007).

The potential negative impact of crises on the mental health of adolescents also has potentially strong consequences for the young children of young adults. Given that a significant percentage of births in the developing world occur to women under the age of 24, the impact of crises on maternal mental health may have lasting effects on current and future generations, as noted in earlier chapters. Maternal mental health is linked to infant growth, survival, preterm delivery, and low birth weight (Prince et al. 2007). It also affects the relationship between the mother and the child. O'Brien et al. (2004), for example, find a significant relationship between postnatal depression and faltering growth (failure to thrive) among children, a relationship partially due to the connection between maternal depression and mother-child interaction. Aizer, Stroud, and Buka (2009) find a robust negative link between maternal stress during pregnancy, as measured through cortisol levels in the blood, and subsequent educational attainment of those infants exposed to elevated levels of cortisol. This last finding is particularly relevant because it suggests that even the transitory impacts of crisis on the psychosocial health of pregnant mothers can have long-lasting effects on children.

Although the effects of parenting on child development are not explored substantially in economics, the psychology literature emphasizes that the quality of parenting is critical for child development, even during adolescence. For a number of reasons, parenting may be altered during times of crisis, in part as a result of its impacts on parental mental health and in part as a result of its effect on time use.[6] Evidence from the rural Midwest of the United States in 1989 suggests that financial pressure affected the emotions of parents. This pressure disrupted parents' childrearing behavior, and adverse moods had harmful consequences for adolescent development (Conger et al. 1994). We will revisit the critical role of parenting in the concluding section.

Patel et al. (2007) identify a range of risk factors for mental health disorders in adolescents, including poverty and social disadvantage, unstable romantic relationships, violence and abuse, poor physical health, and inadequate education. In their study of adults, however, Das et al. (2008) are unable to confirm a relationship between poverty and mental health based on their analysis of survey data on mental health from five developing countries. Along with the risk factors listed above, some evidence also indicates that women are more likely than men to suffer from poor mental health and depressive disorders (Das et al. 2008; Patel et al. 2007). This gender differential is likely to result from a combination of genetic and environmental risk factors (Patel and Kleinman 2003). Engaging family and educational environments (such as parents' encouraging children to express their emotions and schools' providing a safe learning atmosphere), however, can reduce the probability that adolescents will develop mental disorders (Lewinsohn, Rohde, and Seeley 1998; Patel et al. 2007; Saluja et al. 2004).

Evidence of the Impact of Crises on Mental Health

Aggregate economic shocks. Given this background, what impact do we expect financial crises to have on the mental health of adolescents? According to Das et al. (2007), unexpected life events (brought on by either positive or negative shocks) can have a strong effect on mental health. A small number of studies have focused specifically on the impact of economic crises and mental health in developing countries, although none focuses specifically on adolescents. In Thailand after the 1997 financial crisis, rates of suicidal thoughts, severe stress, and hopeless feelings rose dramatically among the recently unemployed (Tangcharoensathien et al. 2000). Friedman and Thomas (2009), using panel data from Indonesia, find a dramatic rise in symptoms related to depression and anxiety due to the Asian financial crisis, particularly among the groups most adversely affected, such as the less-educated, urban, and landless households. This increase appears to persist despite the recovery of other measures of economic welfare such as household income and consumption. Hong, Knapp, and McGuire (2011) look at the impact of the Asian financial crisis on mental health in South Korea from 1998 to 2007. The authors find that rates of suicide and major depression rose after the economic crisis and that the poor were disproportionately affected by mental health disorders.

Natural disasters. If we focus on crisis more generally and incorporate natural disasters, we have a larger body of literature at our disposal; however, that literature provides very limited evidence on adolescents specifically. As with childhood health, one must be cautious in extrapolating these results to financial crises, since the impact of conflict and natural disaster on mental health goes far beyond the effect of a loss in income.

A body of evidence on the impact of Hurricane Katrina on mental health is developing. A survey of adults pre- and post-Katrina suggests that the estimated prevalence of serious mental illness rose significantly after Katrina (from 6.1 percent before to 11.3 percent after) and mild-to-moderate mental illness (from 9.7 percent before to 19.9 percent after) (Kessler et al. 2006). Interestingly, the same study also finds that the prevalence of suicidal ideation and planning was significantly lower post-Katrina due to two dimensions of personal growth that mitigate the impact of large negative shocks on mental health: people's faith in their own abilities to rebuild their lives and the realization of inner strength. According to some evidence, the mental health impacts of Katrina still persisted four years after the disaster, particularly for those who suffered severe financial problems, although the impacts had dissipated somewhat (Picou and Hudson 2010).

In a developing country context, Frankenberg et al. (2008) investigate mental health in Indonesia after the tsunami. They find that posttraumatic stress reactivity (PTSR) was highest for respondents that were most affected by the tsunami. Moreover, they find that PTSR had the highest increase for those between the ages of 15 and 29, suggesting vulnerability in young adulthood.

Positive income shocks. Some evidence on the impact of positive income shocks on mental health also provides further insight into the potential impact of financial crises. Stillman, McKenzie, and Gibson (2009) show that individuals who were selected by lottery to migrate from Tonga to New Zealand (which has higher living standards) exhibited significantly improved mental health outcomes. Gardner and Oswald (2007) provide more direct evidence on the impact of positive income shocks on mental well-being by showing that British lottery winners exhibit significant improvements in mental health. In developing countries, additional evidence on the impact of positive shocks comes largely from the literature on conditional cash transfer programs. Filmer and Schady (2009) present evidence that a cash transfer intervention in Cambodia had a small effect on the mental health of its adolescent beneficiaries. Baird, de Hoop, and Ozler (2011) investigate the impact of a cash transfer program in Malawi on its adolescent female participants. They found that during the two-year program the likelihood of suffering from psychological distress was 17 percent lower in the conditional-cash-transfer arm and 38 percent lower in the unconditional-cash-transfer arm when compared with the control group. The beneficial mental health effects of the cash transfers were limited to the intervention period, however, and dissipated quickly after the program ended.

Economic Crisis and Risky Adolescent Behavior
Mattias Lundberg

Risky Behaviors during Adolescence

Just as the experience of crisis in youth can have lifelong consequences, young people can be similarly affected over the long term by the consequences of their own behavior. The decision to smoke, drink alcohol, or engage in unprotected sex or other dangerous activities may be extremely costly in later life. HIV and tobacco are the only two large and growing causes of death around the world. Smoking kills roughly 5 million people each year; by 2030, that number is expected to double (Jha et al. 2006). Long after tobacco smoking peaked in the United States, tobacco was the single-largest cause of all lung cancer deaths, and about half of those who died were still in middle age. In some developing countries today, close to half of all young men are smokers. Similarly, HIV develops into AIDS with a lag of up to 10 years, taking its toll on people in their prime working ages. In many developing countries, new HIV infections affect young people disproportionately (World Bank 2006).

The Impacts of Economic Crises and Adolescent Risk Taking

Youth is a time of experimentation: young people certainly take more risks than adults, and they make more mistakes than adults. They have less information and less experience and often do not fully understand the future implications of current choices (O'Donoghue and Rabin 2001). However, the link between income, employment, or other measures of socioeconomic status and risk taking are weak; and there is little direct evidence on the impact of changing economic status and risky behavior. In principle, consumption of any normal good—including tobacco, alcohol, and even illegal drugs—will increase when income increases and fall when income falls.[7] The argument that consumption is countercyclical relies on the idea that young people have more idle time or become despondent, leading to more self-destructive behavior (for example, United Nations 2005, 71). There is also increasing evidence of a genetic predisposition to impulsivity, risk taking, and stress response, as well as to vulnerability to addictions (Kreek et al. 2005); these genetic factors may also condition susceptibility to the stresses that accompany economic shocks. We present the evidence, mainly from developed countries (Europe and the United

States) on the links between economic crises and risky behavior as manifest in crime and delinquency, substance abuse, and unprotected sex.

Delinquency and crime. Delinquency, criminality, and violence among youth are generally correlated with levels of poverty and parental unemployment: those young people who commit crimes are more likely to come from poor households and those in which parents have little education and few chances to prosper (Farrington 2009). Little evidence links delinquency and crime to changes in employment or income. Most studies show no effect of unemployment on violent crime and only a weak effect on property crime (Levitt and Lochner 2001).

Research does indicate one important, although indirect, connection between economic shocks and delinquency. A number of studies show that poor parental discipline and harsh parenting are the strongest predictors of delinquency among youth (Smith and Stern 1997) and that fathers who experience severe income loss or unemployment may become more irritable, tense, and explosive in their relationships with children (Elder and Rockwell 1985).[8] Experience of conflict and violence between parents is also correlated with delinquency and criminality among youth (Buehler et al. 1997), while family separation is not a consistent predictor (Farrington 2009). Thus, we can identify possible pathways through which a crisis might increase delinquency.

Smoking and use of drugs and alcohol. The links between socioeconomic status and drug abuse are conflicting: drug use is positively correlated with higher income, but the correlation with higher education is negative (Chassin, Hussong, and Beltran 2009). This positive link with income is not surprising if these are normal goods; education may confer information about the potential harm or may signal differences in human capital investments and time preference.

Again, most studies examine the impact of poverty and employment levels rather than the impact of *becoming* unemployed or poor, and the evidence is generally mixed. While a study in Sweden found that unemployment is a risk factor for increasing consumption of alcohol, tobacco, and illicit drugs, particularly among young men (Hammarström and Janlert 1994), a Norwegian study showed no impact on alcohol consumption in general but a decrease among a high-alcohol-consumption group and an increase in cannabis use (Hammer 1992). On the one hand, research in the United States shows that, when the economy is weak, teenagers increase their use of marijuana and other drugs and are more likely to be involved selling drugs, and there is some indication of higher alcohol consumption (Arkes 2007). On the other hand, recent studies show that the consumption of alcohol, tobacco, and illegal drugs is strongly procyclical, increasing in good economic times (Svensson and Hagquist 2010; Kruger and Svensson 2010; Johansson et al. 2006; Ruhm 2005). Longer duration of unemployment, however, is more consistently associated with illegal drug use, but not alcohol or tobacco, in Scotland (Peck and Plant 1986), heavier drinking in the United Kingdom (Power and Estaugh 1990), and taking up smoking in Sweden (Hammarström and Janlert 1994).

While it is true that young people who experience severe stress are more likely to use alcohol, tobacco, and drugs (Chassin, Hussong, and Beltran 2009; Fletcher and Sindelar, forthcoming), not all young people respond to stress in this way. Evidence suggests that those who are unable to modulate stress response (who may be either hyper- or hypo-reactive) will turn to alcohol and drugs to control responses to stressful situations (Iacono et al. 1999). In addition, Deb et al. (2011) show that individuals who are more likely to respond to job loss by increasing unhealthy behaviors are already exhibiting these problems before losing their jobs. In contrast, emotional distress, such as anxiety or depression, is not consistently correlated with substance abuse (Chassin, Hussong, and Beltran 2009).

Risky sexual activity. In addition to the causal pathways illustrated above, some argue that, especially for young women, economic shocks increase hardship, decrease bargaining power, and leave them vulnerable to coerced and unprotected sex or to sex in exchange for money or gifts. As with the other behaviors discussed here, the evidence is mixed. As Leclerc-Madlala (2003) has shown conclusively, poverty is not usually the main factor leading young women to exchange sex for money or gifts. In fact, no robust, consistent correlation exists between either income or school enrollment and transactional sex. One multicountry study using data from the Demographic and Health Studies (Chatterji et al. 2005) found a negative relationship in Burkina Faso and Togo and a positive relationship in Mali and Nigeria. An in-depth study of young men and women in Ghana and Kenya found no relationship between wealth status and sexual risk-taking behavior for women in either country and a positive relationship for men in Kenya, where wealthier men have significantly more sexual partners than men from lower-income groups (Awusabo-Asare and Annim 2008). Conversely, Arkes and Klerman (2008) show that for 15–17-year-old females in the United States, the rate of pregnancies is higher when the unemployment rate is higher, which is consistent with the countercyclical fertility patterns for this group. For 18–20-year-old males, the results suggested countercyclical patterns of fertility behaviors and outcomes for whites but procyclical patterns for blacks.

While those studies focus on the links between income levels and sexual activity, two studies in South Africa find little evidence of the impact of shocks to the household on sexual behaviors. Dinkelman, Lam, and Liebbrandt (2007) find a small link between condom use and experience of an economic shock within the past two years. Lee-Rife (2008) finds no associations between household shocks and sexual activity, condom use, or the age difference between young people and their sexual partners.

Data from the Demographic and Health Surveys around the world indicate that 13 percent of unmarried women between the ages of 15 and 19 received money or gifts in exchange for sex in the four weeks preceding the survey (Jejeebhoy and Bott 2003). Studies on sex for exchange show that women receive higher returns for unprotected sex and that economic hardship increases willingness to engage in riskier sex practices. Gertler, Shah, and Bertozzi (2005) find that sex workers earn a 23 percent premium for unprotected sex, relative to sex with a condom; and Luke (2006) finds a strong negative relationship between cash transfers and gifts in informal relationships and condom use. In addition, women are more willing to engage in risky acts if they have recently suffered an income shock. Robinson and Yeh (2011) find that women engage in sex-for-money transactions in part to deal with unexpected income shocks and that women increase their supply of riskier, better-compensated sex on days in which a household member falls ill.

Conversely, positive income shocks appear to have a protective effect. Baird et al. (2010) found that a small payment to adolescent girls, conditional on school attendance, led to significant declines in early marriage, teenage pregnancy, and self-reported sexual activity among program beneficiaries after just one year of program implementation. For program beneficiaries who were out of school at baseline, the probability of getting married or becoming pregnant declined by more than 40 percent and 30 percent, respectively. More than a third of all program beneficiaries also delayed their onset of sexual activity by a full year.[9]

Finally, as with drug abuse, crisis and sexual risk taking may be indirectly related, mediated through stress and mental health. In a recent study in Uganda, Lundberg et al. (2011) show that depression is associated with a greater number of lifetime partners and with having concurrent partners, especially among women, and that psychological distress is associated with inconsistent condom use among men.

Summary of Risk Taking in Adolescence

In sum, according to some evidence, economic adversity leads to greater risk taking, but this response is by no means universal; equal evidence argues to the contrary. Although no consistent pattern of impact on average has emerged, there is great heterogeneity around the average. The key is to understand the sources of the heterogeneity, to identify who is more likely to be adversely affected and why in order to target effectively, and to design appropriate interventions to enable protection and recovery, if necessary. For example, stress seems to be a significant mediator for risky behavior. In addition, those at greater risk during a crisis appear to be those who are already at greater risk, whether for economic or for biological reasons. In addition, as discussed earlier, environmental influences, such as families, peers, and neighborhoods, can play a significant role in determining behavioral responses to stressful situations.

Conclusions

This chapter reviewed the literature on how economic crises affect young people's employment and mental health and attempted to understand how shocks might affect their propensity to engage in risky behavior. Studies looking at the short-term labor market impacts of economic crises in most cases find declines in employment. While heterogeneity in some outcomes is quite strong, however, no compelling evidence indicates that young people leave school during crises to work and support the household. Notably, a study of Eastern European countries found that young workers were the first to be let go during this most recent global financial crisis but also were the first to be rehired. Studies of idiosyncratic household shocks reveal much greater heterogeneity, and older youth in particular have a tendency to start working when the household is hit by a shock. Heterogeneity also appears greater over the long term. Long-term impacts depend much on whether a person has furthered his or her education. Furthermore, there is indication that unemployment early on leads to lower income and worse physical and mental health later in life.

Several studies show a rise in mental health issues ranging from stress, hopelessness, depression, and the like in the case of both economic crises and natural disasters. Given the longitudinal nature of the data, a study was able to demonstrate an increase in mental health issues after the financial crisis in Indonesia in the late 1990s, which persisted beyond the crisis years. While these studies were not specific to young people—given their rising awareness of their family's economic situation and of the stigma associated with poverty, as well as their preoccupation with defining their relationships, their identity, and goals for the future—it seems likely that crises do affect young people's mental health.

The link between shocks and risky behavior is not clear. Contextual factors and the capacity for self-regulation thus seem more important predictors of positive adaptation. Nevertheless, while we cannot establish a clear link between crisis and teen pregnancy, teen pregnancy may still be a common phenomenon in some contexts. We should thus worry about how adolescent mental health and exposure to stressors might affect the development of the unborn, as was discussed in detail in chapter 3.

With the three broad salient tasks that shape and guide adolescent transitions in mind, we believe a crisis can affect young people through (1) the availability and predictability of employment opportunities and (2) parental employment and family functioning.

More specifically,

- A crisis may affect a young person's capacity to negotiate their relationships and achieve autonomy through its effect on his or her responsibilities and how it constrains the process of achieving financial independence.
- A crisis is likely to change the context redefining perceptions and aspirations and thus the process of developing an identity as an individual within society.
- A crisis may affect present goals, render them irrelevant or unachievable, or significantly change the parameters for achieving them.

Thus, the outcome indicators reviewed above reflect, at least in part, some of the ways that economic shocks can threaten youth development and a young person's capacity to master these three tasks. The indicators are to a large degree interrelated, and causality may run either way; a young person experiencing socioemotional problems may face greater difficulty in adapting to changes in the environment and be less able to find and keep a job; and, in turn, unemployment can lead to a range of socioemotional difficulties. Differences in internalizing (depression and anxiety, for example) or externalizing (such as violent behavior) adaptive strategies lead to further complexity in understanding the impacts of crises on adolescent development.

What becomes apparent is that young people are increasingly affected by economic crisis directly, that is, through *transmission mechanisms* other than the family or household. While a parent's unemployment may still present one plausible pathway—and can have a myriad of influences on the development of autonomy, identity, and goals—these parameters may also be affected through the young individual's personal perceptions and how these shape his or her aspirations. In other words, while infants are primarily affected by how their caregivers are affected, youth on the verge of transitioning from school to work may be affected even if their family is utterly unaffected.

Thus, it is not surprising that the *timing* of the shock makes a difference; youth close to transitioning to work seem to be most vulnerable and show the greatest long-term consequences. As the literature indicated, young people seem to be hit hardest during crises, and difficulties in this crucial transition can have long-term implications measured in lower income, higher unemployment, and worse physical and mental health. It is thus important to identify those close to this transition.

Like the transmission mechanisms during other stages of development, the shock will be mediated by the *context*. For example, poorer youth seem to be on average harder hit. However, this likely stems from factors associated with lower socioeconomic standards rather than poverty in itself. In other words, some of this impact might stem from contextual factors affecting their capacity for positive adaptation, or resilience, such as high-quality school settings or strong communities that provide support to developing aspirations and goals for the future. In addition, skills for self-regulation may not be entirely developed at the age of 17 when many youth in developing countries are expected to transition to the world of work. If this time happens to coincide with unfavorable labor market conditions, the individual may face challenges exceeding his or her ability to cope.

Chapter 6 will go into more detail on policies and interventions for youth. While adolescence is a time fraught with risks related to future employment and health, it is also a window of opportunity, and, given the support and the resources for positive adaptation, young people can respond by aligning their relationships, identities, and goals with the changing context and constraints.

Notes

1. Future orientation is a cognitive-motivational-affective construct referring to thoughts, feelings, plans, and attitudes about the future. For more detail, see McLoyd et al. (2009).

2. Employment and work as typically measured from household surveys usually excludes household chores. The 2002 study by Skoufias and Parker (2002) is an exception, since the survey collected detailed time-use data. Girls are 18 percent more likely to be involved in domestic work, on average, and various studies have shown that when household work is included in the definition, girls work just as much or more than boys; see, for example, DeGraff and Bilsborrow (2003) for the Philippines; Levison, Moe, and Knaul (2001) for Mexico; Levison and Moe (1998) for Peru; Assaad, Levinson, and Zibani (2007) for Egypt.

3. Verick prefers to examine trends in levels of unemployment rates rather than the ratio of adult to youth unemployment.

4. Cunningham and Bustos-Salvagno examine girls and boys ages 12–15 and 16–17 and find that among the four groups only girls ages 12–15 increased labor supply in response to the aggregate shock. McKenzie's analysis also includes four groups of youth: males and females ages 15–19 and 20–24. Among these four groups, he also finds that only the younger girls ages 15–19 increase their labor supply in response to the aggregate shock.

5. For the case of Norway, this was *predicted* low education, not *realized* low education. The prediction is based on a regression both the ability of the individual and the quality of the institution since it was predicted using a regression of log earnings based on college attended, program of graduation, and years of study, conditional on province of study and cohort year.

6. Evidence from Botswana, Mexico, and Vietnam suggests that a high proportion of parents left young children at home, 50 percent, 33 percent, and 20 percent, respectively, a number that may become substantially higher during times of crisis (Ruiz-Casares and Heymann 2009). This indicates that parents may have less time overall, which can also affect their parenting capacities with adolescent children.

7. Roy (2007) presents evidence that these are normal goods.

8. More recent evidence shows a weaker link between economic downturns and child maltreatment (see, for example, Millet, Lanier, and Drake 2011).

9. Note that behavior may be affected as much by the condition as by the cash.

References

Aaron, R., A. Joseph, S. Abraham, J. Muliyil, K. George, J. Prasad, S. Minz, V. J. Abraham, and A. Bose. 2004. "Suicides in Young People in Rural Southern India." *Lancet* 363 (9415): 1117–18.

Aizer, A., Stroud, L., and S. Buka. 2009. "Maternal Stress and Child Well-Being: Evidence from Siblings." Mimeo. Brown University.

Allison, K., and R. Lerner. 1993. Integrating Research, Policy, and Programs for Adolescents and Their Families." In *Early Adolescence: Perspectives on Research, Policy, and Intervention*, ed. R. Lerner, 17-23. Hillsdale, NJ: Erlbaum.

Arkes, J. 2007. "Does the Economy Affect Teenage Substance Use?" *Health Economics* 16 (1): 19–36.

Arkes, J., and J. Klerman. 2008. "Understanding the Link between the Economy and Teenage Sexual Behavior and Fertility Outcomes." *Journal of Population Economics* 22 (3): 517–36.

Assaad, R., D. Levinson, and N. Zibani. 2007. "The Effect of Child Work on Schooling: Evidence from Egypt." Working Paper 2007-04, Minnesota Population Center, Minneapolis.

Atkin, D. 2009a. "Working for the Future: Female Factory Work and Child Health in Mexico." Manuscript. Yale University.

———. 2009b. "Endogenous Skill Acquisition and Export Manufacturing in Mexico." Manuscript. Yale University.

Awusabo-Asare, Kofi, and Samuel K. Annim. 2008. "Wealth Status and Risky Sexual Behaviour in Ghana and Kenya." *Applied Health Economics and Health Policy* 6 (1): 27–39.

Baird, S., E. Chirwa, C. McIntosh, and B. Özler. 2010. "The Short-Term Impacts of a Schooling Conditional Cash Transfer Program on the Sexual Behavior of Young Women." *Health Economics* 19 (S1): 55–68.

Baird, S., J. de Hoop, and B. Ozler. 2011. "Income Shocks and Adolescent Mental Health." Policy Research Working Paper 5644, World Bank, Washington, DC.

Bell, D., and D. Blanchflower. 2010. "Young People and Recession: A Lost Generation?" Working Paper. Dartmouth College.

Bowman, P. J. 1990. "The Adolescent-to-Adult Transition: Discouragement among Jobless Black Youth." *New Directions for Child and Adolescent Development* 1990 (46): 87–105.

Brandstädter, J. 1992. "Personal Control over Development: Implications of Self-Efficacy." In *Self-Efficacy: Thought Control of Action*, ed. F. Schwarzer, 127–48. Washington, DC: Hemisphere Publishing Corporation.

Buehler, C., C. Anthony, A. Krishnakumar, G. Stone, J. Gerard, and S. Pemberton. 1997. "Interparental Conflict and Youth Problem Behaviors: A Meta-Analysis." *Journal of Child and Family Studies* 6 (2): 233–47.

Burgess, S., C. Propper, H. Rees, and A. Shearer. 2003. "The Class of 1981: The Effects of Early Career Unemployment on Subsequent Unemployment Experiences." *Labour Economics* 10 (3): 291–309.

Central Bank of El Salvador. 2009. *Ingresos Mensuales de Remesas Familiares 1991–2009*, http://www.bcr.gob.sv/estadisticas/series_estadisticas.html.

Chassin, L., A. Hussong, and A. Beltran. 2009. "Adolescent Substance Use." In *Handbook of Adolescent Psychology*. 3rd ed., ed. Richard Lerner and Laurence Steinberg, chap. 21. Hoboken, NJ: Wiley.

Chatterji, M., N. Murray, D. London, and P. Anglewicz. 2005. "The Factors Influencing Transactional Sex among Young Men and Women in 12 Sub-Saharan African Countries." *Social Biology* 52 (1/2): 56–72.

Cho, Y., and D. Newhouse. 2011. "How Did the Great Recession Affect Different Types of Workers? Evidence from 17 Middle-Income Countries." Policy Research Working Paper 5636, World Bank, Washington, DC.

Choudhry, M., E. Marelli, and M. Signorelli. 2010. "The Impact of Financial Crises on Youth Unemployment Rate." Working Paper 79, Department of Economics, Università di Perugia, Perugia, Italy.

Clausen, J. 1991. "Adolescent Competence and the Life Course, or Why One Psychologist Needed a Concept of Personality." *Social Psychology Quarterly* 54 (1): 4–14.

Conger, R. D., K. J. Conger, G. Elder, F. Lorenz, R. Simons, and L. Whitbeck. 1992. "A Family Process Model of Economic Hardship and Adjustment of Early Adolescent Boys." *Child Development* 63 (3): 526–41.

Conger, R. D., and G. H. Elder. 1994. *Families in Troubled Times: Adapting to Change in Rural America*. New York: Aldine de Gruyter.

Conger, R. D., X. Ge, G. Elder, F. Lorenz, and R. Simons. 1994. "Economic Stress, Coercive Family Process, and Developmental Problems of Adolescents." *Child Development* 65 (2): 541–61.

Crockett, L., and R. K. Silbereisen. 2000. *Negotiating Adolescence in Times of Social Change*. Cambridge, UK: Cambridge University Press.

Cunha, F., J. Heckman, and L. Lochner. 2006. "Interpreting the Evidence on Life Cycle Skill Formation." *Handbook of the Economics of Education*. San Diego: Elsevier.

Cunningham, W., and J. Bustos-Salvagno. 2011. "Shocks, Child Labor, and School Dropouts in Argentina." Mimeo. World Bank.

Cunningham, W., and W. Maloney. 2000. "Measuring Vulnerability: Who Suffered in the 1995 Mexican Crisis?" Mimeo. World Bank.

Currie, J., and M. Stabile. 2006. "Child Mental Health and Human Capital Accumulation: The Case of ADHD." *Journal of Health Economics* 25 (6): 1094–118.

Das, J., Q. Do, J. Friedman, and D. McKenzie. 2008. "Mental Health Patterns and Consequences: Results from Survey Data in Five Developing Countries." *World Bank Economic Review* 23 (1): 31–55.

Das, J., Q. Do, J. Friedman, D. McKenzie, and K. Scott. 2007. "Mental Health and Poverty in Developing Countries: Revisiting the Relationship." *Social Science and Medicine* 65: 467–80.

Deb, Partha, William T. Gallo, Padmaja Ayyagari, Jason M. Fletcher, and Jody L. Sindelar. 2011. "The Effect of Job Loss on Overweight and Drinking." *Journal of Health Economics* 30 (2): 317–27.

DeGraff, D., and R. Bilsborrow. 2003. "Children's School Enrollment and Time at Work in the Philippines." *Journal of Developing Areas* 37 (1): 127–58.

Dinkelman, T., D. Lam, and M. Liebbrandt. 2007. "Linking Poverty and Income Shocks to Risky Sexual Behavior: Evidence from a Panel Study of Young Adults in Cape Town." *South African Journal of Economics* 76 (S1): 53–74.

Duryea, S., and M. Arends-Kuenning. 2003. "School Attendance, Child Labor, and Local Labor Market Fluctuations in Urban Brazil." *World Development* 31 (7): 1165–78.

Duryea, S., D. Lam, and D. Levison. 2007. "Effects of Economic Shocks on Children's Employment and Schooling in Brazil." *Journal of Development Economics* 84 (1): 188–214.

Duryea, S., and M. Morales. 2011. "Effects of the Global Financial Crisis on Children's School and Employment Outcomes in El Salvador." *Development Policy Review* 29 (5): 527–46.

Eisenberg, D., and E. Golberstein. 2009. "Mental Health and Academic Success in College." *Berkeley Electronic Journal of Economic Analysis and Policy* 9 (1): Article 40.

Elder, G. H. 1974. *Children of the Great Depression: Social Change in Life Experience*. Chicago: University of Chicago Press.

Elder, Glen H., Jr., and Richard C. Rockwell. 1985. "Children of Hard Times: Perspectives from the Social Change Project." In *Understanding the Economic Crisis: The Impact of Poverty and Unemployment on Children and Families*, ed. Jacques Boulet, Ann Marie DeBritto, and Aisha Ray, 43–63. Ann Arbor: University of Michigan Press.

Ellwood, D. 1982. "Teenage Unemployment: Permanent Scars or Temporary Blemishes?" In *The Youth Labor Market Problem: Its Nature, Causes, and Consequences*, ed. Richard B. Freeman and David A. Wise, 349–90. Chicago: University of Chicago Press.

Erikson, E. H. 1959. *Identity and the Life Cycle*. New York: International Universities Press.

Evans, G. W., P. Kim, A. H. Ting, H. B. Tesher and D. Shanis. 2007. "Cumulative Risk, Maternal Responsiveness, and Allostatic Load among Young Adolescents." *Developmental Psychology* 43: 341–51.

Fares, J., and C. Montenegro. 2011. "Youth Unemployment's Dynamics: Evidence from Brazil (1978–2002) and Chile (1957–2005)." Background Paper for *World Development Report 2007*, World Bank, Washington, DC.

Farrington, D. P. 2009. "Conduct Disorder, Aggression, and Delinquency." In *Handbook of Adolescent Psychology.* 3rd ed., ed. Richard Lerner and Laurence Steinberg, chap. 20. Hoboken, NJ: Wiley.

Festinger, L. 1957. *A Theory of Cognitive Dissonance.* Stanford, CA: Stanford University Press.

Filmer, D., and N. Schady. 2009. "School Enrollment, Selection, and Test Scores." Policy Research Working Paper 4998, World Bank, Washington, DC.

Fishbein, D. H., et al. 2006. "Mediators of the Stress-Substance-Use Relationship in Urban Male Adolescents." *Prevention Science* 7 (2):113–26.

Flanagan, C. A. 1988. "The Effects of a Changing Economy on the Socialization of Young Adolescents' Academic and Vocational Aspirations." Paper presented at the Annual Meeting of the American Educational Research Association, April, New Orleans, LA.

Fletcher, J. M. 2008. "Adolescent Depression: Diagnosis, Treatment, and Educational Attainment." *Health Economics* 19 (7): 855–71.

———. 2010. "Adolescent Depression and Educational Attainment: Results Using Sibling Fixed Effects." *Health Economics* 19 (7): 855–71.

Fletcher, J. M., and J. L. Sindelar. Forthcoming. "The Effects of Family Stressors on Substance Use Initiation in Adolescence." *Review of Economics of the Household* 10 (1): 99–114.

Fletcher, J. M., and B. Wolfe. 2008. "Child Mental Health and Human Capital Accumulation: The Case of ADHD Revisited." *Journal of Health Economics* 27 (3): 794–800.

Frankenberg, E., J. Friedman, T. Gillespie, N. Ingwersen, R. Pynoos, I. Rifai, B. Sikoki, A. Steinberg, C. Sumantri, W. Suriastini, and D. Thomas. 2008. "Mental Health in Sumatra after the Tsunami." *American Journal of Public Health* 98 (9): 1671–77.

Friedman, J., and D. Thomas. 2009. "Psychological Health before, during, and after an Economic Crisis: Results from Indonesia, 1993–2000." *World Bank Economic Review* 23 (1): 57–76.

Galambos, N. L., and R. K. Silbereisen. 1987. "Income Change, Parental Life Outlook, and Adolescent Expectations for Job Success." *Journal of Marriage and the Family* 48 (1): 309–18.

Gardner, J., and A. J. Oswald. 2007. "Money and Mental Wellbeing: A Longitudinal Study of Medium-Sized Lottery Wins." *Journal of Health Economics* 26 (1): 49–60.

Gertler, Paul, Manisha Shah, and Stefano M. Bertozzi. 2005. "Risky Business: The Market for Unprotected Commercial Sex." *Journal of Political Economy* 113 (3): 518–50.

Gregg, P. 2001. "The Impact of Youth Unemployment on Adult Unemployment in the NCS." *Economic Journal* 111 (475): 626–53.

Gregg, P., and E. Tominey. 2005. "The Wage Scar from Male Youth Unemployment." *Labour Economics* 12 (4): 487–509.

Hammarström A., and U. Janlert. 1994. "Unemployment and Change of Tobacco Habits: A Study of Young People from 16 to 21 Years of Age." *Addiction* 89 (12): 1691–96.

Hammer, T. 1992. "Unemployment and Use of Drug and Alcohol among Young People: A Longitudinal Study in the General Population." *British Journal of Addiction* 87 (11): 1571–81.

Hong, J., M. Knapp, and A. McGuire. 2011. "Income-Related Inequalities in the Prevalence of Depression and Suicidal Behaviour: A 10-Year Trend Following Economic Crisis." *World Psychiatry* 10 (1): 40–44.

Iacono, W. G., S. R. Carlson, J. Taylor, I. J. Elkins, and M. McGue. 1999. "Behavioural Disinhibition and the Development of Substance-Use Disorders: Findings from the Minnesota Twins Family Study." *Development and Psychopathology* 11: 869–900.

Jejeebhoy, Shireen J., and Sarah Bott. 2003. "Non-Consensual Sexual Experiences of Young People: A Review of the Evidence from Developing Countries." South and East Asia Regional Working Papers 16, Population Council, New Delhi.

Jha, Prabhat, Frank J. Chaloupka, James Moore, Vendhan Gajalakshmi, Prakash C. Gupta, Richard Peck, Samira Asma, and Witold Zatonski. 2006. "Tobacco Addiction." In *Disease Control Priorities in Developing Countries*, ed. Dean T. Jamison et al., chap. 46. New York: Oxford University Press.

Johansson, Edvard, Petri Böckerman, Ritva Prättälä, and Antti Uutela. 2006. "Alcohol-Related Mortality, Drinking Behavior, and Business Cycles." *European Journal of Health Economics* 7 (3): 212–17.

Kahn, Lisa. 2010. "The Long-Term Labor Market Consequences of Graduating from College in a Bad Economy." *Labour Economics* 17 (2): 303–16.

Kessler, R. C., C. L. Foster, W. B. Saunders, and P. E. Stang. 1995. "Social Consequences of Psychiatric Disorders, I: Educational Attainment." *American Journal of Psychiatry* 152 (July): 1026–32.

Kessler, R. C., S. Galea, R. T. Jones, and H. A. Parker. 2006. "Mental Illness and Suicidality after Hurricane Katrina." *Bulletin of the World Health Organization* 84 (12): 930–39.

Koettl, Johannes, Isil Oral, and Indhira Santos. 2011. "Employment Recovery in Europe and Central Asia." *ECA Knowledge Brief,* World Bank, Washington, DC.

Kreek, Mary Jeanne, David A. Nielsen, Eduardo R. Butelman, and K. Steven LaForge. 2005. "Genetic Influences on Impulsivity, Risk Taking, Stress Responsivity, and Vulnerability to Drug Abuse and Addiction." *Nature Neuroscience* 8 (11):1450–57.

Kruger, Niclas, and Mikael Svensson. 2010. "Good Times Are Drinking Times: Empirical Evidence on Business Cycles and Alcohol Sales in Sweden 1861–2000." *Applied Economics Letters* 17 (6): 543–46.

Larson, J. 1984. "The Effect of Husband's Unemployment on Marital and Family Relations in Blue-Collar Families." *Family Relations* 33 (4): 503–11.

Leclerc-Madlala, S. 2003. "Transactional Sex and the Pursuit of Modernity." *Social Dynamics* 29 (2): 1–21.

Lee-Rife, S. 2008. "Household Disruption and Sexual Victimization among Young South Africans." PhD Dissertation University of Michigan.

Lerner, R. 1993. *Early Adolescence: Perspectives on Research, Policy, and Intervention.* Hillsdale, NJ: Erlbaum.

Levison, D., and K. Moe. 1998. "Household Work as a Deterrent to Schooling: An Analysis of Adolescent Girls in Peru." *Journal of Developing Areas* 32 (3): 339–56.

Levison, D., K. Moe, and F. Knaul. 2001. "Youth Education and Work in Mexico." *World Development* 29 (1): 167–88.

Levitt, S. D., and L. Lochner. 2001. "The Determinants of Juvenile Crime." In *Risky Behavior among Youths: An Economic Analysis,* ed. Jonathan Gruber, 327–74. Chicago: University of Chicago Press.

Lewinsohn. P. M., P. Rohde, and J. R. Seeley. 1998. "Major Depressive Disorders in Older Adolescents: Prevalence, Risk Factors, and Clinical Implications." *Clinical Psychology Review* 18 (7): 765–94.

Lopez Boo, Florencia. 2010. "In School or at Work? Evidence from a Crisis." Discussion Paper 4692, IZA (Institute for the Study of Labor), Bonn.

Luke, Nancy. 2006. "Exchange and Condom Use in Informal Sexual Relationships in Urban Kenya." *Economic Development and Cultural Change* 54 (2): 319–48.

Lundberg, Patric, Godfrey Rukundo, Schola Ashaba, Anna Thorson, Peter Allebeck, Per-Olof Östergren, and Elizabeth Cantor-Graae. 2011. "Poor Mental Health and Sexual Risk Behaviours in Uganda: A Cross-Sectional Population-Based Study." *BMC Public Health* 11 (125): 1–10.

Masten, A. 2007. "Resilience in Developing Systems: Progress and Promise as the Fourth Wave Rises." *Development and Psychopathology* 19: 921–30.

————. 2009. "Ordinary Magic: Lessons from Research on Resilience in Human Development." *Education Canada* 49 (3): 28–32.

Masten, A., and D. Cicchetti. 2010. "Developmental Cascades." *Development and Psychopathology* 22: 491–95.

McKenzie, D. 2003. "How Do Households Cope with Aggregate Shocks? Evidence from the Mexican Peso Crisis." *World Development* 31 (7): 1179–99.

McLoyd, V., R. Kaplan, K. Purtell, E. Bagley, C. Hardaway, and C. Smalls. 2009. "Poverty and Socioeconomic Disadvantage in Adolescence." In *Handbook of Adolescent Psychology*. Vol. 2, 3rd ed., ed. R. Lerner and Laurence Steinberg, 444–91. Hoboken, NJ: Wiley.

Millet, L., P. Lanier, and B. Drake. 2011. "Are Economic Trends Associated with Child Maltreatment? Preliminary Results from the Recent Recession Using State Level Data." *Children and Youth Services Review* 33 (7): 1280–87.

Mroz, T., and T. Savage. 2006. "The Long-Term Effects of Youth Unemployment." *Journal of Human Resources* 41 (2): 259–93.

O'Brien, L. M., E. G. Heycock, M. Hanna, P. W. Jones, and J. L. Cox. 2004. "Postnatal Depression and Faltering Growth: A Community Study." Pt. 1. *Pediatrics* 113 (5): 1242–47.

O'Donoghue, T., and M. Rabin. 2001. "Risky Behavior among Youths: Some Issues from Behavioral Economics." In *Risky Behavior among Youths: An Economic Analysis*, ed. J. Gruber, 29–68. Chicago: University of Chicago Press.

Oreopoulos P., T. von Watcher, and A. Heisz. 2006. "The Short- and Long-Term Career Effects of Graduating in a Recession: Hysteresis and Heterogeneity in the Market for College Graduates." Working Paper 12159, National Bureau of Economic Research, Cambridge, MA.

Patel, V., A. J. Fisher, S. Hetrick, and P. McGory. 2007. "Mental Health of Young People: A Global Public Health Challenge." *Lancet* 369 (9569): 1302–13.

Patel, V., and A. Kleinman. 2003. "Poverty and Common Mental Disorders in Developing Countries." *Bulletin of the World Health Organization* 81 (8): 609–15.

Peck, David F., and Martin A. Plant. 1986. "Unemployment and Illegal Drug Use: Concordant Evidence from a Prospective Study and National Trends." *British Medical Journal* 293 (October): 929–32.

Picou, J. Steven, and Kenneth Hudson. 2010. "Hurricane Katrina and Mental Health: A Research Note on Mississippi Gulf Coast Residents." *Sociological Inquiry* 80 (3): 513–24.

Power, C., and V. Estaugh. 1990. "Employment and Drinking in Early Adulthood: A Longitudinal Perspective." *British Journal of Addiction* 85 (4): 487–94.

Prince, M., V. Patel, S. Saxena, M. Maj, J. Maselko, M. R. Phillips, and A. Rahman. 2007. "No Health without Mental Health." *Lancet* 370 (9590): 859–77.

Raaum, O., and K. Roed. 2006. "Do Business Cycle Conditions at the Time of Labor Market Entry Affect Future Employment Prospects?" *Review of Economics and Statistics* 88 (2): 193–210.

Ramsden, S., F. Richardson, G. Josse, M. Thomas, C. Ellis, C. Shakeshaft, M. Seghier, and C. Price. 2011. "Verbal and Non-Verbal Intelligence Changes in the Teenage Brain." *Nature* 479 (Oct.): 113–16.

Robinson, Jonathan, and Ethan Yeh. 2011. "Transactional Sex as a Response to Risk in Western Kenya." *American Economic Journal: Applied Economics* 3 (1): 35–64.

Roisman, G., A. Masten, J. D. Coatsworth, and A. Tellegen. 2004. "Salient and Emerging Developmental Tasks in the Transition to Adulthood." *Child Development* 75 (1): 123–33.

Roosevelt, Franklin D. 1935. "Statement on the National Youth Administration," June 26. Online by Gerhard Peters and John T. Woolley, The American Presidency Project, http://www.presidency.ucsb.edu/ws/?pid=15091.

Roy, Suryadipta. 2007. "Are Illegal Drugs Inferior Goods in the US?" *Atlantic Economic Journal* 35 (3): 303–14.

Ruhm, Christopher J. 2005. "Healthy Living in Hard Times." *Journal of Health Economics* 24 (2): 341–63.

Ruiz-Casares, M., and J. Heymann. 2009. "Children Home Alone Unsupervised: Modeling Parental Decisions and Associated Factors in Botswana, Mexico, and Vietnam." *Child Abuse and Neglect* 33: 312–23.

Ryan, R., and E. Deci. 2000. "Self-Determination Theory and the Facilitation of Intrinsic Motivation, Social Development, and Well-Being." *American Psychologist* 55 (1): 68–78.

Saluja, G., R. Iachan, P. C. Scheidt, M. D. Overpeck, W. Sun, and J. N. Giedd. 2004. "Prevalence and Risk Factors for Major Depressive Symptoms among Young Adolescents." *Archives of Pediatrics and Adolescent Medicine* 164 (3): 760–65.

Scarpetta, S., A. Sonnet, and T. Manfredi. 2010. "Rising Youth Unemployment during the Crisis: How to Prevent Negative Long-Term Consequences on a Generation." Social, Employment, and Migration Working Paper 106, OECD, Paris.

Schady, N. 2004. "Do Macroeconomic Crises Always Slow Human Capital Accumulation?" *World Bank Economic Review* 18 (2): 131–54.

Seligson, M., and E. Zechmeister 2010. "Americas Barometer Insights 2010," No. 53. LAPOP group at Vanderbilt University, Nashville, TN.

Skoufias, E., and S. Parker. 2002. "Labor Market Shocks and Their Impacts on Work and Schooling: Evidence from Urban Mexico." Discussion Paper 129, International Food Policy Research Institute, Washington, DC.

———. 2006. "Job Loss and Family Adjustments in Work and Schooling during the Mexican Peso Crisis." *Journal of Population Economics* 19 (1): 163–81.

Smith, C.A., and S. B. Stern. 1997. "Delinquency and Antisocial Behavior: A Review of Family Processes and Intervention Research." *Social Service Review* 71 (3): 382–420.

Stein, M. B., and Y. M. Kean. 2000. "Disability and Quality of Life in Social Phobia: Epidemiologic Findings." *American Journal of Psychiatry* 157 (October): 1601–13.

Stevens, K. 2008. "Adverse Economic Conditions at Labour Market Entry: Permanent Scars or Rapid Catch Up?" Job Market Paper, University of Sydney.

Stillman, S., D. McKenzie, and J. Gibson. 2009. "Migration and Mental Health: Evidence from a Natural Experiment." *Journal of Health Economics* 28: 677–87.

Svensson, Mikael, and Curt Hagquist. 2010. "Adolescents, Alcohol-Use, and Economic Conditions: A Multilevel Analysis of Data from a Period with Big Economic Changes." *European Journal of Health Economics* 11 (6): 533–41.

Tangcharoensathien, V., H. Piya, P. Siriwan, and K. Vijj. 2000. "Health Impacts of Rapid Economic Changes in Thailand." *Social Science and Medicine* 51 (6): 789–807.

Thomas, D., E. Frankenberg, J. Smith, K. Beegle, and G. Teruel. 2002. "Wages, Employment, and Economic Shocks: Evidence from Indonesia." *Journal of Population Economics* 15 (1): 161–93.

United Nations. 2005. *World Youth Report.* New York: United Nations Department of Economic and Social Affairs.

Verick, S. 2009. "Who Is Hit Hardest during a Financial Crisis? The Vulnerability of Young Men and Women to Unemployment in an Economic Downturn." Discussion Paper 4359, IZA (Institute for the Study of Labor), Bonn.

World Bank. 2006. *World Development Report 2007: Development and the Next Generation.* Washington, DC: World Bank.

———. 2011. *The Jobs Crisis: Household and Government Responses to the Great Recession in Eastern Europe and Central Asia.* Washington, DC: World Bank.

Yang, Dean. 2006. "Internal Migration, Remittances and Household Investment: Evidence from Philippine Exchange Rate Shocks." Working Paper 12325, National Bureau of Economic Research, Cambridge, MA.

PART III

Policy

CHAPTER 6

Policies to Protect and Promote Young People's Development during Crisis

Alice Wuermli, Kevin Hempel, Larry Aber, and Mattias Lundberg

Introduction to Policies during Economic Crisis

The previous chapters have reviewed evidence on the impact of aggregate economic shocks on developmental processes at various stages of the life course. That review has enabled us to identify the vulnerable stages and domains of particular importance during those stages that are most likely to be affected by economic crises and to identify opportunities for effective intervention, where threats are greatest and where policy can have a larger impact.

This chapter is devoted to addressing the question of how policy can best *protect* and at the same time *promote* young people's development from conception to adulthood in the face of economic crises. Policies include well-established safety net programs, such as cash transfers, public works, or school feeding, which are extensively reviewed in Grosh et al.

Note: Some of the evidence on programs was taken from background papers produced for this purpose by Sarah Baird, Kathleen Beegle, Jed Friedman, Susan Parker, Carly Tubbs, and Suzanne Duryea.

(2008). This chapter builds on the foundation established by Grosh et al. by looking at these programs through the multidisciplinary lens developed in this volume. We revisit selected safety net programs, applying the principles developed in the conceptual framework, nested points of entry (see glossary), substitutability, and targeting as a frame of reference, in an attempt to improve the design and implementation strategies of well-established safety net programs.

Adopting the multidisciplinary approach laid out in this volume and complementing current practices with what we know from the child and youth development field can enhance the performance of policies designed to minimize and alleviate crises in four essential ways:

- *Improve short-term outcomes.* While traditional cash transfers can be very effective at easing the financial constraints experienced during crises by providing the needed income to sustain investments in nutrition and education, they may not sufficiently address the stresses associated with economic hardship. For example, unemployment has significant psychological consequences. Feelings of inadequacy, failure to provide for the family, and loss in social status can all lead to depressive symptoms, anxiety, and substance abuse, which in turn can lead to inconsistent or harsh parenting with negative consequences for the child's development. Adding a specific component to a cash transfer or other safety net program to deal with these associated impacts can significantly enhance the protective effect of the crisis response on human development.

- *Augment long-term outcomes.* Evidence has shown that interventions at specific points in a person's life course can have positive long-term consequences, including better academic achievement, better labor market outcomes, and healthier lives and families. Many commonly implemented crisis interventions, such as public works, have been responsible for only limited sustained improvements in employment or socioeconomic conditions, and, to our knowledge, no such programs in developing countries have evaluated the long-term consequences for participants or their families. Informing crisis responses with developmental insights may be able to change this dramatically by directing our targeting strategy toward cohorts at critical stages of development and by addressing their specific developmental needs. For example, a public works program for out-of-work youth are often largely ineffective at improving postprogram employment perspectives, whereas socioemotional support services and intense mentoring can encourage the development of the competencies needed to participate success-fully in the labor market.

- *Increase cost-effectiveness of crisis response.* Given budget constraints, in particular in times of economic crisis, policy makers are interested in allocating scarce resources most efficiently. Understanding the factors that support positive child and youth development and that increase resilience in the face of adversity can enhance the cost-effectiveness of crisis response programs by informing targeting strategies and accurate delivery mechanisms. For instance, instead of providing costly food or energy subsidies for the population at large, policy makers can adopt well-targeted allowances and other support services to particularly vul-nerable groups, such as pregnant women or adolescents transitioning to work, thus preventing the worst consequences of the crisis while limit-ing the effect on budget exposure. Similarly, where transfers to individual families are either infeasible or ineffective at protecting the develop-ment of children, policy makers may be able to build on the existing infrastructure and promote in- or after-school programs that reach many children at once and that may encourage children to remain in school.

- *Improve political viability and postcrisis sustainability.* There is substantial concern about the ability and political willingness of governments to scale back programs once a crisis has abated. However, a crisis may pro-vide fertile ground for introducing substantial changes in policies and programs that may prove desirable during good times as well as bad. While long-term assistance to the poor may be politically and socially unsustainable, interventions designed to foster good parenting or sup-port cognitive and socioemotional development may be less contentious, as they can be argued to enhance both welfare and long-term growth. For example, after-school programs can provide additional stimulation and promote positive development, while at the same time freeing par-ents' time to engage in job search or training activities and reducing their level of stress. In addition, studies have shown that excessively narrowly defined income- or means-based targeting can erode public support for programs (Gelbach and Pritchett 2002); targeting risk or resilience fac-tors other than socioeconomic status may increase the political viability of the crisis response, especially if these non-income-based characteris-tics are seen as just and fair indicators of need.

This chapter begins by highlighting some of the strengths and limita-tions of traditional crisis responses, such as cash transfer programs and public works, and lays out how taking a developmental approach can help guide policy during an economic crisis. The chapter then provides concrete examples of policy and program designs and implementation arrangements that can mitigate the negative effect of crises on young people's development during early childhood, middle childhood, and adolescence.

This volume focuses on the policies and programs that affect young people and their families directly. Innumerable other factors affect growth, employment, income, and welfare more generally, including both macroeconomic and fiscal policies, such as trade, exchange rates, and taxes. While these do have significant impacts on the development of young people, their impact is indirect: for example, trade policies affect, among other things, relative prices, which affect the returns to investments of labor and capital, in turn affecting incomes and growth. While we certainly agree that a stable macroeconomic environment is of primary importance, there are, for instance, no "youth-specific" trade regimes. In this volume, and in this chapter, we focus on those interventions that can be designed specifically and directly to reach the lives of young people, to correct market failures, to protect young people from harm, and to help them recover and find a healthy path of development in case they fall victim to crisis.

Moving beyond Traditional Safety Net Programs

As Grosh et al. state, "The primary objectives of safety nets in times of crisis are to protect incomes and avoid irreversible losses of physical assets and human capital and to help maintain political consensus around the policies needed to resolve the crisis" (2008, 432). Safety nets include programs that provide temporary income support, such as conditional or unconditional transfers in cash or in kind; temporary income-generation programs such as public works; and programs that protect and enhance human capital. These programs generally target income, but they may also target prices for consumption or investment, such as vouchers, fee waivers, or scholarships.

These programs differ in whom they target, in the degree to which they constrain or manipulate household choices, and in the outcomes they are designed to affect directly. Recipients generally prefer unconditional cash transfers, since they restrict neither behavior nor consumption choices; vouchers, such as food stamps or ration cards, earmark the funds for the purchase of food. School feeding programs are intended to ensure children's nutritional sufficiency, and public works are a short-term response to high unemployment rates. The best option will depend largely on the context, transmission mechanisms, and main effects of the crisis. For example, demand-side interventions such as food stamps or cash in cases where the food supply is disrupted will serve primarily to drive up prices (Cunha, De Giorgi, and Jayachandran 2011), although this phenomenon is more likely to occur in rural areas and areas with poorly developed or integrated markets.

More important, many traditionally designed safety net programs may not be fully able to mitigate the negative effects of economic crises on young people's development. Resource constraints of households experiencing hardship are but one factor affecting children's development. The resulting stress and mental health issues can significantly affect children's development. There is strong evidence on the effects of maternal stress and depression on development in utero and early childhood (for a review see chapter 3 and box 4.1). While the relationship between poverty and mental illness is well recognized, debate continues on what interventions can break this downward spiral. A recent review of interventions found no conclusive evidence on the effect of poverty alleviation programs on mental health, while mental health interventions were all associated with improved economic outcomes of the participants (Lund et al. 2011). For example, Gertler et al. (2003) find that households that had experienced a death were able to insure investments in children's human capital against the purely economic impact of parental loss, but they were unable to insure these investments against behavioral factors related to the presence of a parent in the household. Affected families require more than merely monetary assistance. This suggests that we take a closer look at the effectiveness of safety net programs at addressing mental health concerns.

For example, a direct cash transfer to the family may reach needy beneficiaries in a timely and targeted manner. Furthermore, recent research from Mexico's Oportunidades program finds that maternal depression is lower among participating households and that children in participating households whose mothers exhibited significant depressive symptoms had lower levels of the stress hormones that can have long-term negative impacts on development than children who were not in the program (Fernald and Gunnar 2009). Evidence from Cambodia (Filmer and Schady 2009) and Malawi (Baird, de Hoop, and Özler 2011) also suggests that cash transfers can reduce psychological distress and increase mental health. However, as was pointed out earlier, not all cash transfer programs affect mental health of participants, and there remain questions about the sustainability of these effects (see Baird, de Hoop, and Özler 2011). While the transfer program may succeed in lessening the financial strain on the family, unemployment may still cause stress and other mental health issues affecting one or more people in the household as well as family dynamics and functioning.

Alternatively, in the case of soaring unemployment rates, countries without well-developed unemployment insurance programs often revert to public works. Public works tend to be labor-intensive infrastructure projects whose objective is to keep healthy people—usually men—busy, while providing a subsidy to support household income (for a detailed account, see Grosh et al. 2008). These programs are usually self-targeted by setting the wage lower than the market rate; this facilitates rapid implementation and provides an automatic mechanism for scaling back once the labor market starts to recover. Studies have shown that these programs can function as a cash transfer program and successfully alleviate short-term poverty when the crisis is manifest in high unemployment rates (Galasso and Ravallion 2004). They are, however, less effective when labor market adjustments are made through a general drop in wages. The impact on postprogram employment is inconclusive (Ravallion 1999). Further investigation is needed to better understand the processes driving these mental health outcomes. These programs can be more effective at facilitating the transition to the labor market if they are accompanied by skills development programs or job placement assistance. From a developmental perspective, as the beneficiaries are primarily working-age males and because the cash is transferred to the worker, the additional income may not be allocated in the most effective way to meet the needs of younger household members. In any case, these additional latent developmental threats deserve attention and may require more support services to ensure effective parenting and healthy family functioning.

Identifying the appropriate intervention or combination of interventions to alleviate the hardship that households experience in a crisis will require taking into account the timing with respect to a young person's life course, the specific context and environment of the developing child or adolescent, and the transmission mechanisms and mediators of the shock, all of which are intricately linked and interrelated. It is therefore useful to situate traditional safety net programs in a larger context of tools and interventions that are able to protect and promote young people's development in times of crisis. Figure 6.1 presents a simple graphic depiction of the three parameters from which we derive the three principles for the design of policy and intervention.

Part II of this volume reviewed the evidence on how the impacts of shocks on young people may differ depending on the *timing;* that is,

Figure 6.1   A Developmental Approach to Policy during Economic Crisis

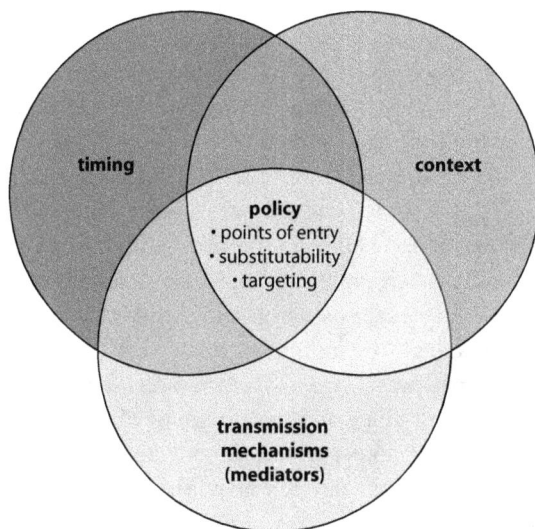

timing

context

policy
• points of entry
• substitutability
• targeting

**transmission
mechanisms
(mediators)**

Source: Authors.

impacts will vary according to the child's stage of development and the historical context and how these two interact. We are able to identify specific points in a young person's life course that are of particular importance and at which time they seem to exhibit particular vulnerability to disruptions, such as those brought on by economic crises. There are distinct differences between the three aggregated age groups—early childhood, middle childhood, and adolescence—in the relative importance of various processes and domains of development, the developmental tasks they face, and the settings in which they are affected. These differences necessitate a more carefully tailored approach to programming for each age group, and it explains why policies and interventions during early childhood tend to focus on health and nutrition, whereas interventions during middle childhood seem more concerned with other factors.

The impact of a crisis on a young person will invariably depend on the *context* in which it occurs. As illustrated through the bioecological model in chapter 2, child and youth development is influenced by many different "contexts," "settings," or "ecologies," such as the family, peers, schools, communities, belief systems, laws and regulations, and the economy. In turn, each of these contexts potentially mediates the influence of the economic shock on the development of the individual. For example, when social policies provide support to communities and households, the effect of a crisis on child and youth development is likely to be much less severe than when those broadly protective policies do not exist. Moreover, the relative importance of social factors varies depending on a young person's life stage. In early childhood, the family is the central setting in a child's life. During this stage, programs targeting the household may be most effective at ensuring a child's well-being. Adolescents, however, while still affected by family processes, are also in the process of developing their own identity and skills in a rapidly changing environment. This situation calls for alternative interventions to address not just family hardship but also those factors that support the ability of young people themselves to adapt to changes while making major life transitions.

There are many pathways, or *transmission mechanisms*, through which a crisis can affect the well-being and development of a young person, financially or psychologically, experienced directly or indirectly through the family or other changes in the environment. Similarly, many factors moderate that impact. Whether the policy response to a crisis is effective will depend crucially on whether it adequately addresses the most prominent transmission mechanisms, or mediators, in a particular situation. Which transmission mechanisms are most important will vary depending on the life stage of the person as well as the context. Table 6.1 presents a range of transmission mechanisms, or factors, that mediate how economic crises can affect children and youth at different stages of their development. The columns segregate the information on possible transmission mechanisms by age group, while the rows categorize the information by "contextual" level.

Table 6.1 by no means claims to be an exhaustive list, and not all the factors listed are equally malleable through policy and might just have to be incorporated as risk or resilience factors into further policy considerations. In particular, this table provides guidance with respect to the principles identified in chapter 2 related to *targeting strategies* and *entry points* and the possible *substitutability* of one type of intervention that may not be feasible for another that supports the same outcomes. Thus, the bullet points roughly represent potential *points of entry* for policy. Policy can consequently counter the effects of a crisis by, for example, preventing household income loss (exo/macrosystem) through a public works program or providing support and guidance, for example, through parenting programs, to maintain effective parenting during stressful times (microsystem). By identifying alternative processes that support the development of specific outcomes—say, socioemotional and behavioral development—certain policies can be substituted through interventions aimed at the same outcomes, for example, school-based programs in lieu of household programs (microsystem). Furthermore, these principles can guide the design and implementation of effective programs in environments with severe budgetary constraints and weak institutional and administrative capacity.

Table 6.1 also provides a great range of targeting alternatives. Instead of income or proxy-means targeting alone, one may choose to target a particular age group at especially vulnerable periods, for example, pregnant women or adolescents on the verge of transitioning from school to work. Or one may target particular mediators, for example, children with weak self-regulation skills identified by behavioral markers in day care or school settings.[1] These principles open up new avenues for intervention that are worthwhile exploring. Outside the realm of the family, for example, universally available school-based or afterschool programs can both increase the likelihood of retention in school and take advantage of the aggregation to deliver ancillary services effectively.

Table 6.2 lists a range of outcomes that can be measured when assessing the impact of economic crises. Measuring such outcomes is useful for assessing both present impacts and the effectiveness of interventions to counter the effect of a shock. Furthermore, understanding the relationship between short-term and long-term outcomes allows us to identify priorities for intervention. As has been pointed out previously, few studies of shocks follow the subjects over a longer time frame. But looking at historical studies, such as the Dutch Hunger Winter of 1944 or the Great Depression in the United States, we can start outlining some of the potential long-term implications of exposure to economic crisis at each of the three life stages represented in this volume.

Finally, experience has shown that policy responses in times of crises seem to be more effective if they can be based on programs or institutional arrangements that were already in place before the crisis hit. The costs and complications of implementing programs during the height of a crisis increase significantly, given the contraction of public budgets and the lack of institutional capacity in many developing countries to collect the necessary data quickly enough and to roll out a coordinated, coherent response in a timely manner. Consequently, one must make a distinction between programs suitable for countries with no significant social protection system in place and programs suitable for countries that can use existing infrastructure for scaling up. In either case, given fiscal and political constraints, targeting the narrower identification of beneficiaries is unavoidable.

Table 6.1 Transmission Mechanisms (Mediators) by Life Stage and System Level

Level	Early childhood	Middle childhood	Adolescence
Macrosystem and Exosystem	• Prices (food, health care, child care, etc.) • Public provision of social services (especially health care and income support) • Parents' workplace/livelihoods • Community ◦ Erosion of community networks and resources (e.g., informal insurance arrangements)	• Prices (food, education, etc.) • Parents' workplace/livelihoods • Public provision of social services (especially education and income support)	• Prices (food, education, etc.) • Social change (structural changes in labor markets, changing skills demand, changes in opportunities, etc.) • Public provision of social services (especially education, school-to-work, mental and sexual/reproductive health) • Parents' workplace/livelihoods

Microsystem	• **Family**
	  ◦ Maternal stress in utero (elevated cortisol levels)
	  ◦ Maternal malnutrition in utero
	  ◦ Severe maternal (parental) stress and inadequate care giving (economic hardship, marital conflict, depression and anxiety, emotional unavailability or inconsistency, lack of positive stimulation)
		• **Family**
		  ◦ Resource investments (especially education and other cognitively stimulating activities)
		  ◦ Parental stress, mental health, and (household) conflict (associated with deterioration of family dynamics, effective parenting; possible increase in substance abuse and domestic violence)
			• **Family**
			  ◦ Parental stress (e.g., manifested in marital conflict, depression, anxiety) resulting in deterioration of family dynamics and parenting
			• **Adolescent's (potential) workplace**
			  ◦ Job loss (or potential job loss)
			  ◦ (Future) job opportunities
			  ◦ Availability of internships or apprenticeships
			  ◦ Job requirements and qualifications
			• **School**
			  ◦ Availability and quality of resources and instructions

○ Inadequate nutrition (economic hardship, insufficient resources, reallocation of funds away from child)

○ Inadequate health care (economic hardship, insufficient resources, reallocation of funds away from child health care)

• **Nonfamily child care**

○ Low-quality child care (economic hardship, need to spend more time generating income, lack of time for child care, need for alternative child care, lack of resources to ensure quality)

• **School**

○ Availability and quality of resources and instruction (e.g., teacher stress, quality of instruction, teacher-child relationship)

○ Availability and access to supervised extracurricular and after-school activities

• **Community**

○ Availability and quality of out-of-school programs

○ Safe and child-friendly environments

○ Teacher-student relationship (e.g., teacher stress, availability and consistency of mentors/positive adult role model)

○ Availability and access to supervised extracurricular and after-school activities

• **Community**

○ Availability and quality of out-of-school programs (providing mentoring relationships, etc.)

○ Safe environments

Individual

• Inadequate nutrition (in utero, infancy)
• Toxic stress
• Epigenetic processes

• Stress-regulatory system
• Cognitive abilities and IQ
• Capacity to self-regulate
• Early stages of socialization (e.g., perceptions, aspirations, etc.)
• Other individual characteristics (e.g., personality and preferences)

• Capacity to self-regulate
• Cognitive abilities and IQ
• Socialization processes (e.g., aspirations, perceptions, identity, discouragement)
• Future orientation
• Efficacy beliefs
• Stress-regulatory system

Source: Authors.

Table 6.2 Negative Outcomes by Life Stage: Time of Exposure and Time of Outcome Measured

	Timing of outcomes		
	Outcomes in early childhood	*Outcomes in middle childhood*	*Outcomes in adolescence*
In-utero exposure to severe malnutrition, stress, and toxins			
	• Low birthweight • Persistent changes in DNA methylation • Congenital anomalies of the nervous system (e.g. spina bifida, hydrocephalus) • Perinatal death and infant mortality	• Major affective disorders • Cognitive development delays (e.g., language abilities and school readiness) • Poorer school performance • Premature school leaving	• Schizophrenia • Major affective disorders • Antisocial personality disorder (especially for young men) • Lower educational achievement • Lower earnings • Higher rates of unemployment • Higher rates of involvement in risky behavior (including substance abuse) • Poorer physical and mental health
Post partum exposure to malnutrition and other stresses to child and caregiver			
	• Stunting • Wasting • Morbidity and mortality • "Failure to thrive" (from emotional deprivation) • Socioemotional and behavioral developmental issues (e.g., insecure attachement)	• Poorer school performance • Premature school leaving • Socioemotional and behavioral developmental issues (e.g., efficacy beliefs, self-regulation, internalizing, and externalizing behaviors) • Cognitive development delays (e.g., language abilities and school readiness)	• Poorer physical and mental health • Unstable relationships • Early pregnancy • Restricted fetal growth during pregnancy • Intergenerational transmission of developmental problems • Socioemotional and behavioral developmental issues (e.g., efficacy beliefs, self-regulation, internalizing and externalizing behaviors)

Exposure during early childhood

Timing of exposure

Exposure during middle childhood	• Cognitive developmental delays • Poorer school performance • Premature school leaving • Socioemotional and behavioral developmental issues (e.g., efficacy beliefs, self-regulation, internalizing and externalizing behaviors)	• Lower educational achievement • Lower earnings • Higher rate of unemployment • Internalizing and externalizing behaviors • Diminished physical and mental health • Increased incidence of risky behavior
Exposure during adolescence		• Lower educational achievement • Job loss • Lack of positive/productive future orientation (pessimism, cynicism, etc.) • Delayed financial independence • Internalizing behaviors (e.g., depression, anxiety, etc.) • Externalizing behaviors and risky behaviors (e.g., aggression, delinquency, substance abuse, unsafe sex, etc.) • Inadequate efficacy beliefs → Long-term implications for earnings, employment, health, productivity.

Source: Authors.

The following sections describe some evidence-based and promising interventions for each age group that could be deployed during times of economic crisis. The discussion is structured roughly along the lines of settings and highlights how they address individual domains of development and support mastery of stage-salient developmental tasks.

Early Childhood

Chapter 3 revealed the long-term consequences associated with exposure to crisis during early childhood on later life outcomes. That chapter identified two main pathways through which young children can be affected: (1) nutritional deficiencies stemming from lack of resources and (2) family dynamics and functioning, including parental and maternal time and mental health, that increase the likelihood of insecure attachments and inadequate stimulation. Nutritional deficiencies during gestation and maternal stress resulting in fetal exposure to high levels of the stress hormone cortisol can have serious long-term implications; attachment and stimulation are especially important during the first 24 months of life. The spectrum of possible consequences arising from food and nutritional shortages during various stages of gestation warrants a serious focus on pregnant women. It is of utmost importance that services for women of child-bearing age and for women during early pregnancy reach their target population. Given the importance of parenting, mother-child interactions, and the family context for children's socioemotional and cognitive development, programs should focus not only on the children themselves but also on the healthy functioning of the entire family.

Health Care Services and Infrastructure: Prenatal and Infant Health and Nutrition

First and foremost, sustain or scale up public health services with particular emphasis on services to pregnant women and very young children. Although in developed countries government spending tends to be countercyclical, this is often not the case in developing countries (Lewis and Verhoeven 2010). The different experiences of Indonesia and Peru illustrate this point (Ferreira and Schady 2009). Indonesia protected government health expenditures during the financial crisis of the 1990s, while Peru did not. Indonesia experienced minimal deterioration in child health outcomes, while in Peru the crisis resulted in approximately 18,000 excess deaths.

Furthermore, while a large share of the world's population does not have access to social insurance, measures to protect families from losing access to health care and other services are crucial (International Labour Organization 2010). Studies of social insurance programs in Ghana (Walsh and Jones 2009), Indonesia (Pradhan, Saadah, and Sparrow 2007), and Thailand (Waters, Saadah, and Pradhan 2003) suggest that these programs can protect and even encourage use of outpatient health care facilities. As these programs might not be specifically targeted to the poor, it may be that the net incidence of public expenditure and benefit is higher among non-poor households (Pradhan, Saadah and Sparrow 2007).

Household Support Programs: Income and Counseling Services to Protect Early Childhood Development

Broaden public works programs to include public service interventions. While effective in transferring cash (or food) to the unemployed and taking advantage of a self-targeting mechanism, traditional public works schemes may not always be effective at ensuring the health and development of the child. Traditional public works tend to be in male-dominated occupations and involve a significant amount of physical labor, although there is growing positive experience with engaging women in traditionally male roles (see Kabeer 2008; Holmes and Jones 2011). As a result, participants will likely be working-age males. Supplementary eligibility criteria can be used to target those, for example, who have young children or a pregnant wife at home. In addition, both the form of payment and the task can be designed to encourage greater participation among women. For example, women may prefer piecework or task-based payments (Subbarao 2003); and women will be encouraged to participate if the program also provides facilities for child care (Sabarwal, Sinha, and Buvinic 2010). Several countries have experimented with an alternative form of public works that provides public services rather than physical infrastructure (for a case study of the crisis response in Argentina, see box 6.1). In the case of Argentina, the majority of enrolled beneficiaries were women. The work could be done in various settings, from community organizations providing child care services to training courses and second-chance education. Public service programs that simultaneously address communities' needs and support social cohesion may achieve a broader range of objectives, including that of ensuring healthy early childhood development (see, for example, Tcherneva and Wray 2005).

Box 6.1

Jefes y Jefas de Hogar Desempleados: Argentina's Response to the 2001–02 Financial Crisis

One of the more prominent and rigorously evaluated crisis response programs was Argentina's public works and service program Jefes y Jefas de Hogar Desempleados (Unemployed Heads of Households). It was conceived and rolled out in the midst of Argentina's worst economic and social crisis in its history and was up and running within approximately three months after the collapse of the banking system and government in early 2002. This public works program targeted unemployed heads of households in which there was at least one child under the age of 18 or a pregnant woman. By the end of 2002, the program covered some 2 million households, 60–70 percent of which were registered as having a female head of household. Galasso and Ravallion (2004) found that the program effectively reduced unemployment, and provided a safety net to many of the households hard hit by the crisis, and reduced the incidence of extreme poverty. The wage was set at 75 percent of the minimum wage, and the requirement for work or training was 4–6 hours a day and no less than 20 hours a week. Municipalities and nongovernmental organizations (NGOs) proposed projects and recruited workers. Participants could work in community projects or microenterprises, go back to school, participate in vocational training, or work in municipal governments or for private employers. The projects included community-organized soup kitchens, bake shops, child care facilities, and other cooperative endeavors. A case study of these activities indicates that the arrangements fostered social cohesion and increased female engagement in activities outside the house, thus enhancing confidence and empowerment (Tcherneva and Wray 2005).

Implement targeted cash transfer programs to help smooth consumption and sustain investments in children's development. Cash transfer programs, both conditional and unconditional, can mitigate the impact of crises by cushioning the effects of the shock on household income (Fiszbein, Ringold, and Srinivasan 2011). On the one hand, evidence shows that conditional cash transfer programs can improve birth weight and child height (Barber and Gertler 2008; Fernald, Gertler, and Neufeld 2008), reduce aggressive or oppositional symptoms among four-to-six-year-olds (Ozer et al. 2009), and improve cognitive and noncognitive outcomes (Macours, Schady, and Vakis 2008). On the other hand, less evidence points to the effectiveness of these programs in protecting health during times of crisis. Moreover, monitoring compliance with conditions is likely to prove difficult during crisis (see, for example, Galasso and Ravallion 2004). A number of new cash transfer programs have emerged during the most recent crisis, including a scaling up of the Benazir Income Support Program in Pakistan, reinstating the Bantuan Langsung Tunai program in Indonesia, and the introduction of a program in Guatemala (Fiszbein, Ringold, and Srinivasan 2011). In most cases, for these programs to be effective, they need to have been in place before the crisis, with the capacity to scale up quickly as needed.

Adopt in-kind or other transfers to support nutrition and food consumption. Food-based programs include those that distribute food directly or indirectly through the provision of vouchers or subsidies for the purchase of food. In principle, these have the advantage of focusing directly on nutrition, freeing up income for other uses, and being generally under the control of women in the household (Rogers and Coates 2002). They also may be easy to scale up in response to a crisis and to scale back afterward. The evidence on the impact of these programs on nutritional outcomes is generally but not universally positive. Some evidence from Ethiopia indicates that a food-for-work program improved food security (Gedamu 2006; Gilligan and Hoddinott 2007) and child weight for height (Quisumbing 2003). However, a food-for-work program in Indonesia in response to the 1997–98 crisis was found to have no impact on child and maternal anemia rates (Moench-Pfanner et al. 2005). In cases where individuals within the household are targeted to receive assistance, the net impact may vary according to the degree to which the household substitutes those benefits for its own resources. This concern is not likely to be large, but evidence among poorer households suggests that children who participate in feeding programs appear to receive less food at home (Jacoby 1997). Specific micronutrient supplementation, for example during pregnancy, may be more effective, as it is less likely to be consumed by other household members. Basic food subsidies or vouchers may be more easily substituted away from the intended target, the child. Caution is thus warranted when using food or other in-kind transfers. Of course, in some true emergencies, such as among refugees and internally displaced people, food transfers may be the only source of food and may constitute the only resources a household receives (Rogers and Coates 2002).

Girls' health may be particularly vulnerable to negative shocks: Rose (1999) reports that favorable rainfall shocks increase the probability that a girl child survives relative to the probability that a boy survives, because girls' consumption is more sensitive to fluctuations in household income. Thus, public policies specifically targeted to protect girls' health and nutrition, particularly during the first year of life, are especially important.

Provide or facilitate access to high-quality child care services. Evidence has shown that food-for-work or cash-for-work programs that provide child care benefit both participating women and young children's development (Fiszbein and Schady 2009). Especially for poorer households, increasing (public works) employment for women has positive impacts on child health over and above its impact of increasing calorie availability through greater income (see, for example, Brown, Yohannes, and Webb 1994). However, women often face significant time constraints due to their (unpaid) domestic and care responsibilities. Thus, the provision of child care at work sites is critical to attracting and enabling women to participate in work activities. Public works participants themselves can be trained to provide these and other services, as in the Jefes y Jefas program (Lal et al. 2010), both providing training and employment for some and freeing up time to pursue other employment for others.

Provide support and guidance on parenting and care. Resource constraints are only one of the mechanisms putting young children's development at risk. Crisis response programs must also address the stress and other mental health issues that may affect people within a household. Parental unemployment and hardship have effects on family dynamics and can hamper healthy family functioning, thus indirectly impeding the development of the child (for a more detailed discussion, see chapter 4 and box 4.1). Policy makers may want to consider additional points of entry to alleviate intrahousehold conflict, reduce parental stress, and improve parenting skills. These may include the provision of conflict resolution skills, parenting advice, or information on where to find support during hard times (see Engle et al. 2011 for a review of 15 parenting programs from around the world; Al-Hassan and Lansford 2010). It may be most useful to incorporate parent-focused interventions into existing programs and services, such as the health care system or community services that engage clients face to face. For example, visits to a health clinic can be a great opportunity to engage with at least one of the parents, most probably the mother and primary care giver, on issues related to child care and parenting. Clinics and health care providers might provide informational materials, emotional support, advice on rearing practices, or hands-on practical guidance on stimulating engagement. But parenting interventions can also be center or community based (see Rebello, Yoshikawa, and Boller 2011 for an overview of implementation arrangements and the role of parenting from a comprehensive early childhood development perspective) or use a home visitation approach (for a review and discussion, see Astuto and Allen 2009). Community-based programs may have added benefits. A randomized trial found that a community-based parenting intervention was six times as cost-effective as an individual parent training program (Cunningham, Bremner, and Boyle 1995). Such environments can foster a sense of belonging and an awareness of support, which reduce the stress perceived and will thus affect family dynamics and parent-child interactions (see also box 6.2 on social resilience).

Provide protective physical and psychosocial services to pregnant women. As Barker (1990) and others have demonstrated, health at birth is a function of the individual's genetic endowment, the health of the mother, and the surrounding environment. The impact of the gestational environment can persist throughout an individual's life. Birth weight, for example, is strongly correlated with achievement and earnings in adulthood (Behrman and Rosenzweig 2004). But not all insults in utero are manifest in birth weight, and severe nutritional deprivation during any stage of gestation can have serious consequences (see Lumey et al. 2007 for evidence from the Dutch Hunger Winter). Interventions can partly compensate for deficits in nutrition during pregnancy: a randomized control trial in Nepal found that giving pregnant women folic acid and iron supplements increased mean birth weight by 37 grams and reduced the prevalence of low-birth-weight babies from 43 percent to 34 percent (Christian et al. 2009). In addition, birth weight and later-life educational outcomes can be affected by exposure in utero to high levels of cortisol resulting from maternal stress (Sarkar et al. 2008; Bergman et al. 2010). Prenatal programs should provide support to counter stress experienced during economic crises. At the same time, programs may also address parenting skills, prevent maternal depression, and affect the quality of the relationship between mother and infant. One program in South Africa that consisted of home visits by previously untrained community workers had a significant positive impact on the quality of the mother-infant relationship and on the security of infant attachment, factors known to predict favorable child development (Cooper et al. 2009).

Box 6.2

Social Resilience and Human Development

Resilience is what allows individuals, groups, or systems to survive, adapt, and even thrive in the face of disruption or other challenges. The concept is found in ecology, developmental and social psychology, and disaster response literature (for example, Masten 2010; Cottle 2001). In child development, resilience generally refers to a child's capacity for positive adaptation in the face of adversity (see box 2.1 for a list of resilience factors). A child's resilience depends, among other things, on the resilience of his or her family, community, and other groups in society; in other words, a child's adaptive capacity is influenced by social resilience. During adolescence, social resilience becomes of direct importance, affecting the development of identity and future orientation. The discussion now looks deeply into social resilience and at how it is built, maintained, and altered while adapting to social change.

Social resilience is the capacity of groups of people—bound together in an organization, class, racial group, community, or nation—to sustain and advance their well-being in the face of challenges. It is an essential characteristic of successful societies (Hall and Lamont 2009) and shapes the ability of people to live healthy, secure, and fulfilling lives. Resilience is dynamic: it is the capacity not only to return to a prior state but also to achieve well-being even when doing so requires significant modifications to behavior or to the social frameworks that structure and give meaning to behavior. In short, it is the capacity of individuals or groups to achieve favorable material, cultural, and emotional outcomes under altered circumstances and, if need be, by new means.

Sources of Social Resilience

People's ability to sustain their well-being in challenging circumstances, such as economic crisis, depends on their access not only to economic resources but also to social resources embodied in networks, social hierarchies, and cultural repertoires, including narratives, rituals, symbols, and ways of seeing the world (Swidler 1986). Moreover, groups do not simply call passively on existing sets of resources, but they engage in more active, creative processes of assembling a variety of tools, including new images of themselves and collective resources, to sustain their well-being in the face of social change.

Resources may be drawn from multiple nested spheres from the family, neighborhood, and local community to the region, nation-state, and transnational

(continued next page)

Box 6.2 *(continued)*

regimes. For instance, a large literature suggests that social networks built on ties to families, friends, and acquaintances constitute social resources from which people can secure information and logistical and emotional support (Liebenberg and Ungar 2009; Berkman 1997; Berkman and Glass 2000; Sampson, Morenoff, and Gannon-Rowley 2002). Social organizations such as trade unions are also an important source of resources (Ancelovici, forthcoming; Barnes and Hall, forthcoming). At a community level, Québec, for example, has been able to sustain aggregate well-being more effectively than other Canadian provinces in part by nurturing a "social economy" characterized by large numbers of cooperatives and enterprises supported by quasi-public organizations (Bouchard, forthcoming). In that respect, Québec resembles the regions of northern Italy and Germany that weathered the economic crises of the 1970s better than others by relying on dense social networks underpinned by a culture of cooperation (Piore and Sabel 1984; Streeck 1991; Herrigel 1996).

Other forms of social connectedness also matter. Societies are bound together not only through social ties but also through *collective imaginaries:* that is, narratives about the chief qualities of a community, its past and future, and its collective orientation and identity (Bouchard 2003, forthcoming). Collective imaginaries often reinforce—and are reinforced by—social organizations and policies. Bouchard (forthcoming), for instance, shows that long-standing myths about the character and history of Québec underpinned social solidarity, sustaining both its social economy and its social safety net. In the Nordic countries, collective imaginaries that promote a sense of shared social responsibility have provided crucial support for the social organizations and policies that contribute to social resilience (Berman 2006; Offe 2011).

Collective imaginaries can also be direct sources of resilience by specifying and supporting collective identities. Stigmatized groups may draw heavily on national collective imaginaries—such as principles of equality in the American creed, a celebration of racial mixing in Brazil, or Zionist identity in Israel—in their strategies to counter racism (Lamont, Fleming, and Welburn, forthcoming). Attachment to a strong collective identity bolsters self-concepts and reduces the adverse psychological impact of experiences of immigration and racial discrimination (see, for example, Feliciano 2005; Oyserman, Bybee, and Terry 2006). The shared cultural references, myths, and narratives embodied in collective imaginaries can buttress an individual's sense of self and capabilities. People depend on these cultural tools to make sense of challenges and to imagine solutions to them

(continued next page)

Box 6.2 *(continued)*

(Small, Harding, and Lamont 2010; Swidler 1986). At stake is their sense of possible futures, both individually and collectively (Markus and Nurius 1986). Chandler and Lalonde (1998) show, for instance, that differences in suicide rates across first-nation communities in British Columbia are influenced by the community's ability to transmit a sense of pride in its collective identity and history.

Many aspects of local cultural orders—such as those prevalent in particular communities or ethnic groups—can also be important for social resilience. People find strategies for action by observing the behavior of those around them. The attitudes toward family violence prevalent in a community, for instance, may condition the resources available to people in family crises. African Americans are less likely than Latinos to seek help finding employment or to recommend co-ethnics for jobs, partly because widespread stereotypes about African American welfare dependency encourage them to invest more strongly in notions of self-reliance (Smith 2010).

Social Resilience and Collective Responses

Social resilience entails not only the features of society on which *individuals* draw to enhance their capabilities but also the capacities of *communities* to respond collectively to challenges. The capacities of the state to redistribute resources, to supply public goods, and to encourage forms of social organization that support employment and social solidarity are important, as are community capacities. For instance, fostering early childhood development requires active cooperation from multiple actors in the local community, ranging from school superintendents to parents and local business people, operating in durable, intersectoral coalitions (Hertzman and Siddiqi 2011).

In a very different setting, Swidler (forthcoming) examines how "collective goods" are supplied in African villages and finds that the institution of the local chief is crucial. She sees the institution of the chief as a culturally constituted resource made possible by the shared narratives of the community. Those narratives accord chiefs a position from which they can seek the cooperation of the members of the community in endeavors to advance its well-being. The chief's authority rests on traditional capacities to allocate symbolic resources, of the sort embodied in attending a funeral, but extends to the allocation of material resources, such as coupons for fertilizer.

The capacity of institutions to enhance a community's social resilience often depends on their interplay with cultural frameworks. Cultural and institutional

(continued next page)

Box 6.2 *(continued)*

structures can reinforce one another, or they can be at odds, as they are in schools where peer-based status orders (that is, how students rank the relative status of their peers) collide with teacher-driven status orders (Carter 2005; Warikoo 2010). This point has special pertinence for efforts to import market-oriented competition and material incentives into local communities. When such experiments ignore local cultural contexts, the results are likely to be misleading; and, when such efforts subvert local cultures, they may destroy rather than create social resources (Swidler and Watkins 2009). Moreover, as ideas about entrepreneurial behavior become more popular, they can shift the cultural frameworks underpinning institutional practices, sometimes for the better but sometimes in ways that erode the capacity of communities to generate collective goods (see also Rao and Walton 2004).

A given set of cultural frameworks does not guarantee resilience. Resilient outcomes usually demand active processes that mobilize people to engage and sustain the appropriate cultural frameworks (Swidler, forthcoming; Bouchard, forthcoming; Hertzman and Siddiqi, 2011). Social resilience ultimately depends on what might be called "cultural frameworks in action" and on institutions that give the relevant actors the "strategic capacity" to formulate concerted responses to challenges and to generate collective goods, protect societies' weakest members, and sustain their well-being.

Source: Prepared by Ryann Manning and Michele Lamont, adapted from from Hall and Lamont (forthcoming).

Middle Childhood

The major concern during middle childhood centers on children's schooling: enrollment, attendance, dropout rate, and grade progression. In theory, during negative financial shocks poorer households are driven to reduce expenditures on education or to increase household income by sending their child to work. Wealthier households may respond to the decreased opportunity cost of the child's time to increase enrollment and attendance. Which effect dominates will depend on the depth of the shock as well as on the household's resources. The evidence reviewed in chapter 4 shows that aggregate economic shocks do not always affect schooling during middle childhood, that the responses may be procyclical or countercyclical, and that no compelling evidence shows that more children start to work. Studies of idiosyncratic shocks, however, do show negative effects on children's schooling. For all households, concerns remain about the broader developmental impacts of crises on cognitive, socioemotional, and behavioral development and their long-term implications for educational achievement, involvement in risky behavior, and labor market success.

Developmental outcomes in middle childhood are determined by the availability of key resources and by proximal processes such as parent-child, teacher-child, and peer-child interactions. Chapter 4 identifies three main transmission mechanisms that may affect a child's development during this stage, given the dominant settings of family and school, within which he or she interacts: (1) parental stress and family functioning; (2) investments in learning and stimulation within the home; and (3) teachers, peers, and the learning environment in schools. We know that shocks affect parental stress and mental health, which, in turn affect the extent to which parents are able to engage in cognitive stimulation and consistent and effective parenting. Economic hardship is also likely to decrease family investments in cognitively stimulating materials and activities in contexts where this is relevant. Reductions in public spending on education can also affect a child's development by affecting the teaching environment and teacher-student relationships. In general, school resources are less important than socioeconomic status in determining attendance and achievement (see Hanushek 1996). Vermeersh and Kremer (2005) show that subsidized school meals yielded greater school participation and higher test scores in Kenya, and Joseph and Wodon (2012) show that greater inputs reduced dropout rates in Ghana. But other studies from Kenya (Glewwe, Kremer, and Moulin 1998), as well as from Guatemala, Mexico, and Peru (Hernandez-Zavala et al. 2006), find that while school characteristics matter, they matter less than family characteristics. All of these factors can have serious and long-lasting consequences for children's healthy cognitive, socioemotional, and behavioral development.

Assuming that poverty is the main constraint to children's education, a government can attempt to reduce the cost of education, as well as the cost of children's time, to prevent school dropout and encourage education and learning despite an economic crisis. These goals can be achieved through cash transfer programs (universal or targeted, conditional or unconditional), scholarships or fee waivers, or subsidized school materials. Policy makers can also try to increase the perceived returns to education by enhancing quality and links to employment; in some cases, simply providing information on the returns to education can increase demand (see, for example, Jensen 2010). However, in the context of an economic shock, perceptions and incentives change, as do the opportunity costs of children's time and intrahousehold relations.

School attendance is only one factor influencing a child's learning and development; interventions aimed at providing families with the means and incentives for school attendance alone may be insufficient to ensure healthy development. In addition, middle childhood is the period when the child's world broadens considerably; he or she increasingly engages in settings outside the family, and these settings will be affected by crises in many different ways. These other settings may pose additional risks or mediate the impact in positive ways. Supportive community settings and healthy peer relationships may offset some of the negative experiences within the family and vice versa. Thus, while many of the common social safety net programs outlined previously apply to middle childhood as well, the nature of this developmental stage opens up other possibilities for intervention. This section reviews the protective effect that traditional safety nets may have during crises, as well as other interventions that can safeguard healthy development during middle childhood.

Household Support Programs: Income and Counseling Services to Maintain Healthy Family Functioning and Investments in Education

Introduce or scale up income support schemes to smooth consumption and sustain family investments in children's development. Mechanisms for the delivery of income support vary significantly, but they are all intended to ensure some minimum level of household consumption for the duration of the crisis. They may provide cash or cashlike vouchers for the purchase of specific goods, or they may provide food directly. They may require some contribution in the form of participation in work or training, or they may require some behavior deemed beneficial to the family, such as school attendance or the consumption of health care services.

In spite of the evidence of the positive impact of public works programs on general welfare, as outlined in the discussion of early childhood, little evidence of their impact on child outcomes in developing countries is available. Several studies of U.S.-based programs show that these programs can support children's development but that the impact depends strongly on program design. For example, Morris et al. (2001) find that programs that require work but provide no extra income and those in which other benefits are cut when incomes increase may leave family income unchanged and have few and mixed effects on children's development. Conversely, programs that increase participants' income, especially if they lift families above the poverty line and do not impose a strict tax on other benefits as incomes rise, have positive (albeit not large) effects on a range of outcomes, from school achievement to problem behavior and health. These programs also affect the development of identity and future orientation, processes that begin in middle childhood and become salient during adolescence (McLoyd et al. 2011). Thus, parental employment status and the ability to improve parents' earning capacity may have longer-lasting effects on children (McLoyd et al. 2011), making well-designed public works program a possible tool for offsetting the household's loss of income during a crisis while simultaneously promoting positive child development.

Conditional cash transfer programs have received great attention recently (for a detailed review, see Fiszbein and Schady 2009). Evidence from two conditional cash transfer programs suggests that such transfers may be effective in mitigating the effect of a shock on children's educational outcomes. The Progresa/Oportunidades conditional cash transfer program in rural Mexico that was in place during the Tequila Crisis in the mid-1990s effectively promoted children's school enrollment among households that experienced a shock, such as unemployment, health, or natural disaster (de Janvry et al. 2006). Similarly, the Nicaraguan Red de Protección Social was effective at increasing school enrollment in coffee-growing areas that were hit by the fall in coffee prices in the late 1990s (Maluccio 2005).

Although some evidence is available on the impact of transfer programs on school attendance, less is available on their impact on learning and other outcomes. Even though school attendance is not a perfect indicator of cognitive outcomes, transfers may alleviate intrafamilial problems such as parental stress and conflict, which inhibit learning even when children attend school. The fact that conditional cash transfers are often given to mothers, however, may also alter intrahousehold relations. The association between income transfers to mothers and intrahousehold relationships is not straightforward, though. How these transfers to mothers affect parent-child relationships and children's well-being is complex and dynamic and may be very context specific (see, for example, Gibson-Davis et al. 2005; Bates et al. 2004; Berger 2005). The subject warrants particular attention to how safety net programs affect family relations and, in turn, children's development, given a particular cultural context.

Conditional cash transfers have other characteristics that make them less attractive as a crisis response tool. If administrative capacity is low, it may not be possible to scale up rapidly enough to meet demand, to manage the complexities of administered targeting schemes quickly, or to scale the programs back once the crisis has abated.

Leveraging the School as a Protective Setting

Maintain public spending on education and ensure timely payment of teacher salaries. Given the amount of time that children around the world spend in schools or nonformal education programs, such institutions are important contexts that may lessen or exacerbate the negative impact of economic crises on educational outcomes. Experience shows that payment of teacher compensation may be at risk during an economic crisis (Knowles, Pernia, and Racelis 1999), increasing the risk of teacher absenteeism and the rates of teacher turnover. To address this issue in the context of conflict zones and natural disasters, which may be equally useful during economic crises, the Inter-Agency Network for Education in Emergencies (INEE) drafted a set of standards that provides a practical framework for various stakeholders on how to train, manage, compensate, and monitor teachers in crisis situations (INEE 2010). These standards could be reviewed and adapted to the context of economic crises to ensure that teacher compensation is maintained.

Reduce the cost to the family of sending children to school. As household incomes fall, families' investments in their children's education may be at risk. Interventions can therefore aim at reducing the burden of schooling for economically strained families and facilitate continued school attendance. Indonesia, for example, implemented a scholarship program in 1998 in response to the regional economic crisis. Cameron (2009) finds that the scholarship program was effective at reducing dropouts at the lower secondary school level, where historically students were most prone to leave school. Sparrow (2007) finds that the program increased enrollment especially for primary school–aged children from poor rural households and helped the households' smooth consumption during the crisis. In addition to fees, the family may no longer be able to provide school uniforms and materials as their incomes fall. School feeding programs can provide additional incentives for children's school attendance as it lessens the family's burden of providing food for the child. See the discussion on early childhood in this chapter for more detail on the pros and cons of feeding programs.

Strengthen in-school and after-school programs to counteract stressful home environments. Even when no apparent change has occurred in consumption patterns or investments in schooling or other outcomes for children, the increased stress on parents may lead to a deterioration in intrafamily dynamics and other contextual influences. These changes may negatively affect children's cognitive, socioemotional, and behavioral development (for a review of the evidence on family stress, see chapter 4 and box 4.1). For example, we know that the socioemotional and cognitive development of primary school–aged children can be particularly affected by intrafamilial conflict stemming from the parent's loss of a job. However, it may be time consuming and costly to design interventions to reach individual families. Instead, implementing new or augmenting existing socioemotional learning programs in schools in times of crisis may serve as a buffer against the potential negative influences in the family context. Reviews have shown that school-based programs can be very effective in enhancing positive social skills, thereby contributing to better learning outcomes, higher self-esteem, and a reduction in risky behaviors, among other effects (see, for example, Cunningham et al. 2008; Bandy and Moore 2011; Durlak et al. 2011). After-school programs and other organized extracurricular activities in schools can provide safe environments and exposure to positive influences, potentially offsetting some of the negative effects of strained home environments (Mahoney, Harris and Eccles 2006). Such after-school activities might be particularly important when parents are working. Furthermore, given the increasing importance of teachers in the lives of children, an intervention that enhances a teacher's ability to cope with the crisis may improve the quality of the learning experience as well as alleviate the burden on children.

Strengthening Community-Based Programs

Provide children with cognitively stimulating learning materials and experiences. Other evidence presented in chapter 4 indicates that household economic pressure may decrease parental investment in cognitively stimulating interaction and materials in the home, a decrease, in turn, which is associated with declines in children's cognitive outcomes (Gershoff et al. 2007). Also, cognitively stimulating home environments affect intrinsic academic motivation in the short and the long term (Gottfried, Fleming, and Gottfried 1998). While further research is necessary to design, implement, and evaluate the feasibility and impact of interventions aimed at increasing cognitive stimulation during middle childhood, that approach may be fruitful and relatively easy to implement for maintaining or improving children's cognitive outcomes during economic crises.

In summary, while supporting family income, consumption, and investment is crucial to protecting middle school–aged children, it is also important to recognize that interventions for this age group need to address other crisis transmission mechanisms, in particular those affecting intrahousehold relations and the school setting. The diverse settings of a child's microsystem do not operate in isolation: events in any one will affect others. It may be possible to design policies and interventions in certain settings (for example, the school) to compensate for negative events or to enhance positive events that occur in a different setting (for example, the family).

Adolescence

Chapter 5 reviewed the evidence on how crises affect adolescent employment, mental health, and risky behaviors. In the short term, economic crises seem to lead to declines in employment among young people, but no consistent impacts on their school attendance are evident. The long-term impacts of economic crisis on educational attainment, employment, and earnings are heterogeneous. We have seen that those who return to or stay in school when faced with a difficult labor market seem to do better in the long run, but we know less about why some young people remain in school and others do not. Access to income or credit matters, but it is not the only determinant of outcomes in a crisis. Given young people's growing independence and increased awareness of the world around them, a crisis may make if more difficult for them to negotiate and master critical developmental tasks.

Much of the research on the impact of crisis on adolescents and the policy responses have focused on the transition to employment. Young people are consistently more vulnerable to economic crises than adults (World Bank 2006), usually because they are often engaged in temporary and less protected work—such as seasonal, temporary, and part-time jobs—or in sectors particularly vulnerable to economic fluctuations, such as construction. Strong evidence indicates that early unemployment has serious long-term effects on income over the lifespan as well as on physical and mental health (see, for example, Bell and Blanchflower 2010).

With long-term objectives and outcomes in mind, chapter 5 outlined the main mechanisms through which crises affect young people:

- The achievement of autonomy and the ability to negotiate relationships with parents and others may be affected by crisis, for example, if it affects the development of financial independence, given increased difficulties transitioning to employment.
- Rapid contextual changes due to economic crisis redefine perceptions and aspirations and hamper the development of an identity as an individual within a society, including the vocational identity.
- A crisis may interfere with the process of setting concrete goals and establishing a strategy to achieve them, as information and environments change rapidly, rendering irrelevant or unachievable previously established objectives or the parameters for achieving them.

While many young people still live with their parents, the factors that influence them broaden continuously, and their goals begin to diverge from those of their parents. Safety nets, such as transfers and employment programs directed at the household, may not completely address the challenges youth are facing. Settings and systems interact, and a young person will shape his or her identity through a wider range of settings than during earlier childhood. For example, decisions about labor market outcomes are jointly made with other important decisions about school investments and other uses of time. Thus, policy makers must consider the impacts of aggregate economic shocks within the broad context of the overall developmental impacts on youth. However, this broader context provides a greater set of possible interventions and tools with which to influence the positive development of young people and to compensate for previous adverse events.

Household Support Programs: Interventions That Encourage Positive Development of Adolescents

Adapt income transfer programs to support healthy parent-child relationships and convey productive messages. Income support programs, such as cash transfers or public works, may replace lost family income, support children's education, and enable parents to maintain effective parenting and supervision. However, income support programs may have a negative impact on the development of vocational identity and future orientation among beneficiaries' children. Adolescents become increasingly aware of the family's socioeconomic status and the stigma associated with welfare benefits. Parental attitudes and work values are strongly associated with the planning behavior and future orientation of their children that lead to social and economic upward mobility in adult life (Clausen 1991), as well as lower incidence of risky behavior (see, for example, Wyman et al. 1992). From a developmental perspective, it is worth considering how safety net programs affect other psychosocial outcomes, such as perceptions and attitudes toward education and work, both among program beneficiaries or participants and among their adolescent children. For example, a synthesis study of pilot welfare programs in the United States found consistently negative impacts of these programs on school performance and grade progression of adolescents (see Gennetian et al. 2004). An experimental evaluation of Wisconsin's New Hope, however, showed positive effects on a range of child outcomes. That program provided working poor adults a choice of benefits, including earnings supplements, child care, and health insurance, conditional on 30 or more hours of work per week. They were also able to access advice and other services from project staff and to hold community service jobs, if no other employment was available. An eight-year follow-up study of children of beneficiaries between the ages of 9 and 19 at the time of the study found positive program impacts on future orientation and employment experiences for boys, particularly for African American boys (McLoyd et al. 2011). While there were no significant changes in employment patterns and earnings during the summer, they did work more during the school year. Boys in beneficiary families were significantly less pessimistic about their employment prospects, less cynical about work, and more involved in employment and career preparation. The higher level of engagement in work during the school year, however, did not seem to affect test scores, academic progress, expectations of completing high school, going to college, or completing college. The study attributes the positive impact on future orientation to key implementation arrangements, such as how the services were delivered, that contributed to an environment of respect and dignity. The study also found that beneficiary children had higher rates of participation in extracurricular activities, bringing them together with adults outside the family who might have acted as mentors and encouraged positive attitudes toward work and the future.

Support Positive Relationships with Adults Outside the Family

Establish mentoring relationships with adults in community, school, and work settings. Mentors, or extrafamilial adult role models, have come to be seen as important figures in the development of children and youth. Mentoring relationships can be established in a variety of settings and through a variety of mechanisms. The International Rescue Committee has successfully used peer mentoring in support of its youth livelihoods programs.[2] The National Guard YouthChallenge program in the United States lets participants identify their mentors in their communities and provided mentors only to those who failed to find their own (Millenky et al. 2011). Other programs provide mentoring services through trained social workers and the like.[3] Success of mentoring programs depends on the quality of the relationships between youth and adults, the regularity and consistency of contact, persistence, and duration of at least one year (Rhodes and DuBois 2006).

Many young people find mentoring-type relationships in community-based programs, such as youth centers, sports, summer camps, and after-school activities. It is thus important for such programs to receive continued funding. In addition, these group settings may not only provide mentoring relationships but also support healthy peer relationships in safe environments, if certain criteria are met. Research has shown that placing at-risk youth in programs and settings with other deviant youth can exacerbate negative peer influences (Dodge, Dishion, and Lansford 2006).

Provide adult-supervised extracurricular opportunities and after school activities. Young people spend a lot of time outside the school environment, and thus how this time is used matters a lot. Structured and supervised activities in youth-friendly spaces can reinforce the development of cognitive, socioemotional, and behavioral skills and characteristics and can provide close mentoring-type relationships with adults outside the family that facilitate the development of more positive future orientation (see, for example, McLoyd et al. 2011). Out-of-school activities can also provide socioemotional support, develop competencies, and improve academic outcomes (Granger 2008).

Such programs can be structured around a wide range of programmatic components, such as academic support, mini-apprenticeships with adult volunteers, health and life skills workshops, and recreational and outdoor activities. They may take place in a variety of settings after school, on weekends, and during holidays; they may be managed by schools, community-based organizations, youth service organizations, or other local stakeholders. Although goals and structures vary across interventions, offering a multitude of services, experiential learning, opportunities, a safe and structured environment, and supportive adult and peer-to-peer relationships are common factors of success (Bowles and Brand 2009). Moreover, alignment with the educational system and collaboration with schools and the community, as well as strong ownership by the local government, provide structural support. Building on the existing personnel and facility infrastructure of the schools and community can help reduce costs and make such interventions viable even in low-resource environments.

Successful examples have been implemented around the world, although less evidence exists for developing countries. In Brazil, for instance, the Open Schools/Abrindo Espaços program has been shown to reduce negative risky behaviors of young people, while in Macedonia the Babylon Youth Centers contributed to increasing the employability of those in the program (Cunningham et al. 2008). A rich experience is also available in the United States, where programs such as the Boys and Girls Clubs or Citizen Schools have improved academic achievement, career aspirations, and prosocial behaviors (Bowles and Brand 2009).

Leveraging the School as a Protective Setting
Prevent youth from dropping out of school and encourage continued education and training. Not all children drop out of school in times of crisis. As chapter 4 notes, crises engender both procyclical and countercyclical responses to schooling. However, young people from poorer households and in poorer settings are more likely to interrupt schooling in times of crisis (see, for example, Duryea, Lam, and Levison 2003). To the extent that parents withdraw children from school for financial reasons, reductions in fees or expenses for uniforms, travel, and supplies may prevent dropout. Lower rates of youth employment in times of economic crisis indicate lower opportunity costs of education; programs incentivizing and supporting further education and training may be particularly effective.

Conditional transfers to the parents, in which the transfer is conditional on school attendance of their child, can protect enrollment but may not prevent parents from increasing children's workload in response to shocks (de Janvry et al. 2006). Furthermore, parents have increasingly less control over their adolescents' school attendance and thus enforcing the condition may prove difficult.

Young people face many conflicting objectives and constraints. They may already carry financial responsibilities either by contributing to their parents' household or by providing for a family of their own, even though they themselves have not yet fully developed neurologically, physiologically, socioemotionally, or behaviorally. Investments at this stage can advance both economic and developmental goals far into the future. For example, a program can direct a cash transfer directly to a young person conditioned on his or her attending school, holding an internship, taking training, or participating in some sort of mentoring or coaching program. Such activities can simultaneously provide income support to a young person and focus on his or her specific developmental needs for long-term growth.

A couple of studies thus far have looked at cash transfers to adolescents rather than to their parents. The results of these studies provide some insights into the importance of agency and the objectives of young people themselves. Riccio et al. (2010) found that incentives paid to early adolescents as part of a conditional cash transfer program in New York City improved the academic performance of the youth who were academically proficient at baseline. Greenberg, Dechausay, and Fraker (2011) conducted an extensive evaluation of how the cash transfers, or "rewards," to both parents and high school students influenced household dynamics, perceptions, and aspirations and culminated in better educational achievements and less cynicism about the future.

Direct transfers to young people can also have impacts beyond schooling. Filmer and Schady (2009) present evidence that a cash transfer intervention in Cambodia had a small effect on the mental health of its adolescent beneficiaries. Baird, de Hoop, and Özler (2011) investigate the impact of a cash transfer program in Malawi on its adolescent female participants. They find that during the two-year program the likelihood of suffering from psychological distress was 17 percent lower in the conditional cash transfer arm and 38 percent lower in the unconditional cash transfer arm when compared with the control group. The beneficial mental health effects of the cash transfers were limited to the intervention period, however, and dissipated quickly after the program ended.

Supporting Adolescents' Transition to Work
Enhance young people's connection to the labor market during the transition to work. Out-of-school and unemployed or inactive youth are of special concern globally. When young people find themselves in a difficult labor market, they may be more willing to engage in training to increase their human capital. However, evidence shows that standard training programs often fail because they are not linked carefully or closely enough to the local labor market. Apprenticeships provide an attractive alternative, especially when the training is subsidized to encourage the participation of employers (see, for example, Hicks et al. 2011).

Cunningham, Sanchez-Puerta, and Wuermli (2010) identify a number of interventions that can have positive impacts, in some contexts, under certain circumstances, and among certain target groups. Solid evidence shows that training programs are more effective among unemployed and disadvantaged youth. Comprehensive programs, such as JobCorps or the Jovenes model in Latin American countries, which combine technical training or education with on-the-job training through internships or apprenticeships and mentoring, are comparatively more effective at increasing employment (Entra21 2009; Wodon and Minowa 2001; Schochet, Burghardt, and McConnell 2006; Ibarraran and Rosas 2009). Entrepreneurship programs, although they may be important for sustainable long-term employment and growth, are unlikely to prove useful for alleviating the youth employment problem during economic downturns. On the other hand, they may provide a solid foundation for rapid and successful entry into the labor market once the economic recovery begins. In addition, this training may provide the "ability to deal with disequilibria" and take advantages of opportunities presented by the crisis (Schultz 1979).

Effective Youth Interventions and Adolescent Development

The important questions are not, Which programs work? but, rather, What type of program is most suitable in a particular context? and How should the intervention be designed and delivered to support the development of the necessary cognitive, socioemotional, and behavioral competencies? While the second question is more general, the first question is particularly important during economic crises when resources and administrative capacity are already strained. Therefore, it is of even greater concern to address the very particular needs of youth to make interventions effective. Young people desire *opportunity* and *purpose*, both of which may be of great scarcity during crises. It is thus of great urgency for interventions to guide and support them on this journey by providing them with the tools to establish and achieve goals and form their identity as workers and citizens.

Adolescents are *not* merely smaller adults. Their physiological, neurological, and psychosocial development is generally incomplete; they require stimulating and rewarding experiences to develop their human capital further. Treating youth like adults, both in expectations of their behavior and in the structure of incentive programs, can distort perceptions and aspirations. A fine line lies between treating youth as the agents they are on the cusp of becoming adults and treating them as the developing person who needs to be protected and guided (see, for example,

Crockett and Silbereisen 2000; Lerner and Steinberg 2009; Silbereisen and Lerner 2007; Elder 1974).

Adolescence is a time in which children seek adult role models outside their family context. Positive role models other than parents can be of great importance in the process of forming identity, developing self-regulatory skills, and setting and achieving goals. Exposure to disillusioned adults or to unhealthy and unproductive behavior can have destructive consequences, for example, by increased exposure to risky behavior (such as unprotected sex or drug and alcohol abuse). To take one rather extreme example, among the interventions for young offenders that have been proved actually harmful is to expose them to older offenders (see World Bank 2006). Grouping at-risk youth together may lead to exactly the outcomes one is trying to avoid. Conversely, engaging youth across different socioeconomic backgrounds together may contribute to strengthening social connectedness.

Developing agency is key; this involves the ability to identify objectives and make plans to achieve them. Learning to set goals and achieve them requires a range of competencies, guidance, and support. Within a "goal setting–goal achievement" process, young people learn about their opportunities and their abilities; they form their preferences, aspirations, and occupational identity; and they actively engage and learn how to strategically plan a process to achieve their goals. At the same time, they learn how to interact in the adult world. Depending on the context, a program may involve short rotating internships through which the young person learns about different occupations, respective prospects, and reasonable expectations and the requirements to actually succeed in a particular job. This process is ideally supported by a mentor or coach, who can provide support and encouragement. Mentors can be peers, employers, other members of the community, or role models who have managed the transition to adulthood in a similar environment (see, for example, the World Bank's Adolescent Girls' Initiative).[4]

Conclusions

This volume builds on a large body of literature from the fields of economics, psychology, and sociology to underscore the crucial importance of childhood and youth for human development. It is by now well established that investments in young people, starting in utero, are the basis for the economic and social development of a country. Conversely, neglecting the human capital of the young generation is not only costly to the

individuals but also to society as a whole. Negative outcomes from insufficient family and public investments in children and youth can include
malnutrition, stunted cognitive and socioemotional development, lower
school performance and attainment, poor health, un- and underemploy-
ment, and an increase in risky behaviors such as substance abuse and
delinquency. The potential economic consequences of such a loss of
human potential, emerging from the direct costs of higher public expenditures and the opportunity costs of lost productivity, are enormous.

While it is challenging for a country to put in place the right mix of
programs and policies to ensure the full development of its young
generation during normal times, it becomes much more difficult in times
of crisis, especially among poorer countries, which are faced with even
higher resource and institutional constraints. Given the potentially severe
short- and long-term consequences of such negative shocks for the development of children and youth, it is in the best interest of each country to
recognize the added vulnerabilities and to adopt a crisis response that
protects and promotes the development of the young generation during
times of economic hardship.

This chapter has summarized a range of program and policy options
that can be adapted or targeted to protect development during early childhood, middle childhood, and adolescence. One overriding lesson is that
economic crises can affect a child or adolescent through a variety of settings, including the family, the school, and the community, in addition to
reductions in public expenditures for social services. This finding suggests
that the developing young person is vulnerable in many different ways and
through different channels other than merely cutbacks in available services. Happily, there are also multiple entry points for interventions that
can mitigate or compensate for the negative effects of an economic shock.
Some settings may be able to act as substitutes for others, and it may, for
example, be an efficient solution to target investments in schools or community programs where many children can be reached at once to mitigate
some of the negative effects experienced within the family. Furthermore,
by adapting the design, changing the targeting strategy, adding a component, or changing the implementation and delivery mechanisms, more
traditional program types can better address the specific needs of children
and youth. The principles of nested points of entry, substitutability, and
targeting provide guidance on how to make these changes.

Moreover, this book has shown that the loss of family income or
wealth that may result from an economic crisis is but one among the
many pathways through which children and youth may be affected.

Therefore, policy makers must consider the impact of traditional safety net programs such as cash transfers or public works on nonfinancial aspects of the crisis. How can these and other interventions be designed or complemented to address, for example, the deterioration of parenting and family functioning and the increased psychological stress that results from greater economic pressures on the household?

While this book has highlighted a multiplicity of possible transmission mechanisms, in practice it becomes crucial to accurately identify the most important constraints affecting individual households and individuals within those households. Every crisis is experienced differently, and different groups are likely to be affected to a different extent by some of the transmission mechanisms in play. For example, while mothers' own health and nutrition and caregivers' investments in health and nutrition of their infants may be a primary concern for all families, the impact on family functioning may not be the same for all households or all socioeconomic groups. Therefore, more sensitive or sophisticated survey instruments and methods may be required than the ones now in common practice to capture fluctuations in income and work status. And more detailed information about parental stress, family coping strategies, and investments of time, as well as of financial resources in the human capital of their children, should be taken into account. Better instruments will facilitate a greater understanding of mechanisms and impacts, as well as more precise targeting and design of interventions and more effective priority setting.

The diversity and complementarity of potential entry points also have implications for the appropriate level of policy intervention of state actors as well as the distribution of responsibilities. Not all interventions described in this chapter can be designed and implemented at the national level. For example, in many countries, policies and programs related to schools are under the authority of regional or local governments. Similarly, community-based programs and services, such as after-school activities or family support services, are usually under the authority of municipalities. When designing policies and programs to protect and promote children and youth in times of economic hardship, policy makers should consider the resource and implementation capacity of all levels of government as well as the NGO sector. Governments and civil society organizations may require donor assistance to maintain essential expenditures as well as technical assistance to absorb and process.

Insights from these different perspectives also provide valuable information for programming and policy making during "normal" economic times. While crises expose vulnerabilities and increase pressures, a deeper understanding of child and youth development—with the variety of relevant settings and the evolving importance over the life course—provides useful guidance whatever the economic context. In fact, the policy implications may be useful in designing targeted interventions for vulnerable children, youth, and families in general, who, even without a macroeconomic crisis, often experience their own idiosyncratic shocks, such as parental job loss or a difficult transition into the labor market. Such experiences impose many of the same pressures as a major economic downturn. Moreover, having the appropriate structures and programs in place during normal times will also facilitate their timely expansion and increase in coverage when economic conditions worsen and the number of children, adolescents, and families in need increases.

Finally, the evidence presented in this volume, while leading to several robust policy conclusions, reveals that we have a great deal left to learn. The major part of the empirical evidence of the impact of shocks on human development comes from the examination of idiosyncratic shocks that affect individual households. Moreover, most of the evidence on the effectiveness of policy responses, as well as most of the evidence obtained using the tools of developmental psychology and sociology, comes from developed countries. Thus, an important research agenda on the effects of negative economic shocks on child and youth development and how best to address them in the context of developing countries remains. In part, this effort will require detailed and sensitive observational data. In addition, understanding the performance of policy interventions will require careful evaluations of alternative tools for protecting and promoting human capital in a crisis, which must be set up quickly as integral components of the crisis response. Understanding how best to protect the development of children and youth will yield great returns in sustained growth from a healthy and productive workforce during normal times, and a faster and less costly recovery from any economic crisis that will inevitably recur in the years to come.

Notes

1. See, for example, http://www.friendsofthechildren.org/.
2. See, for example, http://www.rescue.org/sites/default/files/resource-file/IRC%20MF%20Report%20Final%202010.pdf.
3. See, for example, http://www.npcresearch.com/Files/FOTC/FOTC_Service_Delivery_Report_1109.pdf.
4. See http://go.worldbank.org/ET4S6TEXY0.

References

Al-Hassan, S. M., and J. E. Lansford. 2010. "Evaluation of the Better Parenting Programme in Jordan. *Early Child Development and Care* 181(5): 587–98.

Ancelovici, Marcos. Forthcoming. "The Origins and Dynamics of Organizational Resilience: A Comparative Study of Two French Labor Organizations." In *Social Resilience in the Neo-Liberal Era*, ed. Peter A. Hall and Michèle Lamont. Cambridge, UK: Cambridge University Press.

Astuto, J., and L. Allen. 2009. "Home Visitation and Young Children: An Approach Worth Investing In?" *Social Policy Report* 23 (4).

Baird, Sarah, Jacobus de Hoop, and Berk Ozler. 2011. "Income Shocks and Adolescent Mental Health." Policy Research Paper 5644, World Bank, Washington, DC.

Bandy, T., and Kristin A. Moore. 2011. "What Works for Promoting and Enhancing Positive Social Skills: Lessons from Experimental Evaluations of Programs and Interventions." *Fact Sheet*. Washington, DC: ChildTrends, http://www .childtrends.org/Files/Child_Trends_2011_03_02_RB_WWSocialSkills.pdf.

Barber, Sarah, and Paul Gertler. 2008. "The Impact of Mexico's Conditional Cash Transfer Program, Oportunidades, on Birthweight." *Tropical Medicine and International Health* 13 (2): 1405–14.

Barker, D. J. 1990. "The Fetal and Infant Origins of Adult Disease." *British Medical Journal* 301 (6761): 1111.

Barnes, Lucy, and Peter A. Hall. Forthcoming. "Social Resilience and Well-Being in the Developed Democracies." In *Social Resilience in the Neo-Liberal Era*, ed. Peter A. Hall and Michèle Lamont. Cambridge, UK: Cambridge University Press.

Bates, L., S. Schuler, F. Islam, and K. Islam. 2004. "Socioeconomic Factors and Processes Associated with Domestic Violence in Rural Bangladesh." *International Family Planning Perspectives* 30 (4): 190–99.

Behrman J. R., and M. R. Rosenzweig. 2004. "Returns to Birthweight." *Review of Economics and Statistics* 86 (2): 586–601.

Bell, D. N. F., and D. G. Blanchflower. 2010. "Young People and Recession: A Lost Generation?" Fifty-Second Panel Meeting on Economic Policy, Einaudi Institute for Economics and Finance, October 22–23, Rome, Italy.

Berger, L. 2005. "Income, Family Characteristics, and Physical Violence toward Children." *Child Abuse and Neglect* 29 (2): 107–33.

Bergman, K., V. Glover, P. Sarkar, D. H. Abbott, and T. G. O'Connor. 2010. "In Utero Cortisol and Testosterone Exposure and Fear Reactivity in Infancy." *Hormones and Behavior* 57 (3): 306–12.

Berkman, Lisa F. 1997. "Looking beyond Age and Race: The Structure of Networks, Functions of Support, and Chronic Stress." *Epidemiology* 8 (September): 469–70.

Berkman, Lisa F., and Thomas Glass. 2000. "Social Integration, Social Networks, Social Support, and Health." In *Social Epidemiology*, ed. Lisa F. Berkman and Ichiro Kawachi, 137–74. New York: Oxford University Press.

Berman, Sheri. 2006. *The Primacy of Politics: Social Democracy and the Making of Europe's Twentieth Century*. New York: Cambridge University Press.

Bouchard, Gérard. 2003. *Raison et Contradiction: Le Mythe au Secours de la Pensée* [Sense and contradiction: The myth of aid to thought]. Québec: Éditions Nota bene/Cefan.

———. Forthcoming. "Neo-Liberalism in Québec: The Response of a Small Nation under Pressure." In *Social Resilience in the Neo-Liberal Era*, ed. Peter A. Hall and Michèle Lamont. Cambridge, UK: Cambridge University Press.

Bowles, A., and B. Brand. 2009. *Learning around the Clock: Benefits of Expanded Learning Opportunities for Older Youth*. Washington, DC: American Youth Policy Forum.

Brown, L., Y. Yohannes, and P. Webb. 1994. "Rural Labor-Intensive Public Works: Impacts of Participation on Preschooler Nutrition: Evidence from Niger." *American Journal of Agricultural Economics* 76 (5): 1213–18.

Cameron, L. 2009. "Can a Public Scholarship Program Successfully Reduce School Drop-Outs in a Time of Economic Crisis? Evidence from Indonesia." *Economics of Education Review* 28: 308–17.

Carter, Prudence. 2005. *Keepin' It Real: School Success beyond Black and White*. New York: Oxford University Press.

Chandler, Michael, and Christopher Lalonde. 1998. "Cultural Continuity as a Hedge against Suicide in Canada's First Nations." *Journal of Transcultural Psychology* 35 (2): 191–219.

Christian P., C. P. Stewart, S. C. LeClerq, L. Wu, J. Katz, K. P. West, and S. K. Khatry. 2009. "Antenatal and Postnatal Iron Supplementation and Childhood Mortality in Rural Nepal: A Prospective Follow-Up in a Randomized, Controlled Community Trial." *American Journal of Epidemiology* 170 (9): 1127–36.

Clausen, S. 1991. "Adolescent Competence and the Shaping of the Life Course." *American Journal of Sociology* 96: 805–42.

Cooper, P. J., et al. 2009. "Improving Quality of Mother-Infant Relationship and Infant Attachment in Socioeconomically Deprived Community in South Africa: Randomised Controlled Trial." *British Medical Journal* 338: b974.

Cottle, Thomas J. 2001. *Hardest Times: The Trauma of Long-Term Unemployment*. Westport, CT: Praeger Publishers.

Crockett, L., and R. K. Silbereisen. 2000. *Negotiating Adolescence in Times of Social Change*. Cambridge, UK: Cambridge University Press.

Cunha, J. M., G. De Giorgi, and S. Jayachandran. 2011. "The Price Effects of Cash versus In-Kind Transfers." NBER Working Paper No. 17456. Cambridge, MA: National Bureau of Economic Research.

Cunningham, C., R. Bremner, and M. Boyle. 1995. "Large Group Community-Based Parenting Programs for Families of Preschoolers at Risk for Disruptive Behaviour Disorders: Utilization, Cost Effectiveness, and Outcome." *Journal of Child Psychology and Psychiatry* 36 (7): 1141–59.

Cunningham, W., L. Cohan, S. Naudeau, and L. McGinnis. 2008. *Supporting Youth at Risk: A Policy Toolkit for Middle-Income Countries*. Washington, DC: World Bank.

Cunningham, W., M. L. Sanchez-Puerta, and A. Wuermli. 2010. "Active Labor Market Programs for Youth: A Framework to Guide Youth Employment Interventions." *World Bank Employment Policy Primer* 16, World Bank, Washington, DC.

de Janvry, A., F. Finan, E. Sadoulet, and R. Vakis. 2006. "Can Conditional Cash Transfer Programs Serve as Safety Nets in Keeping Children at School and from Working When Exposed to Shocks?" *Journal of Development Economics* 79 (2): 349–73.

Dodge, K., T. Dishion, and J. Lansford. 2006. "Deviant Peer Influences in Intervention and Public Policy for Youth." *Social Policy Report* 20 (1).

Durlak, J., R. Weissberg, A. Dymnicki, R. Taylor, and K. Schellinger. 2011. The Impact of Enhancing Students' Social and Emotional Leaning: A Meta-Analysis of School-Based Universal Interventions. *Child Development* 81 (1): 405–32.

Duryea, S., D. Lam, and D. Levison. 2003. "Effects of Economic Shocks on Children's Employment and Schooling in Brazil." Mimeo. University of Michigan: Population Studies Center.

Elder, G. H. 1974. *Children of the Great Depression: Social Change in Life Experience*. Chicago: University of Chicago Press.

Engle, P., L. Fernald, H. Alderman, J. Behrman, C. O'Gara, A. Yousafzai, M. Cabral de Mello, M. Hidrobo, N. Ulkuer, I. Ertem, S. Illtus, and the Global Child Development Steering Group. 2011. "Strategies for Reducing Inequalities and Improving Developmental Outcomes for Young Children in Low-Income and Middle-Income Countries." Special issue, "Child Development 2," *Lancet* 378 (October): 1339–53.

Entra21. 2009. "Final Report on the Entra21 Program Phase I 2001–2007." International Youth Foundation, Baltimore, MD.

Feliciano, Cynthia. 2005. "Does Selective Migration Matter? Explaining Ethnic Disparities in Educational Attainment among Immigrants' Children." *International Migration Review* 39 (4): 841–71.

Fernald, L. C. H., P. J. Gertler, and L. M. Neufeld. 2008. "Role of Cash in Conditional Cash Transfer Programmes for Child Health, Growth, and Development: An Analysis of Mexico's Oportunidades." *Lancet* 371 (9615): 828–37.

Fernald, L. C., and M. R. Gunnar. 2009. "Poverty-Alleviation Program Participation and Salivary Cortisol in Very Low-Income Children." *Social Science and Medicine* 68 (12): 2180–89.

Ferreira, F. H. G., and N. Schady. 2009. "Aggregate Economic Shocks, Child Schooling, and Child Health." *World Bank Research Observer* 24 (2): 147–81.

Filmer, D., and N. Schady. 2009. "Are There Diminishing Returns to Transfer Size in Conditional Cash Transfers?" Policy Research Working Paper 4999, World Bank, Washington, DC.

Fiszbein, Arial, Dena Ringold, and Santhosh Srinivasan. 2011. "Cash Transfers and the Crisis: Protecting Current and Future Investments." *Development Policy Review* 29 (5): 585–601.

Fiszbein, A., and N. Schady. 2009. *Conditional Cash Transfers: Reducing Present and Future Poverty.* Washington, DC: World Bank.

Galasso, E., and M. Ravallion, M. 2004. Social Protection in a Crisis: Argentina's Plan *Jefes y Jefas. World Bank Economic Review* 18 (3): 367–99.

Gedamu, A. 2006. "Food for Work Program and Its Implications on Food Security: A Critical Review with a Practical Example from the Amhara Region, Ethiopia." *Journal of Agriculture and Rural Development in the Tropics and Subtropics* 107 (2): 177–88.

Gelbach, J. B., and L. Pritchett. 2002. "Is More for the Poor Less for the Poor? The Politics of Means-Tested Targeting." *B. E. Journal of Economic Analysis and Policy* 2 (1).

Gennetian, L., G. Duncan, W. Knox, E. Clark-Kauffman, and A. London. 2004. "How Welfare Policies Affect Adolescents' School Outcomes: A Synthesis of Evidence from Experimental Studies." *Journal of Research on Adolescence* 14 (4): 399–423.

Gershoff, E., J. L. Aber, C. Raver, and M. C. Lennon. 2007. "Income Is Not Enough: Incorporating Material Hardship into Models of Income Associations with Parenting and Child Development." *Child Development* 78 (1): 70–95.

Gertler, P., S. Martinez, D. Levine, and S. Bertozzi. 2003. "Losing the Presence and Presents of Parents: How Parental Death Affects Children." Mimeo. University of California, Berkeley.

Gibson-Davis, C., K. Magnuson, L. Gennetian, and G. Duncan. 2005. "Employment and the Risk of Domestic Abuse among Low-Income Women." *Journal of Marriage and Family* 67 (5): 1149–68.

Gilligan, D. O., and J. Hoddinott. 2007. "Is There Persistence in the Impact of Emergency Food Aid? Evidence on Consumption, Food Security, and Assets in Rural Ethiopia." *American Journal of Agricultural Economics* 89 (2): 225–42.

Glewwe, Paul, Michael Kremer, and Sylvie Moulin. 1998. "Textbooks and Test Scores: Evidence from a Prospective Evaluation in Kenya." Mimeo. Development Research Group, World Bank, Washington, DC.

Gottfried, A. E., J. S. Fleming, and A. W. Gottfried. 1998. "Role of Cognitively Stimulating Home Environment in Children's Academic Intrinsic Motivation: A Longitudinal Study." *Child Development* 69 (5): 1448–60.

Granger, R. 2008. "After-School Programs and Academics: Implications for Policy, Practice, and Research." *Social Policy Report* 22 (2).

Greenberg, D., N. Dechausay, and C. Fraker. 2011. *Learning Together: How Families Responded to Education Incentives in New York City's Conditional Cash Transfer Program.* New York: MDRC.

Grosh, M., C. del Ninno, E. Tesliuc, and A. Ouerghi. 2008. *For Protection and Promotion: The Design and Implementation of Effective Safety Nets.* Washington DC: World Bank.

Hall, Peter A., and Michèle Lamont. 2009. *Successful Societies: How Institutions and Cultural Repertoires Affect Health and Capabilities.* Cambridge, UK: Cambridge University Press.

———. Forthcoming. "Introduction." In *Social Resilience in the Neo-Liberal Era*, ed. Peter A. Hall and Michèle Lamont. Cambridge, UK: Cambridge University Press.

Hanushek, E. 1996. "A More Complete Picture of School Resource Policies." *Review of Educational Research* 66 (3): 397–409.

Hernandez-Zavala, M., H. A. Patrinos, C. Sakellariou, and J. Shapiro. 2006. "Quality of Schooling and Quality of Schools for Indigenous Students in Guatemala, Mexico, and Peru." Policy Research Working Paper 3982, World Bank, Washington, DC.

Herrigel, Gary. 1996. *Industrial Constructions: The Sources of Germany's Industrial Power.* New York: Cambridge University Press.

Hertzman, Clyde, and Arjumand Siddiqi. 2011. "Can Communities Succeed When States Fail Them? A Case Study of Early Human Development and Social Resilience in a Neo-Liberal Era." In *Social Resilience in the Neo-Liberal Era*, ed. Peter A. Hall and Michèle Lamont. Cambridge, UK: Cambridge University Press.

Hicks, J. H., M. Kremer, I. Mbiti, and E. Miguel. 2011. "Vocational Education Voucher Delivery and Labor Market Returns: A Randomized Evaluation among Kenyan Youth." Mimeo. World Bank, Washington, DC.

Holmes, R., and N. Jones. 2011. "Public Works Programmes in Developing Countries: Reducing Gendered Disparities in Economic Opportunities?"

Paper prepared for the International Conference on Social Cohesion and Development, January 20–21, Paris.

Ibarraran, P., and D. Rosas. 2009. "Evaluating the Impact of Job Training Programs in Latin America: Evidence from IDB Funded Operations." *Journal of Development Effectiveness* 1 (2): 195–216.

INEE. 2010. *Minimum Standards for Education: Preparedness, Response, and Recovery*. New York: Inter-Agency Network for Education in Emergency.

International Labour Organization. 2010. *World Social Security Report 2010/11: Providing Coverage in Times of Crisis and Beyond*. Geneva: ILO.

Jacoby, H. 1997. "Is There an Intrahousehold 'Flypaper Effect'? Evidence from a School Feeding Program." FCND Discussion Paper 31, International Food Policy Research Institute, Washington, DC.

Jensen, R. 2010. "The (Perceived) Returns to Education and the Demand for Schooling." *Quarterly Journal of Economics* 125 (2): 515–48.

Joseph, G., and Q. Wodon. 2012. "School Inputs, School Meals, and Capitation Grants: Impact on Enrollment, Drop-Outs, and Repetitions in Ghana." Mimeo. World Bank, Washington, DC.

Kabeer, N. 2008. *Mainstreaming Gender in Social Protection for the Informal Economy*. London: Commonwealth Secretariat.

Knowles, J. C., E. M. Pernia, and M. Racelis. 1999. "Social Consequences of the Financial Crisis in Asia." Economic Staff Paper 60, Asian Development Bank, Manila.

Lal, R., S. Miller, M. Lieuw-Kie-Song, and D. Kostzer. 2010. "Public Works and Employment Programmes: Towards a Long-Term Development Approach." Working Paper 66, International Policy Centre for Inclusive Growth; Poverty Group, UNDP, Brasilia.

Lamont, Michèle, Crystal Fleming, and Jessica S. Welburn. Forthcoming. "Responses to Discrimination and Social Resilience under Neo-Liberalism: The Case of Brazil, Israel, and the United States. In *Social Resilience in the Neo-Liberal Era*," ed. Peter A. Hall and Michèle Lamont. Cambridge, UK: Cambridge University Press.

Lerner, R., and L. Steinberg, eds. 2009. *Individual Bases of Adolescent Development*. Vol. 1 of *Handbook of Adolescent Psychology*. 3rd ed. Hoboken, NJ: Wiley.

Lewis, M., and M. Verhoeven. 2010. "Financial Crises and Social Spending: The Impact of the 2008–2009 Crisis." *World Economics* 11 (4): 79–110.

Liebenberg, Linda, and Michael Ungar. 2009. *Researching Resilience*. Toronto: University of Toronto Press.

Lumey, L. H., A. D. Stein, H. S. Kahn, K. M. van der Pal-de Bruin, G. J. Blauw, P. A. Zybert, and E. S. Susser. 2007. "Cohort Profile: The Dutch Hunger Winter Families Study." *International Journal of Epidemiology* 36 (6): 1196–204.

Lund, C., M. De Silva, S. Plagerson, S. Cooper, D. Chisholm, J. Das, M. Knapp, and V. Patel. 2011. Global Mental Health 1. "Poverty and Mental Disorders: Breaking the Cycle in Low-Income and Middle-Income Countries." *Lancet* 378 (9801): 1502–14.

Macours, Karen, Norbert Schady, and Renos Vakis. 2008. "Cash Transfers, Behavioral Changes, and Cognitive Development in Early Childhood: Evidence from a Randomized Experiment." Policy Research Working Paper 4759, World Bank, Washington, DC.

Mahoney, J., A. Harris, and J. Eccles. 2006. "Organized Activity Participation, Positive Youth Development and the Over-Scheduling Hypothesis." *Social Policy Report* 20 (4).

Maluccio, John. 2005. "Coping with the Coffee Crisis in Central America: The Role of the Nicaraguan Red de Protección Social." FCND Discussion Paper 188, International Food Policy Research Institute, Washington, DC.

Markus, Hazel, and Paula Nurius. 1986. "Possible Selves." *American Psychologist* 41 (9): 954–69.

Masten, Ann S. 2010. "Ordinary Magic: Lessons from Research on Resilience in Human Development." *Education Canada* 49: 28–32.

McLoyd, V., R. Kaplan, M. Purtell, and A. Huston. 2011. "Assessing the Effects of a Work-Based Antipoverty Program for Parents on Youth's Future Orientation and Employment Experiences." Special issue, "Raising Healthy Children," *Child Development* 82 (1): 113–32.

Millenky, M., D. Bloom, S. Muller-Ravett, and J. Broadus. 2011. "Staying on Course: Three-Year Results of the National Guard Youth Challenge Evaluation." New York: MDRC, http://www.mdrc.org/publications/599/full.pdf.

Moench-Pfanner, R., S. de Pee, M. W. Bloem, D. Foote, S. Kosen, and P. Webb. 2005. "Food-for-Work Programs in Indonesia Had a Limited Effect on Anemia." *Journal of Nutrition* 135 (6): 1423–29.

Morris, P., A. Huston, G. Duncan, D. Crosby, and J. Bos. 2001. *How Welfare and Work Policies Affect Children: A Synthesis of Research.* New York: MDRC.

Offe, Claus. 2011. "Shared Social Responsibility: A Concept in Search of Its Political Meaning and Promise." Paper presented at the Council of Europe and Eurpoean Commission conference "Shared Social Responsibility," March 1, 2011, Brussels.

Oyserman, Daphna, Deborah Bybee, and Kathy Terry. 2006. "Possible Selves and Academic Outcomes: How and When Possible Selves Impel Action." *Journal of Personality and Social Psychology* 91(1): 188–204.

Ozer, E. J, L. C. H. Fernald, J. G. Manley, and P. J. Gertler. 2009. "Effects of a Conditional Cash Transfer Program on Children's Behavior Problems." *Pediatrics* 123 (4): 630–37.

Piore, Michael, and Charles Sabel. 1984. *The Second Industrial Divide: Possibilities for Prosperity*. New York: Basic Books.

Pradhan, M., F. Saadah, and R. Sparrow. 2007. "Did the Health Card Program Ensure Access to Medical Care for the Poor during Indonesia's Economic Crisis?" *World Bank Economic Review* 21 (1): 125–50.

Quisumbing, A. R. 2003. "Food Aid and Child Nutrition in Rural Ethiopia." *World Development* 31 (7): 1309–24.

Rao, Vijayendra, and Michael Walton, eds. 2004. *Culture and Public Action*. Stanford, CA: Stanford University Press.

Ravallion, M. 1999. "Appraising Workfare." *World Bank Research Observer* 14 (1): 31–48.

Rebello Britto, P., H. Yoshikawa, and K. Boller. 2011. "Quality of Early Childhood Development Programs in Global Contexts: Rational for Investment, Conceptual Framework, and Implications for Equity." *Social Policy Report* 25 (2).

Rhodes, J., and D. DuBois. 2006. "Understanding and Facilitating the Youth Mentoring Movement." *Social Policy Report* 20 (3).

Riccio, James, Nadine Dechausay, David Greenberg, Cynthia Miller, Zawadi Rucks, and Nandita Verma. 2010. *Toward Reduced Poverty across Generations: Early Findings from New York City's Conditional Cash Transfer Program*. New York: MDRC.

Rogers, B. L., and J. Coates. 2002. "Food-Based Safety Nets and Related Programs." Social Protection Discussion Paper 0225, World Bank, Washington, DC.

Rose, E. 1999. "Consumption Smoothing and Excess Female Mortality in Rural India." *Review of Economics and Statistics* 81 (1): 41–49.

Sabarwal, S., N. Sinha, and M. Buvinic. 2010. "How Do Women Weather Economic Shocks? A Review of the Evidence." Policy Research Working Paper 5496, World Bank, Washington, DC.

Sampson, Robert J., Jeffrey D. Morenoff, and Thomas Gannon-Rowley. 2002. "Assessing Neighborhood Effects: Social Processes and New Directions in Research." *Annual Review of Sociology* 28: 443–78.

Sarkar, P., K. Bergman, T. O'Connor, and V. Glover. 2008. "Maternal Antenatal Anxiety and Amniotic Fluid Cortisol and Testosterone: Possible Implications for Foetal Programming." *Journal of Neuroendocrinology* 20: 489–96.

Schochet, P., J. Burghardt, and S. McConnell. 2006. *National Job Corps Study and Longer-Term Follow-Up Study: Impact and Benefits-Cost Findings Using Survey and Summary Earnings Records Data*. Princeton, NJ: Mathematica Policy Research, Inc.

Schultz, T. W. 1979. "The Economics of Being Poor." Prize Lecture to the Memory of Alfred Nobel, December 8.

Silbereisen, R. K., and R. Lerner, eds. 2007. *Approaches to Positive Youth Development*. London: Sage Publications.

Small, Mario, David Harding, and Michèle Lamont. 2010. "Introduction: Reconsidering Culture and Poverty." *Annals of the American Academy of Political and Social Sciences* 629 (May): 6–27.

Smith, Sandra Susan. 2010. "A Test of Sincerity: How Black and Latino Service Workers Make Decisions about Making Referrals." *Annals of the American Academy of Political and Social Science* 629 (May): 30–52.

Sparrow, R. 2007. "Protecting Education for the Poor in Times of Crisis: An Evaluation of a Scholarship Programme in Indonesia." *Oxford Bulletin of Economics and Statistics* 69 (1): 99–122.

Streeck, Wolfgang. 1991. "On the Institutional Conditions of Diversified Quality Production." In *Beyond Keynesianis: The Socio-Economics of Production and Employment*, ed. Egon Matzner and Wolfgang Streeck, 21–61. London: Edward Elgar.

Subbarao, K. 2003. "Systemic Shocks and Social Protection: Role and Effectiveness of Public Works Programs." Social Protection Discussion Paper 0302, World Bank, Washington, DC.

Swidler, Ann. 1986. "Culture in Action: Symbols and Strategies." *American Sociological Review* 51: 273–86.

———. Forthcoming. "Cultural Sources of Institutional Resilience: Lessons from Chieftaincy in Rural Malawi." In *Social Resilience in the Neo-Liberal Era*, ed. Peter A. Hall and Michèle Lamont. Cambridge, UK: Cambridge University Press.

Swidler, Ann, and Susan Cott Watkins. 2009. "Teach a Man to Fish? The Sustainability Doctrine and Its Social Consequences." *World Development* 37 (7): 1182–96.

Tcherneva, P., and R. Wray. 2005. "Gender and the Job Guarantee: The Impact of Argentina's Jefes Program on Female Heads of Poor Households." Working Paper 50, Levy Economics Institute, Annandale-on-Hudson, NY.

Vermeersh, C., and M. Kremer 2005. "Schools Meals, Educational Achievement, and School Competition: Evidence from a Randomized Evaluation." Policy Research Working Paper 3523, World Bank, Washington, DC.

Walsh, C., with N. Jones. 2009. "Alternative Approaches to Social Protection for Health in West and Central Africa: Regional Thematic Report 4 for the Study on Social Protection in West and Central Africa." London: Overseas Development Institute.

Warikoo, Natasha. 2010. *Balancing Act: Youth Culture in the Global City*. Berkeley: University of California Press.

Waters, H., F. Saadah, and M. Pradhan. 2003. "The Impact of the 1997–98 East Asian Economic Crisis on Health and Health Care in Indonesia." *Health Policy and Planning* 18 (2): 172–81.

Wodon, Q., and M. Minowa. 2001. "Training for the Urban Unemployed: A Reevaluation of Mexico's Training Program, Probecat." MPRA Paper 12310, Munich Personal RePEc Archive, Munich.

World Bank. 2006. *World Development Report 2007: Development and the Next Generation*. Washington, DC: World Bank.

Wyman, P. A., E. Cowen, W. C. Work, A. Raoof, P. A. Gribble, G. R. Parker, and M. Wannon. 1992. "Interviews with Children Who Experienced Major Life Stress: Family and Child Attributes That Predict Resilient Outcomes. *Journal of the American Academy of Child and Adolescent Psychiatry* 31: 904–10.

Appendix A

The Theory of Human Capital Investment Decisions

Within the analytical framework described in chapter 2, demands for investments in human capital at any point in time reflect the equating of expected present discounted values of marginal (or additional) private benefits and expected present discounted values of marginal (or additional) private costs for human capital investments in a given individual, as is represented by the solid lines in figures A.1 and A.2.[1] The marginal private benefits and costs reflect the objective (welfare, preference) function of the investor, the assets of the investor, and the markets and policy regimes that the investor faces. The marginal private benefit curve depends importantly, among other things, on the expected private gains in productivities (economic productivity or other types of productivity valued by the investor) due to human capital investments. These benefits depend on the marginal impact of the human capital investment on productivities as described in chapter 2 and on the marginal rewards that accrue to the investor because of that impact. For example, the marginal benefit curve is higher, all else equal, if labor markets are expected to reward the human capital investment under consideration (schooling, for example) more, or if the decision maker receives greater welfare from those returns because he or she is more altruistic or has greater direct

Figure A.1   Private Marginal Benefits and Private Marginal Costs of Human Capital Investments, with Higher and Lower Marginal Benefits

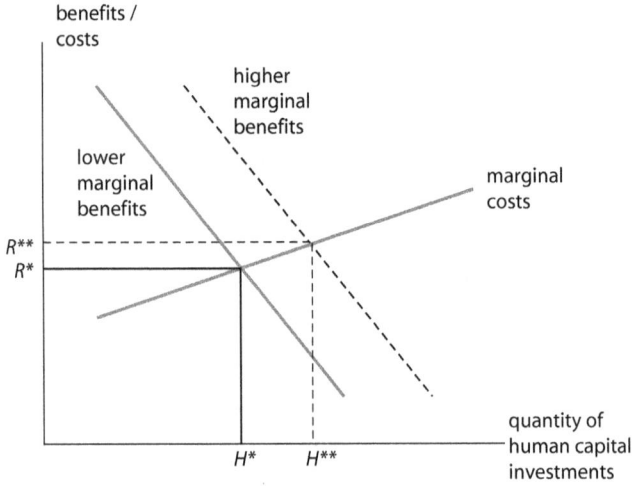

Source: Authors.
Note: Dashed line indicates higher marginal benefits; solid line indicates lower marginal benefits.

Figure A.2   Private Marginal Benefits and Private Marginal Costs of Human Capital Investments, with Higher and Lower Marginal Costs

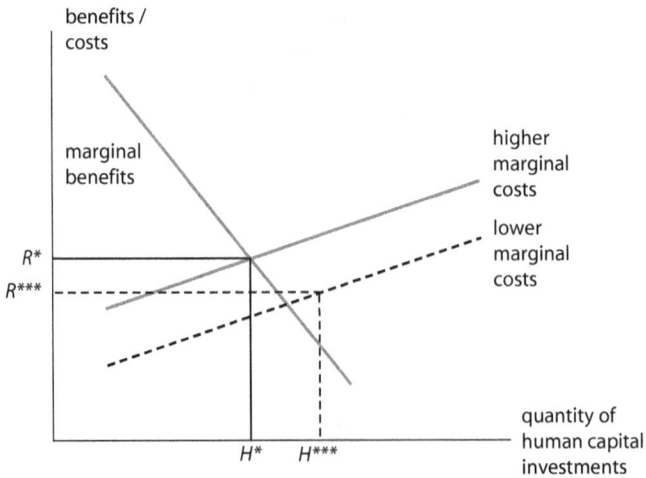

Source: Authors.
Note: Solid line indicates higher marginal costs; dashed line indicates lower marginal costs.

control over the returns. The marginal private benefit curve is downward sloping because of diminishing returns to human capital investments, given genetic and other endowments determined in part by past decisions, including the mating decisions of an individual's parents that affect the person's genetic endowments and aspects of the environment experienced by the individual in earlier life. The marginal private cost may increase with human capital investments because of increasing marginal private costs of borrowing on financial markets or because of increasing marginal costs of time devoted to such investments rather than working, particularly for education.

Privately, from the point of view of the investor, the best human capital investment for this individual is H^*, where the two curves intersect, with both the marginal private benefit and the marginal private cost equal to R^*. It is the marginal or additional benefits and costs that count, *not* the total benefits and costs. For human resource investments lower than H^*, the marginal costs are less than the marginal benefits, so that further gains can be made by increasing investments to the H^* level (and vice versa for human resource investments higher than H^*). This focus on the *marginal* benefits and *marginal* costs is typical for economic analyses of maximizing decisions. The assumption is *not* that individuals are always explicitly making complicated optimizing marginal calculations but that there are pressures to behave as if they were because to do so increases the attainment of their objectives. This equilibrium level of human capital investment at H^* is associated with an equilibrium rate of return, i^*, that equates the present discounted value of expected marginal private benefits with the present discounted value of expected marginal private costs. By comparing this rate of return with those on other investments, the investor can decide whether this investment should be undertaken.

If the marginal private benefit curve is higher for every level of human capital investment as for the dashed line in figure A.1, all else equal, the equilibrium level of human capital investment (H^{**}) and the equilibrium marginal private benefit (R^{**}) both are greater. The marginal private benefit curve may be higher at a point in time for one of two otherwise identical individuals because one individual (or whoever is investing in that individual)[2,3] (1) has greater genetic endowments that are complementary to resources devoted to human capital investments; (2) has lower discount rates so that the future benefits of human capital investments have greater value at the time of the investment decision; (3) is younger so that the postinvestment period in which to reap the returns from the investment is longer;[4] (4) has better health and a longer expected life due to complementary investments, so that the postinvestment period in which that individual reaps the returns to the investment in human development is greater and therefore the expected returns greater; (5) has human capital investment options of higher quality (for example, access to higher-quality public schools or health services) so that the marginal private benefits for a given level of private investment are higher and the equilibrium investment greater;[5] (6) has greater marginal private benefits to a given level of such investments because of discrimination that favors that individual due to gender, race, language, family, village, or ethnic group; (7) has returns to human capital investments that are obtained more by the investor or the relevant decision maker (for example, if traditional gender roles dictate that individuals of one sex, but not the other, provide old-age support for their parents, parental incentives to invest in individuals who are likely to provide such support may be greater);[6] (8) has greater marginal private benefits to a given level of investment because of being in a more dynamic economy in which the returns to such investments are greater; (9) has greater marginal private benefits to a given level of such investments because of greater externalities from the human capital investments of others in the same economy; or (10) lives in a more stable economy so that the discount rate for future returns is lower (because risk is less) and thus the marginal private benefit of future returns is greater.

If the marginal private cost is lower for every level of human capital investment as for the dashed line in figure A.2, all else equal, the equilibrium human capital investment (H^{***}) is greater, with the marginal private benefit (R^{***}) lower at the higher investment level. The marginal private cost might be lower for numerous reasons. Compare two otherwise identical individuals at the same point in time except that one individual (1) has lower private cost access to human development programs related to such investments because of closer proximity to such services or lesser user charges; (2) has less opportunity costs for time used for such investments (for example, such costs may vary among individuals because of differing labor market wages) because of less developed labor markets or negative economic shocks in those markets; (3) is from a family with greater access to credit (or less need for credit) for financing such investments because of greater wealth or status or better connections; or (4) is from a group that is favored for such investments because of private discrimination or policies.

This maximization process leads to demands for human capital investments in individual i that depend on all relevant prices P and on all relevant resources R and on all the parameters of the relevant production functions (including those for the production of human capital) and on preferences:

$$H_i = H(P, R \mid \text{production parameters, preference parameters}).$$

The prices include all those that enter into the investor's decision-making process, including the prices paid for human development–related services and other consumption and investments and for transferring resources over time (that is, the interest rate) and for insuring against uncertainty. At the time that any human capital investment decision is made, these prices include all past and current prices for these goods and services (perhaps embodied in current stocks of human capital), as well as expected future prices (including expected future returns to human capital investments and variances in those expected returns due to possible shocks). These prices are not just monetary costs, but all costs, including the cost of time. The resources include all resources of the individual, family, educational and health institutions, and community that affect the family's decisions. These resources include human capital that reflects past investments and related decisions, financial resources, physical resources, genetic endowments, and general learning and health environments.

Notes

1. Discounting makes possible the comparison of two streams of costs and benefits over time, each defined in terms of constant prices, by converting them into their present or current values. Discounting is critical for comparing investments in which there are different lags between the investments and the payoffs. A gain of one dollar in 15 years, for example, is worth only $0.47 now if the appropriate discount rate is 5 percent and only $0.22 if the appropriate discount rate is 10 percent. More generally, the present discounted value of a dollar received or paid in n years is $1/(1+r)^n$. The failure to discount for comparing events that happen at very different points in time can lead to quite misleading interpretations (for example., overstating considerably the present value of more distant future gains due to current human resource investments in comparison with gains that will be realized with lesser lags). For simplicity, in what follows we refer to *marginal benefits* and *marginal costs* without always qualifying them explicitly by the phrase *present discounted value,* but it should be kept in mind that making events that occur across time comparable is essential for analyzing costs and benefits of investments in human capital (as well as other investments).

2. For the last three of these comparisons, the otherwise identical individuals would have to live in different economies or at different times.

3. Some of these examples, both on the marginal benefit and the marginal cost side, depend on there being imperfect capital and insurance markets. For example, if insurance markets are perfect and insurance is costless, risk does not affect families differentially. But it is widely perceived that capital and insurance markets for human resource investments are quite imperfect.

4. For this reason, investments in schooling and training tend to be made relatively early in the life cycle. The economics literature has tended to focus on such investments. But investments also have costs, so that if certain investments do not have returns until later in the life cycle, there also are incentives to put off these investments (and their costs) into the future closer to the time at which the returns might be realized.

5. If the investor must pay for greater human capital service–related quality, however, investment does not necessarily increase with a higher-quality option. What happens to the equilibrium investment depends upon where the marginal private cost curve is for the higher-quality option, in addition to the location of the marginal private benefit curve.

6. Although this tendency may be offset if, for example, human capital substitutes sufficiently for financial and physical transfers in marriage markets (for example, Rao 1993; Behrman et al. 1999).

References

Behrman, Jere R., Andrew Foster, Mark R. Rosenzweig, and Prem Vashishtha. 1999. "Women's Schooling, Home Teaching, and Economic Growth." *Journal of Political Economy* 107 (4): 682–714.

Rao, Vijayendra. 1993. "The Rising Price of Husbands: A Hedonic Analysis of Dowry Increases in Rural India." *Journal of Political Economy* 101 (4): 666–77.

Appendix B

Measurement and Identification of Aggregate Shocks: Problems of Comparability between Studies

How are aggregate economic shocks defined, and why do we distinguish between aggregate and idiosyncratic shocks? Ferreira and Schady (2009) focus on aggregate shocks, defined as macroeconomic shocks that result in a "substantial temporary reduction in production and income levels." (For a more detailed discussion, see chapter 2.) Ferreira and Schady argue that idiosyncratic shocks primarily have income effects, whereas aggregate economic shocks have both income and substitution effects. The income effects derive from a fall in available household resources and income, which in turn reduces investments in children's schooling. Substitution effects derive from decreases in real wages, which reduce the opportunity cost of schooling and have the potential effect of increasing schooling. The overall net effect of macroeconomic crises on schooling is thus ambiguous.

How are the impacts of aggregate shocks or crises measured? Some studies take advantage of variation in the likely impact of the shock on different populations. Nevertheless, many studies of aggregate shocks treat the shock as though it affects the entire population in the same way. A feasible methodological approach then is to compare school enrollment in crisis years with school enrollment in noncrisis years, perhaps including controls for the socioeconomic characteristics of individual households. This is based on the assumption that conditional on the control variables, the economic crisis is responsible for all changes in school relative to that in the noncrisis years. In other words, in the absence of the crisis, school enrollment would have been similar to that in the noncrisis year.[1] Where the crisis affects all households, there is no obvious way to test this proposition. One would like to have clear pre- and postcrisis data on schooling, as well as information on other variables that are likely to affect schooling (for instance, public scholarship programs). If these policy variables did not fundamentally change during the crisis, one can use variation in implementation arrangements, funding, eligibility, or other criteria to identify the impact of the shocks. This type of analysis often requires detailed institutional knowledge of both the country context and the history during the crisis as well as the country's education sector. An excellent example of a study that fulfills these criteria is Thomas et al. (2004) in Indonesia. The second wave of the Indonesian Family Life Survey was completed just before the severe economic crisis that began in 1997. The researchers were quickly able to implement a follow-up survey among a subsample of households during the height of the economic crisis. The study thus includes two consecutive years of data, one before and the other during the crisis. This quick timing reduced the possibility that changes in conditions other than those associated with the macroeconomic crisis are conflated with the effects of the crisis.

However, even when one can credibly assume that changes observed from one year to the next are really due to the economic crisis, this aggregate approach does not identify the particular aspects of the crisis that might most affect household-level outcomes. Many macroeconomic crises are characterized by increases in unemployment, higher prices, exchange rate devaluations, decreases in real wages, and changes in government spending not only on education but also on most other areas as well. This aggregate approach may not shed light on which aspects of economic crisis are potentially most harmful. The deficiency of the aggregate approach— and a fundamental problem with the examination of truly aggregate shocks within one country—is that it is difficult to identify which aspects of economic crises are the most harmful for investment in children's schooling, since they all occur together. This also limits the identification of interventions. If we knew that increases in adult unemployment had the greatest impact on enrollment (conditional on all the other things that happen in a crisis), we could design specific programs to compensate or mitigate, such as unemployment insurance or temporary employment programs. This suggests that studies of idiosyncratic shocks—such as the effects of parental unemployment on investment in children's schooling—may be more useful for making concrete policy recommendations.

Note

1. One can also compare changes in school enrollment during the crisis period to changes in pre- or postcrisis years, rather than levels.

References

Ferreira, F. H. G., and N. Schady. 2009. "Aggregate Economic Shocks, Child Schooling, and Child Health." *World Bank Research Observer* 24 (2): 147–81.

Thomas, D., K. Beegle, E. Frankenberg, B. Sikoki, J. Strauss, and G. Teruel. 2004. "Education in a Crisis." *Journal of Development Economics* 74 (1): 53–85.

Glossary

Allele: a form or variant of a gene that is present on a particular chromosome. The combination of different alleles determines some inherited traits such as blood type and eye color. Another allele, the seven-repeat D4 allele, has been associated with heightened environmental susceptibility.

Congenital: a condition that is present at birth, regardless of it being inherited or not.

Differential susceptibility: the theory that some children are more susceptible, or sensitive, to environmental influences such as child-rearing experiences, due to neurobiological processes that arise from genetic or epigenetic variation. Children who are predisposed to greater susceptibility will exhibit worse behavioral problems when a mother is highly insensitive but will exhibit fewer behavioral issues when a mother is highly sensitive, compared to children without this predisposition.

Dynamic complementarity: see path dependence.

Epigenetics: the study of heritable changes in gene expression other than through changes in the underlying DNA sequence. In other words, it is the study of how much phenotypic variance, or variance in observable characteristics or traits, results from genetic versus nongenetic (environmental) influences.

Executive functioning: the set of cognitive abilities or mental processes used when engaged in goal-directed behaviors and capacities such as behavior modification, problem solving, attention, concept formation, and abstract thinking.

Exosystem: refers to the links and processes taking place between two or more settings, at least one of which does not contain the developing person, that indirectly influence the immediate setting or microsystem in which the developing person lives. In other words, the exosystem involves events that do not directly affect the child but that influence the child's interactions within his or her microsystem. For example, parents' experiences in the workplace do not involve the child directly but can influence parent-child interactions by affecting the parent.

Expected marginal private benefit: the total value, considered today, of the sum of all future benefits enjoyed by a household (or firm) from consuming, producing, or investing in one more unit of a good or service, minus the sum of all of the costs incurred in doing so.

Externalizing behaviors: problematic reactions or behaviors that are directed toward others, commonly as the result of stressful or negative experiences. Examples of externalizing behaviors in Western cultures include disruptiveness, hyperactivity, and aggression. Substance abuse has variously been conceived of as both an internalizing and an externalizing behavior.

Genetic moderation: when the association between an environmental risk factor and a person's response or outcome is conditional on genetic factors. For example, evidence suggests that maternal insensitivity during infancy predicts later childhood externalizing behaviors conditional on the presence of the seven-repeat D4 (DRD4) allele.

Human development: describes myriad complex, interactive, interdependent systems and processes at all levels of human functioning, from the molecular to the cultural, that unfold over time in continuous interactions. Human development as an outcome is often associated with actualizing the person's genetic potential, or *nature*, through adequate nutrition, cognitive stimulation, and social and emotional support, or *nurture*.

Internalizing behaviors: problematic reactions or behaviors that are directed inward toward the self, commonly as the result of stressful or negative experiences. Examples of internalizing behaviors in Western cultures include withdrawal, anxiety, and depression.

Knowledge spillover: when innovations in one firm or market stimulate improvements in another. This can occur through the exchange of ideas among individuals or firms, usually in geographical proximity.

Macrosystem: broadly describes the culture in which individuals live, including the belief systems, knowledge, material resources, customs, lifestyles, opportunities, hazards, and life-course options available to the developing individual, which reciprocally influence other systems, including the micro-, meso-, and exosystems. Phenomena in the macrosystem, such as economic shocks, affect child and youth development through shifts in these systems and settings.

Mesosystem: comprises the links and processes taking place between two or more settings that involve the developing person directly, such as the interactions between the school setting and the family setting. Settings can interact in the mesosystem in opposition to or in harmony with each other. For example, acting out to impress the peer group may be in conflict with behavioral expectations within the classroom.

Microsystem: comprises the settings with which the developing person has direct contact. Settings in the microsystem (for example, family or school) directly affect the child's development through proximal processes.

Myelination: the process by which a myelin sheath forms around the axon (nerve fiber) of a neuron, enabling the nerve cell to transmit information more quickly and efficiently. This neurological process is part of synaptogenesis, whereby a connection or synapse between neurons is formed.

Nested points of entry: the possible options or entry points for intervention, corresponding to key points along the pathways through which a shock is transmitted to the individual child.

Neuroendocrine moderation: when the association between an environmental risk factor and a person's response or outcome is conditional upon neuroendocrine factors. For example, in families characterized by high stress and conflict, children showing low parasympathetic nervous system reactivity evidenced greater improvements in academic competence over the course of the kindergarten year than children with highly reactive parasympathetic nervous systems.

Neuroplasticity: the ability of structures and functions of the brain and nervous system to change in response to experiences across the life span, often through processes such as synaptogenesis and pruning.

Parasympathetic nervous system: the part of the autonomic nervous system that promotes maintenance of the body when at rest, including through digestion, salivation, and deceleration of the heart rate. In contrast, the sympathetic nervous system is responsible for activities associated with the "fight or flight" response, including acceleration of the heart rate and constriction of the blood vessels.

Path dependence: Path dependence, or dynamic complementarity, refers to the notion of "limited substitutability" between investments at different points in time. In other words, returns to present or future investments will depend on past investments, and forgone investments are not easily made up for.

Present discounted value: refers to the value today of some income or asset obtained in the future, once these have been discounted to take account of the time until the income or asset is received.

Production function: is a technical relation that describes the maximum output that can be produced with a given set of inputs by a firm (or a household or other production unit).

Proximal processes: refer to a developing person's increasingly complex interactions with people, objects, and symbols within contexts or settings of the microsystem that promote the realization of the genetic potential for effective development.

Pruning: the process by which the number of neurons and synapses in the brain is reduced, increasing the efficiency of the neural and synaptic configurations that remain. In general, frequently used synapses are retained, while less active synapses are eliminated.

Settings: different contexts or environments to which an individual can be exposed throughout the life course. Settings in a child's microsystem include, among others, family, school, and the peer group, whereas settings in the same child's exosystem might include a parent's workplace or a sibling's school.

Synaptogenesis: the process by which neurons connect to other neurons or cells (form synapses), allowing them to communicate. This process is particularly active during early childhood.

www.ingramcontent.com/pod-product-compliance
Lightning Source LLC
Chambersburg PA
CBHW070600270326
41926CB00013B/2380